GOLD COAST DIASPORAS

BLACKS IN THE DIASPORA

EDITORS

Herman L. Bennett
Kim D. Butler
Judith A. Byfield
Tracy Sharpley-Whiting

GOLD COAST DIASPORAS

IDENTITY, CULTURE, AND POWER

WALTER C. RUCKER

INDIANA UNIVERSITY PRESS

Bloomington & Indianapolis

This book is a publication of

INDIANA UNIVERSITY PRESS
Office of Scholarly Publishing
Herman B Wells Library 350
1320 East 10th Street
Bloomington, Indiana 47405 USA

iupress.indiana.edu

The paper used in this publication
meets the minimum requirements of
the American National Standard for
Information Sciences–Permanence of
Paper for Printed Library Materials,
ANSI Z39.48–1992.

*Manufactured in the
United States of America*

*Cataloging-in-Publication Data is
available from the Library of Congress.*

ISBN 978-0-253-01694-2 (cloth)
ISBN 978-0-253-01701-7 (ebook)

1 2 3 4 5   20 19 18 17 16 15

For Bayo, Na'eem, and our new shining light, Ayinde.

CONTENTS

ACKNOWLEDGMENTS

Over the long, winding, and sometimes meandering transatlantic path I took in completing this project, a series of four watershed moments helped to anchor my thoughts and interpretations and facilitated my scholarly rebirth as an early-modern Black Atlantic specialist. The first moment occurred during a panel at the 1999 American Historical Association meeting in Washington, D.C. Rosalyn Terborg-Penn's helpful challenge to me then, not to forget about women in my historical analyses, played a shaping role in the interpretive directions I have taken since the publication of my first book. A year later, at the inaugural Association for the Study of the Worldwide African Diaspora (ASWAD) meeting in New York, Kim Butler's public praise of my embryonic work on slave resistance and culture in antebellum South Carolina was the second moment. The third moment happened as I reversed the middle passage in a very personal way during my first visit to Ghana in the summer of 2002. Facilitated by a good colleague—Leon Caldwell—as well as funding from the University of Nebraska–Lincoln (UNL) and a National Endowment for the Humanities Summer Stipend, my trip to and through Ghana provided a Black Atlantic frame for my evolving understandings of Atlantic history, cultural change, memory, and trauma. The fourth and final moment—pivotal in my reincarnation as an early-modern Black Atlantic historian—was the 2009 ASWAD conference in Accra, Ghana, where I presented my first paper on this project.

This book owes debts, of a variety of sorts, to several people. First and foremost, a small group of colleagues and friends whom I hold in the highest esteem—all are also the smartest people I know—provided support, much-needed and timely criticism, and platforms upon which

I could safely try out new ideas. This cadre includes Leslie Alexander, Jason Young, and Bayo Holsey. In addition, I am fortunate to be part of a group of Morehouse College alumni who all earned history Ph.D.s between 1996 and 2002 and who are tenured at a range of universities across the United States and the world. The "Morehouse Scholars Collective," including Jeffrey O. G. Ogbar, Jason Young, Hasan Kwame Jeffries, Fanon Che Wilkins, Charles McKinney, David Canton, and Frederick Knight, helped shape every step I have taken in becoming a historian and a published scholar. Ogbar encouraged my shift in major from computer science to history in 1990. Two others, Young and Knight, were graduate student colleagues with me in Riverside, California. Jeffries was a close colleague and friend during my eight years at the Ohio State University (OSU). Finally, McKinney, Wilkins, Canton, and Ogbar were role models and mentors—the veritable elders of the cohort. Within our collective are multiple department chairs and program directors, a vice provost, and authors and editors of more than a dozen books. "Steadfast, honest, true," and, yes, we plan to take over black academe.

Graduate students enrolled in a range of readings courses and seminars at OSU—Comparative History of the African Diaspora, Black Atlantic Communities and Cultures, Seminar in West African Society and Culture, and Slavery in Comparative Context—allowed me to assign books I needed to read in preparation for this project. We also had dozens of stimulating discussions about historiographic, historical, and theoretical matters that, in the end, facilitated my fluency in Black Atlantic studies. Through brief chats, words of encouragement, questions after presentations and invited talks, and emails, this project benefited from the support and collective wisdom of a range of scholars, including Ray Kea, Gwendolyn Midlo Hall, John Thornton, Mike Gomez, Rebecca Shumway, Vincent Brown, Rosanne Adderly, Mia Bay, Herman Bennett, Carolyn Brown, Margaret Washington, Jim Sweet, Ahmad Sikainga, Alton Hornsby, Jr., Marcellus Barksdale, Deborah Gray White, Ann Fabian, Jemima Pierre, Peter Hudson, Heather Williams, Bill Ferris, Amrita Myers, Ousman Kobo, Lisa Lindsay, Fatimah Jackson, Judson Jeffries, Lupenga Mphande, Franco Barchiesi, Jerma Jackson, Genna Rae McNeil, Ike Newsum, Michael Lambert, the late Nick Nelson, Linda Myers, Curtis Austin, Andrea Davis, Julius Nyang'oro, Bereket Selassie, Ken

Goings, Kenneth Janken, and Akinyele Umoja. I am thankful especially for the generosity of John Thornton, who shared with me translations of Dutch documents related to Gold Coast history and the transatlantic slave trade. I also owe debts that I may never be able to repay properly to the two anonymous readers; to Herman Bennett and other editors of the Blacks in the Diaspora series; and to Bob Sloan, Jenna Whittaker, and Darja Malcolm-Clarke at Indiana University Press. I have had many experiences with university and academic presses over the years, but none surpass the care, attention to detail, and professionalism of the editorial and production staff at Indiana.

I extend special thanks to UNL, the National Endowment for the Humanities, OSU, and the University of North Carolina at Chapel Hill (UNC) for grant funding and a research leave I received to support this project. Financial support from the Research Council and the Layman Trust (UNL); three Arts and Humanities Grants and a 2010–2011 research leave (OSU); and funding from the University Research Council, the Institute for African American Research, and the Department of African, African American, and Diaspora Studies (UNC) made possible a series of research trips to Barbados, Trinidad, Ghana, the UK, New York, and Louisiana. The staffs of the following libraries and archives were particularly helpful: the Amistad Research Center at Tulane University, the Pointe Coupee Parish Courthouse, the New-York Historical Society, the New York Public Library, the Southern Historical Collection, the Barbados Museum and Historical Society, Balme Library Special Collections at the University of Ghana–Legon, the National Archives at Kew, Lambeth Palace Library, Oxford University's Bodleian Library, and the British Library.

Though the 2009 ASWAD meeting in Accra represents a moment in my reinvention as a Black Atlantic specialist, it was also the venue at which I met my partner, Bayo Holsey. Her keen intellect and supreme patience shaped this book in immeasurable ways. For the gifts of love, laughter, and new life, I dedicate this book to her.

GOLD COAST DIASPORAS

Introduction

The tribe of the Middle Passage . . . was the tribe created by the
rapacity of African elites, the territorial expansion of strong states,
and the greed, cruelty, and arrogance of white men possessing
the world. It was the tribe of those stolen from their natal land,
stripped of their "country marks," and severed from their kin.

SAIDIYA HARTMAN, *LOSE YOUR MOTHER* (2007)

Private Don Juan's military discharge on July 10, 1846, was nothing more
than a routine matter at the time. After twenty-two years of distinguished service in Her Majesty's 2nd West India Regiment of Foot, the
regimental board and the surgeon appointed to inspect his physical and
mental condition deemed Don Juan "unfit for further service," ending
his career as a soldier at the age of forty. Wellington Poole, the assistant
surgeon in medical charge of the regiment, certified him as permanently
disabled because he had been "worn out." Suffering from chronic rheu-
matism and having survived well beyond the life expectancy of black
laborers in the nineteenth-century British Caribbean, Don Juan had
outlived his usefulness. Extolled by his commanding officers as a "good
Soldier . . . trustworthy & sober" who rarely visited a hospital, never
complained about work or injury, nor took time off duty, Don Juan more
than paid back the British Crown for his 1824 release from bondage.[1]

When he agreed to join the 2nd West India Regiment, Don Juan claimed to be from "Coromantee in Africa." This reported place of origin refers to two Fante-speaking towns, Upper and Lower Kormantse, and a nearby trading factory in Atlantic Africa's Gold Coast—a region coterminous with modern-day Ghana. Don Juan's claim to a Coromantee natal origin can be traced from his recruitment at age eighteen until his military discharge at forty. No one recording his memory of a Coromantee origin had grounds to question Don Juan's authority or authenticity. Upon cursory physical examination, Assistant Surgeon Poole noted that Don Juan's face was "covered with Country Marks." Three marks each at the corner of the mouth and cheek and several marks on his forehead signaled to any contemporary observer Don Juan's birth in Atlantic Africa. His reported Coromantee home, and even notes in the discharge papers about Don Juan's service as "a good Soldier" who never visited the hospital for treatment nor complained about injury, left little room for doubt in the minds of his commanding officers about his geographic and ethnolinguistic origins. Coromantees had well-earned reputations for physical fortitude—a combination of bravery, pain tolerance, and martial prowess—that had proved troublesome in their anti-slavery activities throughout the seventeenth- and eighteenth-century circum-Caribbean.[2]

Don Juan's claims to a Coromantee natal origin placed him in odd and even ironic scenarios as he traversed the Gold Coast diaspora in service to the British crown. During his tour of duty, Don Juan served in the Gold Coast and throughout the British Caribbean—sites of Gold Coast diaspora origin and the processes leading to Coromantee ethnogenesis in the Black Atlantic. Indeed, his first and only military campaign occurred during the 1824 Anglo–Asante War, during which Don Juan's regiment aided in the defense of Cape Coast Castle—a former British slave trading factory—and other fortifications in the Gold Coast. When Lieutenant-Colonel Sutherland arrived with a forty-man detachment of Don Juan's regiment on May 18, 1824, they joined a Fante force of three thousand and the Royal African Company corps to counter a marauding Asante army about ten thousand strong. Despite a series of skirmishes launched by the Asante military, the garrison at Cape Coast held, and Don Juan's Atlantic journey continued.[3] After a brief assign-

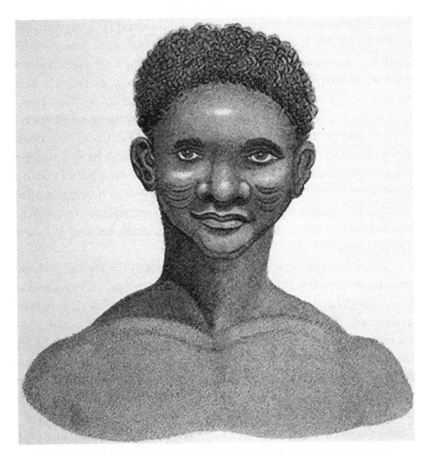

0.1. Country marks depicted on the face of a Coromantee youth, circa 1820s.
Source: Cuvier, *The Animal Kingdom*, opposite 96.

ment in Sierra Leone, he spent the next few years in Nassau, Honduras, and Jamaica—traversing parts of the Gold Coast diaspora and, perhaps, connecting with other Coromantees along the way.[4]

What could have been coursing through the mind of an eighteen-year-old soldier who voluntarily took up arms to defend a former slave castle from which he could have embarked on a slave ship as a young child? How did he understand the circumstances leading up to his return to the Gold Coast only to fight, shoulder-to-shoulder, with Fante soldiers and Royal African Company personnel—forces possibly responsible for his earlier transformation into an Atlantic commodity? How did Don Juan interpret his own claim to be from "Coromantee in Africa" while helping to garrison a British-controlled fortress less than a dozen miles from his reported place of origin? Did he understand his home to be a specific Gold Coast locale or an ambiguous, borderless, and imagined geography in the Black Atlantic where an ever evolving set of socio-cultural and political principles defined his very existence? This book seeks to address these and related questions. Though he spent many years abroad in the Gold Coast and other locales in West Africa and the Caribbean, Don Juan's discharge took place July 1846 in Kingston, Jamaica. As far as extant records reveal, he never returned to West Africa, electing instead to stay in Jamaica—among a sizable number of fellow Coromantees—for the remainder of his years.[5]

Throughout his career as a soldier, Don Juan quite ably and perhaps consciously performed Coromantee identity and embodied, in the words of Douglas Chambers, the "master recursive metaphor" of Coromantee as the brave, stoic, and noble warrior—a trope of Coromantee masculinity invented and perpetuated in the European mind by Aphra Behn in her 1688 novel *Oroonoko*. Indeed, Behn—who had personal experience in Suriname and first-hand knowledge of Coromantee performances there—depicts her title character as a former "Coramantien" war captain with a "natural inclination to arms." As one of the "bravest soldiers," Oroonoko had a "real greatness of soul," and Behn further described him as epitomizing "honour," "gallantry," and courage. "Without a groan or a reproach," the former Coramantien war captain and prince dies at the end of the novel after having his ears, nose, and arms amputated as punishment for an act of rebellion.[6] While Behn contributed to the trope of Coromantee masculinity in the seventeenth- and eighteenth-century European mind, this recursive metaphor was reinforced continuously by frequent performances of Coromantee and "(A)mina" resistance in the British, Dutch, and Danish Americas.[7]

At the time of Don Juan's discharge in 1846, Coromantee identity had been in existence and continual development for two centuries in the Western Hemisphere. By the mid-nineteenth century, Coromantee and its attendant associations were mere shadows of their original forms—emptied of some of their earlier meanings and filled with others.

In the seventeenth and eighteenth centuries, "Coromantee" referred to people from any number of coastal and inland slave procurement or "catchment" areas in the Gold Coast. Linked together in the Americas by a common tongue—Akan—and the deployment of a range of shared cultural technologies, Coromantees became a feared contingent of enslaved Atlantic Africans in English and Dutch Western Hemisphere colonies due to their alleged propensity for violent resistance. While it was an ethnic stereotype, the ubiquitous idea of Coromantee rebelliousness may have reflected the fact that, given the long history of expansion, military conquest, and growth in the number of commoners in armies and local militias in the principal catchment areas of the Gold Coast by the 1760s, many people who became Coromantees in the Americas had been soldiers with training in the arts of war.[8] At the time of Don Juan's discharge, however, "Coromantee" may have been more a generic label—emphasizing a particular kind of masculine "toughness"—than an ethnolinguistic or regional identifier.

Just as the term "Spartan," over many centuries, made the etymological turn from a reference to a militarized ancient Greek polity to mean, in a broader sense, self-disciplined, austere, and courageous, "Coromantee" followed a similar trajectory.[9] By the mid-nineteenth century and certainly later, this neo-African ethnic identifier connoted a much more general notion of martial prowess and fearlessness. Coromantee no longer carried the same specific cultural meaning it once held in the seventeenth and eighteenth centuries. In this sense, Don Juan could be Coromantee in the nineteenth century without having to originate from a specific Gold Coast town nor embarking on a slaver at Fort Kormantse.[10] Indeed, being Coromantee for Don Juan did not necessarily mean a facility with the Akan language nor a personal engagement with a range of Coromantee cultural technologies including blood oaths and obeah—a ritual practice centered around the power of ancestral spirits. Don Juan enlisted in the 2nd West India Regiment on March 24, 1824, as an eighteen-year-old. The Slave Trade Act, which passed Parliament on March 25, 1807, ended British participation in the slave trade roughly a year after Don Juan's birth. In this case, four possible scenarios exist. First, Don Juan could have been a toddler when he arrived by slave ship in the British Caribbean in 1807. Second, Don Juan was possibly imported into Jamaica illegally after the end of the British slave trade. Third, he may have been a liberated African from a Spanish slaver captured by the Royal Navy at some point after 1807. Finally, he could have been born to "Coromantee" parents in the British Caribbean. Even if Don Juan was born shortly before the Slave Trade Act passed, boarded a slave ship as a toddler, and disembarked in the British Caribbean in 1807 or 1808, Coromantee could have been nothing more than an American invention for him. Being from Coromantee, in this case, was more about an American present for Don Juan and others in the nineteenth century circum-Caribbean than a specific Gold Coast past.[11]

All of the possible pasts for Don Juan trouble and disrupt the meaning of "Coromantee" in the nineteenth-century British Caribbean. In this case, we should move beyond understanding the term as designating a physical place of origin in the Gold Coast. Instead, it formed part of a liminal space situated somewhere between social death and separation from Gold Coast communities and the social resurrections experienced by Akan, Ga, Adanme, and Ewe speakers and their American-born creole descendants in the Western Hemisphere. Coromantee identity—particularly by the 1840s—represented a sociocultural invention in Jamaica, Barbados, Antigua, and elsewhere.

Don Juan's life, then, represents a temporal waypoint Atlantic Africans and their American-born descendants traveled in their centuries-long sojourn from ethnicity to race. Coromantees, Eboes, Congos, and other neo-African ethnic groups mingled and engaged in a variety of cultural negotiations and transformations in the Caribbean, South America, and North America. Out of many, they became one in complex, multi-staged, and prolonged transitions from neo-African ethnicity to American "race." Before they "exchanged their country marks," these groups appropriated and continually redefined a range of ethnic labels in the Americas, which they filled with varying meanings over time. This book tracks a portion of their story. In short, it explores the cultural and sociopolitical dynamics of a set of Atlantic African peoples—linked by common geography, ties of trade and political or military domination, and overlapping languages and cultural ways—cast collectively into the hell of chattel and racial slavery in the Western Hemisphere. They originated from various catchment regions of the eighteenth-century Gold

Coast and suffered a series of social deaths and disruptions to become, in the words of black expatriates living in modern-day Ghana, the "tribe of the Middle Passage."[12]

Forcibly torn from home, kith, and kin and packed on slave ships, many enslaved Gold Coast Africans followed social death with physical death either in the Middle Passage or shortly after arrival in the Americas. While that part of the larger narrative is important, this book focuses on those who survived to create new lives and to develop communities in the Western Hemisphere. Known widely as Coromantees or (A)minas, enslaved Gold Coast Africans exported to the Americas came from a number of littoral and inland polities and language groups—including speakers of Akan, Ga, Adanme, and Ewe. By understanding these groupings as forming polyglottal and geographically defined diasporas, as opposed to a monolinguistic or "ethnic" diaspora, a sharper and more defined picture emerges of the ways in which they (per)formed culture, ethnicity, and identity in the Americas. This tribe of the Middle Passage, "stolen from their natal land, stripped of their 'country marks,' and severed from their kin," reinvented themselves as Coromantees and (A)minas, in part, to make sense of, and develop survival strategies in, the new worlds in which they were disembarked.[13]

This study begins with the premise that the ethnic labels attached to particular diasporic groupings, however problematic and inaccurate, held meaning for those who identified with those labels and who redefined them over time. While some scholars understand "Coromantee" and "(A)mina" as false ethnonyms and constructions of European derivation, others, such as Douglas Chambers, James Sidbury, and Jorge Cañizares-Esguerra opt for more nuanced approaches. Like a range of enslaved Atlantic Africans imported into the Americas, Gold Coast Africans originated from culturally fluid littoral or coastal societies, and this context shaped their New World experiences and ethnic transformations. New ethnic labels like Coromantee and (A)mina—by-products of ethnogenesis and cultural plasticity—were used and embraced actively in ways that inform how enslaved Atlantic Africans began the process of developing new concepts of group identity.[14] In addition to tracking the meaning and significance of Coromantee and (A)mina over time, I forward a theoretical frame that assesses sociopolitical, or class, dimensions in the creation of these new ethnic identities in the Gold Coast diaspora. Missing from most historical analyses regarding the circulations of people, cultures, and ideas throughout the Black Atlantic is the notion that enslaved Atlantic Africans originated from particular sociopolitical circumstances that shaped their sense of New World identity and consciousness as much as—if not more than—their cultural and linguistic backgrounds.

This study tracks the evolution of what I call a commoner consciousness—a set of sociocultural motifs and forms that embodied and embedded critiques of power and empowered elites. Spawned in the context of chattel and racial slavery in the Americas, this consciousness developed into anti-slavery, egalitarian, and revolutionary articulations that drew upon familiar Gold Coast cultural forms. To be sure, not all enslaved Atlantic Africans came from commoner backgrounds, nor did they all contribute to the development of commoner consciousness in the Western Hemisphere. The case of enslaved African Muslims, some of whom embraced the legitimacy of slavery to the degree that they could be entrusted with managing plantations or work gangs, serves as a useful counterpoint to commoner consciousness. In certain instances, the elite and aristocratic backgrounds of African Muslims nurtured a sense of religious, intellectual, and even racial supremacy that separated them from the non-Muslim enslaved masses.[15] Even among those who claimed Coromantee or (A)mina identity, some hailed from elite backgrounds in the Gold Coast, and this former status informed their sense of being in the environment of racialized slavery in the Americas. The example of the 1733–34 Amina revolt in Danish St. John, discussed at length in chapter 4, points in the direction of the formation of an "elite consciousness" that embraced human bondage and that legitimized Atlantic commerce while contesting European hegemony. The political revolution led by the St. John Aminas, however, stands in stark contrast with the many attempts at social revolution throughout the seventeenth- and eighteenth-century Gold Coast diaspora.[16]

Across a series of interconnected themes, this book assesses how enslaved and displaced Gold Coast non-elites used preexisting and evolving cultural scripts about power as a means of understanding, defining, and resisting new manifestations of oppression in the Western Hemisphere. Performances of Coromantee and (A)mina identity involved a common set of sociopolitical concerns and the creation of the necessary "weapons" to combat racial and chattel slavery in the Americas. As spiritual, social, and political means of empowerment, these weapons formed a cultural and sociopolitical arsenal for Coromantees and (A)minas who deployed them often and effectively in the early-modern circum-Caribbean. The ennoblement of former commoners to create New World Coromantee and (A)mina political orders; the activation of ancestors through obeah, blood oaths, and related ritual technologies; the development of Gold Coast diaspora masculinity with an attendant set of rules that moved many toward violent resistance; and the empowerment of women as political leaders, warriors, and ritual specialists represent concepts that sharply broke from their original applications and forms in the Gold Coast while helping to construct and define the New World present. Gold Coast Africans reinvented, redefined, and transformed Gold Coast cultural materials and deployed them in unprecedented ways in the Americas.[17] In tracking how Coromantees and (A)minas (per)formed their identities, this book seeks to elucidate and assess both discontinuities and continuities across the Black Atlantic.

FROM SOCIAL DEATH TO SOCIAL RESURRECTION

Death has been employed by a growing range of scholars as an interpretive and theoretical frame from which the slave trade, slavery, and the Atlantic African diaspora in the Americas can be understood. This trend, beginning largely with the work of Harvard sociologist Orlando Patterson and continuing with recent iterations by historians, focuses on "demographic catastrophe" and social dislocation inhibiting the formation of sociocultural forms in the Americas that drew upon, and that were sustained by, Atlantic African materials. These works tend to emphasize sharp sociocultural breaks and discontinuities with the Atlantic African past, since death, in its many incarnations, disrupted the ability of the enslaved to form—at the very minimum—coherent communities in the Western Hemisphere.[18]

In his pioneering 1982 analysis titled *Slavery and Social Death*, Patterson—a specialist in British Caribbean slavery—offers a theoretical framework that seeks to understand slave societies across space and time. Working from a broad and theoretical foundation, the concept of "social death" emerges as one of the most significant and influential interventions in the study of New World slavery in the past few decades.[19] In agreement with the work of Claude Meillassoux, Patterson contends that "the slave is violently uprooted from his milieu. He is desocialized and depersonalized." After this process of "social negation" and natal alienation, in which the enslaved were separated from kin, kith, and community, they either became permanent internal enemies or fallen insiders—criminals or prisoners of war. In either case, the social death that led humans to be transformed into commodities also meant a continual living death, as the enslaved could not be fully incorporated into their new societies.[20]

In the hands of historians of Atlantic World slavery, this sociological theory has led to a range of implications and has become the subject of a number of recent historiographic interventions.[21] In addition to the employments of social death, another historiographic trend has been the veritable explosion of scholarly interest in the various ethnic, linguistic, religious, or geographically defined diasporas emanating out of early-modern Atlantic Africa. Since the publications of John Thornton's *Africa and Africans in the Making of the Atlantic World* (1992), Michael Gomez's *Exchanging Our Country Marks* (1998), and Colin Palmer's "Defining and Studying the Modern African Diaspora" (2000), practically every region of Atlantic Africa has been the starting point for book-length explorations into the formation of various kinds of Western Hemisphere diasporas.[22] Despite an enormous corpus of extant and available archival sources, scholars of the Black Atlantic have only recently turned their interpretive gaze to the formation of Gold Coast diasporas. Indeed, the first three book-length historical treatments appeared just in the past decade. Two of the more influential works include Stephanie Smallwood's *Saltwater Slavery* (2007) and Vincent Brown's *The Reaper's Garden* (2008)—both activating or engaging Patterson's conceptualization of social death. More recently, Kwasi Konadu's *The Akan Diaspora in the Americas* (2010) has entered the historiographic fray.[23]

In *Saltwater Slavery*, Smallwood describes the creation of Gold Coast diasporas in the Americas variably as the result of an "unprecedented social death" and of "demographic catastrophe." Facing social and physical death in their continual "death march" to British Caribbean plantations, Gold Coast Africans were, in this view, "doomed to failure" in building networks of kinship and community in the Western Hemisphere. Smallwood does theorize a social life "counterbalance[d] [by] the alienation engendered by . . . social death," which took the form of "the elaboration of specific cultural content and its transformation to meet the particular needs of slave life in the Atlantic system." Without detailing this cultural content beyond broad and abstract categories, Smallwood concludes that invention, experimentation, growth, and change were the hallmarks of the cultural practices of the New World Gold Coast diaspora. In sum, the narrative formed by *Saltwater Slavery* begins with social death and demographic catastrophe in the Gold Coast, on slave ships and throughout the process of commodification, followed by the creation of new peoples with new cultural forms in the Americas. Smallwood rightfully troubles monolithic and monolingual ethnic formations and "modern Western anthropological constructions" such as "Akan," "Angolan," and "Biafran." However, she does not see that the "disaggregated lots" that disembarked from slave ships in the British Caribbean could and did form neo-African ethnicities like Coromantee and Eboe. Despite an explicit focus on "saltwater" or new enslaved Atlantic African imports, Smallwood largely ignores these new ethnic labels in her analysis.[24]

Vincent Brown's *The Reaper's Garden* masterfully activates death as a historical agent that shaped the lives of black and white Jamaicans. In doing so, he cautions against "viewing 'social death' as an actual state of being." Indeed, he rightly distills Patterson's definition of social death as "the absence of inheritance"—cultural and social.[25] Despite dealing with Atlantic African and, specifically, Gold Coast–inspired cultural technologies and forms in eighteenth-century Jamaica—obeah, transmigration, loyalty oaths, and death inquests—Brown also cautions against tracking specific cultural traits to "distinct 'ethnic' groups, traced back to their places of origin, or to describe cultural change in terms of linear progress toward settled New World patterns." Instead, he favors an emphasis on cultural creativity and "the politics of practical behavior" over the notion that "people's sole aim was to achieve a distinct cultural identity."[26]

Dislocated, socially alienated, and dying, Atlantic Africans brought to Jamaica came from diverse backgrounds and developed "deeply entangled" cultural practices as they "borrowed, stole, and mimicked" from each other. For Brown, attempts to disentangle this culture or explain the Africanity of particular practices serve little purpose. He does not wish, in his words, to "sustain a 'cult of continuity,' as some would have it, but to animate a politics of regeneration for a fluid world." The emphasis on death, crisis, flux, chaos, and discontinuity shapes much of the insightful narrative of *Reaper's Garden*. While allowing for a process of "social reconnection," activated by concerns about death, Brown does not provide thicker descriptions of these reconnections and rarely offers an effective counterbalance to social death. Indeed, the Atlantic African historical background is rendered as an indecipherable and mostly unknowable terrain throughout the book.[27]

If Smallwood and Brown represent a spectrum of historical engagements with the "social death" theoretical frame, Konadu's *The Akan Diaspora in the Americas* can be understood as making an argument for "social immortality." In many ways his work is a historiographic outlier, harkening back to the earlier anthropological studies of Melville J. Herskovits. Konadu maintains that an unbroken and pure "composite Akan culture" has existed from the sixteenth century to the present. Impervious and impermeable to the interventions of Islam, Christianity, and modernity, this culture, Konadu contends, was carried to the Americas by "Akan persons or culture bearers"—a people with a "shared (genetic) language, ethos, calendrical system, traditions of origin, sociopolitical order, and a high degree of ideological conformity." Despite the ravages of time and the demographic and geographic variances in the regions in which they were dispersed, the "Akan" kept their "distinct and largely homogeneous" culture intact throughout the Western Hemisphere. If any scholar is guilty of employing the "tribal" approach, as outlined and critiqued by David Northrup, Konadu would be the principal suspect. In his assessment of the construction of group identities in the early-modern Americas, Northrup argues against a recent historiographic trend that contends "that something closely resembling the ethnolingusitic 'tribes' of twentieth-century nationalist politics emerged in the Americas and made important contributions to the development of African-American cultures."²⁸ Northrup targets Douglas Chambers, John Thornton, and Mike Gomez in this regard; however, this assertion misses the mark as all three scholars recognize that New World African-derived identities and ethnic labels bore little resemblance to ethnolinguistic groups in Atlantic Africa. While Northrup may have misinterpreted the works of Chambers, Thornton, and Gomez—all of whom focus to varying degrees on ethnogenesis and cultural (re)invention—his pointed critique of the "tribal" approach captures Konadu's essentialist views of the persistence and continuity of Akan culture in the Black Atlantic.²⁹

Konadu dismisses the notion that enslaved peoples actively embraced or employed "Coromantee" or "(A)mina" as identifiers, contending instead that these "trademarks" were simply impositions by Europeans. Certainly, Europeans invented and first applied these two ethnonyms to Gold Coast Africans. Konadu, however, denies that enslaved Atlantic Africans appropriated and redefined these labels for their own purposes. In addition to his analysis of ethnic labels, Konadu contends that the "composite" Akan culture in the Americas—as static, bounded, and flat—was neither the product of ethnogenesis nor of cultural mixing and intermingling with Europeans or even other Atlantic Africans. In this view, the Akan never suffered social death but, instead, maintained a continuous sociocultural existence from their natal homes in the Gold Coast to Jamaica and other Western Hemisphere locales—even into the twenty-first century.³⁰

Somewhere between the interpretive extremes of social death and social immortality lies a generative middle ground, what I call "social resurrection."³¹ Mirroring to some extent Vincent Brown's "regeneration" and James Sweet's "recreation," resurrection embodies certain kinds of continuities and discontinuities while relying heavily on understandings of Gold Coast and Atlantic African historical backgrounds.³² In doing so, this interpretive middle ground grapples with "Coromantee" and "(A)mina" as new ethnic groups in the Americas that actively drew upon the old and the new—Atlantic African sociopolitical positioning and cultural technologies as well as the realities of chattel bondage in the Western Hemisphere. I analyze the dynamic ways in which Coromantee and (A)mina communities formed, changed, and were sustained over time. In recognizing that, in specific instances, Gold Coast diasporic communities actively integrated Akan, Ga, Adanme, and Ewe speakers, this book elucidates some of the mechanisms by which Atlantic Africans from different language cohorts negotiated with each other in the prolonged transition from ethnicity to race. Importantly, this transformation of diasporic identities was neither instantaneous nor linear. Instead, this constant shift from ethnicity toward race occurred over centuries and should be characterized as dynamic, nonlinear, and chaotic. In the tempestuous sea of change in the Gold Coast diaspora, "Coromantee" and "(A)mina" provided anchors of identity and meaning—at particular times and in specific locales. Understanding these meanings and tracking their changes helps us map a part of the convoluted cultural geography of the Black Atlantic.

What Smallwood, Brown, and Konadu can agree on in their interpretations of Gold Coast diasporas is that ethnic labels had little to no meaning in the Americas. At worst, these labels marked a Eurocentric ethnic nomenclature and taxonomy of African "types" similar to eighteenth-century descriptions of slave behavioral traits. At best, "Coromantee" and "(A)mina" reflect ever-shifting and moving targets that are impossible to define, understand, or historicize. In "rescuing" and seeking to track the changing meaning and values of these two ethnic identifiers over time, I embrace ideas articulated by Colin Palmer, John Thornton, Michael Gomez, Paul Lovejoy, Gwendolyn Midlo Hall, and Robin Law. As summarized by Kristin Mann, they collectively contend that "persons born in Africa carried with them into slavery not only their culture but also their history, and that if we understand the experiences of slaves and the histories of the societies from which they came, then we will be able to trace these influences into the diaspora."[33]

This "African-centered" focus, as articulated by Lovejoy, frames the history of transatlantic slavery and slave trading as extensions of Atlantic African history in the Americas. In defining the methodology of the study of African diasporas, Colin Palmer wisely notes, "The African continent—the ancestral homeland—must be central to any informed analysis and understanding of the dispersal of its peoples . . . [and] the peoples who left Africa and their ethnic group, coerced or otherwise, brought their cultures, ideas, and worldviews with them as well."[34] In similar fashion, Roquinaldo Ferreira contends that the Atlantic Ocean should be understood as a bridge—not an insurmountable divide—that connected together histories in Atlantic Africa to the Americas.[35] The claim I make is that while enslaved Gold Coast Africans stopped being citizens of polities and suffered social death, they did not cease making Atlantic African history—even as they were becoming Coromantees or (A)minas. Embedded within each of their stories were the continuities and discontinuities of experience that shaped and defined Atlantic African diasporas.

In the interpretive frame of this work, both death and resurrection become generative tropes that encompass the many transformations Gold Coast Africans and their American-born descendants underwent in Western Hemisphere slavery. By the seventeenth century, a sociopolitical system akin to feudalism developed in the Gold Coast in which hereditary nobles monopolized political authority, social power, and various modes of wealth generation. Within this sociopolitical order, human bondage was normative and slaves became one of the earliest and most accessible forms of private property. The political, social, and economic distance maintained between the class of hereditary nobles and the commoner masses was made possible by retainers—slaves and bonded commoners—who provided nobles with labor and helped them generate wealth. Involvement in Atlantic commerce by nobles and other elites deepened the divide and, over time, placed growing numbers of commoners in danger of being enslaved and transported to the Americas.[36] Within this sociopolitical order, commoners who had the access and wherewithal to engage in Atlantic commerce and, thus, aid in the enslavement of others did so with few qualms. Even former slaves or bonded commoners could become slave raiders, traders, or owners in their own right.

While slavery may have been a normal aspect of life in the early-modern Gold Coast, the processes of capture, warehousing, commodification, transport, disembarkation, and seasoning in Western Hemisphere colonies represented, qualitatively, a different set of experiences altogether. These processes and the immersion of the enslaved into new worlds where racialized bondage held sway represented the transition from social life to social death highlighted in the first part of this book. Social death, indeed, occurred in the trauma of the transatlantic experience. In combination, forced removal of individuals from their natal homes and experiences with racial slavery represented quite radical breaks from the prior existence of Gold Coast commoners. Moreover, these former commoners—forcibly transformed into Atlantic commodities—were forever separated from hereditary elites and the familiar social and political hierarchies of their home polities.

As harrowing as their experiences were, transportation to the Americas offered enslaved Gold Coast Africans opportunities to make their worlds anew. The realities of racial slavery demanded the development of new practices for survival and resistance. The absense of hereditary nobles meant that these practices could represent radical innovations. They developed a new sense of identity and a revolutionary, anti-slavery, commoner consciousness that drew inspiration from an array of materials in their immediate Gold Coast pasts. As much as racial slavery in the Americas accelerated transformations in identity and consciousness, neither social death nor "soul murder" could be permanent states of being.[37] In the Western Hemisphere, social death quickly gave way to social resurrection. The creation of Coromantee and (A)mina peoples and the commoner consciousness marked a new cultural geography in the Black Atlantic and the genesis of a new political discourse. Their concepts of freedom, autonomy, and egalitarianism did not, however, emerge out of early-modern European intellectual movements—the Enlightenment and classical liberalism.[38] In crafting a new sense of Black Atlantic citizenship and articulating a new collective consciousness that questioned the legitimacy of human bondage, Coromantees and (A)minas cannot be understood as liberalized or liberal subjects molded by Europe's Age of Reason.[39] They developed ideas of liberty and autonomy that favored the corporate or collective over the individual. Moreover, the very paths Coromantees and (A)minas took to obtain freedom, autonomy, and sovereignty were facilitated and informed by Atlantic African rather than European contexts and cultural technologies.

In sum, Gold Coast commoners remembered their natal homes and thus drew from memories of Atlantic Africa to confront the harsh and suffocating realities of Western Hemisphere slavery. In doing so, they forged an abolitionist consciousness. As outlined in the second part of the book, this consciousness—activated through their ideas about state formation and governance, spirituality and the ancestral realm, women and regeneration—demonstrated both discontinuities and continuities with the past and framed their ongoing "resurrections" as new ethnic groups in their New World present. As they (per)formed Coromantee and (A)mina identities and cultures, enslaved Gold Coast commoners embodied the tribe of the Middle Passage. Separated from their natal homelands and kin, they actively and consciously remade themselves within the crucible of American slavery.

PART 1
SOCIAL LIFE AND DEATH

ONE

Gold Coast Backgrounds

We were a people in motion still . . .

AYI KWEI ARMAH, *TWO THOUSAND SEASONS* (1973)

This chapter provides a historical optic through which the Gold Coast diaspora in the Americas can be better understood. If we can embrace notions forwarded by Gomez, Palmer, Thornton, and others that diasporic peoples carried their histories with them across the Atlantic, then understanding those histories helps contextualize the societies they encountered, confronted, and recreated in the Americas.[1] Social death, then, may have been real and consequential. However, the forced separation of Atlantic Africans from the societies of their birth and their subsequent diasporic dispersals did not lead to mass amnesia nor, for that matter, a series of cultural holocausts. They did not forget the range of familiar political, social, and cultural geographies from their immediate pasts, nor could they continue their previous lives in unaltered forms. Physical separation from natal societies and life in chattel bondage in the Americas represented real historical watersheds and the frames within which the enslaved could engage in the invention and formulation of new sociopolitical traditions. Simply put, social death gave way to social resurrection as diasporic Atlantic Africans actively and continuously reinvented themselves using concepts with which they had strong familiarity.

In this view, the Gold Coast past mattered in their New World present. In order to grasp the processes of resurrection and reinvention in the Americas, Gold Coast backgrounds become key starting points for this study. The goal here, however, is not to project static conceptualizations of Atlantic Africa—histories without complexities, layers, and motion—or broad categories of continuities in the Americas. Instead, this chapter seeks to describe and understand the complicated and fluid "terrains"—physical, ethnolinguistic, and political—inhabited by diverse peoples throughout the early-modern Gold Coast with a particular focus on speakers of the Akan, Ga, Adanme, and Ewe languages. Within these ever-moving and shifting terrains, Gold Coast peoples and polities became linked through a number of ongoing political, commercial, and cultural processes. These connections, including the "Akanization" of Ga-, Adanme-, and Ewe-speaking polities by the early-eighteenth century and the spread of Akan—along the coast and into near hinterland regions—as a political and commercial lingua franca, resulted from identifiable historical processes and not from some ethereal sense of a shared or "genetic" Gold Coast or Akan cultural "heritage" existing in the region since time immemorial.[2] Manifestations of cultural cross-fertilization, particularly the spreading influence and political domination of Akan-speaking peoples, meant that between 1700 and 1765 most of the Gold Coast Africans sucked into transatlantic slave trading vortices knew Akan as a primary, secondary, or tertiary language. This common linguistic thread and the heavy concentrations of Gold Coast Africans in specific Caribbean and mainland colonies in the Americas served as catalysts to ethnogenesis and the creation of Coromantee and (A)mina identities and cultures throughout the eighteenth century.

In sum, this chapter surveys Gold Coast history through the mid-eighteenth century. The northward expansion of the Asante kingdom during and after 1760 radically altered the ethnolinguistic composition of the Gold Coast slave trade as more and more non-Akan speakers were drawn into Atlantic commercial orbits. While some previous studies employ Asante-centric assessments of the Gold Coast slave trade and the formation of Gold Coast diasporas in the Americas, this bias toward the hinterland leads to underestimations of the number of Akan, Ga, Adanme, and Ewe speakers from littoral zones embarking on slavers during the early decades of the eighteenth-century—a period when Coromantee and (A)mina ethnic groups formed in the Americas.[3] Since the larger study assesses the formation of the Gold Coast diaspora from the 1680s to the 1760s, limiting the chronological focus of this chapter allows for keener assessments of the links between littoral histories and geographies in the Gold Coast and the broader Atlantic World. In seeking to illuminate as much of the relevant and usable Gold Coast past as possible, the goal in this chapter is to recreate a part of the transregional history of eighteenth-century Atlantic Africa. As articulated by Kristin Mann, the diasporic paradigm employed here requires "a model that begins in Africa, traces the movement of specific cohorts of peoples into the Americas and examines how, in regionally and temporally specific contexts, they drew on what they brought with them as well as what they found in the Americas to forge new worlds for themselves."[4] From this frame, we can better judge and assess the nature of a range of continuities and discontinuities that became part of the multiple worlds inhabited by Gold Coast Africans in the Western Hemisphere.

PHYSICAL AND ETHNOLINGUISTIC GEOGRAPHIES

No discussion of the Gold Coast can begin without some description of its physical terrain and topography. Historically, the area lacked a common place name among its inhabitants; the Gold Coast moniker was originally adapted by European traders in the sixteenth century from the Portuguese *Costa da Mina* (the Coast of Mines) due to the lucrative trade in gold in the coastal regions. The region includes just over three hundred miles of coastline in Atlantic West Africa situated between the Comoé River in the west and the Volta River in the east—encompassing parts of modern-day Ghana, Côte d'Ivoire, and Togo. Depending on the century, or decade in some instances, the Gold Coast extended inland to the Volta basin in the north and—at least in terms of potential slave procurement or catchment areas—as far north as modern Burkina Faso. Much of the northern reach of the Gold Coast depended on the expansion and wide-ranging political influences of the Asante kingdom, particularly during the course of the mid- to late-eighteenth century.[5]

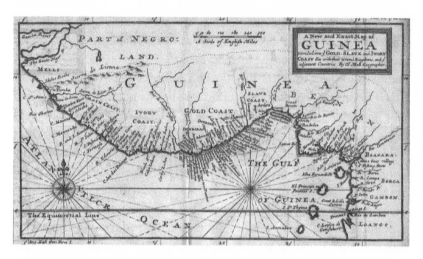

1.1. A map of Guinea divided into the Gold, Slave, and Ivory Coasts, circa 1680s. Source: Bosman, *A New and Accurate Description,* opposite 1. Courtesy of the Manuscripts, Archives, and Rare Books Division, Schomburg Center for Research in Black Culture, New York Public Library, Astor, Lenox, and Tilden Foundations.

Despite its small size relative to other coastal regions in Atlantic Africa, the Gold Coast was a land of stark contrasts. Within its diverse and shifting boundaries, the Gold Coast included three vastly differ- ent ecological zones—coastal grasslands, forests, and savannas. From south to north, flat coastal lands, salt marshes, and lagoons give way to hills, mountains, and dense forestation—representing a seemingly impenetrable "bush" in the early-modern European imaginary. In the view of Ludewig Rømer, a trader stationed at Christiansborg Castle in the 1740s, "Africa (the sea coasts excepted) is still wholly unknown," a fact he blamed on "Nature herself," which created thick stands of forest and bushes that even the inhabitants had difficulty managing. The land was not as foreboding and impenetrable as outsiders believed, though its tropical disease ecology—complete with such lethal afflictions as malaria and yellow fever—made the Gold Coast, and much of Atlantic Africa by extension, truly a "white man's grave."[6]

Despite its lethality to Europeans, the fertile coastal lands and in- land savannahs sustained life to the degree that high population and settlement densities led to the wide proliferation of settled agricultural communities and large towns in the Gold Coast prior to 1600. On this note, Gerard Chouin and Christopher Decorse contend that as early as 800 CE, Akan-speaking peoples in the southern Gold Coast created a "pre-Atlantic" agrarian order in which they carved out—with iron tools no less—agricultural spaces and dwellings from the dense inland forests. Within these habitations, people cultivated palm oil and yam and used iron digging tools to create the entrenched earthwork settlements they lived in between 800 and 1500 CE. The Chouin-Decorse model is an open challenge to one forwarded by Ivor Wilks in which European contact and the start of Atlantic commerce in the fifteenth and sixteenth centuries served as catalysts driving sociopolitical complexity in the southern Gold Coast. Joining and, for the most part, corroborating Chouin and Decorse in their counter to Wilks, A. Norman Klein introduced DNA and radiocarbon evidence that dates the presence of Akan-speaking agrarians in the forests of the southern Gold Coast by 700 CE. The pre-Atlantic agrarian order, however, collapsed abruptly as the possible result of epidemic disease that caused a demographic catastrophe and served a devastating blow to the rise and growth of polities in the Gold Coast when it struck. In the wake of rapid population collapse, a new "Atlantic agrarian order" emerged that coincided with the arrival of the Portuguese in the fifteenth century. In this case, the Gold Coast was still recovering from the demographic and sociopolitical legacies of epidemic disease, and the previous earthwork settlements and agrarian spaces of the pre-Atlantic agrarian order were largely reforested by the late 1400s.[7]

By the 1600s, both populations and agrarian settlements had rebounded. Indeed, the Gold Coast witnessed a veritable demographic explosion, perhaps as a result of the natural process of recovery from epidemic disease and not, as argued by Wilks, a new shift to crop cultivation. Wilhelm Müller, a Lutheran pastor residing at a Danish fort near Cape Coast from 1662 to 1669, described various "large and populous" towns in the region, including Efutu, Wimba (Winneba), Enkinne-Fu, and Ando-Crum. Reporting historical narratives passed on to him by the Ga-speaking residents of eighteenth-century Accra, Rømer noted, "The old Blacks tell us about millions of people once living on the Accra coast.... It was not only the coast that was densely populated.... where the mountains begin, [the district] was full of towns and people everywhere." In sum, the Gold Coast was "full of people" in Rømer's view, owing to a number of causes. "Blessed" and fertile land as well as efficient modes of agricultural production and labor mobilization combined to help sustain high population and settlement densities that later represented deep "recruitment" pools from which Europeans extracted enslaved Atlantic African labor.[8]

The peoples of the Gold Coast were just as diverse as the physical geographies they inhabited. The four largest ethnolinguistic clusters in the region, both numerically and in terms of geographic expanse, include Akan or Volta-Comoé (Fante, Twi, Guang), Ga, Adanme, and Ewe. These language groups were joined by a range of others—including Gur in the north and Etsii, Efutu, Eguafo, and Asebu in the south. Particularly in the coastal south, some of these smaller ethnolinguistic groupings became amalgamated by larger language clusters through complex processes of ethnogenesis, often as the result of military conquest or the political exigencies arising from the threat of northern invasion. In part, the current study seeks to work against the bias toward Akan speakers in historical accounts on the Gold Coast—Asante in the hinterland and Fante in the coastal south. Even if Akan speakers represented a numerical majority in the southern Gold Coast, they lived among and interacted with speakers of Ga, Adanme, and Ewe, and the resulting cultural formulations played out in revealing ways in the Western Hemisphere diaspora. In this specific sense, they created something in the Americas that went beyond an "Akan" diaspora, and both Coromantee and (A)mina were amalgams of the languages and cultures of a range of peoples living in the littoral and near inland regions of the Gold Coast.[9]

As John Parker notes, only a handful of historians "have paused to consider the history of the Ga-Dangme coast between Accra and the River Volta, yet it divides two of Africa's most intensively researched cultural agglomerations: the Twi-speaking Akan kingdoms to the west, and the Aja- and Yoruba-speaking kingdoms in the east." The lack of historical attention to Ga, Adanme, Ewe, and—to a lesser extent—Fante speakers in the central coast has a lot to do with the historical "weight" associated with centralized and expansionist kingdoms in Atlantic Africa—particularly Asante, Dahomey, Benin, and Kongo.[10] Those who lived in decentralized societies and small polities constituted a majority of the people in the Gold Coast and throughout Atlantic Africa and, by the fact of their relative powerlessness vis-à-vis centralized kingdoms, they were overrepresented among the enslaved, the (dis)embarked, and the dispersed. It is for this very reason that their collective stories form an important aspect of the Gold Coast diaspora.

Before 1700, Akan was the most widely spoken language throughout the Gold Coast. It also had, by far, the largest geographic scope and spread. By the seventeenth century, the range for Akan speaking peoples encompassed much of the coastal portion of the Gold Coast, reaching northward beyond the region between the Afram and Volta rivers. From west to east, Akan speakers inhabited the area between the southeastern portion of what is now Côte d'Ivoire and parts of the coastal region east of the Volta River's outlet into the Gulf of Guinea—in the western portion of modern-day Togo. Certainly, given the long history of human migrations and the rise and fall of powerful states throughout the Gold Coast, the region in which Akan speakers lived experienced constant expansions and contractions, rendering it difficult if not impossible to convey a sense of a stable ethnolinguistic geography. They, like others, were a people in continuous motion. Even the mapping of Akan-speaking habitation patterns in the seventeenth and eighteenth-century becomes more complicated when we take into account the Akanization of people from a variety of language communities conquered by Akan polities or through the more benign adoption of Akan as a political or commercial lingua franca. As a result of a number of intersecting political and sociocultural processes, many peoples throughout the littoral and near-inland regions of the Gold Coast were familiar with Akan or a mutually intelligible dialect and could likely speak it as a secondary or tertiary language by the early eighteenth century.[11]

Though many Akan traditions of origin speak of ancestors who descended from the sky or from under bodies of water, the corpus of "terrestrial" genesis traditions—in which the first people originated from underground—point in useful historical and archaeological directions. Due to the precision of the geographic locales at which Akan ancestors sprang from the ground, Wilks hypothesized that they represent the "exact sites where farming began" in the thirteenth or fourteenth century. Quite a number of these sites pointed the way to valuable archaeological findings producing some of the earliest known Akan materials, including ceramics and samples of charcoal. However, carbon dating pushes back the chronology from Wilks's earlier estimates to 800–930 CE. These sites of Akan origins may have represented more than places where they began a new agricultural mode of production. In the "long memory" represented by Akan oral traditions, the sites where their ancestors emerged from the ground may have been geographic way points representing regions they settled after lengthy migrations from elsewhere.[12] From afar, it may have seemed as if their ancestors emerged from holes in the ground, given how deeply rooted Akan speakers were to become in the forest fringe of the Gold Coast.

Using a fragmentary evidentiary base, a handful of writers—namely W. T. Balmer, Eve Meyerowitz, and J. B. Danquah—theorized that the ancestors of the Akan speakers who populated the Gold Coast originated from the ancient empire of Ghana. While this theory had a great deal of currency when the Gold Coast became independent in 1957—serving as the basis for the choice in name for the new republic—not much extant evidence supports the claim. Even more unsubstantiated have been the assertions of Akan connections to, in the words of Danquah, an "ancient heliolithic culture which once flourished in the Mediterranean and the Ancient East." This particular theory originated with Thomas E. Bowdich in 1817 during the British mission to Kumasi—the capital of the Asante kingdom. In this case, Bowdich discovered what he thought were similarities between the laws and customs of ancient Egypt, Abyssinia, and nineteenth-century Asante. While origin stories and histories linking Akan-speaking peoples to migrations from Ghana and Egypt require imaginative leaps, a handful of oral traditions make more reasonable claims that Akan speakers originated somewhere in the north from either the "Great White Desert" or the sahelian and savannah regions of Atlantic Africa.[13]

Another set of traditions focus on the town or state of Adanse. Originating from the north to inhabit the forest fringe, Akan speakers arrived at what became Adanse and created a permanent settlement. Other traditions tell of Adanse as the very site of Akan-speaking origin and the place where their sky god, Jancómpon, began the project of creating the world and humanity. Situated south of Kumasi, east of

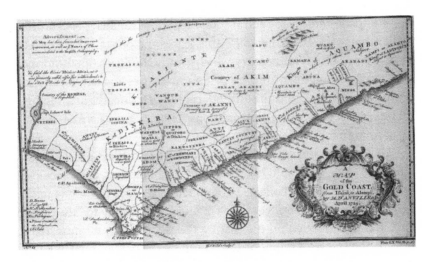

1.2. A map of the Gold Coast from Assini to Alampi, 1729.
Source: J. Greene, *A New General Collection of Voyages and Travels* 2: plate 60,
between 564 and 565. Courtesy of the Rare Books Division, New York Public
Library, Astor, Lenox, and Tilden Foundations.

Denkyira, and west of Akyem, Adanse's central locale in what became
the Akan heartland perhaps explains its central place in oral traditions
as the home of most Akan clans. Adanse appears in a number of oral
histories, and now in written accounts by professional historians, as
one of the five great towns of pre-Atlantic Akan-speaking states. Seven-
teenth- and eighteenth-century map makers frequently located "Acanij"
or "Akanni"—the alleged home of the Akani or Akanist community of
gold merchants—at or near Adanse. Whether Adanse was previously the
capital of a centralized Akan kingdom or a pseudonym for an "Akanni"
state may not be as important as the place in the collective Akan consciousness of this region as birth home to most, if not all, icons of Akan
political culture—including court linguists (*akyeame*) and swords of
state. Even now, many Akan-speaking clans trace their origins to Adanse, which is often said to be the "first Akan state" or the place where
Akan speakers built the first houses in oral traditions. Recent archaeological findings support some of these claims. According to Brian Vivian, archaeological analyses conducted in the 1990s "from the site of
Adansemanso indicate that a significant level of cultural complexity

was attained within the central forest region of Ghana 2–3 centuries earlier than previously thought." This places the origins of Adanse in the twelfth or thirteenth century, which greatly conflicts with the former view held by a range of historians that Akan polities first developed near the forest fringe as late as the fifteenth century. In sum, the archaeological record and the various oral traditions about the primacy and centrality of Adanse mostly concur.[14]

Ga speakers inhabited a much more circumscribed and less fluid ethnolinguistic geography. According to Carl Reindorf, a Ga-speaking Basel missionary who collected a number of Ga oral traditions in the early- to mid-nineteenth century, Ga refers specifically to "the people and country bounded on the east by the lagoon Tshemu near Tema, west by the [Lesser Sakumo River], south by the sea, and north by the Akwapem mountains." Representing about thirty miles of coastline and radiating out from its political and geographic center at Accra, the region inhabited by Ga speakers—the Accra Plains—was tiny in comparison to the lands of their far more numerous and geographically spread Akan-speaking neighbors. Their close physical proximity to, and long historical domination by, their Akan neighbors shaped fundamental aspects of Ga-speaking littoral communities. One example, among many, appears in the very naming of the Ga capital at Accra. The Ga name for the polity Accra is "Ga"; among Akan speakers, both the town and people were called "Nkran" (Accra)—a reference to a particular species of swarming ant and an Akan translation of the word "Ga." As a "powerful wandering tribe" that invaded other lands and subdued their inhabitants, Ga speakers named themselves after a species of invasive dark-brown ants that "wander about in great swarms and invade houses, killing and devouring every living thing they meet," according to Reindorf. While Ga speakers used the reference to swarming ants to connote military prowess and their ancient conquest of Guang speakers residing in the Accra Plains, the Akan-speaking appropriation and translation of this metaphor had a less than generous meaning. Instead of viewing Ga speakers as a formidable military force, the Akan-speaking term "Nkran" cast Ga peoples as pests or nuisances to be controlled or exterminated.[15]

Both linguistic evidence and Ga oral traditions concur that Ga speakers migrated from what is now northern Nigeria, presumably to escape military and religious incursions by a Fulani sovereign. Another set of oral traditions claim that Ga and Adanme speakers migrated together or separately from either Tetetutu or Sameh in the east—both western tributaries or provinces of the kingdom of Benin. According to Parker, the fact that no archaeological findings support the linguistic evidence and oral traditions may mean that we should interpret the migration trope as a metaphor for "their gradual rise to demographic, linguistic, and political ascendancy over neighboring Guang-speaking peoples." Traditions of migration, movement, and motion, including less likely traditions linking Ga to ancient Egypt or the biblical Hebrews, have become ubiquitous elements in the consciousness and sense of historical trajectory for Ga-speaking peoples and many of their Gold Coast neighbors. Though Ga is now lumped in with Akan, Adanme, and Ewe as part of the Western Kwa family of languages due to vast similarities in vocabulary, phonology, and grammar, this modern classification muddles a historical process in which Ga-speaking peoples and polities suffered military defeat at the hands of, and political domination by, a sequence of expansionist Akan-speaking polities. Over the course of three centuries, Ga speakers absorbed aspects of the cultures of their conquerors and neighbors. The significant amount of cross-fertilization and linguistic intrusion between Ga and Akan obfuscates modern-day language classification systems that may not take into consideration the probability of a divergent linguistic past. We can make a plausible case that strong linguistic links between Ga, Adanme, and Ewe—for example—point to an earlier common proto-language that originated to the east of the Gold Coast. In this scenario, Ga, Adanme, and Ewe may have more ancient, historical connections between each other that were not shared with Akan before the fourteenth or fifteenth century.[16]

Closely related to Ga, Adanme—a language Reindorf claims was the "mother dialect" of Ga—had an even smaller ethnolinguistic geography in comparison to its close neighbor. Situated to the east of Accra, along the coastal area between Kpone and Ada—on the western lip of the Volta's outlet to the Gulf of Guinea and enclosed by the Volta River to the north—Adanme speakers inhabited an area roughly half the size of Greater Accra. Despite the tendency in modern parlance of treating Ga and Adanme as a single linguistic unit (thus, "Ga-Adanme"), this simplifies a more complex ethnolinguistic and political geography. While Ga and Adanme may be closely related, sharing an extensive amount of vocabulary and linguistic structure, these two languages or dialects of a much earlier proto-language were not quite mutually intelligible. In this case, we have to understand Ga- and Adanme-speaking cohorts and their polities as separate and unique. This is something recognized in at least a handful of oral traditions that offer an origin story for Adanme speakers separate from the trajectory of Ga speakers. In this case, Reindorf relates that Adanme speakers originated from "[Sameh], a country situated between two rivers, Efa and Kpola, near the Niger." Squeezed by continued expansion of two powerful Slave Coast kingdoms—Oyo and Dahomey—Adanme speakers trekked through Hwatshi and Togologo before their contingent divided into three groups upon crossing the Volta. One group, led by Akroye—sister of the future sovereign of Krobo—settled with her followers at Lashibi Island. Akroye's husband, the future king of La, left for the coast. The third group, led by Akroye's brother, settled at the foot of a mountain to the north and established the Krobo polity. From these three groups, Adanme speakers migrated farther west and settled in existing Ga-speaking towns or created their own small settlements.[17]

To the east of the Ga- and Adanme-speaking diasporas, peoples, and polities and encompassing portions of modern southeastern Ghana, Togo, and southwestern Benin, the region inhabited by Ewe speakers was relatively vast and diverse. Indeed, Ewe speakers bridged two major Atlantic African coastal zones—as defined and imagined by Europeans—with significant settlements in both the Gold Coast and the aptly named Slave Coast. Where the Volta forms a natural east-west divide—at the border between modern-day Ghana and Togo—Ewe speakers resided in the region since at least the mid-seventeenth century. Like their Ga- and Adanme-speaking neighbors, Ewe speakers tell of earlier migrations, movements, and linguistic diasporas that resulted in some of their forebears crossing the Volta from the east.[18]

Their oral traditions recount an early migration from a town named Ketu, where Ewe speakers settled after temporary residence in Oyo and Belebele in what is now Nigeria. After local wars convulsed the region, they abandoned Ketu and split into three groups with each one estab-

lishing its own town—Tado, Notsie, and Dogbonyigbo. An internal dispute in Dogbonyigbo led to the departure of the ethnolinguistic group
known later as the Fon, who settled in what became Grand Popo near
Benin. The predecessors of the Anlo-Ewe also abandoned Dogbonyigbo
and settled among other Ewe speakers in Notsie, perhaps around the
early seventeenth century. The residents of Notsie soon left after a series
of disputes with a neighboring town and, in their exodus, Ewe speakers split again into three main bodies—the northern (western), middle,
and southern groups. The northern group moved west from Notsie to
the hills of Togo. From there they continued to migrate both north and
south where some, the Krepi, settled in the Anum hills and Kyerepon.
Others of the original northern group moved as far north as Akpafu
where they settled in preexisting Guang-speaking communities. The
middle group migrated south after arriving at a set of hills, eventually
settling near Ho and Adaklu. The southern group of Ewe-speaking migrants split in two. One group, led by Amega Wenya, moved southwest
and settled at Keta near the lagoons to the east of the Volta outlet to the
Gulf of Guinea. Sri, Wenya's nephew, led the second southern group and
settled in the area between the Keta Lagoon and the Volta. Later, both
Sri and Wenya founded the Anlo state—the southernmost Ewe-speaking
polity in the Gold Coast.[19]

Linguistic evidence complicates the historical trajectories of Ewe
speakers as conveyed in their oral traditions. Despite a number of studies
conducted by ethnolinguists seeking to connect Ewe to Yoruba—thus
verifying Ewe traditions of migration from what is today Nigeria—the
data is far from conclusive. Indeed, interpretations have run the full
gamut from establishing a definitive link between Ewe and Yoruba to
claims that Ewe has no trace of an earlier linguistic connection to Yoruba and is, instead, strongly linked to Akan, Ga, and Adanme. While
the idea of a migration from a Yoruba-speaking region as far east as
modern Nigeria cannot be supported by the linguistic evidence, studies
of Ewe dialects provide some support for the story of the Notsie exodus.
Dialectical studies, for example, tend to divide the Ewe language into
three dialect clusters—the western (inland or interior dialects, Glidyi,
and Anlo), central (Watyi, Ge, and Adja), and eastern sections (Gũ,
Fon, and Mahi). In the oral traditions, Fon speakers separated from the

Anlo-Ewe at an early point and settled in Grand Popo. As a dialect, Fon is so distinct from Anlo and other Ewe dialects that many ethnolinguists classify it as a separate language group altogether. As Sandra Greene summarizes, "Watyi, the dialect spoken in Notsie among other places is said to be 'substantially the same as Anlo'; the western dialects which 'are more closely related to each other than to the rest of the cluster' conforms in part with the groups which are said to have left Notsie with the Anlos."[20] Thus, some of the linguistic or dialectal trajectories match the historical trajectories contained in Ewe oral traditions.

Many historians would claim Anlo and the Ewe-speaking populations of the southeastern Gold Coast as part of the specific geography of the Slave Coast—a region including the coastal portions of modern Togo, Benin, and western Nigeria—and its attendant slave trading networks. However, the Anlo-Ewe in particular were drawn into the activities of Akan-speaking Akwamu—an expansionist kingdom that conquered Anlo in 1702—pulling other Ewe-speaking peoples and polities into orbits of both the Gold Coast and the Slave Coast slave trading networks. In this case, disaggregating Ewe speakers from processes occurring in the Gold Coast assumes that the neat lines drawn on historical maps by Europeans had real meaning for the people and processes on the ground. In addition, the activities of various slave trading enterprises further complicates the matter. During the 1678–79 voyage of the French Compagnie du Sénégal slaver *Soleil d'Affrique,* the ship's captain procured most of his human cargo on the Gold Coast and visited as far east as Allada in the Slave Coast to fill his hold. Likewise, the English Royal African Company defined the Gold and Slave Coasts as a contiguous trading zone—stretching from Axim in the west to Whydah in the east—by the 1680s. In 1692, the Dutch West India Company received a letter from Jan Ainsworth suggesting that the *St. Clara* acquire a full "load of slaves in the area between Craa [Accra] and Fida [Whydah]." "Coasting," or the pattern of making two or more stops at slave trading posts in the Gold Coast and in Whydah and Allada, became a ubiquitous practice for much of the slave trade. In fact, to trade "à Costy" for slavers employed by the Dutch West India Company meant to trade along the contiguous region from Costa da Mina to the Slave Coast, in the parlance used by the company in the period after 1730. Combined, the very nature of seventeenth- and eighteenth-century Gold Coast political geographies, as well as the existence of trade networks that intersected and crossed the imaginary divide between the Gold Coast and the Slave Coast, meant that Ewe speakers often joined cargoes of Akan, Ga, and Adanme speakers in their journeys across the Atlantic.[21]

One concept the four ethnolinguistic groups analyzed in this study shared—above all else—were stories in their oral traditions about movement and motion through space and the creation of miniature diasporas in the Gold and Slave Coasts. Over the *longue durée* of early modern to modern history, movement—through a desert, forests, savannahs, and across an ocean—became an ever-present theme throughout the Gold Coast and its diaspora. The ubiquity of migration traditions in Ghana, especially among Ewe and Fante speakers, moved Ivor Wilks to create and critique an entire category of Gold Coast origin stories that had a number of common features. Among these shared themes, he included "the abandonment of one homeland and the establishment of a new one at some relatively distant location" and, upon arrival, new groups either "succeeded in establishing their domination over pre-existing populations" or they created their own settlements in previously uninhabited or sparsely populated areas.[22] Perhaps, then, the domination of Gold Coast cultural technologies in particular Western Hemisphere colonies and the creation of Coromantee maroons in Jamaica and Suriname can be framed within the context of the themes emerging out of Gold Coast origins stories.

Perhaps the one element that separated earlier dispersals and diasporas from the later and larger transatlantic one would be that the migrations internal to the Gold Coast and adjoining regions were often led by political leaders and elites. Thus, Akan, Ga, Adanme, and Ewe speakers settled new towns or in towns occupied by others and then replicated—in whole—political and social hierarchies of their immediate pasts. Within this frame, the fluidity of their movements between and across physical (e.g., the forest, the savannah, or the Volta River) and cultural borderlands was not matched by correspondingly fluid sociopolitical forms in their new or temporary homes. This particular historical pattern would not be broken until the transatlantic trade separated Gold Coast commoners from elites. With very few exceptions, Gold Coast elites did not join the mass dispersals of peoples across the Atlantic to the Western Hemisphere. This transatlantic movement set the stage for the creation of new sociopolitical orders, visions, and realities discussed in the second part of this book.

Another common theme in the traditions of Akan, Ga, Adanme, and Ewe movement, migration, and diaspora was the amount of cultural mingling and sharing that spurred the creation of new cultural forms and spawned new ethnolinguistic configurations. Seemingly, new peoples and polities were created continuously throughout the broad outlines of Gold Coast geography and history. These new peoples and polities emerged often as the result of new or reconfigured cultural alignments as powerful forces—epidemic disease, expansionist polities, and Atlantic commerce—continuously dispersed coastal and near-inland communities. The key mechanisms for this type of ethnogenesis came in substantial historical waves at times. No better example of this exists than the creation of Fante language, ethnicity, and multistate alliances during the early eighteenth century as described in Rebecca Shumway's path-breaking *The Fante and the Transatlantic Slave Trade* (2011) and discussed later in this chapter.[23]

The themes of motion, diaspora, and ethnogenesis were not new to Gold Coast Africans who suffered the natal separation and alienation of social death caused by enslavement. They were all products of movement, dispersal, identity (trans)formation, and cultural innovation long before setting foot upon New World shores. These historical patterns and processes prefigured the creation of Coromantee and (A)mina in the Americas as well as (re)invented cultural performances like the ritual practice of obeah or the use of older Gold Coast sociopolitical concepts in new ways.[24] As unique and dynamic as these New World inventions and applications were, they should be seen as extensions of long-standing Gold Coast and Atlantic African realities. The contestations that convulsed Akan, Ga, Adanme, and Ewe peoples and polities created shifting political terrains in which war, predation, dispersal, and enslavement became ever-present realities for many Gold Coast commoners. As destabilizing and destructive as these circumstance were, they provided the frame within which those shipped across the Atlantic constructed new and revolutionary worlds in the Americas.

POLITICAL GEOGRAPHIES

While Akan-centric approaches have dominated the field of precolonial Gold Coast studies, in some ways, the historical and political processes underway in the region after 1600 lend credence to this bias. The expanding political, commercial, and cultural networks of Akan-speaking states had significant implications for all inhabitants. Focusing on the formation and expansion of Akan states in depicting complicated and shifting political geographies becomes necessary—despite the potential for denying the historical agency of Ga, Adanme, and Ewe speakers, among others. Widespread Akanization, or the adoption of Akan cultural forms, political institutions, and social structures among many non-Akan speakers in the Gold Coast by the eighteenth century, is simply historical fact. Explaining Akanization in the early-modern Gold Coast requires assessments of the historical role of Akan states in facilitating a level of regional interconnectedness that prefigured the formation of geographically defined, as opposed to "ethnic" or ethnolinguistic, diasporas in the Americas.[25]

Akan oral traditions identify five progenitor Akan-speaking kingdoms or *Akanman piesie anum*—Adanse, Akyem, Assin, Denkyira, and Asante. In this order, we arrive at a rough chronology of the rise and fall of at least three of the four larger expansionist kingdoms in the Gold Coast by the seventeenth and eighteenth centuries. By the midseventeenth century, Akwamu, Akyem, and Denkyira became the most significant polities in the region, to be followed by Asante after 1701. The coalition of Fante states that emerged during the first half of the eighteenth century was a decentralized alliance of polities and, by definition, was not expansionist. The states of Akwamu, Akyem, Denkyira, and Asante were examples of what Ray Kea refers to as a "social formation" or "a historically concrete society whose structure, organization, and historical development were conditioned by specific systems (modes) of material production." In this case, one particular mode of production— the tributary mode—necessitated state control and ownership over land resources and state collection of tribute in both kind and specie from commoners and peasants as a means of channeling agricultural surplus and other commodities from rural peripheries to elite-dominated urban cores. While this produced what Kea describes as "the conflict between the peasantry and the ruling class over the appropriation of the agricultural surplus," it was also a mode of production characterized by ever-expanding networks of tribute-producing peasant labor.[26] Not only does this type of suzerainty create a provocation for territorial expansion as a means of drawing more peasant labor into the grasp of landed and city-dwelling elites, but also it creates a recruitment pool of excess labor to be sold later to Europeans arriving at the coast with valuable and highly coveted trade goods.

In addition to the Akan social formation, we can describe an Akan "political formation" with structures, methods of organization, office-holders, and other state functionaries that form critical dimensions of Akan political culture. At the generative center of this political formation was the hierarchically arranged *oman* (*aman* plural), or polity, itself. While a cast of personnel assisted in administering an oman, no one person or office trumped the political stature of the *ohene* (*ahene* plural), or king. In a mid-seventeenth century description of Efutu, Wilhelm Johann Müller—Lutheran Chaplain of Danish Fort Fredericksburg—noted ahene never ruled without the consent of "senior personages of the kingdom and the most important *panyin* [elders] of the people." The political system headed by the ohene was more akin to an aristocracy than an absolute monarch, given the existence of notable checks and balances on the extent of their political authority. Among the checks on the power of ahene, in the view of Müller, was the fact that they were often elected for their wisdom but not as a result of their affluence. As Müller concludes, this structure allowed the "grandees" of Efutu to select "a king in order that their authority, might, and power may continue and be preserved, i.e. that they may rule much and he little."[27] In any event, even as a political figurehead for more powerful economic interests, an ohene headed an influential family of hereditary nobles and could wield supreme military and political authority over all others in a given polity.

The fact that ahene wielded real power can be corroborated by the icons, objects, and accoutrements with which they were typically associated. Otherwise mundane objects possessed or used by ahene represented a type of "paraphernalia of power" that collectively symbolized their transcendent political and ritual might. Quite literally, the "seat" of Akan political power was the royal stool (*ahennwa*)—a symbol of royal heritage, or ennoblement, and state power. Royal stools served dual purposes. Not only were they the sacred personal possessions of ahene, but also they held symbolic significance as the "soul" or "spirit" of a polity and all of its subjects. Thus, in the commission of a war, the act of capturing an enemy royal stool had profound implications beyond the political act of conquest.

Many royal officials and others of high status employed the hammocks and canopies or umbrellas that became so emblematic of Akan-speaking political leadership. These items signified sociopolitical hierarchy in obvious ways and were imbued with particular kinds of transcendent meaning. The very conveyance of royalty and especially ahene in hammocks by groups of subordinates symbolized political authority as much as the rare blankets, rugs, and imported fabrics used in their construction. Similarly, the shade provided by canopies or umbrellas separated royalty and court officials from the commoner masses who often toiled in the unrelenting heat without protection from the sun. Again, whether elevated and conveyed in a hammock or shaded from the sun, royalty and elites could always call upon the service of retainers, a specialized class of subordinates, to aid in their comfort.

Swords of state, or as Müller describes them, "precious sabres" made of the finest silver, gave "the most distinguished and richest men in the country an air of dignity, for they are carried in front of them on the head of a slave." Finely crafted iron and steel blades, often decorated on the pommel with horse-tails purchased from European merchants and sheathed in scabbards made of expensive and imported fabrics, jewels, "blood-red seashells," and the heads of lions or leopards, represented highly coveted adornments and were part of the standard accoutrements of the rich and powerful. In some instances, an actual sword of state became a symbol of a royal line, an ohene, or the oman much in the same way as a royal stool.[28] In addition to swords, canes or staves—usually of European manufacture and given as gifts by merchant company agents to kings and court officials—became symbols of royal power. In a 1704 agreement between the Dutch and Aquando, the king of Akwamu (or *Akwamuhene*), a stipulation appears that states "nobody shall be allowed to make palaver but those who are legally authorized to do so on behalf

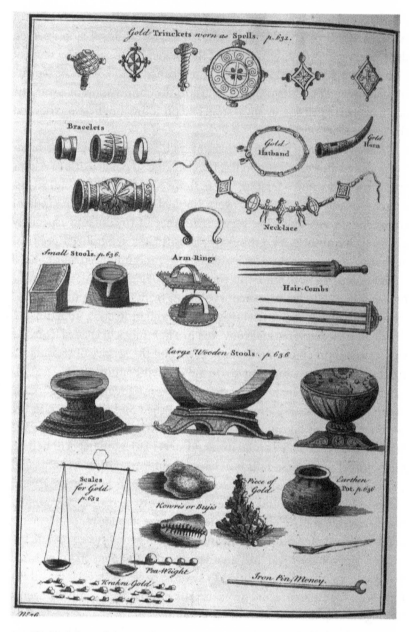

1.3. Akan stools, tools, musical instruments, jewelry, gold pieces, royal heralds, and other items, circa 1680s. Source: Barbot, *Coasts of North and South Guinea* III: opposite 251. Courtesy of the Rare Books Division, New York Public Library, Astor, Lenox, and Tilden Foundations.

of the King by showing his cane or staff." Royal heralds, staves adorned with a carved *fitiso* or animal "totem," were often used to represent a particular royal lineage or clan. In this case, the bearer of the king's staff carried the authority to "make palaver," or to initiate an agreement or resolve a range of disputes.[29] Though uniquely located in the worlds of Akan-speaking concepts of sociopolitical hierarchy and order, the paraphernalia of power—stools, canopies, hammocks, swords of state, and staves—would be appropriated and activated later by enslaved Gold Coast commoners in the making of new worlds in the Americas.

Below ahene, and in no particular order, were a range of officehold-ers and state administrators who played varying and even alternating roles in the military, religious, and commercial affairs of the oman they served. *Akyeame* (*okyeame* singular), often reduced in European sources to translators, could serve as chief counsels to kings, command royal guards, or negotiate trade and military agreements as ambassadors. Müller designates the "obcjámmi" as the state chancellor who served as the "first royal counselor" and, in essence, represented the first in com-mand after the ohene of Efutu. As the official bearers of royal heralds and staves, akyeame were ubiquitous features in and around the courts of Akan polities. Next to, or in some cases paralleling, the position of the okyeame, the office of *day* served as treasurer and chief administrator of state—at least in seventeenth- and eighteenth-century Efutu. According to Jean Barbot, a commercial agent in the employ of the French Compag-nie du Sénégal, days were high treasurers, viceroys, and essentially prime ministers serving as the "officers next [to] the king of Fetu." Perhaps in the eighty years that separated the observations of Efutu by Müller and Barbot, the office of day expanded to eclipse or equal the *okyeame*. As Barbot notes, the day "is almost inseparable from the king's person, and accompanies him [wherever] the necessity of affairs requires his pres-ence." Perhaps this role of being "inseparable from the king's person" was reflected in a 1659 commercial treaty between Efutu, Denmark, and the Danish African Company. In this instance, the king of Fetu was accompanied by a delegation including his captain of the royal guard (*fetero*), the day, and a *braffo* (military commander). Another Efutu del-egation appearing at Elmina Castle in June 1689 included the *Efutuhene* (King of Efutu) and his "Fetaire, Dey and Samin of Fitu" to demand from the Dutch director-general a loan of 120 to 130 bendas of gold to aid in their war against the Esebu state. In addition to being present with the ohene, the day served as the chief deputy in the king's absence and had the authority to make civil and military decisions as necessary.[30]

Beyond the actual administration of the oman, another set of officials provided security for the royal court and various court constituencies. Entrusted with the protection of an ohene, the captain of the royal guards, or *fataira*, accompanied kings on military expeditions and could be "[raised] so high as to be sometimes advanced to the throne, upon vacancy." Sword- and shield-bearers, often the princes of conquered and vassal states, had a number of responsibilities beyond the obvious. For example, they conveyed messages between a king and visitors to the royal court and, as Barbot notes, sword-bearers in particular were "sometimes sent [as] ambassadors to foreign countries." In many ways, employing a prince from a vassal polity as a sword- or shield-bearer served as insurance against an uprising by their home state. They were, in effect, hostages or pawns to be used to force the compliance of tributary states. Finally, court eunuchs or "attendants" prevented the king's wives from being "debauched," in Barbot's words. In polities lacking a treasurer, these attendants were "commonly intrusted with the king's wealth, the keys whereof they always keep . . . and consequently after the king's death, they are liable and obliged to give an account of it to the successor."[31]

Braffo, defined variably as a "commander-in-chief," "military commander," "or standard-bearer," served under an ohene and had a combination of political, military, and commercial responsibilities. Müller describes an event on April 22, 1663 in which the "bràfu" of Efutu led an armed party into Cape Coast Castle "under the guise of good friendship" to take control of the fortress from the Swedish and seize gold and all merchandise they found. This specific action was authorized by the "king and other grandees" of Efutu and undertaken by the braffo due to the inability of the Swedes to maintain a steady flow of trade goods into the region—as the result of a Dutch naval blockade. Taking Cape Coast Castle by force allowed Efutu to "sell" the fortress to the highest bidder. Though the English and Danes tried through negotiations with Efutu to possess the castle, the Dutch won the bidding war and assumed control in May 1663. From Müller's description of this event, the Efutu braffo assumed military authority over the castle for the sake of the commercial interests of the polity.[32]

Rømer defined braffos as military generals or "individuals who exercise the highest command over the entire nation," but the term could more broadly refer to high-ranking court or town officials, commercial agents, and priests or followers of particular deities or shrines. In some instances, *braffo* and *caboceer* became interchangeable terms or represented political, military, or commercial officeholders of roughly equal rank. From the Portuguese "cabociero," meaning headman or official, a caboceer in the Gold Coast context could be anything from the leader of a town or smaller settlement to a commercial agent working as a go-between for either an ohene or European merchant companies. The three caboceers—Pregatte, Sofphonije, and Apanij—who negotiated with Brandenburg agents to allow them to build a trading post in 1681, swore Akan oaths to not trade with English or French interlopers in the region between Axim and Cape Three Points. In this case, these three men may have combined the roles of town leaders, with the political authority to make a binding oath with a foreign nation, and commercial agents. Caboceers also had other roles and connotations. In his reflections on Gold Coast religion in the eighteenth century, Rømer describes one informant named Caboceer Putti who was the chief priest (*obosomfo* or *okomfo*) of the "most important oracle on the Gold Coast" at the Ga-speaking town of Labadi. Either Putti (Okpoti) was both a priest and a caboceer or, as Rømer intimates, he was a caboceer because he was a chief priest. With a variety of meanings over time and across the far-flung geography of the Gold Coast, both *braffo* and *caboceer* might have been references to something akin to the rank of "captain" or the titles "head" and "chief" (e.g., captain of troops, town head, chief priest, or captain of trade).[33]

In addition to ahene, akyeame, days, braffos, and caboceers, Akan-speaking aman relied upon priests (*akomfo* and *abosomfo*); elders (panyin); hereditary nobles, lords, or "big-men" (*ofan, abirempong,* or *awura*); and merchants (*batafou*) in varying degrees for state administration and to maintain an interconnected web of attendant power structures. While these titles and ranks carried imprecise and shifting meanings across time and space, the overwhelming role of men as court and state officeholders remained constant in the Gold Coast—at least through the early decades of the nineteenth century.[34] Beyond brief mentions of prominent priestesses, wives or concubines of ahene, and a small handful of queens, politically empowered women in the sixteenth-, seventeenth-, and eighteenth-century Gold Coast are absent in both European records and local oral traditions. For instance, a small handful of references to individual queens who ruled Akan-speaking polities in the Gold Coast appear in contemporary travel accounts and oral histories recorded in the twentieth century. In many of these cases, these women lacked sufficient power, authority, and autonomy to be much more than subordinates to male regents.[35]

Even in Müller's extensive vocabulary of seventeenth-century Efutu, no mention of *ahemma* (*ohemma* singular), or queen-mothers, as coregents appears despite the fact that he discusses a host of other royal functionaries and officeholders. The "ohinne-düfu" (*ohene-düfu*), or principal wife of the king, is the closest approximation to the office of ohemma found in either his narrative or his extensive seventeenth-century Akan-Efutu vocabulary. Beyond Müller, all other seventeenth- and eighteenth-century Gold Coast travel accounts and Akan vocabularies fail to reference ahemma—even in sources that extensively and closely detail state actors and functionaries in the region. While Shumway surmises that this silence reflects "early modern European notions of gender roles or simply a lack of accurate information among European agents on the coast," this runs counter to the existence of a real and long-standing "precolonial gaze"—in this case, a series of lurid interpretations of black female bodies that became ubiquitous in early-modern European travel accounts in Atlantic Africa. Beginning in the sixteenth century, European travelers generated a corpus of quasi-ethnographic commentary about the bodies, sexuality, and childbearing practices of Atlantic African women, and this "gaze" played a role in early rationales for African enslavement. Some of these travelers visited the Gold Coast, writing extensively about women in all areas of life in Akan-speaking polities. Given the many tropes of difference, defect, and dysfunction appearing in works written by many of these early-modern European travelers, the presence of empowered women in Gold Coast polities would have been quickly seized upon in their imaginings.[36] Extensive analyses by modern historians as well as seventeenth-century accounts of Queen Njinga of Ndongo in West-central Africa and eighteenth-century observations about Dahomey's queen-mothers (or *kpojito*) and gun-wielding women warriors provide insightful counterpoints to the evident trends in the Gold Coast.[37] If examples of politically empowered and otherwise powerful women can be found in the records related to other early-modern Atlantic African coastal regions, why has there been such silence about the existence of their counterparts in the Gold Coast?

Another explanation may help resolve issues regarding the many silences in the historical record about politically empowered Gold Coast women in the seventeenth or eighteenth century. Using interpretive constructions from extant historical records and oral traditions, we arrive at the conclusion that Akan-speaking women neither wielded significant levels of political power nor held political offices as queen-mothers, merchants, caboceers, and town leaders in early-modern Gold Coast polities. Instead, these roles may have been relatively recent nineteenth- and twentieth-century sociopolitical inventions—perhaps as one of many consequences of the growing demographic power of Gold Coast women caused by the transatlantic slave trade. Practically all historical references to "queen-mothers" in the Gold Coast originate in, or refer to, the nineteenth and twentieth centuries. The earliest known historical reference to a female co-regent of an Akan-speaking polity—with the level of power and autonomy to balance or check an ohene—appears to be Ohemma Ama Sewa, who led the state of Dwaben against Asante in the 1830s. Yaa Asantewaa, the *Ejisuhemaa* (e.g., queen-mother of the Ejisu state near Kumasi), commanded Asante's armies against the British in 1900 and, as a result, became the most famous example of an empowered woman political leader in the Gold Coast.[38] For pre-nineteenth-century examples of empowered women in the Gold Coast or its diaspora, we have to look to seventeenth- and eighteenth-century slave and maroon communities forming in the British, Dutch, and Danish circum-Caribbean colonies discussed at length in chapter 6.

In combination, oral traditions, political maps, archeological evidence, and written accounts by individuals living in or visiting the seventeenth- and eighteenth-century Gold Coast aid in the reconstruction and description of the shifting political geographies of the region. One synchronic snapshot of this political terrain appears in a 1629 Dutch map created by Hans Propheet that includes approximate locations and notations about a range of inland and coastal polities including Akwamu (Aquemboe), Accra (Great Acara), Akyem (Akim or Great Acanij), Borbor Fante (Fantijnn), Efutu (Afutu), Ahanta (Ante), Eguafo (Great Kommenda), and Esebu (Sabeu). Relying upon the testimony of knowledgeable coastal inhabitants and the travel accounts of Dutch traders, Propheet also provides locations for important coastal towns— Kormantse (Cormantijn), Anomabu, Seccundi (Saconde), and Mankessim (Maquesanquie). From the cartographical evidence alone, a few interrelated historical factors become crystal clear. First, the Gold Coast was densely populated, with more than forty settlements ranging from large towns to smaller hamlets in just a three-hundred-mile stretch of coastline. Second, some of the larger polities were connected to commercial enterprises associated with gold mining and the procurement of forced labor by the early seventeenth century. Perhaps because of this, Gold Coast and Dutch informants characterized these states with particular behavioral attributes—the "thievish" and "predatory" Awkamus or the "rascal" Kwahus—that imply the predation upon the weak by the powerful was already a normative experience throughout the region.[39]

By 1650 three Akan-speaking powers—Akwamu, Akyem, and Denkyira—had emerged in the Gold Coast perhaps due to, as Fynn notes, "the determination of some enterprising families to organise a formidable state capable of controlling the gold, slave, ivory and kola nut resources in the Gold Coast interior." Whatever may have been the reason for the expansion of these and other polities, the frequent contestations over tributaries, resources, and trade routes had significant social and political reverberations for decades to come. Described in Propheet's 1629 map as a "predatory nation," Akwamu and its origins were shrouded in mystery until it became one of the principal military and commercial powers on the coast. Before Akwamu rose to become one of the largest kingdoms in the history of the Gold Coast, it began near the eastern portion of the Gold Coast, north of Accra and in very close proximity to its fierce rival Akyem to its immediate west. Situated at or near vital trade routes from the interior to the coast, Akwamu's reputation as a predatory, "warlike," or "thievish" polity would become well-earned in the period between 1650 and 1730.[40]

Oral traditions regarding the origin of Akwamu tend to focus on an early migration of Akan-speaking peoples from Adanse across the Ofe and Pra rivers to settle at or near Twifo-Hemang. From this early settlement, the peoples who would later establish the Akwamu state moved again, due to pressures exerted by Akyem, to inhabit a region north of Ga-speaking Accra. According to Reindorf, the Akwamu state had very humble beginnings as a tributary or vassal to the Ga kingdom of Accra. In his rendition of the history of Akwamu, a prince of the polity named Odei served in the court of the king of Accra as part of the "ritual of conquest" so ubiquitous in the Gold Coast. In this instance, Prince Odei—like many princes from vassal states before and after him—served as a horsetail-, sword-, or shield-bearer in the court of King Okai Koi. In addition to these outward acts of the subjugation of vassal polities, the princes of conquered states received instruction in politics and martial affairs. This guaranteed two potentially conflicting eventualities. The intensive study of politics and warfare promoted the rise of a group of polished and capable leaders to lead vassal states in the future. It also created potential enemies with the requisite skills to destabilize an expansionist kingdom. In this particular case, it was the latter that facilitated the collapse of Ga-speaking Accra as a sovereign Gold Coast state. As Reindorf concludes, Prince Odei had "brought about the ruin of the Akra kingdom" by employing "the usual ability of the Twi princes for gaining power . . . the kings of Akwamu easily managed by war and plunder to extend their dominion over the surrounding [polities]." In 1530, Akwamu rebelled against Accra to establish itself as an independent state. By 1646, the former power relationship between the two polities had been reversed; Akwamu was receiving a tribute in gold from Accra as payment to allow Ga-speaking merchants access to trade at Adanme-speaking Latebi.[41]

Between 1640 and 1710, Akwamu expanded wildly, bringing into its orbit various regions and states such as Agona, Guang, Ga-speaking Accra, and Adanme-speaking Latebi. Its expansion moved south and east due to the existence of its rival, Akyem, to the west and a newly forming Fante coalition of coastal states to Akwamu's southwest. The most attractive prize, Ga-speaking Accra, represented lucrative commercial opportunities at the coast for Akwamu as trade companies and agents from five European nations had set up operations there. Much of Akwamu's history, particularly its rise and expansion, can be explained by the need to access or control trade routes from the interior to the coast. In Accra between 1576 and 1679, the Portuguese, Dutch, English, Swedes, and Danes established and fought for control over lodges, forts, and one castle in or near the Ga-speaking polity. As a result, guns, powder, gold, and slaves circulated with some ease in Accra, making it a prime target for predatory neighbors to the north. To this end, Akwamuhene Ansa Sasraku forged an alliance in 1677 with Agave, Agona, and Akron in an offensive against Greater Accra—the Ga inland capital near Ayawaso—as a means of gaining some measure of control over trade routes to the coast.[42] Another explanation for the attack offered by Rømer and repeated later by Reindorf centers on the story of Akwamu Prince Odei, who, during his stay at the court of King Okai Koi of Accra, submitted to a Ga circumcision ceremony. Lacking his foreskin and being scorned as an *akotja* or amputee by his own subjects, Prince Odei could not assume the stool vacated by his deceased father. After several unsuccessful entreaties to Accra to have the foreskin returned, Akwamu attacked Greater Accra. In any event, King Okai Koi and his oldest son were captured and beheaded in 1677.[43] By 1681 Akwamu's armies overran the rest of Accra, forcing the surviving Ga royalty to flee east to settle in Adanme-speaking Ladoku and Ewe-speaking Anlo or establish their own communities across the Volta at Little Popo and near Whydah. This dramatic power shift led William Pley, a Royal African Company factor based at James Fort in Accra, to note in August 1681 that the "Quomboes" became the nation upon "whome almost our whole trade depends." Two decades later, the lines between Akwamu and Accra were so blurred that a Dutch West India Company report mistakenly referred to Akwamu as "a great kingdom at Accra." Accra's 1681 defeat inaugurated 140 years of continuous domination of Ga-speaking peoples in the Gold Coast by a succession of Akan-speaking states—Akwamu, followed by Akyem and then Asante.[44]

Shortly after Akwamu's conquest of Ga-speaking Accra, their sheer military domination over the region allowed the Akwamuhene to become so brazen as to order the capture of Christiansborg Castle from the Danes in 1693. Caboceer Asameni, leading a group of merchants on the pretense of purchasing firearms, entered the castle and had his men hide shot and powder in their clothing. Once in the castle, the group loaded the firearms they were to purchase, disarmed and imprisoned several Danes, and assumed control of Christiansborg for a year. After the Danes agreed to pay 50 marks of gold and to not seek reparations for their substantial commercial loses, Akwamu relinquished control of the castle despite keeping the gate keys and making them the permanent stool property of the kingdom.[45]

In addition to forcing Ga-speaking polities into vassalage and imposing humiliating concessions on European trade companies in Accra, Akwamu extended its influence over Adanme polities to the east as well as states and territories to the north near the Akwapim range by the 1680s. Departing West Africa in 1682, Barbot reported that the kingdom of Ningo, whose prince bore the title of king of Adanme-speaking Ladoku, had "an [entire] dependence on the king of Aquamboe, who lords over them absolutely, that the slightest faults are often [punished] with death."[46] As a conquered vassal state, Ladoku's royalty and territorial holdings were initially left intact and Akwamu ruled the polity indirectly requiring annual or semiannual tribute payments and soldiers for its armies. By 1702, this relationship shifted when Akwamu sent an expeditionary military force, including Ga-speaking soldiers from Accra, to crush an embryonic anti-imperial movement led by the Ladoku king. After this campaign, the power of the Ladoku king diminished and the kingdom itself became divided into a number of smaller provinces—Ada, Ningo, Kpone, and others—controlled directly by Akwamu stools. From the time of the Ladoku campaign, Akwamu extended its domain eastward some 150 miles from its capital all the way to the Volta River and beyond. By 1702, Akwamu forces had overrun Little Popo and even entered Whydah—deep into what was then the Slave Coast. Akwamu became, at this point, a vast expansionist state controlling 250 miles of coastline from Agona to Whydah—easily rivaling Benin and Dahomey in the Slave Coast and Denkyira in the Gold Coast in military might and geographic expanse.[47]

Perhaps the lengthy Akwamu domination over peoples living near the Volta, including Ewe speakers in Anlo, may explain the Anlo-Ewe oral traditions that speak of Ewe, Ga, and Akan-speaking Akwamus all originating together from a common region called Ketu in the Niger River delta. This aspect of Anlo-Ewe oral tradition could also be the result of the various immigrant and displaced populations appearing in Anlo due to Akwamu's wars of expansion. Between 1677 and 1688, Ga- and Adanme-speaking populations arrived in waves in Anlo and beyond—bringing Ewe speakers into intimate contact with a range of language communities and peoples that had long settled in and around the Accra Plains. On April 10, 1702, Akwamu's expeditionary force passed through Anloga, the capital of Anlo, and brought Anlo under the administrative control of Akwamu. This began more than a century of close contact, governance, and military alliance between Akwamu and Anlo lasting until 1813. Through military conquest, expansion, and the related displacement of thousands of people, Anlo would have Akan, Adanme, Ga, and Ewe speakers as inhabitants by the early 1700s—an ethnolinguistic configuration that would be replicated in various locales in the Western Hemisphere by the eighteenth century. Other regions of the Ewe-speaking Volta came under Akwamu control in short order. Between 1707 and 1708, Krepi, Ho, and Kpandu were conquered and re-duced to vassal states of Akwamu, followed by Kwahu in July 1710. These campaigns against Ewe-speaking polities near the Volta would mark the end of Akwamu's expansionist wars. Until its collapse and defeat by longtime rival Akyem and a coalition of aggrieved states and some of its own citizens in 1730, Akwamu was the second most powerful coastal polity in the history of the Gold Coast.[48]

To the immediate west of Akwamu, Akyem had origins similar to its neighbor. Oral traditions refer to migrants from Adanse who left in a number of waves to settle in the region known to Europeans as "Akim," "Great Akanny," or "Akimse Akkany." In what later became Akyem Abuakwa by 1715, migrants from Adanse built an Akan-speaking polity between the Pra and Birem rivers in the 1500s. Rich from the territory's sources of pure gold, the early inhabitants of Akyem established a powerful inland state by the first few decades of seventeenth century. Known for its "delicate people" and described as "rich in slaves," Akyem benefited from close proximity to Assin, which featured gold mines and gold trading routes from the interior to the coast frequented by the Akani Trading Organization.[49] Indeed, it may have been the rich gold mines in the region they exploited that provided a foundation for Akyem's political and commercial growth. Michael Hemmersam, a goldsmith and employee of the Dutch West India Company visiting the Gold Coast from 1630 to 1645, noted that the gold from Akyem was "supposed to be the best in the country." Willem Bosman—chief factor of the Dutch West India Company during the 1690s—corroborated Hemmersam's claim when he noted that Akyem "furnishes as large Quantities of Gold as any Land I know and that also the most valuable and pure of any that is carried from this Coast it is easily distinguishable by its deep colour."[50]

Though Propheet described the people of Akyem as "delicate" in his 1629 map, by the 1690s this emerging state may have been one of two Gold Coast polities that could effectively check the military power of Akwamu. Johannes Rask, a Danish Lutheran priest stationed at Christiansborg Castle in 1708, claimed that despite the ability of Akwamu to field ten thousand men on short notice, "they are only vassals of the [Akim], from whose lands the gold evidently comes . . . and the [Akim] are more than twice as powerful as they" despite the ability of Akwamu to block access to coastal trade.[51] Both Barbot and Bosman, reflecting on the decades leading up to the 1690s, concur on the ability of Akyem to serve as a balance to Akwamu's regional influence. "These Aquamboes are naturally brave, resolute and warlike," Barbot observes, adding that Akwamu had been "for the most part at variance with [Akyem], by whom they for many years past had been much infested; they having made several inroads into Aquamboe, destroying all with fire and sword. They are now at peace, which 'tis likely will not last long, there being such a natural aversion to each other."[52] Bosman notes, for example, that "the Aquamboe Negroes are very haughty, arrogant, and War like, their Power is also very terrible to all their Neighbouring Countries except Akim."

Perhaps due to its own burgeoning military might, Akyem tried to demand an annual tribute from Akwamu, "pretending a Feudal Right" over their long-standing regional rival. This "tribute" may have been reference to an amount of gold Akwamu borrowed from Akyem to purchase weapons during its offensive against Ga-speaking polities between 1677 and 1681. In a version of this story offered by a Dutch West India Company agent stationed at Accra in 1700, Akwamu had paid a considerable sum to Akyem. However, after "4, 5, or 6 months . . . the aforesaid Akims would make new claims" extending further the debt owed by Akwamu. Akwamuhene Ansa Sasraku failed to pay back this debt to the satisfaction of Akyem and, upon his death, Akyem transferred the debt to his successor—Akwamuhene Basua. Neither Basua nor his successor, Akwamuhene Ado, acknowledged the validity of the debt until Akyem attacked three Akwamu towns between 1699 and 1700, taking scores of war prisoners.[53] This war had the unintended consequence of disrupting trade to the degree that the Dutch West India Company abandoned their once-lucrative gold and slave trade operations at Kpone on the grounds that they had "little value" due to the regional conflict. Akwamuhene Ado paid Akyem about thirty pounds of gold, thirty slaves, and fifty crates of brandy, but the "Akims rejected his offer, saying that they had the rights to the entire inheritance of [Basua]; and though they had the goodness to leave the Aquamboes in the possession of it, they claimed such great sums, that it was impossible for the Aquamboes to pay them." By March 1700, this conflict over the loan repayment had not concluded, leading a West India Company agent to state "we shall have to leave the outcome of this affair to time."[54]

Throughout the seventeenth and eighteenth centuries, tensions between Akwamu and Akyem would spill over into all-out warfare. In 1659, Akyem joined with Accra in a campaign against Akwamu and Agona. An Akyem force of twelve thousand battled an Akwamu contingent of equal strength in October 1682 just thirty miles north of Accra. Six years later, Akwamuhene Ansa Sasraku initiated an offensive against Agona upon suspicions that this former ally had formed a new military pact with Akyem. Taking advantage of the circumstance, Akyem opened a second front in the 1688 war by attacking Akwamu forces near their northern capital—an action that forced Akwamu to withdraw troops used to assault Agona in the coastal town of Winneba. Though Akyem's forces were quickly dispatched in the 1688 conflict, Akwamu suffered heavy losses in Agona and would never again seek to expand westward. The capture of the aforementioned Akwamu towns between 1699 and 1700 during the dispute over the gold debt owed to Akyem represented a significant turning point in the balance of power in the region.[55]

By late 1703, an uneasy peace settled over the region as the conflict between Akwamu and Akyem came to a temporary halt. Willem de la Palma, who was from 1702 the director-general of the Dutch West India Company, noted in October 1703 that "at present there is a reasonable prospect for general peace, and to our knowledge none of the black Nations between Axim and Accra is at the moment in arms." Though this brief pause in warfare reflected a reality, de la Palma's assertions that the Dutch brokered a deal with "the powerful King of Aquamboe" to lay down arms belie a supreme overconfidence in the ability of Europeans and their agents to determine the course of events in the Gold Coast interior. While traders from D'Inquira (Denkyira), 'tJuffer (Twiffo), Assjante (Asante), and other Akan-speaking polities declared they "were equally tired of war," this had more to do with its deleterious effects on trade than some notion that the Dutch had become the "master of the balance, peace, and quietness of the Gold Coast."[56] Despite this supposed mastery by the Dutch over the Gold Coast, de la Palma reported within a year that "of all the areas of foreign trade, none is as uncertain as that of the Gold Coast." He supported this change of opinion by noting that Denkyira and Akyem possess gold, but "robbery of their merchants," "closure of the [trade] paths, the levy of heavy tolls and public wars" prevent them from freely accessing the coast.[57] The difficulties Akyem faced gaining access to coastal trade led directly to renewed warfare in the interior by 1715.

Though Bosman described Akyem as "an extraordinary large Country" with a "Monarchical Government," this was not to be the case for long. By 1715, Akyem split into two separate and sovereign polities—Akyem Abuakwa under Ofori Panin and Akyem Kotoku led by Ofosuhene Apenten. Though working as sovereign states, Abuakwa and Kotoku acted in concert when it came to foreign affairs and wars. In 1715, armies from both states marched against Akwamu and Agona in an effort to open trade routes to Winneba in the central coast. With trade access to the coast, both Akyem states could purchase firearms in preparation for a planned assault against Asante—a new threat in the forest fringe. Understanding that the offensive against Akwamu and Agona was simply the prelude to an Akyem war against Asante, Asantehene Osei Tutu recalled his forces to Kumasi in December 1715 in preparation. By 1717, Asante launched a full-scale war against the two Akyem states. During the course of this war, Akyem handed Asante its most significant defeat punctuated, no less, by the death of Asantehene Osei Tutu in battle at the Pra River. The end of the Asante–Akyem war of 1717 led to a temporary peace treaty and military pact by the former combatants against the Akwamu, who were blamed for the death of the Asante king.[58] In 1730, Akyem defeated Akwamu and took control of Ga- and Adanme-speaking polities in the south and the entire western portion of Akwamu. Their reign as successor to Akwamu was brief; Asante defeated Akyem in 1742, taking control over Accra and other nearby Ga and Adanme polities. Under Asantehene Opoku Ware and subsequent kings, Asante expanded to control a region larger than modern-day Ghana.[59]

As a contemporary with Akwamu and Akyem, Denkyira's rise and fall does not fit into a neat and linear chronology of Gold Coast polities. Indeed, for the purposes of this chapter, a discussion about Denkyira only sets the stage for an explanation of the rise and rapid expansion of Asante after 1699. Unlike Akwamu, Akyem, and Asante, Denkyira's vassal and subjugated states did not include large numbers of Ga-, Adanme-, and Ewe-speaking peoples and polities and, as such, its history is not directly tied into to the larger processes under study in this book.

Denkyira first appears as "Dunkeries" in European records in 1681 and would not be noted by European cartographers in their various renditions of the political geographies of the Gold Coast until the early eighteenth century.[60] Described by Barbot as "formerly a country of a small compass, and not very populous," Denkyira quickly grew until it became the dominant power in the Ofin-Pra river basin by the 1680s. Just five days north by foot from Elmina, Denkyira had shared the commercial advantages and disadvantages of other inland polities. Like Akyem, Denkyira's location in or near the source of very rich gold mines—in part through the conquest of Adanse—generated enormous assets for coastal trade and helped the kingdom grow, in Bosman's words, "so improved in Power, that they are respected and honoured by all their Neighbouing Nations; all which they have taught to fear them, except Asiante and Akim." Similar to Akyem and Akwamu, Denkyira did not fully control the trade routes from the forest fringe to the coast, which allowed bandits, commercial interlopers and middlemen, and predatory coastal polities to factor into the ability of the rulers and merchants of Denkyira to benefit from such ready access to gold mines and the immense wealth they could generate. In addition to the more human impediments to coastal trade, the roads and trade routes from Denkyira—particularly the roads to Axim and Elmina—proved a laborious feat to navigate. As Bosman and Barbot note, the trade roads from inland Denkyira to Axim and Elmina at the coast were so poorly constructed and winding that it doubled the normal time of travel than if the roads were in good repair and straighter.[61]

Between the 1670s and the early 1690s, a series of wars initiated by the Denkyirahene sought to resolve the kingdom's commercial dilemma through expansion. In doing so, Denkyira conquered and pulled into its political orbit both gold-producing states and territories and states near trade roads reaching the coast—Wassa, Sefwi, Inkassa, Igyina, and Aowin. This series of expansionist wars granted Denkyira an even larger monopoly over gold production and trade in the region, leading Bosman to note that Denkyira's gold alone "satisfied the demand of the whole Coast from Axim to Sekondee." This stranglehold on the southwestern Gold Coast trade through military expansion also sowed the seeds of future regional discord. As Reindorf notes, it was "by trade and plunder they grew rich and powerful [and] they became so arrogant that they looked with contempt on other nations, esteeming them as slaves, and on this account they were disliked." The largesse and ostentation of the Denkyirahene became well known throughout the forest fringe and beyond. One king reportedly instituted a royal harem for the Denkyirahene complete with eunuchs and guards, while greatly increasing the number of royal fan- and horsetail-bearers. Another had two golden stools forged to serve as symbols of the Denkyira state and commissioned twelve gold-headed staves for use by his akyeame. Denkyirahene Boamponsem I ordered new gold ornaments to be made for every state or royal ceremony and refused to use the same ornament twice, proudly earning the royal epithet *Boamponsem a odi sika atompenada*—"Boamponsem who uses gold but once." During his reign as Denkyira king, the state stool had gold adornments, or *sika ware,* added to it. Gold became, for obvious reasons, a critical component of Denkyira's "paraphernalia of power."[62]

Denkyira fought a series of wars during the 1680s and 1690s with the aim of further opening up and controlling trade routes to its south. In 1688, Denkyira assisted Agona—at the coast near Winneba—against an imminent invasion by Akwamu. The same year, Denkyira forces threatened Efutu, and only a bribe of a significant amount of gold paid by the Dutch West India Company director at Elmina prevented what might have been a disastrous conflict—for both Efutu and the Dutch. Between 1698 and 1700, Denkyira conquered Assin in decisive victories that opened up trade access to additional coastal regions. Through the Adanse-Assin trade route, for example, Denkyira merchants had direct access to Cape Coast and Elmina castles. In 1700, Denkyira attacked Twifo and demanded a bribe of a hundred gold bendas—forcing the Dutch West India Company into an awkward position. If they paid the bribe for Twifo in an attempt to end the conflict and return coastal trade to normal levels, the Komenda state "would yet keep the [trade] passages closed" in fear of upsetting Denkyira. This result could, in turn, focus Denkyira's ire against the Dutch at Elmina. Denkyira's victory of Twifo expanded its access to coastal trade and, to the relief of the Dutch, created renewed flows of trade from the interior. In this case, "no goods [were] more current than firearms," according to Dutch West India Company agents. The agents reasoned that despite the unpredictability of Denkyira, their need for guns substantiated rumors that "they either want to fight with the [Asante], or with the [Fante], the Twifo, Adomse, Wassase or the inhabitants of the [Ancobra] river."[63]

In expanding south with the goal of gaining unfettered access to the coastal roads to Elmina and Axim, Denkyira's military was stretched thin. This expansion also drained the gold resources of the kingdom, leading to added demands on tributary states to produce more gold to support the largesse of Denkyira kings and to finance the military control over southern trade roads. The increased demands on vassal states backfired by the time of the reign of Denkyirahene Ntim Gyakari beginning in 1694. A coalition of northern tributary states—Kwaman, Kokofu, Dwaben, Nsuta, Mampon, Juaben, and Bekwai among them—contested the authority of Denkyira in a collective act that would profoundly shape the course of Gold Coast history. Among the deprivations faced by these states was one, the ritual of conquest, which again proved a double-edged sword for expansionist polities. Similar to the service of Akwamu Prince Odei in the court of Accra King Okai Koi as a shield-bearer, Osei Tutu—nephew and chosen successor of the Kwamanhene Obiri Yeboa—served in the Denkyira court as a shield-bearer for Denkyirahene Boamponsem I at some point before 1694. The ritual of conquest, a ubiquitous feature in tributary relationships throughout the Gold Coast, allowed for the nephews or sons of the kings of vassal states to receive some instruction in military and political affairs. In this case, like Prince Odei, Tutu would prove a formidable foe to his conquerors as he used his training to rally allies and defeat Denkyira by 1701.[64]

According to oral traditions, when Tutu left the court of the Denkyirahene he sought refuge in Akwamu—then ruled by Akwamuhene Ansa Sasraku. Reindorf claims that under the tutelage of the Akwamuhene, Tutu "had the opportunity of mastering the politics of the two principal powers then existing, Dankyera and Akwamu." Not only did Ansa Sasraku augment Tutu's knowledge of political and military affairs, he granted him two additional gifts, according to Asante traditions. First, Tutu received a personal retinue of thirty soldiers—though other versions of the story claim that the number was three hundred. Importantly, these Akwamu soldiers were trained in the use of firearms and would prove a decisive factor in the war against Denkyira. Second, Tutu met and befriended Anokye, a powerful *okomfo*, or priest, who would accompany the future Asantehene back to Kwaman. While there is some conjecture among historians about whether or not Okomfo Anokye existed, the traditions surrounding Tutu may have been metaphors for the military, technological, and ritual assistance he drew upon after his brief stay in Akwamu. One thing is certain: during his time in Denkyira and Akwamu, Tutu became aware of the reliance by both on gold production and slave procurement for Atlantic commerce, including the purchase of firearms and powder, and thus the need for undeterred access to the coast as the route to regional influence and military might.[65]

Upon his return to Kwaman, Tutu began the work of crafting a new state to rival Denkyira. The northern vassal states of Denkyira had long been primed to contest the ever-increasing tribute demands and related humiliations. A May 20, 1701, Dutch West India Company report noted, "The Dinkirase have since long been very bellicose and proud of their victories, and so they have become unbearable to their neighbors." As Denkyira had "ruined" Assin, Twifo, Adom, Wassa, and Aowin, the report concluded, "it is their turn to take revenge on the Dinkirase."[66] A confederation of northern states, then, could be forged from the common hatred they shared for the Denkyirahene and the kingdom he led. In Asante traditions, the story of the moment the northern confederation became the Asante Union centers around Okomfo Anokye and the *Sika Dwa Kofi*—the famed Asante Golden Stool. At a Friday meeting of northern confederation kings in Kwaman, Okomfo Anokye conjured the Sika Dwa Kofi from the heavens to rest on the lap of Osei Tutu. After this miraculous feat, Okomfo Anokye stated that the Golden Stool contained the spirit of the entire Asante nation, and the kingdom would exist as long as the stool remained under their protection. He also struck a sword in the ground at the spot where the Golden Stool descended from the heavens and proclaimed that if it were ever removed, the Asante nation would cease to exist.[67] This story is imbued with metaphorical meanings and symbols of both regional and ritual power. The meeting of northern kings, held on a Friday, paralleled the actions of the Akan sky god—Jancómpon—who breathed life into humanity on the fifth day of creation. The stool descended from heaven, from the sky god himself, to rest on the knees of Osei Tutu to symbolize his divine selection and right to rule. The stool itself, adorned with gold, may have been a reflection on the link between gold and political power demonstrated by the rise of three regional and inland states—Akwamu, Akyem, and Denkyira. Even the sword struck in the ground by Okomfo Anokye, a sign in the region for peace, symbolized the ability of the northern kings to unite in their efforts against Denkyira military and political domination.[68]

By the 1690s, Tutu changed Kwaman's name to Kumasi and merged the vassal states of Kokofu, Nsuta, Beckwai, Dwaben, and Mampon into the Asante Union. With its capital at Kumasi, the Asante Union agreed that Tutu would be the first Asantehene, due to his political savvy and charisma. He quickly proved the wisdom of this decision, leading the military of the Union, with assistance from Akwamu, to victories against Domaa, Amakom, Tafo, and Ofeso—smaller polities within a few miles' radius of Kumasi. Once the Union consolidated its territo-

rial base, Asantehene Tutu turned toward Denkyira by 1699. Engaged
in the south in an attempt to control the coastal trade roads, Denkyira
faced the Asante Union's offensive in the north, forcing the kingdom to
fight on two fronts. Initially, Denkyira repulsed Asante's forces, driving
them north from Adunku, Aboatem, and Aputuogya. In a pivotal 1701
battle, Denkyirahene Ntim Gyakari led his army, with assistance from
Akyem, to face Asantehene Tutu's main force at Feyiase. In short order,
Asante's forces routed the Denkyira army and Ntim Gyakari died on
the battlefield. Asante forces sacked Abankeseso, the Denkyira capital,
looting it of its massive gold reserve. A Dutch West India Company agent
lamented that, despite their hopes that a Denkyira defeat would initiate
renewed gold and slave trading at the coast, Elmina Castle did not have
"even 2 marks of gold in cash" at the conclusion of the Denkyira–Asante
war. According to a report by Van Sevenhuysen, this was "because the
Assjanteese are so full of the rich loot of the Dinquirase, that they do not
think of trading, but rather spend their days lustily in the defeated country of Dinkira." From this point forward, Asante became the dominant
power in the Ofin-Pra river basin and, over the course of the eighteenth
and nineteenth centuries, consolidated the entire Gold Coast and beyond under its political control.[69]

Asante's expansion was swift and determined. Between 1713 and 1715,
Asante allied with Wassa in successful military campaigns against Twifo
and Aowin to open trade access to European castles, forts, and lodges
on the coast. Asante's war against Akyem in 1717 came at the cost of its
founding Asantehene—who died rather unceremoniously at the Pra
River. While the war ended as one of Asante's first and greatest defeats,
it did not deter the kingdom from further expansion. Much of this can
be credited to Asantehene Opoku Ware's thirty-year reign. As Reindorf
notes, Ware "extended the Asante dominion more than any of his predecessors or successors." Enstooled around 1720, Ware began his reign
by instituting the Ntam Kese, or Great Oath, as a measure to rebuild mo-
rale after the resounding defeat by Akyem and to maintain the Asante
Union. This oath recalled the day (Saturday) and place (Kormantse) at
which Tutu was slain during the Asante–Akyem war and served as a vow
to meet enemies of the kingdom without fear or cowardice, upon pain of
a torturous death. The oath served to consolidate and ensure the loyal-
ties of vassal ahene (omanhene) of Asante; any king breaking the Ntam

Kese would face the wrath of the Asantehene and all other vassal ahene of the Union. This move proved critical as a number of former Denkyira provincial states—Aowin, Sefwi, Wassa, and Twifo—had taken the opportunity of Asante's 1717 defeat to declare their independence from Asante and a few had even joined sides with Akyem—the long-time ally of Denkyira. In 1718, Sefwi became brazen enough to attack the Asante capital at Kumasi, and its forces killed all but two of the Asante royal family in residence. Assuming Akwamu's complicity in the 1717 defeat to Akyem and the subsequent death of Osei Tutu, Asantehene Ware broke the long-standing military pact with Akwamu and formed a temporary alliance with Akyem. Despite claims of real grievances against Akwamu, this move by Ware proved his strategic savvy.[70]

As Asante was struggling to deal with the northern provinces formally under the dominion of Denkyira, renewed warfare against Akyem could prove disastrous to the Asante Union. By forming a pact with Akyem, Ware could pit the two largest regional powers against each other with the hopes that a much-weakened victor could be more readily crushed by Asante Union forces. This was not the only benefit of an alliance with the state that handed Asante its most decisive defeat culminating in the death of the Union's founder. While Akyem and Akwamu fought each other to exhaustion, the Asante Union could concentrate all of its military resources on consolidating the breakaway provinces in the north. This interpretation finds corroboration in Rømer, who notes that when Akyem declared war against Akwamu—at the urging of Asante—they offered five hundred slaves to Asantehene Ware in exchange for a promise that he would not take the occasion of this war to invade Akyem territories. With most of their forces committed to an offensive to the east, an Asante invasion of Akyem from the west would open up a second war front that would undermine their war aims. Reportedly, Ware consented to the request but only agreed to a five-month non-aggression pact with Akyem. We do know, from practically all extant sources, that once Akyem attacked Akwamu in 1730, the Asante Union neither invaded Akyem nor helped defend their former ally—Akwamu.[71]

Given the Akyem–Asante alliance that lasted from about 1720 to 1730, the Asante Union managed to use the opportunity to crush northern resistance. Two years after the sacking of Kumasi, Asante forces led by Amankwa Tia—commander of Kumasi's military—initiated a punitive campaign against Sefwi. In the course of just a few weeks, Asante crushed Sefwi's army, killed the Sefwihene Ebirim Moro, and annexed all of their territories into the Asante Union. By 1722, Sefwi was effectively erased as the territory, now known as Ahafo, became a game reserve for future Asantehene. Ware then led Asante forces in a series of battles against gold-rich Aowin between 1721 and 1722, culminating in the defeat and complete subjugation of the rebel state. In the aftermath of this war, Asante merchants sold hundreds of Aowin captives at Cape Coast, Anomabu, and Elmina. Shortly following the defeat of Aowin, the Asante Union and Asantehene Ware used brute force and subterfuge to defeat or claim the territories of Nzima, Tekyiman, and Wassa by 1731.

Following these campaigns, Ware turned to the growing regional power of, and military threat represented by, Akyem after its resounding defeat of Akwamu in 1730. Probably hoping that the victor of the Akyem–Akwamu war would emerge greatly weakened, the Asante Union had to be alarmed by the increasing military power of Akyem after gaining control over Accra and direct access to multiple European trade partners. Collecting rent from the Danish, British, and Dutch based in and around Accra meant a steady flow of firearms, shot, and powder into the hands of the Akyemhene at a time when Asante had exhausted much of its military resources in a protracted campaign against Wassa. The conflict between Asante and Akyem, brewing ever since the 1717 death of Osei Tutu, came to a head in 1742 when Asante Union forces simultaneously assaulted Akyem Kotoku and Akyem Abuakwa. By April 1742, the defeat of the two Akyems was complete and Asante forces moved south to secure Accra and to force tribute payments from the Danes and Dutch. With the defeat of Akyem, Asante stood alone as the dominant power in the Gold Coast interior. By 1744, Asante further extended its territories by invading Gonja and Kong in the north. Having gained control over and consolidated the northern Gold Coast and the former territories of Denkyira, Akyem, and Akwamu, Asante—in its size, military might, and commercial influence—rivaled or exceeded Dahomey, Benin, Kongo, or any other centralized polity in early-modern Atlantic Africa.[72]

While Asante became the dominant inland polity, a coalition of Fante states along the coast between Winneba in the east and Eguafo to the west controlled a large swath of the southern Gold Coast and stood virtually alone, from 1750 until 1807, against the ever-encroaching power of the Asante kingdom. Indeed, as Shumway contends, the region inhabited by the Fante coalition—the central portion of the southern Gold Coast—was one of the few areas to avoid domination by Asante during the eighteenth century. By the late 1600s, however, the possibility of this coalition would have seemed far-fetched given the frequent and internecine wars between a number of polities included on Propheet's 1629 map—Commendo or Guoffo (Eguafo), Futu (Efutu), Sabeu (Asebu), Fantijnn (Borbor Fante) and Agwano (Agona). Indeed, some of the divisions went beyond the political realm as at least three distinct language groups—Guang, Etsii, and Akan—made the central coast their home. With a common threat and common commercial interests, these polities and peoples experienced a remarkable ethnogenesis in which Fante language, identity, and culture were born. This ethnogenesis coincided with and helped generate a new multistate formation—the Fante coalition—and both processes reveal patterns that would be replicated across the Atlantic in the Gold Coast diaspora.[73]

The polity "Fantijnn" appearing on Propheet's 1629 map formed as the result of the migration of the Borbor Fante from the Brong region to the coast in the 1300s. According to Fante oral traditions, three "founding fathers"—Oburumankuma, Odapagyan, and Osun—led the migration to the central coast and settled at the town of Mankessim, which became the central hub of a small polity by the fifteenth century. The role of these early Fante settlers and state-builders in commercial activities at the coast helped blend Akan, Portuguese, and other languages in the region to create the Akan dialect known as Fante. The creation of this language and its use as a regional lingua franca became central in the forging of Fante identity and culture. Before this development, the central coastal region experienced a series of destructive wars within and between states that would eventually be subsumed under a unifying Fante ethnolinguistic banner. In 1688, Borbor Fante joined with Asebu in an offensive against Efutu. From 1687 to 1688 and again from 1694 to 1700, Efutu, Asebu, Eguafo, Borbor Fante, Ahanta, Acron, Adom, Assin, the British Royal African Company, and the Dutch West India Company became embroiled in a series of conflicts known as the Komenda Wars that convulsed the central coast. By 1704, Eguafo erupted in a civil war that threatened to tear apart the polity. In many of these conflicts, polities or factions within polities fought over the control of gold trading routes and access to coastal markets, just as Akwamu, Akyem, Denkyira, and Asante expanded to monopolize centers of gold production and access to coastal trade. Coastal trade and the presence of European merchants, then, became one of many catalysts responsible for the rise and fall of a number of states in the eighteenth century Gold Coast.[74]

By the first decade of the eighteenth century, the polities of Eguafo, Efutu, Asebu, Acron, and Agona had lost their sovereignty as the seventeenth-century political order, centering as it did on kings, had shifted dramatically. As Shumway contends, "While the institution of kingship was dissolving, however, Borbor Fante warlords grew increasingly influential in trade, diplomacy, and military affairs in the region."[75] In sum, the formation of what became the Fante coalition was forged with iron, fire, and blood. The Borbor Fante attacked Asebu and Efutu in 1708, a conflict that ended in the beheading of the Asebuhene. Victories by Borbor Fante against Efutu in 1720 and Agona in 1724 permanently ended the sovereignty of both states. A new leadership cadre represented by Borbor Fante warlords such as Kwegya Akwa replaced kings in the political order of the eighteenth-century central Gold Coast. These new leaders based their power on military might, which ostensibly became an attractive trait in the destabilizing times that accompanied the expansion of the transatlantic slave trade. From this foundation, the new military leadership created a coalition government by the 1730s and, within a decade, began to increase their combined strength through military pacts and alliances with inland polities—Wassa and Twifo. By the time Asante defeated Akyem and expanded to Accra in the 1740s to 1750s, the Fante coalition was the "only autonomous polity that survived in a region that had otherwise been appropriated by the Asante Kingdom."[76]

Along with this political formation, the cultural formation of "Fante" centered around concerns about Asante invasion and mutual defense. As Shumway contends, three unique cultural inventions that formed part of this new Fante identity had martial dimensions. Fante, as a common dialect and lingua franca spoken throughout the member polities in the coastal coalition by the eighteenth century, combined Akan, Guang, and Etsii dialects and helped consolidate and bridge ethnolinguistic and cultural divides in the central coast. In this case, the development of a common language became a critical component of Fante ethnogenesis and served as a unifying factor that could only aid in the ability of peoples in the central coast to act, at times, with singular purpose. Another unique aspect of the newly forming Fante culture was the *asafo* company. Essentially community or town militias, asafo companies became ever-present features in coastal Fante polities during the eighteenth century.[77] Asafo companies, in addition to providing security and protection, "enabled people in southern Ghana to form bonds with their immediate neighbors in spite of cultural differences that would otherwise have prohibited the kind of close cooperation needed to protect neighborhoods from the threats of raiders and kidnappers."[78] Finally, the shrine of *Nananom Mpow* (Grove of the Ancestors) was a sacred grove near Mankessim at which Fante akomfo consulted with ancestral spirits and, later, their war god. Oral traditions contend that this sacred grove includes the site where the three founders of Mankessim and by extension Borbor Fante, were interred and that Nananom Mpow contains the ancestral spirits of Fante peoples. During the uncertain and destabilizing times of the expansion of the transatlantic slave trade in the Gold Coast, this sacred grove became a Fante war oracle or god and served as a source of guidance and protection by the 1750s.[79]

Combined, Fante language, the formation of asafo companies, and the Nananom Mpow war shrine solidified alliances and provided protection as part of a complex ethnogenesis that produced Fante culture, identity, and peoples. The political and cultural formation of "Fante"—which is now understood as a "stable" ethnolinguistic group in modern Ghana—provides a blueprint for tracking processes that would continually occur throughout the Gold Coast and its American diasporas. When former enemies become one, under a unifying political and cultural identity, the process of be(com)ing Fante serves as a helpful and generative frame within which Coromantee and (A)mina in the Americas can be understood and assessed. Indeed, the themes of motion, migration, diaspora, ethnogenesis, and the formation of multilingual polities or political alliances repeated throughout this chapter provide clear evidence that Atlantic Africans carried their histories—both distant and recent—with them to the new worlds they would encounter in the Western

Hemisphere. Likewise, the social destabilizations, violence, and constant sense of threat caused by military expansion and Atlantic commerce provided a generative set of experiences that shaped responses to racial and chattel slavery in the Americas. Natal and social alienation—the hallmarks of social death—may have marked a portion of the passage between the old and new worlds in the Black Atlantic, but the distant and immediate pasts of Gold Coast Africans helped frame a collective liminal experience part and parcel to their resurrections in the Americas.

TWO

Making the Gold Coast Diaspora

Our people who are no longer of us
Also pleaded and waited fearfully
For the truth of betrayal:
They too got carried away.

KWADWO OPOKU-AGYEMANG, "IN THE SHADOW OF THE CASTLE,"
CAPE COAST CASTLE: A COLLECTION OF POEMS (1996)

Perhaps the first real evil of the transatlantic traffic in flesh was the social death suffered by its many victims. Nothing captures this truth better than the story of a Fante youth who went on to become one of the most strident abolitionist voices of the eighteenth century. When Quobna Ottobah Cugoano, "born in the city of Agimaque (Ajumako), on the coast of Fantyn" in 1757, remembered his life before his forced Atlantic sojourn and the months of toil on a Grenada slave gang, his focus centered on forever severed familial and social relations. Indeed, his recollections of his Gold Coast home moved immediately to his father, who served as a close companion and confidant to the Ajumakohene, perhaps in the capacity of caboceer or other court official. When the king died, his successor—Ajumakohene Ambro Accasa—sent for the young Cugoano to live with him at the royal court among his own children. After about two years in Accasa's court, Cugoano departed for an extended visit with his uncle, who had a residence three day's journey to the west of

2.1. Possible portrait of Quobna Ottobah Cugoano, late eighteenth century. In
the original, neither the sitter nor the painter was identified by name, and the oil
portrait was long assumed to be of Olaudah Equiano. Courtesy of the Royal Albert
Memorial Museum, Exeter, Devon, UK/Bridgeman Images.

Ajumako near Assini. Three months with his uncle led Cugoano to consider returning back to his family and friends in Ajumako, but he notes, "By this time I had got well acquainted with some of the children of my uncle's hundreds of relations." In extending his stay with his uncle and other kin, Cugoano became caught up in the machinations of Atlantic commerce.[1]

Captured in 1770 at the age of thirteen with some twenty other children, Cugoano was sold to a European factor for a gun, a bolt of cloth, and some lead shot. His transformation from subject to object, from person to thing, and from social life to death continued after being warehoused at an unnamed fort and, later, at Cape Coast Castle. His vain hopes that Ajumakohene Accasa would learn about his plight and redeem him led to heartbreaking despair when the realization of his fate finally dawned upon the young Cugoano:[2]

> Let it suffice to say, that I was thus lost to my dear indulgent parents and relations, and they to me. All my help was cries and tears, and these could not avail; nor suffered long, till one succeeding woe, and dread, swelled up another. Brought from a state of innocence and freedom, and, in a barbarous and cruel manner, conveyed to a state of horror and slavery: This abandoned situation may be easier conceived than described. From the time that I was kidnapped and conducted to a factory, and from thence in the brutish, base, but fashionable way of traffic, consigned to Grenada, the grievous thoughts which I then felt, still pant in my heart.[3]

However, the anguish of social death was not a totalizing experience for enslaved captives. This notion, present in so much of the historiography, limits the possibilities and range of human agency. For Cugoano, though he deemed it a personal shame that some among his own "countrymen" had captured and sold him to Europeans, his new life in Grenada was perhaps made slightly more bearable by the many new companions with whom he could speak Akan and form new connections and even a new sense of community citizenship. No longer did Fante, Ajumako, or Assini have currency or serve as viable identities or identifiers in Cugoano's mind. By the time this "Son of Africa" penned his autobiographical account in 1787, he would proclaim a new identity as "A Native of the Gold Coast, Africa."[4] This shift from natal alienation and physical separation from Ajumako to a diasporic citizenship in the Black Atlantic based on a broad Gold Coast geography found resonance with many untold thousands following similar Atlantic journeys.

This chapter addresses the mechanisms that, in a literal sense, made the Gold Coast diaspora to the 1760s. Through a focus on linguistic and cultural Akanization, Gold Coast cultural geographies, slave procurement and trading, and the regions of disembarkation in the Americas in the period between the early seventeenth and the mid-eighteenth centuries, a clearer picture of the Akan-speaking provenance of Coromantees and (A)minas emerges.[5] Indeed, there were very traceable patterns of the many flows and fluctuations of Gold Coast and Atlantic commerce that produced concentrations of peoples familiar with Akan languages and cultures in specific locales throughout the Western Hemisphere. The very mechanisms of slave procurement employed in the region before about 1765 determined the fact that a significant proportion of enslaved Africans involved in this phase of the Gold Coast slave trade would be Akan, Ga, Adanme, and Ewe speakers from a range of coastal and near-inland regions. From this relatively narrow geographic band, enslaved Gold Coast Africans were largely concentrated in British, Dutch, and Danish colonies in the Americas during the eighteenth century—a point corroborated by the Du Bois Institute slave trade dataset. In the century between 1665 and 1765, for example, 78 percent of all Gold Coast Africans embarked on slave ships were destined for British, Dutch, and Danish possessions in the Western Hemisphere.[6] The common bond they shared in the Americas was Akan, and this would mean that the existence of broad language communities they encountered on slave plantations would facilitate the ethnogenesis of Coromantee and (A)mina.

In illustrating the common and linked geographies of slave trading in the Gold Coast and the Americas, this chapter also details the Akanization of Ga-, Adanme-, and Ewe-speaking peoples and polities and the spread of Akan as a political and commercial lingua franca. Thus, the contention forwarded here is that most Gold Coast Africans transported to the Americas knew Akan as a primary, secondary, or even tertiary language. This common thread and the heavy concentrations of Gold Coast Africans in specific circum-Caribbean and mainland colonies served as catalysts to ethnogenesis. Moreover, the dominance of Akan cultures in the Gold Coast meant that the influence of Akan-speaking peoples and polities went well beyond their languages. Aspects of their naming practices, religions, folkloric traditions, and political cultures became overlays in addition to—but not replacing or obliterating—the cultures of Ga, Adanme, and Ewe speakers. These levels of cultural interplay and exchange prefigured the kinds of collaborative enterprises Akan, Ga, Adanme, and Ewe speakers engaged in after their New World sojourns.

Here, also, I focus on the linguistic and sociocultural threads that ultimately made the Gold Coast diaspora possible. Instead of the slave trade joining together previously unconnected and purposefully randomized peoples from one continent only to deposit them—again randomly—in another, distinct historical patterns emerge demonstrating that Gold Coast commoners had identifiable points of sociocultural connection long before embarking on European slavers. Specifically, the unique political geographies existing in the seventeenth- and eighteenth-century Gold Coast produced thorough cultural and linguistic blending throughout the coastal and close inland regions. Akanization, then, was a real force and historical process that would ensure, at the minimum, that the many Ga, Adanme, and Ewe speakers shipped across the Atlantic had more than marginal familiarity with Akan language, dialects, and cultures. For all three language groups, this reality was shaped by the fact of the conquest, subjugation, and relegation of their polities to the status of vassals by a succession of Akan states—Akwamu, Akyem, and Asante. Whether by force or through more benign measures, the sociocultural and linguistic threads that bound them together in the Gold Coast past became essential parts of Coromantee and (A)mina tapestries in their Western Hemisphere present.

By paying careful attention to the actual patterns and geographies of slave trading, from procurement to disembarkation, this chapter strengthens recent interpretations that work against the notion that purposeful ethnic and linguistic randomization characterized the flows of Atlantic Africans to the Western Hemisphere. In this regard, struggles to gain coastal access by inland and coastal polities in the Gold Coast meant that slave procurement regions were, by definition, geographically circumscribed. Not until the expansion of the Asante kingdom to the northern reaches of the Gold Coast beginning in the period after 1744 did the procurement of enslaved captives range to areas in which Akan was not a principal language.[7] Even then, the focus on coastal and close inland sources for slaves did not decidedly shift until the decade of the 1760s.

Within the temporal range of this book's analysis of the creation of Coromantee and (A)mina peoples in the Western Hemisphere (1680 to 1760), most enslaved captives from the Gold Coast did not originate from what is now northern Ghana or Burkina Faso. Instead, as argued in this chapter, the majority of Gold Coast captives embarking on slave ships before 1765 originated within the largely Akan-speaking linguistic geography of the littoral or coastal and near inland regions. Linguistic Akanization across a broad region explains the fact that between 1680 and 1760 most enslaved peoples from the Gold Coast had either a working familiarity with Akan or spoke it as one of a range of languages.[8] In addition, patterns of castle, fort, and lodge trading as well as ship or "coasting" trade engaged in by European merchant companies determined that Atlantic Africans from a narrow geographic band in the Gold Coast embarked on European slavers and were shipped to a small range of locales in the Western Hemisphere. Combined, the military, political, and commercial activities of Gold Coast polities and European merchant companies narrowed the geographic scope of both the slave procurement regions and the locales of disembarkation in the Americas by the 1760s—facts born out in documentary evidence and empirical data sets.

The ever-shifting and constantly moving political geographies of the Gold Coast serve as precursors to the processes that would facilitate the continued dispersals and diasporas of Akan, Ga, Adanme, and Ewe speakers in the Western Hemisphere. Dislodged from their home societies due to the constant game of stools—the rise, expansion, and fall of polities, the creation of multistate military pacts, and contestations over trade routes to the coast—Gold Coast commoners swept up into Atlantic streams depositing in Antigua, Suriname, and Louisiana suffered what many scholars would consider a series of social deaths. This chapter explores the process of social death, in part, by connecting the local and particular political geographies of the Gold Coast with broader geopolitical and commercial forces and connections between the continents linked by the Atlantic.

CULTURAL GEOGRAPHIES AND AKANIZATION

Historicizing cultural formations and processes can be a difficult endeavor. The very nature of human cultures, constantly changing, expanding, and adding or even shedding layers, defies attempts to employ fixed or static categories, terms, and theoretical frames in assessing them. Not all scholars have conveyed these complexities in their work, and a number have fallen back to essentialist and essentializing approaches to Atlantic African cultures, particularly in the "Africanisms" debate. The tendency toward essentialist understandings of cultures as timeless, bounded, and resistant to change can be seductive at times. Even scholars as careful with cultural matters as anthropologists Sidney Mintz and Richard Price, who defined the creolist position that has been championed by scores of historians since the 1980s, theorized the existence of a seemingly timeless and static "cognitive orientation" as a means of assessing broad categories of cultural continuities between Africa and African America.[9]

In quite a few discrete examples, we can locate a cultural continuity that transcends large temporal, if not geographic, distances. When, for example, Pieter de Marees describes a handshake greeting between two acquaintances in the Gold Coast in his 1602 account, it reads as all too familiar for anyone who has visited Ghana and other parts of West Africa in recent years: "They will take each other in their arms and give each other the first two fingers of the right hand, putting them together and making them click (snap) twice or thrice against each other."[10] Six decades later, Müller witnessed a similar phenomenon in Efutu, noting: "It is the general custom among them, when someone offers his hand, to grasp with his thumb and middle finger the finger and the thumb of the other person and press them firmly together, so that as the fingers are withdrawn, a little click is produced. The louder this little click sounds, the higher it is esteemed as a sign of friendship."[11] The same handshake greeting in modern Ghana and beyond serves as one example, among many, of cultural continuities existing in the region across long stretches of time.[12]

In the same vein, cultures have the capacity to quickly change, absorb, expand, and contract for myriad reasons. Coastal and border cultures tended toward cultural plasticity, given the need for peoples originating from different regions or continents to communicate and their desire to engage in commercial transactions. In the case of the Gold Coast, sustained contacts with Portuguese navigators and merchants beginning in the fifteenth century explains the many Iberian loan words in coastal Akan dialects. For example, personal pronouns (*me* and *wo*) and other Portuguese loan words associated with commercial actors and activities—*caboceer* (from *cabociero,* meaning headman), *dash* (from *doação,* meaning gift, donation, or bribe), *panyar* (from *penjaré,* meaning seize), *palaver* (from *palavra,* meaning speak or negotiate), and *viador* (from *vedor,* meaning overseer or manager)—became engrained in Fante and other coastal Akan dialects. Indeed, many coastal peoples became fluent in Portuguese creole, or what was then referred to as "Negro-Portuguese," by the eighteenth century. Portuguese creole became a commercial lingua franca in the Gold Coast to the degree that coastal polities developed unique institutions like the *piaffu*—a personal attendant of the king of Efutu "employed as an interpreter (when something is conducted in Portuguese)." Rømer adds, "When anyone wants to negotiate a deal with the Negroes, it definitely must be done in the Portuguese language, or, more correctly, in Negro-Portuguese."[13]

The level of cultural change representative of coastal and borderland regions of the Atlantic could also become a weapon of exploitation in the hands of elites. In this regard, de Marees relates an account in which coastal merchants, fluent in Portuguese creole, used their linguistic dexterity to take advantage of less cosmopolitan commoners. In this example, Gold Coast merchants allowed commoners who had items to trade to accompany them onboard a Dutch ship. After inviting them onboard, the merchants typically asked the commoners "how much money they have," as a means of measuring how much could be swindled from them in subsequent transactions. They then made sure to let the Dutch factor know that the "Peasant . . . cannot speak Portuguese" and further instructed the Dutch traders to avoid speaking "'the black language [Akan], for he is a Peasant', indicating with these words that they want to cheat [the peasant] and rob him of his money." Lacking familiarity with the motion of an anchored European ship, the commoners quickly became seasick, "lying on board and vomiting like Dogs." In their sickened state and ignorant of both Portuguese and Dutch, "they leave it to these Brokers to carry on with the transaction, telling them what goods they wish to have for what weights of Gold." The ruse also centered around the fact that prices for trade goods were set long before the party boarded the ship, but the coastal merchants pretended to vigorously negotiate in Portuguese creole. In the end, the coastal merchants and the Dutch traders split the amount they bilked from the commoners. As de Marees summarizes, "Thus it often happens that (through such practices) they steal not less than a third of what was due to the Peasant."[14] Perhaps because Portuguese creole had been a language used to rob them and that played a role in the transactions that transformed many Gold Coast captives into Western Hemisphere slaves, it could not be a central part of the sociocultural arsenal of those who became Coromantees and (A)minas.

The cultural plasticity of coastal populations has long mesmerized European traders and explorers as well as many modern historians. William Snelgrave, an English captain and merchant involved in the Atlantic African slave trade during the 1720s and 1730s, notes that "in this part called the Gold Coast, the Natives near the Sea side are much civilized, by their conversing with the Europeans, at their Settlements; and by going on board so many Ships to trade, as frequent this part of the Coast."[15] Aside from the obvious ethnocentric overtones in this assessment, Snelgrave's statement reveals the effect of a set of cultural processes set into motion when the Portuguese first made landfall in the Gold Coast in 1471. Just over a decade after this initial contact, King João II of Portugal commissioned a flotilla, under the command of Dom Diogo de Azambuja, to sail to the Gold Coast and negotiate with Edinahene Caramansa to build a permanent settlement at Elmina.[16] From this set of encounters and the sustained contacts they fostered beginning in 1482, Atlantic creole culture was given birth in the Gold Coast and, a quarter of a millennium later, Snelgrave could marvel at the "civilized" nature of coastal populations. Furthermore, these "civilized" blacks have drawn an inordinate amount of scholarly attention by historians of late as a number of works about Atlantic Africans and their diasporas have been drawn into the gravitational pull of Eurocentricity. When Atlantic Africans begin speaking European languages, consuming European goods, practicing Catholicism, or embracing European intellectual trends, they reach the level of serious scholarly contemplation for many.[17]

Close commercial and physical proximity to Portuguese merchants allowed for a veneer alongside the many layers that comprised seventeenth- and eighteenth-century coastal Atlantic African cultures. Examples of linguistic and cultural dexterity among the populations inhabiting the Gold Coast in particular may have been the only cultural "constant" in the long history of interactions, migrations, and dispersals occurring in the region. The concept of cultural "dexterity" captures best the spread of Akan cultures throughout the coastal and near-inland regions during the seventeenth and eighteenth centuries. Not only were Akwamu, Akyem, Asante, and the Fante coalition multilingual polities or political formations, but the non-Akan speakers they forced into vassalage or alliance absorbed and adopted many of the cultural ways of Akan speakers. Given the Akan-dominated political geographies—resulting from the military expansion of Akwamu, Akyem, and Asante—mapping the cultural geographies of the Gold Coast becomes an essential aspect of discussing the Akanization of Ga-, Adanme-, and Ewe-speaking peoples. In this case, focusing on relevant aspects of seventeenth- and eighteenth-century Akan language, naming practices, religion, folklore, and aspects of political culture provides a basis for understanding cultural adaptation, change, and continuity.

Due to the flows and interactions that became ubiquitous components of the Atlantic World, coastal peoples in the Gold Coast, by necessity, became culturally dexterous and multilingual. By the time de Marees visited the Gold Coast in the early 1600s, these factors had been true for more than a century. On this note, he remarks that along the Gold Coast lived "black people who trade with all nations, and because they trade and communicate with many foreign nations, they are able to speak many languages."[18] Though he listed a number of European languages in this regard, including English, French, Dutch, and Portuguese, the fact of multilingualism in the Gold Coast also encompassed Akan, Ga, Adanme, and Ewe—among others. In describing the regions along the coast from Ahanta in Côte d'Ivoire eastward to the village of Senya Beraku near Winneba, de Marees observes that "up to here all the places mentioned above speak one and the same language."[19] In his assessment, more than two-thirds of the coastal and near-inland regions of the Gold Coast spoke Akan dialects so mutually intelligible that de Marees claimed they formed a single language. This view finds support in the travel narrative of Samuel Brun, a Swiss surgeon residing at Dutch Fort Nassau in Mori from 1617 to 1620. In his account the Akani gold traders from the interior "speak no language except Acanish, and so they use people from Accara [Accra] as their interpreters." Brun bore witness to an early, if limited, example of linguistic Akanization of Ga-speaking peoples seven decades before the conquest of Accra by Akwamu. In this case, at least a few residents of Accra were familiar enough with Akan (and probably Portuguese and Dutch) to be employed by Akani gold merchants as their principal interpreters in trade negotiations with Dutch factors based at Accra and Mori.[20]

Combined, multilingualism, linguistic Akanization, and the sheer cultural weight of Akan dialects as lingua francas across large regions shaped a number of realities in both the Gold Coast and its diaspora. The very nature of the political geographies outlined in the previous chapter meant that no ethnolinguistic group was in isolation from others and, in a few identifiable cases, the language of conquerors replaced or became the existing political and commercial linga francas across broad geographic bands. This historically based assessment runs counter to and disrupts the claims made by Mintz and Price in *The Birth of African-American Culture*. Working from the perspective of a limited range of available sources, they could still definitively claim that while some enslaved Atlantic Africans may have been bilingual or trilingual, they could "assume with confidence that the *initial* aggregates of slaves in particular New World enterprises usually did not constitute speech communities."[21] The specific realities within the Gold Coast diaspora—in which many were familiar with Akan—serves as useful counterpoints to what was an essential contention of the creolist position.

Barbot, Bosman, Rask, and Rømer offer more insights into the nature of multilingualism and linguistic Akanization.[22] During Barbot's two visits (1678–79 and 1681–82), he made note of the fact that the Keta kingdom in the Slave Coast—in the region east of the Volta and near Anlo—"is in a sort of confederacy with Aquamboe. . . . Their economy, politicks, and religion are much the same as on the Gold Coast . . . and as to their dialect, it differs little from that of Acra." In this case, Ga speakers who fled east after the conquest of Accra by Akwamu populated this region to the degree that many in Keta spoke Ga and possibly Adanme. In addition to Keta, Barbot made a similar assessment about the links between the polities, religious cultures, and languages of the peoples of Little Popo and Accra.[23] In sum, the political geographies of the Gold and Slave Coasts shaped resulting cultural and linguistic geographies across broad swaths of territory.

Bosman, whose stay in the Gold Coast lasted thirteen years (1689–1702), offers a more sophisticated and nuanced perspective on regional languages. Though Barbot would rely heavily on Bosman in many other areas, to the extent that versions of his *Description* published after 1688 plagiarized large sections of Bosman, the two differed in their conclusions about language. This was possibly due to the length of their respective stays in the region or their exposure to particular coastal language clusters. Noting the relatively small size of the Gold Coast, Bosman begins his assessment of regional languages by noting their diversity: "We find there seven or eight several Languages, so different that three or four of them are interchangeable unintelligible to any but the respective Natives." In his view, the languages of the western portion of the Gold Coast—"Egira, Abocroe, Ancober, and Axim"—had vast and seemingly unbridgeable differences. As a long-time resident at Elmina Castle, in the central coast region, Bosman was constantly surrounded by Akan speakers. In this context he noted, "The other Coast Negroes, those of Aquamboe only excepted, generally understand one another." This Bosman contended after claiming that "more shocking is [the language] of Acra, not having the least Similitude with any of the rest."[24]

Though Bosman understood that Akan language and dialect clusters in the central coast had linguistic links to inland polities like Denkyira, Akyem, Assin, and Adom, his ear was not keen enough to draw the language spoken by the peoples of Akwamu into the Akan linguistic circle. He did, however, note the distinction between Ga-speaking residents of Accra and the majority of coastal Akan speakers. Not having spent a great deal of time in Accra, Bosman had no real opportunity to witness or comment upon multilingualism and Akanization in Ga- and Adanme-speaking regions in and around the Accra Plains. Being most familiar with the languages and dialects of the central coast, Bosman bore witness to the emergence of Fante as a lingua franca and the ethnogenesis of Fante peoples—thus his claim that central coast peoples generally understood each other. Indeed, the "Fanteization" of the central coast presents an illuminating parallel to the Akanization of other regions as the result of the rise and expansion of Akwamu, Akyem, and Asante after 1688. Combined, both processes facilitated the spread of Akan dialects along coastal and near-inland regions between Axim and the Volta by the early decades of the eighteenth century.

For Rask, at Danish Christiansborg Castle near Accra, the case for Atlantic African multilingualism and Akanization was much more clearly articulated. Living in the Gold Coast continuously over a five year span (1708–13) and encountering speakers of Ga, Adanme, and Akan on a daily basis, he observed that "most of them have good abilities and quick minds when it comes to learning a number of languages, such as Dutch, English, Danish—with the greatest difficulty—French, Portuguese and all manner of Negro languages, which are countless, and often very different from one another."[25] He further elaborated, adding, "The languages of Guinea are very many, but even though each people in that country, live indeed scarcely 1 or one and one-half miles from each other, be they Infanties [Borbor Fante], Akanies [Assin], Akras [Ga-speaking Accra], Aquvamus [Akwamu], Kræpees [Ewe-speaking Krepi], Qvahus [Ewe-speaking Kwahu], Qvitas [Keta], Harders, Popos, Fidas [Whydah] . . . each of whom has his own special language that they use among themselves. . . ."[26] This impossible linguistic diversity recounted by Rask must be qualified by two important factors. First, much of his understanding about the diversity of languages was shaped by his reading and understanding of Olivier Dapper, who never visited Atlantic Africa and—instead—relied heavily upon the travel accounts of others in his analyses of ethnolinguistic groups in the Gold Coast. Second, even Rask casts doubt on the accuracy of Dapper when he concludes, "It is Aqvambuish that is, so to speak, their chief language, in which almost 100 miles above Akra, and nearly as many miles below they can communicate."[27]

For Rask, "Aqvambuish" or Akan served as a lingua franca in and well beyond Accra due to the territorial expansion of Akwamu and because of the more general linguistic sway of Akan among the coastal and near-inland populations in the Gold Coast. The notion that Akan could be understood throughout the Gold Coast finds confirmation in the writings of Jacobus Elisa Joannes Capitein, a native Akan speaker from the Gold Coast born between 1717 and 1718. By the 1740s Capitein had been educated in Holland and returned to Elmina Castle in the employ of the Dutch West Indies Company. Author of one of the first texts written in Akan, Capitein wrote a catechetical described by him as composed in the "Negro language" spoken from "Abrowarie to Afam"—regions then defining much of the Gold Coast.[28] Both Rask's "Aqvambuish" and Capitein's "Negro language" demonstrate that while there was no common name for the Akan language and its related cluster of dialects in the eighteenth-century Gold Coast, as John Thornton notes "it was certainly widely spoken, by whatever names it might be called. Indeed, Akan was a lingua franca, being spoken as a second language by many speakers of other languages, living to the east of the Gold Coast."[29]

Further complicating things, Rask includes a number of words in his "Aqvambuish" vocabulary that are actually Ga in origin. The Ga words he lists for tobacco pipe (*bele*), knife (*gakang*), ear (*toi*), nose (*gungo*), mouth (*onabu*), and head (*ito*) are intermixed with a much lengthier list of Akan words, signaling the fact that residents of Accra spoke both Ga and Akan interchangeably and with relative ease.[30] Rømer, who served at Christiansborg Castle for a decade (1739–49), confirms some of the conclusions made by Rask. Noting the standard greeting given to Europeans, he states that the mostly Ga-speaking residents of Accra would say "Jo aussi" (*Yo Kwasi*) which translates roughly to mean "All right, Sunday's child." This custom began with a bit of cultural misunderstanding regarding Christian ways. Due to the fact that Europeans from five different nations residing in or near Accra would noticeably "dress up more on Sundays than otherwise," Ga speakers thought Europeans were celebrating their birthdays and thus all Europeans were assumed to have been born on Sunday. In this case, the greeting assigns all Europeans the Akan day-name for a boy born on Sunday (Kwasi) and "yo" roughly translates to mean "yes, certainly, all right, or OK." In a rather seamless fashion then, Ga-speaking residents of Accra employed both Akan language and understandings of Akan-derived day-names.[31]

From both Rask's *Brief and Truthful Description* and Rømer's *Reliable Account* we arrive at widespread multilingualism and linguistic Akanization as real cultural forces throughout the coastal and near-inland regions by the first few decades of the eighteenth century. By mid-century, linguistic Akanization was simply a fact throughout the Gold Coast. Thomas Thompson, an Anglican missionary residing at Cape Coast Castle from 1752 to 1755, recalled that among the coastal languages "Fantee" was "the most extensive . . . of any of the Coast Tongues, which is the sole Dialect of the Cape Coast Blacks . . . as far as betwixt Cape Apollonia to the River Volta, that is, about an hundred Leagues."[32] The end result of linguistic Akanization witnessed by Thompson—among many others—can be seen in eighteenth- and nineteenth-century Ga and Ewe vocabularies. For example, Ga words for nobleman (*oblempon*), king (*omanhene*), polity (*man*), linguist (*otsiami*), master (*owula*), money (*sika*), rich man (*sikatse*), militia (*asafo*), and a court official's household (*jase* or *gyase*) all derive from Akan words. Indeed, even as far away as the Volta, similar Akan loan words seeped into Ewe by the nineteenth century. Ewe words for noblemen (*abirempon*) and militia captains (*asafohene*) have origins in Akan, and even a handful of Ga and Adanme words entered the everyday vocabulary of the Ewe-speaking residents of Anlo.[33] The fact that many of these loan words relate to commerce and either economic or political power should come as no surprise given centuries of Akan-speaking dominance over Accra, Anlo, and their surrounds.

When Rømer wrote, "It strikes me as strange that the Negroes' languages differ so much from each other," he was referencing what he perceived to be the vast differences in language between the Gold Coast and the Slave Coast. Given his daily experiences with Ga and Adanme speakers under Akan domination, this statement has to be understood within the context of the effect of decades Akanization in Accra. Rømer did not note how much the languages in an around Accra differ, probably because by the 1740s the level of Akanization and the linguistic dexterity of Ga and Adanme speakers would make the language(s) spoken in Accra impossible to differentiate to the untrained ear. Though Rømer's words, found in a section about "Benin influences" in Accra, seem to undermine the notion that Ga and Adanme speakers regularly spoke Akan or that a significant amount of linguistic Akanization could characterize the populations in and around Accra, there is a more viable construction on what may seem to be an odd claim on his part. In this instance, his statement may have been in reference to the difference in languages spoken by the Ga-, Adanme- and Akan-speaking peoples he interacted with constantly at Christiansborg Castle and in Accra and the languages spoken by groups near and to the immediate east of the Volta—namely, Ewe, Fon, and Yoruba speakers.[34]

Having traveled to the Slave Coast as far east as the kingdom of Benin, Rømer's observations of "Benin influences" and the linguistic differences between the Gold and Slave Coasts reflected both his personal knowledge of the two regions and his frequent encounters with enslaved Ewe-, Fon-, and Yoruba-speaking workers imported from the Slave Coast to work at Gold Coast castles and forts. Importing castle slaves—that is slaves who worked in the employ of European merchants and trade companies but who were not designated for transatlantic shipment—from regions adjoining the Gold Coast was a long-standing practice. In August 1684, for example, the director-general of Dutch Elmina Castle noted that "the Noble Company is ill-provided with work-slaves here on the Gold Coast, and . . . most of these Negroes still remaining are slaves who have been bought here on the Gold Coast, who consequently are inclined towards running away and seeking their freedom." In response to this circumstance, the director-general suggested that it would be best to commission a ship and "send it to Ardra [Allada] . . . in order to buy a number of 80 Ps. Slaves." Since these enslaved Ewe, Fon, and Yoruba speakers would be new to the Gold Coast, "those slaves, being strangers, are less likely to run away."[35]

The Portuguese began the practice of importing enslaved peoples from Allada to Gold Coast castles, forts, and towns to the degree that imported slave laborers—no matter their origin—were generally known as "Alatas" by the late seventeenth century. As Reindorf recounts, Alata was "a Fante name for people of Lagos, Yoruba, &c." Within each coastal town, Alatas "formed their own district in connection with the town's people, and were acknowledged as citizens of the place by joining the established band of the town." Indeed, Accra was—according to this practice—divided into "Kinka or Dutch Alata, English Alata, and Osu or Danish Alata" as early as 1672. Even now, a major subdivision of modern-day Accra near James Town Fort is known as *Ngleshie Alata* (a Ga corruption of "English Alata")—attesting to the continuing memory of the Ewe-, Fon-, and Yoruba-speaking workers who built and inhabited large sections of the coastal town.[36] Clearly, a sizable number of castle slaves and other laborers working at Christiansborg Castle in Osu (or Danish Alata) originated from the Slave Coast in Rømer's time. He had ample opportunity, therefore, to draw comparisons between the residents of Accra and workers imported from the Slave Coast in his understanding of linguistic diversity in Atlantic Africa.

Within the geographic range of the Gold Coast, we can assert claims for both linguistic diversity and linguistic homogeneity. The "impossible diversity" thesis embraced by advocates of the creolist school has been shown, by John Thornton and others, as linked to the tendency to associate a unique cultural identity to every language or dialect spoken in Atlantic Africa.[37] In the case of the Gold Coast, these assumptions and tendencies ignore the many historical realities forged by unique ethnolinguistic and political geographies. Multilingualism, partly the result of Akanization or Fanteization; the trajectories of ethnolinguistic groups that divided, merged, and moved constantly in the region; and the emergence of political and commercial lingua francas all combined to explain why so many enslaved and exported Gold Coast commoners would adopt Akan as their common tongue in the Americas. While no precision on this matter is possible, we can estimate that more than three-quarters of all Gold Coast Atlantic Africans arriving in the Americas by the mid-eighteenth century knew or were familiar with Akan as a primary, secondary, or tertiary language. The development of a common tongue and Akan speech communities are prime examples, among many, of common ties in the Gold Coast that would become even more evident in the diaspora.

Connected directly to language and linguistic Akanization, the spread and adoption of the Akan day-naming system throughout the Gold Coast represents another cultural tie linking what should be vastly diverse peoples and polities. Again, Rømer mentioned and explained the typical greeting given to Europeans living in and near Accra that was based on the assumption that all Christians were born on a Sunday. Whether or not day-naming began as a uniquely Akan-speaking concept before spreading to others in the Gold Coast and beyond may be impossible to discover, especially given how intimately tangled cultures and peoples in the region became over time and through sustained contact. With this stated, it is likely that the Ga and the later Ewe adoptions of day-names had their genesis among Akan-speaking neighbors and conquerors. Clues to this are embedded in Ga oral traditions claiming that the Ga-speaking settlers at Accra originally developed a calendrical system based on an eight-day week. By the eighteenth century, Ga speakers not only adopted a seven-day week, but also used the seven days of the week as the basis for part of the naming process for newborns. From his time in Ga-speaking Accra, Rømer notes specifically that "each week every Negro has his own sacred day, the day on which he was born."[38] Paul Erdmann Isert, a much later authority than Rømer on naming practices in Ga-speaking Accra, wrote in 1788, "When a child is fourteen days old a feast is held in order to give him a name. . . . Normally they have two names: the one taken from the day on which they were born, and the other given by the family."[39]

Bosman, primarily interacting with Akan speakers to the west of Accra, noted, "As soon as the Child is born . . . it hath three Names bestowed on it . . . the first is that of the Day of the Week on which it was born."[40] Among Akan speakers, the day of one's birth became an important layer of identity. Thus, day-names, or names assigned based on the day of the week on which a child was born, become not only a unique mark of Akan cultures in the Gold Coast, but also a cultural vector that helps trace the extent of Akanization (see table 2.1). Perhaps the most insightful example of the use and embrace of Akan day-names among non-Akan speakers is the story of Cudjo (Kojo), a chief broker and caboceer of the Royal African Company based at James Fort in English Accra and the first *Alata Akutso Mantse* (or Alata division head). Cudjo, originally a Yoruba speaker from Allada named Ojo, was imported to Accra to serve

Table 2.1. Akan Days of the Week and Day-Names.

| Days of the Week | | Akan Day-Names | |
English	Gold Coast (17th Century)	Male	Female
Sunday	Quassi-da, Quachirath	Kwasi, Kwesi	Akosua
Monday	Egwju, Edouwera	Kwadwo, Kojo	Adwoa
Tuesday	Ebbenada	Kwabena	Abenaa, Abenaba
Wednesday	Eckura	Kweku, Kwaku	Ekuwa, Akua
Thursday	Ejuada	Kwaa, Yaw	Aba, Yaa
Friday	Efi-da, Efira	Kwefi, Kofi	Efiwa, Afua
Saturday	Ennemad	Kwame, Kwamena	Amba, Amma

Sources: de Marees, *Historical Account of the Gold Kingdom*, 255; "Müller's Description of the Fetu Country, 1662–9," in Jones, *German Sources*, 278; Pitman, "Slavery on British West India Plantations," 641; DeCamp, "African Day-Names," 139; Handler and J. Jacoby, "Slave Names and Naming," 699.

as an enslaved worker at James Fort. Mastering English, Ga, and Akan, Cudjo quickly rose through the social ranks from enslaved laborer to wage-earning linguist and, ultimately, Royal African Company cabo-ceer. By 1748, he ascended to a royal stool in Accra, becoming the head of the Alata quarter in James Town—a position his descendants continue to hold to this day.[41] Not only did Cudjo adopt the Akan day-name for a child born on Monday, but also he embraced the annual Akan Odwira festival procession.[42] In many ways, the story of Cudjo epitomizes the degree and type of cultural transmutations characteristic of coastal and border cultures throughout Atlantic Africa.

In the intersecting realms of religion and folklore, Akan concepts dominated the Gold Coast regions in which Akan-speaking peoples and polities spread by the eighteenth century. This aspect of culture assumes elevated importance, as one eighteenth-century observer noted, because "a people's nature and customs usually flow from their religion."[43] In the case of Akan religions in the Gold Coast, the lack of a uniform under-standing of the otherworldly among their varied adherents—partly as the result of the absence of a unifying set of sacred texts—did not prevent a number of European observers from making extensive and sometimes insightful commentary. Though, as Rømer notes, "opinions as distinct from one another as east is from west" existed in the Gold Coast about spiritual matters, we can identify broad practices and discuss, with some degree of specificity, seventeenth- and eighteenth-century beliefs and the wide range of adherents of Akan religious cultures and folkloric "traditions."[44]

Observing the religious values of the mostly Ga-speaking inhabitants of Accra, Rømer demonstrates the penetration of Akan spiritual concerns and beliefs among non-Akan speakers as well as the multiple intersections between folklore and religion. In his discussion of the "universal spirit" and creator of the world among "All the negroes" in the Gold Coast, Rømer states that this being's name was known as "Niumboo." Rask, another resident of Accra, noted that "The Akras call god Jungo, and the Aqvambues call god Jankumpung."[45] In other seventeenth- and eighteenth-century records, the various renderings of the name of the sky god of creation in the Gold Coast include "Jan Commae,"[46] "Jan Commé,"[47] "Jancómpon,"[48] "Iuan goemain,"[49] "Iancome,"[50] and "Yancúmpong."[51] In the modern Ga and Akan orthography, the sky god is rendered as *Nyoŋmo* (Ga), *Nyɔnmɔ* (Ga), *Nyankoŋ* (Akan), or simply *Nyame* (Akan).[52] Across Dutch, Danish, German, English, and French sources, the name of the Ga and Akan god of creation have the same etymological roots and a similar range of associated attributes.

Given the Akwamu conquest of Accra, this Akan cultural overlay comes as no surprise. The shifting regional power relationships caused by this conquest had direct ramifications for Ga and Adanme religious worldviews. Indeed, Rømer provides further evidence for this conclusion in his interview of Caboceer Okpoti of Labadi. Serving as the principal priest of the Lakpa oracle in the Ga- and Adanme-speaking town of Labadi, Okpoti admitted to Rømer the relative weakness of his oracle in comparison to the Fante war shrine Nananom Mpow. When Rømer asked Okpoti if Lakpa could "lift an ox or cow up into the air, as the Fante [oracle] can," the priest replied with a rather laconic response: "The ancestors of the Fantes were all with God, but their own (the Labodes') had died in war." Pressing Okpoti further on what his statement meant, Rømer received and recorded a fascinating aspect of the interpenetrations of Gold Coast politics and religions: "Don't you know, master, that the Blacks cut each other's heads off in war, and do you think that God receives people without heads? Can he not get enough people who die in their homes and are buried with their heads on?"[53] So, from Okpoti's perspective, the Ga defeat at the hands of Akwamu and the failure of their beheaded ancestors to properly ascend to the sky god resulted in the spiritual subordination of their most important oracle to Nananom Mpow.[54] In this way, the political and religious subordination of Ga-speaking peoples and polities to their Akan-speaking neighbors went hand in hand.

The revelations made by Okpoti to Rømer underscore another aspect of Akan religious beliefs and either the Akanization of Ga-speaking spiritual worldviews or a set of independent cultural inventions that resonated within and beyond Akan, Ga, and Adanme cultural circles. Okpoti's statement about the Fante ancestors residing with the sky god points to a ubiquitous religious concept throughout the Gold Coast and much of Atlantic Africa—namely, the immortality of the human soul. In some cases, belief in the soul's life beyond physical death led to the development of religious systems that embraced ideas of transmigration or reincarnation. Apparently, in the seventeenth- and eighteenth-century Gold Coast, no real consensus could be found by European observers or their Atlantic African informants. In this regard, Rask and Bosman concur that both Ga and Akan speakers believed in the immortality of the soul and a type of life after death.[55] On the other hand, Rømer observes, "They have many differing opinions on their condition after death." Giving two concrete accounts of people he encountered who explicitly believed in reincarnation, Rømer was fascinated by the response of a company slave named Qvacu (Kwaku) who remarked, "When I die, I shall ask God not to send me back into the world as the slave of the Whites." The priest Okpoti, who served as Rømer's principal informant, offered an interpretation of death and the afterlife that seemed more akin to Christian concepts of judgment and heaven. In this case, Jancómpon weighed the "pious" soul to see if it could be deemed "worthy to be received to Himself."[56] Despite unsupported claims made by Kwasi Konadu that "the Akan," after centuries of contact with Arab Muslims and European Christians "never became Islamic or Christian (until the twentieth century, and even then with resistance)," Okpoti's statement is in line with other Christian and European interpenetrations in Akan religions by the eighteenth and nineteenth centuries.[57]

In addition to the appearance of the Akan god of creation in the religious worldviews of Ga and Adanme speakers, one of Jancómpon's subordinates—Ananse or Nanni—provided a vital bridge between religion and folkloric traditions. First mentioned in European accounts by Bosman as "Spider Ananse," this mysterious entity often appears associated by Akan speakers and others with the creation of humanity and with a set of didactic tales. While Bosman and other supposedly "better informed" Europeans sought to instruct Akan speakers they encountered about the impossibility of a spider creating the first humans, he bemoaned the fact that "a great Number . . . remain of that Opinion, out of which Folly they are not to be reason'd." In his words, their faith in the powers of Spider Ananse was the "greatest Piece of Ignorance and Stupidity," especially considering that the Christian logic of edenic gardens, forbidden fruits, and talking serpents should have been much more convincing to any reasonable listener.[58] In sharp contrast, Rømer offers a more extensive and nuanced commentary about the figure he refers to as "Nanni," explaining in full the religious and folkloric dimensions of the trickster spider.[59]

Rømer's version of Nanni came to him by way of Ga speakers in Accra, though the story has clear ties to Akan religious concepts and cultures. In this rendition, Nanni creates humanity out of woven cloth at the behest of the Akan sky god Jancómpon. Instead of humanity appreciating Nanni, they ran in fear upon seeing her. With the extra cloth remaining, Nanni created another being—a male spider in her own image—and even named the new entity Nanni. It was this anthropomorphic spider, the male Nanni, who would become the subject of a corpus of didactic folktales in Akan-, Ga-, and Adanme-speaking regions of the Gold Coast. Compared by Rømer to Ulenspeyl, a prankster character in German literature, Nanni ultimately becomes a trickster; his stories were acted out "in moonlight, sitting out of doors, fifty in a circle, while the old people tell the young about this Nanni." In the sample of a Nanni story given by Rømer, Nanni does not resemble his more heroic diasporic counterpart in the eighteenth- and nineteenth-century

British Caribbean. Instead of being depicted as a clever and witty hero, champion, and rebel against those who would abuse their power over the weak, Nanni in the story presented by Rømer is wealthy, with many wives and children, yet lazy and greedy. In the end, Nanni has his hands amputated after a particularly petty and selfish act of theft. When his wives threaten to leave due to his weakened state, Nanni impersonates the voice of an oracle to convince them to return.[60] In sum, Nanni and his associated tales serve as both a measure of the Akanization of populations in and near Accra and as a backdrop against which diasporic folktales about Ananse the Spider—imbued, as they were, with the commoner consciousness—can be compared.

With some certainty, we can trace the presence of Jancómpon and Nanni among Akan peoples and polities and regions touched by Akanization throughout the early-modern Gold Coast. Seventeenth- and eighteenth-century Akan religions and spiritual worldviews lacked any sort of uniformity, making a comprehensive description using contemporary sources close to impossible. In very broad outlines, Akan religions as practiced during the height of the Atlantic slave trade may have incorporated a handful of common features. The world of Akan speakers was filled with spiritual forces to the degree that a sense of spiritual causality could explain most abnormal events. As Bosman observed, many coastal peoples believed in "nothing uncommon ever happening which is not attributed to some Miracle or another." He concluded that even "Death is never without a Cause."[61] Mysterious deaths, illnesses, and bad or good fortune could be attributable to the activation of spiritual forces or the ancestors by an aggrieved party. Accidents or luck, therefore, would always have spiritual explanations. In these worldviews, there was no sharp line of distinction between the material and spiritual planes of existence. Few boundaries, if any, existed between the realms, allowing spiritual forces to permeate every area of life for Akan-speaking peoples and others in the Gold Coast. In this regard, while Jancómpon was the omnipotent sky god, this entity remained distant and removed from his creation. Few if any priest- or priestess-hoods, shrines, and sacred groves honored the sky god directly. As one seventeenth-century observer noted, because Jancómpon was "righteous and good" and could do "no-one any harm," adherents of Akan religions deemed it unnecessary to worship or pray to him.[62] Instead, a constellation of personal, local, and lesser deities, ancestral spirits, and oracles—collectively known as *bossum* (or *obosum* in the modern orthography)—became the recipients of prayers, sacrifices, libations, and requests of various sorts by supplicants. Bossum, or "fetisso," could represent an entire polity (as in the cases of Nananom Mpow or Lakpa), a lineage, or a household; they provided protection or could be activated as weapons to be used against enemies. Bossum played important roles in a hierarchically arranged spiritual universe among Akan speakers and others in the seventeenth- and eighteenth-century Gold Coast.[63]

Another spiritual force that had personal uses and applications was a category known as *sumán*. While bossum and sumán seemed to overlap, at least in the mind of Müller, the latter refers to a more general type of protective spirit used as a "special domestic idol." Whereas bossum were attended to by a host of priests and priestesses—known variably in the seventeenth century Gold Coast as *o-bossum-fù, comfu,* or *sophu*—and had shrines or sacred groves constructed in their honor, sumán can be understood as personal ritual objects imbued with varying levels of spiritual power. This belief system was decentralized and mostly unregulated by polities; any supplicant could inherit, purchase, steal, or otherwise acquire a sumán. Once activated, these objects had the potential of allowing anyone—from peasants to nobles—to tap into empowering and powerful forces.[64] According to Müller, sumán were the domain of a unique priesthood known as the *summàn-fù,* who were "highly honoured, but not as highly as o-bossum-fu," probably because they lacked state sanction and approval.[65] Given the personal, quotidian, and even democratic nature of beliefs associated with sumán, this complex of spiritual concepts survived Atlantic passages to the Americas and became a vital base for the worldviews of Gold Coast Africans in the New World. Sumán and the Western Hemisphere system known as obeah became dimensions and extensions of the commoner consciousness as articulated throughout the eighteenth-century Caribbean and mainland.[66]

Beyond religion and folklore, another aspect of Akanization and the spreading influence of Akan-speaking polities becomes readily apparent in the political cultures throughout the Gold Coast. As far east as the Volta region, Akan concepts of matrilineal descent, stools, military formations (e.g., the three-wing formation innovated by Akwamu), and asafo companies became hallmarks of Anlo-Ewe political and military culture by the early nineteenth century. Certainly, the Akwamu conquest and absorption of Ewe-speaking states to the west of the Volta—Anlo, Keta, Little Popo, and Krepi—and its later and long-standing alliance with Anlo played a significant role in the adoption of Akan political and military cultures among Ewe-speaking polities.[67] In similar fashion, Ga- and Adanme-speaking polities extensively borrowed aspects from the military and political cultures of their Akan neighbors and conquerors. Indeed, given the longer history of Akan suzerainty in and around the Accra Plains, the interpenetration of Akan cultures was deeper among Ga- and Adanme-speaking people and polities. Ga- and Adanme-speaking polities, for example, adopted asafo companies and other forms of Akan military organization, matrilineal descent systems, and the Akan "paraphernalia of power"—stools, state swords, umbrellas, and palanquins.[68]

As in the Ewe case, the adoption of Akan matrilineal descent was a sharp break from the cultural patterns established by both Guang and Ga speakers in Accra. Reindorf notes, for example, that "originally the inheritance in both the Guan and Ga races was by male line; but this was converted into the Twi [Akan] system during the time of the temporal reigns of Ofori and a few of the Akan kings."[69] Such a fundamental change in sociopolitical culture among Ga speakers and other residents of Accra signals how deeply Akan and Ga concepts became intertwined with each other. Indeed, Reindorf—a Ga-speaking resident of Accra who collected a number of Ga oral traditions in composing his *History of the Gold Coast and Asante*—credits a range of Asantehene with the creation of Accra asafo "bands" organized in every Ga-speaking town in the Accra Plains. Not only was the very organization of asafo militia companies in Ga towns an Akan cultural intervention, but the company names, their "symbolical mottoes," and their sigils or various "designs displayed by the bands . . . in the flags, swords, and state umbrellas" all bore the stamp of coastal Akan cultures.[70]

Above and beyond all other markers of Akan political cultures in the Gold Coast, state and personal oaths and oathing ceremonies became central features, serving, ideally, as inviolable contracts for states, state and commercial actors, or armies. In most cases, taking an oath was a sacred act that involved eating or drinking substances believed by adherents to contain sufficient spiritual potency to kill anyone taking the oath on false pretense or breaking the terms of a sworn agreement.[71] The ubiquitous practice of eating or imbibing during an oathing ritual led to the European description of an Akan oath as "eating fetish."[72] In some descriptions, someone wishing to prove their innocence when accused of a criminal offense would be subjected to an oathing test or ordeal in which they would eat salt or bread on top of a ritual object—probably a personal sumán of the accuser or the "fetisso" or bossum of a town or larger polity.[73] In Müller's description, "If he does, and for three days experiences no harm, he is recognised as innocent."[74] Sumán, bossum, and other ritual objects figure into Reindorf's description of loyalty oaths. He observes that "the powerful fetish of the country or town" is washed with water, producing a "potion" that is offered to an oath taker to imbibe during an elaborate and sacred ceremony.[75]

As in Reindorf's description, most accounts of seventeenth- and eighteenth-century Gold Coast oathing ceremonies involve the creation of special drinks made from a variety of substances—green leaf juice, gunpowder, water, blood, ground millet, and rum or other spirits—to help seal commercial contracts, to consecrate peace treaties between nations, or to ensure the loyalty of soldiers and their commanding officers to the war aims of a polity. In all these cases, drinking "fetish," or the oath drink, accompanied severe sanctions for the dishonest or disloyal.[76] As Bosman notes, "They oblige the Priest to swear first, and drink the *Oath-Draught,* with the Imprecation, that the *Fetiche* should punish him with Death, if he ever absolved any Person from their Oath without the unanimous Consent of all interested in that Contract."[77] According to Christian Whit, a Ga-speaking informant for Johannes Rask who served as a drum major at Christiansborg Castle, each item in the oath drink signified a different form of death for those who violate the terms of a sacred contract: "Water means an unhappy death in the sea . . . the blood means a violent death by gunshot or sword . . . the [millet] that all the blessings of the earth's fertility will be denied him, if he breaks the oath."[78]

The ubiquity of oathing ceremonies, as described in a range of sources, obfuscates the origins of this aspect of Gold Coast political cultures. Practiced among Akan-, Ga-, Adanme-, and Ewe-speaking peoples and among language cohorts in regions adjacent to the Gold Coast, loyalty oaths may have been universally employed throughout Atlantic Africa—particularly in regions with expansionist states that needed the security of inviolable contracts to lengthen their political and commercial reach. Whether or not loyalty oaths can be categorized as uniquely Akan-speaking practices that spread to other language cohorts through military conquest and political domination is probably unknowable. Perhaps the form that loyalty oaths took in the Gold Coast originated among Akan-speaking peoples and polities; they could have also come to Gold Coast language cohorts from a common foreign vector.[79] The point here is that one would be hard pressed to find a people or polity in the region that did not embrace the meaning and significance of "eating fetish" and oathing ceremonies. This becomes more evident when considering the frequent references to loyalty oaths throughout the Gold Coast diaspora—particularly in the formation of Coromantee or (A)mina polities in the Americas or in the execution of conspiracies and revolts against colonial slaveocracies.

While Akanization and the sway of Akan-speaking cultural practices throughout the Gold Coast allowed for and facilitated a set of connections between Akan-, Ga-, Adanme-, and Ewe-speaking peoples in the Western Hemisphere diaspora, it does not follow that all peoples exported from the Gold Coast should be simply reduced to Akan "culture bearers."[80] Military conquest and political suzerainty may explain why many adopted aspects of Akan cultures; nevertheless, a number of unique practices and worldviews continued under new cultural layers resulting from Akanization. Ga speakers in and around Accra, for instance, maintained the Ga language, the practice of male circumcision, and annual Homowo festivals in August as continuing aspects of their unique cultural identities.[81] Likewise, Ewe speakers residing near the Volta kept their languages, their mastery over intricate cloth weaving techniques known as Kente (to be later appropriated by, and associated with, the Asante kingdom), and the characteristic Anlo-Ewe clan structure (hlo).[82] Combined, the ability of Ga and Ewe speakers to simultaneously adopt the cultures of others and maintain their own unique cultural markers exemplifies the types of cultural crosscurrents profoundly shaping their Black Atlantic experiences. Along with enslaved Akan speakers who joined them in their westward sojourns into bondage, this capacity of Ga, Adanme, and Ewe speakers to both adapt to and resist new cultural interventions facilitated their collective transformations into Coromantees and (A)minas in the Americas.

This approach to identity transformation may seem, on the surface, to be related to a series of compelling claims made by Vincent Brown in his widely celebrated *The Reaper's Garden* (2008). Noting that "it can be misleading to attribute cultural traits to distinct 'ethnic' groups, traced back to their places of origin," Brown concludes that the aim of Atlantic Africans in diaspora was not "to achieve a distinct cultural identity." He adds that by assessing the behavior of enslaved peoples we can make note of a range of performances and beliefs that transcend the "cultural history of identity."[83] I contend that, in the case of Gold Coast Africans in the Americas, while they were certainly not cultural nationalists seeking to forge New World identities deeply rooted in a particular Atlantic African ethnicity, they clearly were not forgetful of the useful elements of their past in framing their new lives in the Americas. The "changing same" that allowed a former Ga speaker from Accra to claim the title of "king" of the Antiguan Coromantees in 1736—employing Akan-speaking political and cultural performances to recruit followers—implies processes of identity formation different, in varying degrees, from ones outlined by Brown, David Northrup, and Philip Morgan.[84] Coromantees and (A)minas should not be understood as being concerned with "cultural purity,"[85] nor did they represent "pre-packaged static cultures."[86] Instead, a hallmark of their cultural identities in both Atlantic Africa and the Americas was the plasticity that allowed them to incorporate or accommodate new ideas while resisting others. Their genius was in their ability to simultaneously remember and forget, or to stand still while moving, in the constant race toward new ethnic and sociocultural constructions in the Western Hemisphere.[87]

SOCIAL DEATH, SLAVE PROCUREMENT, AND THE GEOGRAPHIES OF SLAVE TRADING

In a tangible sense, the related processes of capture and enslavement can be best symbolized as a sort of death for those suffering this fate. Following the logic of Orlando Patterson and others, the levels of violence and disruption involved in being torn from kin and kith only to be redefined as commodities to be traded and bartered—a sharp and abrupt discontinuity of a former existence—can only be described with the finality implied by death. As soul-rending as the processes of capture and enslavement had to be for their many victims, we should avoid overestimating the effects of social death as part of the continuity of experiences for Gold Coasts commoners throughout the Black Atlantic. Cugoano, for instance, found some semblance of community among his Akan-speaking countrymen in Grenada and a sense of a transnational community citizenship in his life in freedom in the wider Black Atlantic. His example was representative of larger realities for many in the Gold Coast diaspora.

Outside of nobles enslaved after the defeat or collapse of their polity, the vast majority of those who suffered social death in the Gold Coast came from the lower orders of what were rigidly hierarchical societies. The five degrees or classes of Gold Coast peoples, as discussed by Bosman, did not suffer enslavement, humiliation, and social death evenly. Indeed, the first, second, and third degrees—kings, caboceers, and nobles, or *obirempong*—instigated expansionist wars, controlled political offices, collected tribute payments, and bartered with European factors and merchant companies to the disadvantage of the commoners and slaves who inhabited the fourth and fifth degrees. In reaping the benefits of those who were "imployed in the Tillage of Wines, Agriculture and Fishing" while forcing others into slavery through foreign acquisition and purchase, war, and debt, the various classes of Gold Coast elites presided over systems of exploitation that generated expanding pools of dependent and forced labor.[88] Peasants living in rural hamlets undergirded expansionist city-states and kingdoms as the product of their collective labor fueled and fed wars that were often initiated by the wealthy and high-born, but fought by the poor and dependent.

As Kea notes, there were "two categories of people that determined the continued social-economic existence of the *abirempon* [hereditary nobles] and the *afahene* [wealthy elites] as an upper class: retainers and free commoners."[89] Within the hierarchical and corporatist structure of seventeenth- and eighteenth-century Gold Coast states, kings, caboceers, and nobles conceived of their polities as "families" in which social lessers—servants, retainers, and slaves—became part of a metaphorical kin simply as a means of providing the labor and social wealth necessary for elites to maintain their status and power. They were, in this sense, the hands that tilled and the feet that transported goods to market sustaining a body politic headed by ennobled economic and political elites.[90] Though not comprising a class of dependent labor, even free commoners could be considered as essential elements in the ability of elites to define and retain power. In many ways, commoners became "pawns" to be acquired by nobility and other elites through the control of political offices. As a "class of political dependents or subjects," commoners—including petty farmers, fishermen, craftsmen, soldiers, market sellers, and low-ranking priests and priestess—generated revenues for political elites in the form of levies, tribute payments (in specie and in kind), and through a variety of specialized labor services.[91] In the course of the slave trade, it would be among the poor, the downtrodden, the political or economic dependents, and the non-elite that new worlds across the Atlantic would be built. What would link them together would not just be a common range of dialects, languages, and broadly defined cultural practices. They became connected through a common consciousness that could be defined by a set of cultural and political performances that articulated distinctively subaltern worldviews.

Ultimately, the Gold Coast slave trade was made through commercial interests and networks on both sides of the Atlantic. In the castles and forts, the holds of slavers, and the slave pens and plantations, enslaved Gold Coast commoners became keenly aware of their new circumstances. In the process of Atlantic commerce, they proved the possibility of a social life after social death—forming connections with ever-widening circles of captives that went far beyond the shipmate bonds discussed by Mintz and Price.[92] Slave ships were, in this sense, means of conveyance from one continent to others. They can even be understood as preindustrial "factories" that produced labor for plantation societies in the Americas. However, imaginings of slave ships literally giving birth to African American peoples and cultures go a bit too far. The reality for Gold Coast Africans was that they were warehoused, shipped, and disembarked with others from the same speech communities and, in some cases, the same polities, villages, and even kinship groups. Their cultures would not be forged in the belly of Atlantic sea-faring beasts or the liminal space represented by the middle passage, but within the context of both the Gold Coast past and the New World present.

In the continuum of realities that existed during the course of the Atlantic slave trade, there seem to be two radically different yet characteristic historical poles. On one end of the spectrum, the specific and patterned trade link between one Atlantic African port of call and another in the Americas allowed for heavy concentrations of particular language cohorts in distinct Western Hemisphere regions. This appears to be the case in the much studied link between Bunce Island off the coast of Sierra Leone and the coastal and Sea Island regions of South Carolina in the period between 1740 and 1800. The influx of rice producers from Greater Senegambia in general and Sierra Leone specifically meant that the resulting cultural matrix—Gullah and Geechee—was not due to the purposeful randomization of Atlantic African language or ethnic groups by European slavers and planters. While Gullah and Geechee borrowed a substantial amount of cultural material from West-Central African charter generations who predominated before the 1739 Stono revolt, the number of Mande loan words, the reliance on the knowledge of rice cultivation and livestock herding, and other markers of these unique cultures point to a Greater Senegambian provenance for the more recent threads woven into these rich cultural tapestries in the South Carolina Lowcountry. Ironically, Greater Senegambia may have been one of the most linguistically and culturally diverse Atlantic African slave trading regions. This diversity, however, was outweighed—at least in the case of coastal and Sea Island South Carolina—by the very focused and narrow Atlantic connections formed in the eighteenth century.[93]

Sharply contrasting with the trade networks linking Greater Senegambia to South Carolina would be the much more chaotic trading experiences associated with various West-Central African ports of call and the destinations they "fed" with black flesh throughout the Western Hemisphere. In this case, over a number of decades the slave trading networks reached far into hinterland regions in West-Central Africa, bringing dozens of peoples and polities into the pull of transatlantic commerce. The combined coastal and inland regions of West-Central Africa totaled more than 2.5 million square kilometers, and it was from this massive region that enslaved captives were drawn. Even if many of the language cohorts in this vast region spoke Bantu dialects, these were not always mutually intelligible and the amount of cultural homogeneity in the region has been greatly exaggerated by a range of scholars. Over time, the slave trade in West-Central Africa produced increasingly heterogeneous enslaved crowds shipped to the Americas. Likewise, enslaved West-Central Africans experienced much more scattered dispersal patterns in the Western Hemisphere, owing in part to their overrepresentation in the import and disembarkation statistics for the entire slave trade. As they accounted for more than 40 percent of all Western Hemisphere imports throughout the course of the slave trade, it would be difficult to show how they could be principally concentrated in any region outside of Brazil.[94]

The Gold Coast trade, in the continuum of slave trading experiences, can be situated between the two poles represented by Greater Senegambia and West-Central Africa. If Greater Senegambia represents a culturally diverse yet focused Atlantic stream—especially into South Carolina, Georgia, and Louisiana—and West-Central Africa a less culturally diverse and more scattered import pattern, the eighteenth-century Gold Coast trade was both less diverse (owing to Akanization and the smaller scale of its coastal and inland trade networks) and meticulously patterned with heavy disembarkation concentrations in eighteenth-century British, Dutch, and Danish circum-Caribbean colonies. With this said, three identifiable phases of the Gold Coast trade characterized the involvement of the region with Atlantic commerce from the time of the early Portuguese interactions beginning in the 1480s. In the first phase (1480–1700), the Portuguese and other European interlopers traded European goods and later enslaved peoples from the Slave Coast and West-Central Africa in exchange for gold mined in the Gold Coast forest belt. As mentioned in the first chapter, it would be during this phase that a number of near inland and coastal polities sought to gain control over trade roads—the vital commercial arteries in the region—to the coast and mines in the forest interior as a means of maximizing their economic, political, and military dominance over others.[95]

Expansionist Akan-speaking polities in the Gold Coast—through their very actions—helped to inaugurate a shift in trade patterns with European interests along the coast and the rise of a new phase (1700–

1760) in their involvement in Atlantic commerce. Polities that fought over control of trade roads, attempting to monopolize the commercial networks connecting interior gold mines to European factors and merchant companies at the coast, shifted to procuring and selling captives. During this second phase, the Gold Coast became a net exporter of slaves for the first time. In addition, the principal Gold Coast slave catchment areas shifted from the Slave Coast to the coastal and near-inland regions of the Gold Coast. This limited geographic zone for slave procurement meant that most of the enslaved peoples exported to the Western Hemisphere during this period knew Akan, facilitating their ability to connect with others from the Gold Coast shortly after disembarkation and to create viable language communities in the Americas. It was during this phase of the Gold Coast slave trade that the heavy concentrations of Akan-speaking peoples in particular locales in the Americas would spawn the creation of Coromantee and (A)mina identities and cultures.[96]

The second phase of the slave trade shifted to a third and final phase (1760–1807) due to the actions of the Asante kingdom and expansionist Asantehene beginning with Opoku Ware. As the kingdom widened its sphere of influence, two related processes shifted the slave catchment regions from the coast and near inland to the northern reaches of the Gold Coast. First, the Asante kingdom expanded north, conquering a number of polities and establishing a new "recruitment" pool for slave labor. In this case, hinterland slave markets like Salaga in Burkina Faso grew rapidly as the Gold Coast north and the Asante kingdom's capital at Kumasi became important hubs of transatlantic commerce in black flesh. Along the coast, the multistate Fante coalition—which formed earlier in the eighteenth century—stood as the only force that could effectively repulse military incursion and political domination by Asante. With the spread of community and state militias or asafo companies, many towns and smaller polities along the coast and near inland developed defense mechanisms against slave raiding and "panyarring" (kidnapping) that had plagued them between 1700 and 1760. The northern shift that characterized this final phase of the Gold Coast slave trade meant that a growing number of enslaved peoples embarking on European slavers came from non-Akan speaking groups—including Tchamba speakers and others—in the northern regions.[97] As a result, part of the lasting discourse of the slave trade in the imaginary of modern Ghanaians is that all or most slaves—during the long chronology of the slave trade—were northerners not directly related to coastal and mostly Akan-speaking populations. They were deemed collectively to be *donkor,* a term that implies northern Gold Coast origins and other more unfortunate attributes, including barbarian, stupid, and uncouth.[98] As Saidiya Hartman notes, nineteenth-century Asante law held that by definition the term *donkor* was "applied strictly to any man or woman, other than an Asante, who had been purchased with the express purpose of making him or her a slave."[99] They became the quintessential "other"—a group that could be alienated and enslaved without generating sympathy or remorse in the more contemporary discourse about the slave trade and its many legacies in the former Gold Coast.

The Du Bois dataset corroborates the claim that export streams from the Gold Coast were much more narrow and focused than previously assumed. As Douglas Chambers shows, 76 percent of all Gold Coast Africans embarked on European slavers destined for the Americas at just two ports—Anomabu and Cape Coast Castle. In this circumstance, the trade activities of both Fante and British traders become central to commercial patterns emanating from the eighteenth-century Gold Coast.[100] While many scholars have emphasized the role of the Asante kingdom in the Gold Coast trade, the Asante did not ascend to military and political dominance in the region until the reign of Asantehene Opoku Ware. In addition, it was not until 1744 that Asante controlled the major trade roads from the Gold Coast interior to the coastal trade centers. In sum, because Asante did not monopolize the supply end of the slave trade until after the 1750s, an unspecifiable but sizable majority of Gold Coast Africans involved in the slave trade between 1680 and 1760 were Akan-speaking or from regions along the coast and the near inland that had experienced a significant amount of Akanization.

Though the Gold Coast was a net importer of slaves through the 1690s, this reality quickly changed during the first decade of the eighteenth century.[101] This picture becomes acutely obvious when assessing the outflow of enslaved peoples embarking on ships at particular Gold Coast ports of call. In the fifty-year period after 1700, the number of slaves embarked on European ships at Cape Coast, Elmina, Accra/Chris-

Table 2.2. Gold Coast Africans Embarked by Port

Embarkation Port	1651–1700	1701–1750	% Increase
Elmina	6,610	62,076	939%
Cape Coast	5,999	33,650	560%
Anomabu	43,745	122,558	280%
Christiansborg*	1,316	8,277	629%
Unspecified	35,218	96,713	275%

Source: *Voyages: The Trans-Atlantic Slave Trade Database.*
*The Christiansborg embarkation numbers include estimates for all of Accra.

tiansborg, and Anomabu grew exponentially—ranging from two- to ten-fold increases (see table 2.2). This massive expansion in slave trading operations did not result in more scattered patterns of dispersal in the Western Hemisphere. Instead, there were clear patterns of import clustering in colonies linked to the merchant companies housed at the many castles, forts, and lodges built along the Gold Coast. In addition, enslaved Gold Coast Africans became highly coveted in the slave markets in the Americas—a factor that influenced import concentrations and the active reshaping of import populations through the transshipment trade.[102]

On both sides of the Atlantic, the Gold Coast slave trade—both exports and imports—can be characterized as regular and patterned, particularly during the second phase (1700–1760) of this commercial network. While the slave trade can be characterized as patterned, allowing for clusterings of coastal and near inland peoples in the Gold Coast on European slave ships, this patterned flow of people across the Atlantic was mirrored in the ports of disembarkation in the Western Hemisphere. Enslaved Akan, Ga, Adanme, and Ewe speakers from the Gold Coast became concentrated in British, Dutch, and Danish colonies in the Americas during the course of the eighteenth century; strong evidence for this can be found in the Du Bois slave trade dataset. As mentioned earlier, in the century between 1665 and 1765, more than 78 percent (286,755 of 369,165) of all enslaved Gold Coast Africans boarded ships destined for British, Dutch, and Danish colonies in the Americas. More specifically, between 1700 and 1765, Gold Coast Africans represented significant percentages of Atlantic Africans disembarked in Curaçao (14.8%), the Dutch Guianas (25%), Antigua (19%), Barbados (22.4%), Jamaica (26.9%), British Guiana (31.7%), and the Danish West Indies (46.6%).[103]

These import figures reflect the dominating positions British, Dutch, and Danish trade companies had over the many castles, forts, lodges, and other trading posts along the Gold Coast during the eighteenth century as well as the coastal ship trade near Fante-controlled Anomabu. In addition, these import figures include free traders, not connected to specific trade companies, from a range of Europe nations. However, disembarkation figures from the slave trade dataset only offer a partial window into a much more complex demographic terrain in the Gold Coast diaspora. For a range of reasons, Gold Coast import estimates are skewed downward, and heavier concentrations of enslaved peoples with some knowledge of Akan language were more likely to be the historical reality in the British, Dutch, and Danish Caribbean and mainland.

Alone, the disembarkation percentages of enslaved Gold Coast Africans do not tell a complete story. If we were to rely solely on those estimates, the enslaved Gold Coast contingent in disembarkation regions like Jamaica, Antigua, Curaçao, and Suriname would seem inconsequential in comparison to the numbers of Atlantic Africans from other regions. Even in eighteenth-century British, Dutch, and Danish Caribbean and mainland colonies, disembarkations from the Gold Coast could be dwarfed by imports from the Bight of Biafra and West-Central Africa. However, three factors augment the importation and disembarkation percentages for Gold Coast Africans—perhaps to the degree that their seemingly disproportionate role in the affairs of these colonies can be reasonably explained. First, disembarkation figures do not take into account the long-standing practice of slavers "coasting" from Gold Coast forts and castles to the adjoining Slave Coast to fill their cargo holds before departing across the Atlantic to the Americas. In this instance, a ship receiving a portion of its cargo at Christiansborg Castle near Accra and completing its quota in human flesh in Allada would be recorded in the slave trade dataset as embarking from the Slave Coast or the Bight of Benin, not the Gold Coast. In view of this reality, a portion of Slave Coast/Bight of Benin traffic has to be counted in the Gold Coast embarkation figures—particularly considering the outflow of captives from Ewe- and Ga-speaking polities east of the Volta River who would have been familiar with Akan language and cultures. Combined, the ubiquitous practice of trading "à costy," or the coasting trade, and the presence of Ewe and Ga speakers in the Slave Coast transatlantic traffic require a readjustment of the importation figures for the Gold Coast (or at least an expansion on what is meant by a "Gold Coast" embarkation). Jamaica, a disembarkation region receiving more than 40 percent of all Atlantic Africans imported into the eighteenth-century British, Dutch, and Danish Caribbean and the Guianas, witnessed a total of 741,563 enslaved Africans disembarking there between 1700 and 1780. Of this total, enslaved Atlantic Africans from the Gold Coast (27%), the Slave Coast/Bight of Benin (11%), the Bight of Biafra (31%), and West-Central Africa (16%) represented the four largest import streams. Shifting just 20 percent of the Slave Coast/Bight of Benin traffic to the Gold Coast import figures produces an additional 63,956 enslaved individuals and drives up the Gold Coast disembarkation rate from 27 to 36 percent.[104]

A second issue unaccounted for in disembarkation estimates would be the extensive transshipment network in the Americas—epitomized by the *asiento* traffic—which redirected many enslaved Atlantic Africans to other colonies after brief stays in the British Caribbean. As the destination of about 37 percent of all slavers arriving in the eighteenth-century British Americas, Jamaica hosted a transshipment or re-export trade to Spanish colonies via the asiento outstripping that of other locales in the circum-Caribbean; this trade reveals patterns that can yield insights. Beginning in the seventeenth century, about 20 percent of all enslaved Africans recorded as disembarked in Jamaica were redirected ultimately to Spanish colonies. This peculiar trade relationship peaked after 1700, followed by a significant decline between 1748 and 1783. From 1700 to 1748, the asiento trade redirected a disproportionate number of Atlantic Africans originating from the Bight of Biafra and West-Central Africa to Spanish colonies. As a highly coveted enslaved cohort, Gold Coast Africans had higher value in the eyes of Jamaican planters. In light of his estimate that up to "three quarters of all slaves retained in Jamaica before 1725 probably were from the adjacent Gold Coast and Slave Coast," David Eltis asserts that this strong preference for Gold Coast Africans helped determine an identifiable pattern in asiento traffic and other transshipments from Jamaica.[105]

While Jamaica represented the epicenter of the Caribbean transshipment trade, both the Dutch and Danes used their West Indies possessions to transship disembarked Atlantic Africans to other locales—particularly in the Spanish Americas. Curaçao, for example, was frequently used by the Dutch to build a lucrative transshipment trade connected to the Spanish mainland colonies. The Dutch West Indies Company conducted asiento traffic between 1699 and 1701 using Curaçao as a base of operations. Even during the French (1701–13) and British (1713–50) asiento tenures, the Dutch continued to illicitly redirect imports intended for Curaçao to the Spanish mainland, to the degree that Johannes Potsma concludes that "the vast majority of the slaves landed at Curaçao ended up as Spanish subjects." Another sizable contingent was transshipped from Curaçao to other Dutch possessions in the Caribbean and Guiana. Likewise, in Danish possessions in the Caribbean—namely St. Thomas and St. Croix—enslaved Atlantic Africans were routinely transshipped to other Caribbean and mainland destinations.[106]

A third factor helping to provide some explanation for the disproportionate influence of Gold Coast Africans in British, Dutch, and Danish colonies in the eighteenth-century Western Hemisphere may also shed light on why so many disembarked Atlantic Africans from the Bight of Biafra and West-Central Africa were redirected and transshipped to other colonies. The lack of interest in enslaved Biafrans and West-Central Africans on the part of British planters in the Caribbean might have been the result of the deplorable physical condition they were in upon disembarkation in the Americas. Both Alexander Byrd and Joseph Miller discuss the length of journey to and from slave trade ports in Biafra and Angola and the impact this had on the morbidity and mortality rates for Atlantic Africans from those regions. Enslaved Atlantic Africans from the Biafran interior, for example, often originated several hundred miles in the hinterland, requiring many months on foot to reach coastal factories. Upon transfer to European factors and merchant companies, Biafran captives could wait up to three months in fetid holding pens on the coast or in the holds of Guinea slavers. Indeed, Byrd comments: "The Bight of Biafra was the sickliest, deadliest stretch of western Africa, averaging in the first half of the eighteenth century levels of mortality twice as high as the rest of Atlantic Africa." Thus, even before the Middle Passage, enslaved people in the holds of ships at port in Biafra suffered mortality rates as high as 40 percent. After an average of seventy days onboard ships traversing the Atlantic, captives from the Bight of Biafra disembarked in the Caribbean in very poor physical and psychological condition. This contributed to the widely held opinion among British planters that Biafrans were "refuse slaves"—inherently weak and more prone to despondency, suicide, and early death than other Atlantic African imports in the eighteenth-century Western Hemisphere. Likewise, the *tumbeiros,* or "floating tombs," plying the slave trade between West-Central Africa and the Caribbean experienced the longest transatlantic voyage and one which passed through a particularly "hazardous zone of unreliable winds along the equator." As mentioned earlier, the West-Central African "slaving frontier" reached deep into the remote interior or hinterland regions and paralleled the lengthy overland journeys faced by captives from the Biafran interior to the coast.[107]

In Biafra and West-Central Africa, long overland journeys from remote interior regions, lengthy and lethal stays in the more densely populated coastal regions and onboard docked slave ships, and the two longest middle passage voyages from Atlantic Africa to the Caribbean resulted in higher mortality rates after disembarkation for people from these regions in comparison to enslaved Gold and Slave Coast Africans. Enslaved peoples from the adjacent Gold and Slave Coasts arrived healthier, lived longer, and were retained by planters at higher rates than their Biafran and West-Central African counterparts. In sum, the disembarkation percentages offered by the Du Bois slave trade dataset does not account for these factors and, as a result, skews decidedly away from the historical and demographic reality of larger numbers and concentrations of Gold Coast Africans in British, Dutch, and Danish colonies over the course of the eighteenth century.

In addition to the above, the principal mechanisms of slave procurement employed in the Gold Coast in the period before the 1760s—panyarring (or kidnapping), banditry, judicial enslavement for offenses ranging from adultery to witchcraft, and the many dislocations caused by the rise, expansion, and fall of states—determined the fact that many involved in the 1700–1760 phase of the Gold Coast slave trade would be from a range of coastal and near-inland regions.[108] Indeed, the many deprivations of the Akwamu state in the first three decades of the eighteenth century helped produce a new vocabulary for Gold Coast and European slave traders. The so-called "siccadingers" were organized paramilitary bands of men commissioned by Akwamu to engage in state-sponsored panyarring and the seizure of trade goods. Under two separate Akwamuhenes—Akwonno (1703–25) and Ansa Kwao (1725–30)—hundreds of siccadingers kidnapped people in and around Akwamu and as far away as neighboring territories in Krobo for sale to European merchants and company operatives at the coast. Possibly serving in the role of debt-collectors, these bands did not range too far from the borders of Akwamu's jurisdiction, and thus their activities were generally confined to the coastal and near-inland areas of the Gold Coast. Rømer goes as far as to claim that "the Aqvamboe Siccadinger did not leave their own country, fearing injury in the country of strangers, so they stole their neighbour's children and their friends, and sold them." This particular practice, however, precipitated the collapse of Akwamu as it compelled the formation of a coalition of some of Akwamu's own citizens and the armies of neighboring polities during the 1730–31 Akwamu-Akyem war. In some measure, this war accompanied an internal reordering in Akwamu in which commoners rebelled against the very mechanisms that saw so many of their friends and neighbors enter Atlantic bondage.[109]

In the context of the Gold Coast, commercial and historical forces in the region determined a circumscribed geography for panyarring and banditry. By the middle decades of the eighteenth century, both of these practices occurred mostly near well-established gold trade routes from the interior to the coast, reflecting patterns that existed during the era in which the Gold Coast was a net exporter of gold and net importer of slaves. In the period before the exponential rise of the Gold Coast slave trade, bandits routinely attacked traders and their gold-laden caravans on trade roads to the coast. This seventeenth-century pattern served as the foundation for similar depredations in the period between 1700 and 1760 when bandits, highwaymen, and kidnappers turned their attention to the forced capture and sale of enslaved peoples. This shift can be gauged by the frequent references in the reports of Europeans about the means by which some of their slaves were acquired. The director-general of Elmina, for example, noted in an April 4, 1710 complaint to the English governor—Sir Dalby Thomas—his concerns regarding the "robberies and panyarrings committed lately by the Fantyns" near the coast against company operatives who were then sold to the English at Cape Coast Castle. In sum, bandits and robbers would find little benefit in their operations ranging too far from coastal trade roads and the company-controlled trade castles and forts. By the very definition of this range of activities, they occurred as close as possible to coastal and near-inland "recruitment" pools and European factories, merchant companies, and ships stationed at the coast.[110]

As a direct consequence of these procurement and trade patterns, "nations" or neo-African ethnicities known as the Coromantee or the (A)mina, having clear Gold Coast origins, formed in the eighteenth-century British, Dutch, and Danish Americas. These new ethnic groups combined together Akan, Ga, Adanme, and Ewe speakers who were previously connected in the Gold Coast as a result of common geographies, shared and interlacing commercial networks, political domination, military conquest, or much more benign mechanisms of contact discussed earlier. Given the amount of multilingualism, the military domination of a long line of Akan-speaking states over Ga, Adanme, and Ewe peoples and polities, the use of Akan as a trade and political lingua franca over vast regions of the Gold Coast and cultural Akanization, we may conclude that many embarking on ships in the Gold Coast and destined for lives of slavery in the Americas had previous linguistic and cultural ties or common linguistic foundations from which Akan language communities could be developed. In the Americas, communities with strong and coherent concentrations of Akan, Ga, Adanme, and Ewe speakers formed in the British, Dutch, and Danish circum-Caribbean and mainland. These ties and common geographies of embarkation and disembarkation prefigured identity and cultural formations in the Western Hemisphere with profound implications for decades to come.

Captured, enslaved, and sold to European traders, Gold Coast commoners were remarkable in their ability to formulate unique and even separate spaces in the Americas. They established maroon societies in a number of colonies in the Caribbean and South America; their cultural and sociopolitical worldviews informed core aspects of slave communities from Suriname to New York City; and their presence in slave conspiracies and revolts made them a feared contingent among the numerous Africans dispersed in the Americas. This sense of cultural and political cohesion, expressed through their collective actions, was a relatively new phenomenon. As citizens of separate, hostile, or even warring states in the Gold Coast, Akan speakers and others certainly had little, if any, notion of solidarity in Atlantic Africa upon arrival in the Americas, despite the many points of linguistic, cultural, and political contact and convergence discussed previously. By the late sixteenth century, the Gold Coast, like the rest of Atlantic Africa, was thoroughly balkanized. In the context of Western Hemisphere slavery, however, Gold Coast Africans experienced an unprecedented transformation; former enemies became allies and a divided people became—more or less—one. Like Cugoano, they developed a new sense of Black Atlantic citizenship and community—representing a sharp departure from their past lives in the Gold Coast. The next chapter explores the emergence of these new identities and the continual transformations of Gold Coast commoners in the Americas.

THREE

Slavery, Ethnogenesis, and Social Resurrection

Coramantien, a country of blacks . . . is very warlike and
brave, and having a continual campaign, being always in
hostility with one neighbouring prince or other.

APHRA BEHN, OROONOKO (1688)

In the autumn of 1736, hundreds of the inhabitants on the British Caribbean island of Antigua witnessed a series of events purported to be the
culmination of months of clandestine planning. Court, an enslaved man
in the employ of Thomas Kerby, became the widely recognized leader of
a "Coromantee" contingent and he helped forge an alliance with "Eboes"
and island-born creoles. Captured and enslaved in the Gold Coast at the
age of ten, Court reportedly hailed from a "considerable" family—likely
in Ga-speaking Accra—though he was not of royal blood. Despite his
high-born natal origin, the leveling influences of capture, social death,
and chattel slavery—along with his youth at the time of his transatlantic
journey in 1711—reduced Court's status to that of other Atlantic Africans
and creoles he encountered after disembarking in Antigua. Over the
course of a quarter century, Court—described in trial records as "artful,
and ambitious, very proud, and of few Words"—accumulated money,
influence, and an elevated status that led him to assume, "among his

Countrymen . . . the Title of King, and had been by them [addressed] and treated as such." Court's stature as New World royalty among the Coromantee was evident in the chant his retinue routinely performed in his presence. With raised wooden cutlasses, they would cry "*Tackey, Tackey, Tackey, Coquo Tackey* which signifies, King, King, King, great King, which Words are used in the *Coramantee* Country every Morning at the King's Door." Indeed, Court was referred to by his Coromantee title "Tackey"—a Ga royal lineage or office—so often that it was mistaken by contemporary witnesses and more recent historians for his personal, Gold Coast name.[1]

On Sunday, October 3, 1736, at two o'clock, Court participated in an elaborate coronation ceremony centered around an *ikem* (or shield) dance, loyalty oaths, and a range of other activities. Court consciously employed Coromantee "cultural technologies," in part to solidify his hold on the leadership of the burgeoning movement and, perhaps, to gauge the size and destructive potential of his rebel army. Complete with many of the markers of eighteenth-century Akan political cultures and the paraphernalia of power discussed in chapter 1, Court was to be carried aloft by bearers, shielded from the sun by a canopy of umbrellas, and accompanied by drummers to signify his appointment as the king of the Antiguan Coromantees. His officers and lieutenants, known collectively by the conspirators as *braffo*, facilitated the military planning and administration of a series of duties and tasks under their regent. When Court assumed his royal seat, he was surrounded by "his Generals . . . his Guards on each side, his *Braffo* and Marshal clearing the Circle." His retinue even included a personal chamberlain named Quashey—assuming the title of *Asseng* among the Antiguan Coromantees—who served as a horsetail bearer, swatting flies and keeping other pests away from King Court.[2]

In addition to embracing and employing symbolic elements of Akan statecraft, Court wisely evoked powerful ancestral forces through the active use of three obeah doctors—Caesar, John Obia, and Quawcoo. As with many slave conspiracies in the eighteenth-century Western Hemisphere, religion and spirituality—in the form of Vodun, Kongo Christianity, and Islam—served as catalysts in inspiring involvement in dangerous undertakings. Indeed, these syncretic religious and spiritual practices represented a wider range of Atlantic African cultural technologies that became ubiquitous within enslaved communities. In the Antiguan case, the obeah doctors employed by Court presided over several loyalty oath ceremonies involving the consumption of ritual draughts composed of rum, blood, and grave dirt. Quawcoo specifically was known in contemporary documents to be "a Negroe Obiaman, or Wizard, who acted his Part before a great number of Slaves . . . and assured them of Success." He was such an imposing figure that Quamina—an enslaved man who betrayed the plot by turning king's witness—confessed to court officials: "By God if you had not Catched me I would not have told you now. I am afraid of this Obey Man now, he is a Bloody fellow, I knew him in Cormantee Country."[3]

In addition to utilizing the ritual expertise of obeah doctors, the conspirators also relied on a language of secrecy they called "Coromantee," which played a vital role in their many loyalty oaths and other secular rituals. Referred to as either Coromantee or "Accartin" by the trial justices, many of those involved in the plot could speak and understand this language. Johnno, another conspirator who turned king's witness against his former comrades, reported to court officials that his close friend, Secundi, had "Spoke to him in Cormantee; Drank to him and Said, Here Country Man (Chawa Worra Terry) i.e. Cutt your Masters head Off." Along with other Akan words that appear in the 1736 conspiracy trial records (e.g., *braffo, abeng, ikem*), this remarkable transcription of eighteenth-century Akan language in the Americas represents a significant and precise cultural carryover from the Gold Coast. Using seventeenth- and eighteenth-century Akan vocabularies, *chawa worra terry* translates into English as roughly "cut off master's head." In this case, the seventeenth-century "Guinean" vocabulary compiled by de Marees includes *tua* (to cut), *eteri* (head), and *owura* (sir). Müller includes the words *etyr* (head) and *aurarre* (lord or master) in his seventeenth-century Fetu vocabulary. The linguistic connections between the eighteenth-century Coromantee phrase (*chawa worra terry*) and the seventeenth-century Akan equivalent (*tua owura eteri*) point to the fact that the Antiguan court justices used the services of Akan-speaking translators to understand the precise meaning of Coromantee phrases and words appearing in trial testimonies. This also corroborates an Akan-speaking base for the Coromantee languages that developed in Antigua, Jamaica, Suriname, and Barbados.[4]

In combination, the various elements that frame the narrative of the 1736 Antigua Conspiracy can seem confusing if not approached from a Black Atlantic and Gold Coast historical perspective. King Court, a Ga-speaking leader of an Akan-speaking contingent, actively employed elements of Akan statecraft and a syncretic spiritual system in obeah—itself a probable fusion of Akan-speaking *bayi* and Igbo-speaking *dibia*. Moreover, the trial records include examples of Gold Coast-born Akan-speakers who frequently spoke in Coromantee, yet were acculturated enough to give their entire testimonies in English. The court proceedings also detail island-born creoles—some with Akan day-names—who were fearful of the power of obeah doctors, who imbibed Coromantee ritual draughts and who, in some cases, believed in the spiritual sanctions that would follow breaking loyalty oaths.[5] The 1736 Antigua Conspiracy, like other examples throughout the Gold Coast diaspora, represents active reconfigurations of identity, culture, and consciousness that were integral to the creation of the Coromantee, the (A)mina, and other diasporic neo-African ethnic enclaves. Polyglottal and multicultural formations such as these played foundational roles in the creation of the many variants of "African-American" or "Black Atlantic" cultures in the Western Hemisphere.

This chapter analyzes the mechanisms that spurred the ethnogenesis of Gold Coast Africans and their descendants in the New World diaspora beginning in the seventeenth century. With a focus on the formation of Coromantee in Anglophone Caribbean and mainland colonies and Delmina (Dutch Berbice), Amina (Danish Virgin Islands), or Mina (Spanish and French Louisiana), I forward the claim that the slave trade and chattel slavery in the Western Hemisphere became catalysts for the process of ethnogenesis among and between Atlantic African cohorts. Gold Coast Africans transformed, over time, from divided and even hostile subunits into relatively integrated aggregates in the Americas. They were not, in this case, cultural nationalists only interested in preserving a pure and distinct monolingual "Akan" culture in the Americas. In sociological terms, they moved from crowds as they boarded slave ships in Atlantic Africa to polyglottal groups in the Western Hemisphere. Within

the frame of this sort of ethnogenesis, discrete cultural values and principles were augmented to the point that they became associated with
the Coromantee and the (A)mina over time. These reinvented cultural
forms and technologies include blood oaths and other loyalty contracts;
expressive plays, dances, and coronation ceremonies; the ritual practice
of obeah; Ananse the Spider tales; and belief in spiritual transmigration
that prefigured mass suicides. Together these Coromantee and (A)mina
sociopolitical and cultural scripts, diasporic tropes, or performances
form the substance of the social resurrection or rebirth experienced
collectively by Gold Coast Africans in the diaspora. Coromantees and
(A)minas, in effect, remade themselves while forging troubled lives in
New World bondage.

"COUNTRY" AND "COUNTRYMEN" IN
THE GOLD COAST DIASPORA

Evidence supporting the claim that Gold Coast Africans created inten-
tional communities with their fellow countrymen can be found throughout the eighteenth-century Americas. In this regard, a revealing incident
took place in New York City at noon on Wednesday, March 18, 1741,
when fire alarms sounded at Fort George—headquarters of British royal
government in colonial New York. Beginning on the roof of the governor's residence, flames spread rapidly to a number of nearby and sus-
piciously strategic buildings, including the king's chapel and the troop
barracks. Within two hours, these buildings collapsed into smoldering
heaps. Citizen volunteers and a timely rainfall saved the city from further destruction. In the months following this blaze, New Yorkers witnessed ten more fires that consumed private homes and public buildings
throughout Manhattan. Already in the midst of investigating a criminal
theft ring involving black street gangs and white fences, local authorities
turned their attention to the possibility of an arson conspiracy devised
by the city's enslaved inhabitants.[6]

On April 11, the Common Council of New York City proposed rewards for the capture of suspected arsonists and their accomplices. Supreme Court hearings of a number of suspects began on April 21. White
tavern owner John Hughson, under arrest for his alleged role as a fence

for stolen goods in a criminal theft ring, was implicated by an indentured servant as chief instigator and co-conspirator in a city-wide arson plot. About a month before the fire at Fort George, Hughson reportedly presided over a loyalty oath ceremony attended by a number of enslaved co-conspirators. The trial testimony of Bastian Vaarck revealed that the conspirators—including Cuffee (Philipse), Quacko (Roosevelt), Cuffee (Gomez), Cajoe (Gomez), Caesar (Peck), Billy (Ward), and Quash (Rutger)—swore to burn New York City, kill most of its white inhabitants, and establish a biracial ruling regime. To seal the oath, Hughson and the enslaved conspirators partook of a loyalty drink or "punch" composed primarily of rum.[7]

According to additional testimony, Hughson told the enslaved conspirators present at this oathing ceremony "that they must not attempt to draw in any one that was not their countryman; that if they met with any countrymen, they must tell them so; and if they found they were likely to come in, then they might tell them of the plot." This, Hughson implored, after the conspirators agreed that Quacko (Roosevelt) would set the initial fire at Fort George. When Hughson warned that conspirators include only their "countrymen" in the plot, the fact that he told men named Cuffee, Quacko, Quash, and Cajoe indicates the location of this "country" within the diasporic imaginary. Aside from a shared hatred of slavery, these particular men had Akan day-names, and possibly Gold Coast natal origins, in common. As the trial record reveals, the country from which a number of conspirators originated was indeed Coromantee. Thus, the enslaved and their white allies understood and embraced the term Coromantee as a meaningful label and identifier.[8]

During the course of the 1741 New York conspiracy trials, the court implicated a total of eleven people with Akan day-names: two Cudjos, three Cuffees, three Quacks, a Quamino, a Quash, and a woman named Cuba. Trial records include two additional individuals—Caesar (Peck) and Jenny (Comfort)—claimed to be Coromantee by co-conspirators and court officials. Two others had direct links to the Gold Coast diaspora—Harry, a possible obeah doctor, and Billy (Ward). Billy, in particular, revealed to court officials his role in two major acts of resistance on the part of enslaved Gold Coast Africans in the Western Hemisphere prior to his arrival in Manhattan in 1737.[9] Taken together, the Antigua and New York conspiracy trial records reveal details about the complex, dynamic, and transformative cultural processes evident throughout Atlantic African diasporas. They particularly demonstrate a unique ethnogenesis that led to the rise of polyglottal Coromantee and (A)mina identities and ethnicities in the Western Hemisphere.

Gold Coast Africans managed to create unique social spaces and revolutionary political visions in the New World that open windows into the inner workings of their diasporic imaginations. These spaces and visions combined together speakers of Akan, Ga, Adanme, and Ewe from a range of polities and, in doing so, marked sharp discontinuities with the Gold Coast past. Political fragmentation, the rise of small regional states and multistate alliances, became part of a normative set of experiences for most people living in the seventeenth- and eighteenth-century Gold Coast. Even the existence of larger states or alliances—Akwamu, Akyem, Asante, and the Fante coalition—meant a political geography characterized by expansionist wars, serial regicide, and violent attempts to monopolize trade routes. While Akan culture and language created some sense of connection, peoples and states in the Gold Coast often peered at each other across vast political divides. In the context of Western Hemisphere slavery, however, Gold Coast Africans experienced radical transformations as former enemies became new allies. Their new allegiances were to Coromantee and (A)mina—neo-ethnic constructs not associated with specific Gold Coast polities; their new enemies were white slaveholders. In the process of this transformation, previous political divides became less important either immediately or over time. Their shared social backgrounds as commoners in the Gold Coast, their new enemies in the form of Western Hemisphere slaveholders, and the existence of a lingua franca in the New World served as connecting points in what became Gold Coast diasporic ethnicities.

Understanding this ethnogenesis requires an excavation of the origins of Coromantee and its associated cultural technologies. Coromantee, as referenced in the Antigua and New York conspiracy trials, points to a handful of locales in the early-modern Gold Coast. The correct term, *Kormantse*, specifically refers to two Fante-speaking coastal towns and a trading fort established by the Dutch in 1598 (see figure 3.1). Fort Kormantse (now Fort Amsterdam) was destroyed in 1645 and rebuilt later

3.1. Fort Amsterdam (Fort Kormantse) courtyard, 2006. Photo by author.

by the English. It became the first of many English trading posts along the coast of the Gulf of Guinea. From Fort Kormantse and other coastal factories, the English exported Atlantic Africans principally to their Caribbean possessions in Barbados, Antigua, and Jamaica throughout the seventeenth and eighteenth centuries. During the second Anglo-Dutch War, Fort Kormantse was seized by the Dutch West Indies Company and renamed Fort Amsterdam. As a result of the combined Fante, English, and Dutch commercial activities at Kormantse, enslaved Africans exported from this region of the Gold Coast became generally referred to as Coromantees by English slave traders, factors and ship captains during the seventeenth and eighteenth centuries. While "Coromantee"—combining natal, linguistic, and ethnic connotations—has many ambiguities, it refers to mostly Akan-speakers from the Gold Coast. Similar connections can be made between (A)mina as an ethnic label in the Danish Virgin Islands (Amina), Dutch Berbice (Delmina), Louisiana (Mina), and other locales in the Americas and São Jorge da Mina (El-

3.2. Three Gold Coast forts, including Fort Cormantin in upper left and right, circa 1680s. Source: Bosman, *A New and Accurate Description,* opposite 58. Courtesy of the Manuscripts, Archives, and Rare Books Division, Schomburg Center for Research in Black Culture, New York Public Library, Astor, Lenox, and Tilden Foundations.

3.3. Fort Cormantin, Gold Coast, circa 1560s. Source: Dapper, *Description de l'Afrique,* between 284 and 285. Courtesy of the Picture Collection, New York Public Library, Astor, Lenox, and Tilden Foundations.

mina Castle) in the Gold Coast.[10] The Mina of Portuguese Brazil, however, were the product of very different historical and cultural forces.[11]

Though Coromantee and (A)mina denoted Gold Coast origins in the minds of European factors, slavers, and plantation owners, these labels were appropriated by Gold Coast Africans in the diaspora. This is clear in the cases of the Antigua and New York conspiracy trial records, in which, on a number of occasions, those providing testimony used the term "Coromantee" as a means of either self-identification or identifying comrades and co-conspirators. Examples in which Coromantee or (A)mina as a Gold Coast language, polity, country, or ethnic label was actively embraced and employed by the enslaved abounds in records related to acts of resistance in eighteenth-century Jamaica, Barbados, Danish St. John, Louisiana, and New York City.

This identification with terms imposed upon them by Europeans raises an important question. Cast out into *Abrokyire*—the not-so-mythical western lands beyond the Gold Coast horizon—how did crowds of

3.4. Elmina Castle and Neighboring Village, Gold Coast, circa 1670s.
Source: Dapper, *Description de l'Afrique,* 435b. Courtesy of the General Research
and Reference Division, Schomburg Center for Research in Black Culture, New
York Public Library, Astor, Lenox, and Tilden Foundations.

captives, outcasts, and exiles from varying polities, language groups,
and clans create a sense of group consciousness and cohesiveness over
time? They transformed themselves from crowds into groups, in part,
to insure mutual survival in hostile and enemy spaces in the Western
Hemisphere and to create unified fronts in combating the daily viola-
tions they experienced in racial and chattel slavery. At the very minimum, this transformative ethnogenesis complicates understandings of
early slave resistance efforts in the Americas.

Monica Schuler, Orlando Patterson, Eugene Genovese, Michael
Mullin, and others have fallen into the interpretive trap of detailing
"ethnic" slave rebellions in the period before the 1791 Haitian Revolution. This formulation flattens a much more complex set of historical
realities. The Coromantee, in contrast to interpretations forwarded by
Patterson and Mullin, were not an unvariegated, monolithic, and mono-

3.5. Elmina Castle, 2006. Photo by author.

linguistic Atlantic African nation. In this case, Coromantee should not be understood as solely a reference to Akan-speakers born in the Gold Coast.[12] Though they became an ethnic group over time in the Americas, they were not previously an ethnicity, a nation, or, worse, a "tribe" in the Atlantic African context. Clear examples of Ga-speaking "Coromantees"—the Tackey who led the 1736 Antiguan Coromantees and the Tackey who led the Jamaican Coromantees in 1760—as well as even the many Akan-speaking members of this new ethnic group who originated from hostile, warring, or competing Gold Coast states undermine the idea of a singular political, cultural, or even linguistic provenance for the Coromantee in the Western Hemisphere.[13] This being the case, I contend that conditions evident under racialized slavery spurred an emerging commoner consciousness and facilitated the production of pan-regional and even pan-African conceptualizations of identity and ethnicity taking root in the Americas. In this conceptualization, social resurrection represented a watershed in reimaginings and reformulations of ethnicity in the Atlantic African diaspora.

Likewise, contrary to the claim made by Gwendolyn Midlo Hall, the Mina of Louisiana were not composed of people with a singular linguistic, ethnic, or geographic origin—mostly Ewe-speakers and others from the Slave Coast. Instead, they represented a polyglottal ethnolinguistic formation that included Akan, Ga, Adanme, and Ewe speakers, and others from both the Gold Coast and the adjoining Slave Coast.[14] Using a range of evidence, the Minas inhabiting eighteenth-century Pointe Coupee Parish in Louisiana can be identified as a Gold Coast diaspora grouping. Among the "prisoners" tried during the 1791 Mina plot, a handful had clear Akan or Ga names (two Atas and a Cofi) while others had names related to Akan day-names (two Jacós or Quacos). Though the majority of those tried for involvement in the conspiracy were listed as Mina in the trial record, even those who were not had origins in or links to the Gold Coast. In this instance, the list of prisoners included a Chamba-speaking man (or a Tchamba-speaker possibly from the northern Gold Coast) named José and an English-speaking Jamaican creole named Caesar—a possible Coromantee turned Mina. In the 1791 inventory of one plantation, the Olivo estate in Pointe Coupee, all of the enslaved peoples originated from the Bight of Benin (the former Slave Coast), but none of them were identified as being Mina. By 1795, the Mina of Point Coupee included a free black man named Antonio Cofi and a range of enslaved people with Akan day-names—including Coffi (Poydras), Jacco (LaCour), Jacco (Allain), and Jacco (Farars). As a Mina leader who, through a variety of means, connected this enclave from New Orleans to Pointe Coupee, Antonio Cofi encountered a Chamba man from the Gold Coast named Tham who could speak "a little Mina." Also, when eighteen-year-old Joseph Mina was sentenced to the gallows for his role in the 1795 plot, he met his death laughing and waving to his comrades—embodying a central element of Coromantee and (A)mina masculine performance.[15]

The example of Gullah is instructive in this regard. With distinct and discrete elements from West-Central Africa and Greater Senegambia, the Gullah in coastal Carolina and Georgia epitomize the type of cultural matrix framing the ethnogenesis of Coromantee, (A)mina, and other neo-African ethnic groups such as Lucumí, Eboe, and Nâgo. In essence they were not previously ethnic groups in Atlantic Africa, but—over time and through close proximity, common condition, and a common enemy in the Americas—they became an ethnicity. In sum, no neat transition between ethnic African and creole slave rebellions existed in the Western Hemisphere. While imported crowds were continuously reshaping into more cohesive groups on plantations in the Americas, the resulting cultural and identity formations (and formulations) were—by necessity—multidimensional, multilayered, dynamic, complicated, and fluid. Importantly, this was not a phenomenon limited to plantation societies in the Americas, as numerous Atlantic African polities—small and large—experienced the effects of military expansion, cultural absorption and assimilation, political domination, and other forms of cultural exchange. The Yoruba *Orisha,* or pantheon of gods (including Edo and Fon deities), the presence of Akan day-names among Ga and Ewe speakers, Akan Ananse the Spider tales in Sierra Leone, and Kente cloth weaving or the use of *adinkra* symbols—Ewe and Fante creations respectively—throughout the former Gold Coast all testify to the reality of dynamic cultural processes and exchanges in Atlantic Africa before, during, and after the slave trade. Evidence of such levels of cultural interplay at work in Atlantic Africa greatly complicates the idea of ethnicity in the African context and problematizes creolization, as a unique process of mixing between peoples and cultures originating from different continents, in the Western Hemisphere.[16]

The significant amount of cultural interplay in Atlantic Africa did not equate to political cohesion nor the creation of pan-regional ethnic identities. Indeed, given the presence of a long sequence of Akan-speaking expansionist polities, cultural interplay and exchange were often linked directly to the fears or realities of military conquest and political domination. Thus, in this case, a singular and monolithic Akan "people" never existed before colonialism, given the sheer amount of political fragmentation and balkanization evident in the early-modern Gold Coast. Despite certainties regarding "Coromantee" or "(A)mina" culture, identity, or even behavioral traits expressed by eighteenth-century observers or twentieth-century historians, the "Akan" cultural background from which they derived was clearly a false monolith meant to encompass a multitude of sociopolitical groupings under a single linguistic banner. While the term Akan offers slightly more precision than references to the "Ashanti" by modern historians or the Coromantee by eighteenth-century writers, it still falls well short of the goal of creating an effective ethnic nomenclature and taxonomy. Indeed, the origin and proper use of the term Akan has been a topic of long-standing and contentious debate among Africanists.[17] While individuals embarking on slave ships along the Gold Coast may have spoken Akan and its regional variants as a primary, secondary, or tertiary language, they could often be grouped together with others from hostile states. Before arrival in the Americas, the only real shared dimensions of their identities were the common range of languages or dialects they spoke and related cultural framings.

Enslavement at the hands of Europeans helped blur the lines of social and political distinction. To be certain, both intra- and inter-group divides continued to find expression in a range of diasporic communities and contributed to strife, violent conflict, or hierarchical formulations among enslaved African aggregates. An example of intra-group dissension appears in the Dutch colony of Berbice in 1763. During the planning of a colony-wide revolt, the "Delmina" army was split in two—seemingly along lines of natal or linguistic origin. This Gold Coast contingent had initially elected an Akan-speaking man named Cuffy to serve as their "Governor," with a Ga-speaking insurgent insightfully named Accara (Accra)—after the Ga-speaking state in the Gold Coast—to be a subordinate "Captain." This arrangement paralleled the long-standing political subordination of Ga-speaking Accra to a series of Akan states in the seventeenth- and eighteenth-century Gold Coast. Eventually Accara broke ranks with Governor Cuffy and supported others in electing another "Governor"—in this case, a man named Atta, who appointed subordinate officers with natal origins in the Gold Coast and at least one from West-Central Africa.[18] At this critical moment, in this particular space in the Western Hemisphere, a unified and all-encompassing Gold Coast diasporic identity that effectively combined together Akan and Ga speakers came in fits and starts. At the very minimum, embracing the Delmina neo-African ethnic banner did not completely quell internal discord.

An example of inter-group division can be found in the court proceedings following the 1791 Pointe Coupee, Louisiana, conspiracy. In July

1791, a contingent of enslaved Africans known as the Minas—of mostly Gold and Slave Coast origin—organized a series of so-called Mina Balls in which they danced, sang songs in Atlantic African languages, and elected a "king" who led and inspired them. This community extended from Pointe Coupee to New Orleans due to the activities of a free black man named Antonio Cofi Mina, who organized the Mina Balls for the two decades leading up to the 1791 plot. Like their Coromantee counterparts in Antigua, the Minas of Louisiana used elaborate and expressive dances, what specialists refer to as "plays," as opportunities to organize and plan for resistance.[19]

Inter-ethnic conflict became a real problem in Pointe Coupee as a tenuous coalition of Minas and "Edos" from the Slave Coast frayed at the early inception of the conspiracy. An Edo-speaking woman named Venus, after being approached by Dique—an Edo-speaking countryman—about the planned revolt, asserted, "You are not a Mina. You are an Adó like me. Do not join them."[20] Venus, along with members of her family—both Edo and country-born creoles alike—warned their holder about the conspiracy, and local authorities, in short order, arrested and tried the Mina plotters. During the subsequent court trials, officials revealed that another neo-African ethnic group, in this case the Bambara, had also been approached by Mina conspirators and were asked to join the revolt. With no record of enslaved Bambaras either arrested or charged with conspiracy, we can assume that they refused to join with the Gold and Slave Coast Minas. Clearly, the notion that enslaved peoples shared a common ancestry, destiny, and enemy had not yet dawned on the many Edos, Bambaras, creoles, and others residing in Pointe Coupee Parish in 1791. Four years later, in 1795, however, this reality had changed significantly and a pan-African resistance movement emerged—similar to the 1791 Haitian Revolution.[21]

Over time, however, both intra-group and inter-group divides mostly collapsed. In creating a common foe and a shared debased condition, chattel slavery in the Western Hemisphere provided the means by which Coromantees and (A)minas formed and constituted new ethnic identities. In this process of ethnogenesis, Gold Coast Africans developed, reinvented, and utilized a range of cultural technologies shaped by a commoner consciousness—itself a response to the new world reality of racial and chattel bondage. Some of these cultural forms and technologies borrowed from other African language cohorts, were shared across multiple groups, or represented new formulations altogether. Importantly, these cultural practices and principles can be traced throughout the Gold Coast diaspora. In analyzing one dimension of the polyglot that became "African American" culture, we can project a more historically precise image of the processes of acculturation or creolization which, over centuries, led to the rise of many variations of "African American," "Black Atlantic," or "Diasporic African" cultures.

THE BIRTH OF AN AFRICAN AMERICAN CULTURE

Despite eloquent statements made by Sterling Stuckey, Sidney Mintz, and Richard Price, African American cultures were not born in the belly of the wooden beasts that plied the transatlantic slave trade.[22] While these scholars stand, oddly enough, at opposite ends of the interpretive spectrum regarding cultural and acculturative processes underway in the Black Atlantic, they combine to imagine Atlantic African cultures and peoples as hopelessly diverse and divided, and the ethnogenesis of "African Americans" as something facilitated in the forced combinations of Africans onboard slave ships. For this to be true, the types of intricate, interwoven, fluid, and dynamic cultural geographies in the Gold Coast discussed in earlier chapters could not exist. To imagine Atlantic Africans standing across distinct, clearly delineated, and unbridgeable "cultural lines" blurred only by Atlantic commerce and transport is to embrace notions of African tribalism. Within the historical frame of this book, captured and enslaved speakers of Akan, Ga, Adanme, and Ewe did not meet for the first time during the processes in which they became Atlantic commodities and dehumanized "pieces," units, or heads.[23] As discussed in the preceding chapters, long before they encountered European merchants, slave castles, and slavers on the coast, Gold Coast language clusters experienced movement, the formation of new diasporas and ethnicities, and intermingled cultural ways. Enslavement and overseas transport accelerated or greatly focused some of these ongoing processes, but sale and shipment did not create or give birth to them.

The ethnogenesis of Coromantee and (A)mina peoples in the Americas, then, was not a product of embarkation or disembarkation; the slave ship was not the first time Akan, Ga, Adanme, and Ewe speakers met and mingled. While they may have represented the "Tribe of the Middle Passage," their cultures were forged between two worlds—Atlantic Africa and the Americas. The creation of Coromantee and (A)mina can be seen as a Western Hemisphere extension of an ongoing cultural process that reached back deep into the *longue durée* of Gold Coast history. The formation of these neo-African ethnic groups came out of a need for community and served as a foundation for a number of cultural technologies in which Akan-speaking or, more broadly, Gold Coast cultural formations were refashioned to suit the needs of a new whole. The invention of Coromantee specifically, at least in the minds of Europeans, began in the associations that English and Dutch merchants drew between the coastal Fante towns of Kormantse (or its nearby namesake Fort Kormantse) and the captured and enslaved men and women exported to their New World possessions from the Gold Coast. While the specific historical origin of this association may be difficult to ascertain, we do know that by 1688— the year Aphra Behn's *Oroonoko* appeared in print—Coromantee (and a wide range of spelling variations) as an ethnic referent in the Americas was already in wide circulation in the English colonies of Barbados and Suriname. Her possible encounters with real "Coramantiens" during a stay in Suriname during the 1660s means that this ethnonym and all of its connotations may have been in wide use very shortly after the English established Fort Kormantse in the 1630s.[24]

Despite Behn's role in popularizing the term Coromantee and its associated behavioral characteristics, Gold Coast Africans in the Western Hemisphere diaspora were not a people existing and framed solely within the European imaginary. While Europeans may have invented the use of Coromantee as a Black Atlantic ethnonym, they did not invent the people; any claim to the contrary is an attempt to strike a blow against the agency, ingenuity, and perseverance of peoples responsible for the re-creation of a range Gold Coast cultural technologies that left indelible stamps on New World societies. As previously mentioned, the many "landmarks" in the sociocultural geography inhabited by Coromantees and (A)minas in the Americas—obeah, Ananse the Spider, loyalty oaths, Akan day-names, and items of material culture, among others discussed later in this book—point in the direction of Gold Coast origins or cultural reformulations that drew upon Gold Coast and other Atlantic African backgrounds.

The concept of Coromantee underwent a radical transformation over the course of three centuries. Over time, it became filled with meanings added by both Europeans and Gold Coast Africans, until Coromantee became a real ethnicity in the Western Hemisphere. In tracking this rather complicated ethnogenesis, I begin with some of the earliest mentions of Coromantee in European written records and Gold Coast oral histories. By 1601, "Kormentain" was little more than a Dutch trading place not worthy of a visit by Pieter de Marees. The same was true in 1614, when Samuel Brun made his second voyage to the Guinea Coast onboard the *Weisse Hund.* "Carmandin," for Brun and the mostly Dutch crew, was a meeting point for other ships in their employer's fleet. By the early seventeenth century, Kormantse served as a place name for two separate locations—Upper or Great Kormantse and Lower or Little Kormantse. Before the advent of Fante ethnogenesis in the early eighteenth century, the peoples inhabiting the region were a mixture of Akan, Guang, and Etsi speakers. Described by de Marees as a village "situated on a hillock" with "a tall Tree in the middle of the Market," Great Kormantse was the northern and larger neighbor of Little Kormantse—located at the coast. In de Marees's estimation, Kormantse "used to be one of the most important trading places on the whole Coast; but nowadays it is not held in much esteem." This would significantly change over the next three decades as Kormantse assumed an increasing importance, both commercially and as part of a new Atlantic African ethnic nomenclature in the minds of British and Dutch merchants. After 1645, the British established Fort Kormantse as their Gold Coast headquarters until it was overrun by forces under the command of Dutch Admiral Michiel Adriaenszoon de Ruyter on February 8, 1665. By the 1680s, Barbot could confidently report that the "village [of Cormentin] is the most import one on the [Fante] coast, both on account of the number of inhabitants . . . and on account of its advantageous location." Kormantse's simultaneous rise as both a commercial and population center in the central coast by the 1680s combined to help create a new lexicon of ethnicity in the Gold Coast and its diaspora of peoples.[25]

For the residents of Greater and Little Kormantse, the name of their respective villages probably did not serve as an ethnic identifier—no more than Efutu, Asebu, or Eguafo did for the residents of these small and moderate-sized polities in the central coast region. In the local jargon, one could be *from* Kormantse, but being Kormantse (or Coromantee) would have been a foreign concept. More likely than not, the residents of the two Kormantses may have referred to themselves simply as Fetu by the seventeenth century and Fante by the eighteenth century—the latter being the result of a unique ethnogenesis arising from the political consolidation of central coast polities by the 1730s.[26] The initial thrust in the process of "naming" Coromantees came from the British and Dutch until their actual ethnogenesis took on a momentum and life of its own in the Americas. On this note, Douglas Chambers has drawn links between references to Coromantee in English and Dutch Suriname and the Great Oath of Asante—"*Kromanti Miminda.*" More recently, Kwasi Konadu has attempted a similar historiographic intervention. As mentioned in chapter 1, the 1717 Asante–Akyem war ended with the unceremonious death of the founding Asantehene, Osei Tutu, at a river crossing near the Pra. Under the reign of Asantehene Opoku Ware, the Great Oath was instituted by 1720, and its very name recognized both the day (Saturday or *Miminda*) and place (Kormantse) of Tutu's death. However, linking the Great Oath of Asante to the creation of Coromantee as an ethnic identity requires quite a few interpretive leaps. First, by 1720, Coromantee was already in wide circulation as an ethnic referent in the Americas and among Dutch and British ship captains plying the Atlantic trade in enslaved peoples. Second, while the place of Tutu's death (Kormantse) seems to correspond to the coastal town or village of the same or similar name, what we know about the geography of this region helps cast doubt on there being any direct connection. Tutu died at a crossing of the Pra River more than thirty-five miles north of Upper or Greater Kormantse. In short, the geography of the region testifies against a definitive link between the Great Asante Oath and the creation of the ethnonym. Finally, it is highly doubtful that commoners near the coast would have positively identified with an Asante oath in which they would have specifically pledged to fight enemies of the Asantehene without retreat or demonstration of fear upon pain of death. In the end, neither Chambers nor Konadu convincingly connects the Great Oath to the formation of Coromantee identity in the Americas.[27]

In the late-seventeenth century British Caribbean and South American mainland, Coromantee could evoke an almost instantaneous set of mental images and assumptions of behavioral characteristics. The details of the 1675 Barbados plot led by "Cormantee or Gold Coast Negro's"—when combined with Behn's colorful description of the Coromantee of Suriname—further reinforced the idea of them as a group of noble and brave savages. Indeed, the governor of Barbados at the time of the conspiracy, Jonathan Atkins, noted that the plot was hatched "especially amongst the Cormantin negroes, who are much the greater number from any one country, and are a warlike and robust people." On June 12, 1675, the Barbados Coromantees crowned a king named Cuffee, "an Ancient Gold [Coast] Negroe," precipitating a plan to set fire to sugar cane fields and kill as many whites as possible. This "Design amongst them the Cormantee Negro's to kill all the Baccararoes or White People in the Island within a fortnight" was betrayed when a young Coromantee woman named Fortuna overheard one of her countrymen attempting to recruit other Gold Coast Africans into the rebellious designs. After a series of trials, a number of the ring-leaders were found guilty, and the courts sentenced thirty-five to a variety of torturous executions. When one conspirator, chained to a stake and awaiting death by fire, attempted to divulge the details of the plot, he was chided by a fellow countryman named Tony, who gave a grisly reminder of the fate of those already found to be connected to the plot: "Thou Fool, are there not enough of our Country-men killed already? Art thou minded to kill them all?" To this the betrayer fell silent and the crowd of spectators—incensed by the effect of Tony's words—taunted, "We shall see you fry bravely by and by." Tony's response reveals the source of Coromantee bravery and tolerance for pain and torture; he replied, "If you Roast me to day, you cannot Roast me tomorrow." The person recording this exchange between Tony and the white onlookers opined that Coromantees believe "that after their death they go into their own Country." Transmigration, assessed later in this book, played a critical role in helping constitute one of the key behavioral traits associated with Coromantees and (A)minas in the Americas—their famed physical fortitude and pain tolerance.[28]

"Coromantee," as an ethnic term and as part of a growing typology and ethnic nomenclature of Atlantic Africans, can be found in a range of seventeenth-century references beyond the 1675 Barbados conspiracy. In the aftermath of the planned rebellion in Barbados, for example, Henry Drax—a wealthy sugar planter who owned two estates there—still felt an attachment to "the Caramantines, and Gold Coast slaves" since they "always stood and proved best" on his plantations. Drax's preference for Gold Coast Africans finds some explanation in the 1686 correspondence sent by Edwyn Steed and Stephen Gascoigne in Barbados to Royal African Company agents posted at Cape Coast Castle. "As one of the greatest services can be done the Company," Steed and Gascoigne requested "that you will send us as many good Gold Coast and Cormanteen Negroes as possible can be got, those comeing always in good condition, also well accepted here."[29] As mentioned in the previous chapter, it is entirely likely that—in comparison to captured and enslaved Atlantic Africans from the Bight of Biafra and West-Central Africa—Gold Coast Africans arrived in the Americas in better health and physical condition. This might be especially true considering the close proximity of Barbados, as the easternmost island in the Caribbean, to the Atlantic coast of West Africa.

Given the dangers associated with importing concentrations of particular language clusters from Atlantic African embarkation regions, planters in Barbados began the process of carefully noting what they thought were behavioral characteristics and traits of peoples from the Slave Coast, the Gold Coast, the Bight of Biafra, and Angola—moving beyond preferences based simply on the physical condition of new arrivals. By 1693, when Steed penned an account of Barbados slave imports for the Royal African Company, "Coromantins" had been categorized as the quintessential noble savages—proud, courageous, and prone to violent resistance. While this may have been one of many legacies of the 1675 Barbados plot, these views found a great deal of corroboration throughout the seventeenth and eighteenth centuries. Though heavy concentrations of Gold Coast Africans could become a cause for concern, they were also deemed a likely source of good, able-bodied laborers, and they continued to be highly preferred over Congos, Eboes, and others. This notion finds resonance in the writings of Captain Thomas Phillips, who visited the Slave Coast on a Royal African Company charter in 1693–1694. Though purchasing most of his human cargo at Whydah, he noted "The negroes most in demand at Barbadoes, are the gold coast, or, as they call them, Cormantines, which will yield 3 or 4 *l.* a head more [than] the Whidaw, or, as they call them, Papa negroes."[30] Coromantees, therefore, were both highly coveted as a labor force in the British Americas and feared due to their alleged propensity to seek vengeance. In the complex algorithm of Atlantic commerce, the potential profit Coromantees could generate outweighed the great risk they posed in disrupting plantation economies though violence.

By the turn of the eighteenth century—precisely at the point the Gold Coast shifted toward specializing in the exportation of slaves—the idea and meaning of Coromantee further crystalized in the European mind. For Christopher Codrington, Governor of the British Leeward Islands, Coromantees may have been "the best and most faithful of our slaves, but are really all born Heroes." This he felt compelled to say in light of the murder of a Major Martin in Antigua on December 27, 1701, at the hands of a Coromantee he had mistreated. Neither "raskal nor coward" could be counted among any of this nation; indeed, Codrington adds that they were "intrepid to the last degree," and every Coromantee man would "stand to be cut to pieces without a sigh or groan, grateful and obedient to a kind master, but implacably revengeful when ill-treated." Thus, the master recursive metaphor of Coromantee masculinity—theorized by Douglas Chambers—may have been based on clear-eyed observations about phenomena and behavioral traits made by a range of contemporary witnesses.[31]

William Snelgrave, an English ship captain plying the West African slave trade during the first three decades of the eighteenth century, experienced three shipboard revolts, at least two of them involving Coromantees. Most of his voyages occurred without incident, but Snelgrave observes that "sometimes we meet with stout stubborn People amongst them, who are never to be made easy; and these are generally some of the Cormantines, a Nation of the Gold Coast." His observations of their intractability notwithstanding, Snelgrave added that among all Atlantic

Africans, the Coromantees could be distinguished as "the stoutest and most sensible Negroes on the Coast." In addition, Snelgave concluded that Coromantees "despised Punishment, and even Death itself," as evidenced by mass suicides in Barbados and the belief among them that "if they are put to death and not dismembered, they shall return again to their own Country."[32] The potentially lethal combination of their strong minds and bodies, sensible and obstinate dispositions, and fearlessness made Coromantees ideal noble savages in the European mind.

In the 1760s, Jamaican planter Bryan Edwards offered strong corroboration that the reputation of Coromantees as able-bodied and fit, if recalcitrant and even courageous, enslaved peoples had spread beyond slave ship captains and planters in Barbados and Suriname. In the aftermath of a massive slave revolt in 1760 and the many revelations made about its inner workings during a series of court proceedings, Edwards noted: "The circumstances which distinguish the Koromantyn, or Gold Coast negroes, from all others are firmness both of body and mind; a ferociousness of disposition; but, withal, activity, courage, and a stubbornness, or what an ancient Roman would have deemed an elevation of soul, which prompts them to enterprizes of difficulty and danger; and enables them to meet death, in its most horrible shape, with fortitude or indifference."[33] Also noting the actions of the Coromantees during the 1760 Jamaica conspiracy, fellow planter Edward Long observed that the plot "had originated (like most or all the others that had occurred in the island) with the Coromantins; whose turbulent, savage, and martial temper was well known." This notable level of recalcitrance and rebelliousness represented through frequent Coromantee plots and revolts in Jamaica prompted the Assembly of Jamaica to introduce legislation aimed at attaching higher import duties on "all Fantin, Akim and Ashantee Negroes, and all other commonly [called] Coromantins." In the end, this measure did not receive much support, owing to the "conceit"—in the words of Long—of several planters who believed strongly in the "superior strength of the Coromantins, and greater hardiness to support field labour" which outweighed legitimate concerns regarding "public tranquility and safety." Five years later, another Coromantee uprising—this time in Westmoreland—demonstrated the ever-present danger Jamaica's slaveocracy continued to face.[34]

The ethnogenesis of Coromantees, in the minds of British and Dutch slaveholding interests in the Americas, followed a complicated and multistaged process. What began as observations about the physical condition of imported Gold Coast Africans mobilized an ethnic nomenclature and taxonomy, beginning with planters in Barbados and Suriname, that spread through the Anglophone and later Dutch-speaking circum-Caribbean. Because Coromantees accompanied a set of cultural technologies originating mostly from the Gold Coast—obeah, blood oaths, trickster spider folktales, and belief in the immortality of the human soul—their identity as an ethnic group became increasingly fixed over time. Edward Long, in particular, outlines aspects of Coromantee as an ethnicity in his 1774 account. In his description, Coromantees "are brought from the Gold Coast" and originate specifically among the "Akims, Fantins, Ashantees, Quamboos, &c. from the towns so called, at whose markets they are bought." In the Gold Coast, they "were marked with the same characters, which authors have given to the natives of this part, who are said to be the most turbulent and desperate of any on the coast of Guiney." In addition to their warlike dispositions, Long added that Coromantees were easily identifiable in the Black Atlantic given their characteristic employment of "obeiah-men," blood oaths, lively music, martial dances, and expressive plays.[35]

Coromantees were not, however, entirely "invented" peoples, existing only in the minds of slave owners and merchant company agents in the Atlantic World. Many Coromantees (and [A]minas) came from overlapping cultural and linguistic frontiers and, upon disembarkation in the Americas, immediately established language communities and further elaborated and negotiated the cultural markers that would define them as a unique group. In this sense, Coromantee and (A)mina should not be understood as genetic or immutable attributes. Over time, they became increasingly multilingual and culturally inclusive, as the boundaries between them and, say, Eboes, Congos, Chambas, and others blurred or were erased altogether. People in the circum-Caribbean were continuously becoming Coromantee, to the degree that by the nineteenth century, the concept and associated cultural and performative connotations lost some of their original meaning and form. Evidence of this level of cultural intermingling can be tracked through a number of historical examples in Antigua, New York City, Jamaica, Suriname, and Danish St. John.

By the early 1700s, for example, a Jamaican Maroon enclave led by Cudjoe in the west-central portion of the British Caribbean colony represented a multiethnic formation incorporating enslaved Africans from regions quite far from the Gold Coast. Dominated by "Cormantins," this group was joined by a contingent of enslaved people originating reportedly from Madagascar. Whether or not they actually came from the island off the East African coast may not matter as much as the long memory of how this group became incorporated into Cudjoe's Coromantee Maroons. According to details provided in one description, the Madagascar runaways were "distinct in every respect; their figure, character, language, and country, being different from those of other blacks"—particularly the Coromantees. Indeed, some of the descendants of this maroon group "remember that their parents spoke, in their own families, a language entirely different from that spoken by the rest of the negroes with whom they had incorporated." Despite these differences, the cultural weight of Coromantee prevailed as "The Coromantee language . . . superseded the others, and became in time the general one in use."[36]

The combination of the "Nations of Carmantee and Pappa" in the 1712 New York City revolt came as no surprise given the close proximity and shared political and cultural geographies connecting Akan-speakers from the Gold Coast and the Ewe, Fon, and even Ga speakers residing in and near Popo, east of the Volta River in the Slave Coast.[37] Likewise, the amalgamation of Akan, Ga, and Adanme speakers in the 1733–1734 Danish St. John "Amina" revolt may have simply reflected phenomena and long-standing cultural intermixing existing in the Gold Coast and its diaspora of peoples.[38] The examples of the Coromantees and Pappas of New York and the St. John Amina, when added to Tackey Court's leadership of the Akan-speaking Coromantees in 1736 Antigua, demonstrate just how multilingual the neo-African ethnic constructions were in the Americas. Indeed, during the 1760 Jamaican slave revolt, another Tackey led a contingent of mostly Akan-speaking Coromantees, providing more support for the claim that Coromantees in the Americas drew from over-lapping and even contested geographies—linguistic, cultural, and politi-cal—that brought them together as one in the Western Hemisphere.[39]

While a common sense of Gold and Slave Coast geographies, as well as common knowledge of Akan language, may have drawn together Coromantees and (A)minas when they met in the New World, these newly emerging ethnic constructs and sets of performances embraced cultural technologies and peoples from a much broader physical geogra-phy. Obeah, discussed at length in chapter 5, combined ritual practices and the cultural technologies from peoples embarked on slavers in the Gold Coast and the Bight of Biafra. This was one of many manifes-tations of the cultural negotiations and agreements enslaved Atlantic Africans engaged in as they encountered new and unfamiliar peoples. Other syncretic ritual forms, including Vodun, Candomblé, Santería, represent similar negotiations—mostly between peoples originating from the Slave Coast and West-Central Africa—that were part of the continuous process of be(com)ing one of many neo-African ethnicities in the Americas.[40]

Over time, the ways in which Europeans understood, defined, and wrote about the meaning of Coromantee changed radically. A parallel process of cultural change occurred simultaneously among Atlantic Africans and their American-born descendants as Coromantee, (A) mina, and their many associated cultural forms were in constant mo-tion. This process took on local shapes and forms throughout circum-Caribbean colonies. The limitations of the archive in diachronically tracking cultural processes undermines any attempt at precision in this case. Perhaps the only meaningful way of describing this change over time and across various Western Hemisphere geographies would be to conclude that these shifts in meaning, substance, form, and function of Gold Coast diaspora ethnonyms and their related cultural technolo-gies were uneven and chaotic. As with any cultural phenomena, change was the only constant as the meaning of Coromantee in the minds of Europeans, Atlantic Africans, and creoles transformed sharply between the eighteenth and nineteenth centuries. Prime examples of these con-tinual transformations can be tracked through the meanings associated with specific Akan day-names in the Americas. Cuffee (Kofi), the Akan day-name for a male born on a Friday, transformed into a much more general referent—particularly in eighteenth- and nineteenth-century North America. At some point before 1880, Cuffee became synonymous with a generic African American. Thus, a line from a popular New York Pinkster celebration song referenced "Cuffee, with protruding lip" as early as the American Revolution. In a June 20, 1859, letter, Edward Pollard laments to Horace Greeley—editor of the *New-York Tribune*—"the coarse insolence displayed by Cuffy." In the same year, Harriet Beecher Stowe remarked that both "Sambo and Cuffy" had the ability to adapt to the "varying soil and circumstances" in North America. By the time Zora Neal Hurston encountered "Cuffee" in the twentieth century, the name had become a self-lacerating epithet used among African Americans in the U.S. South: "If it was old cuffy down with it!" and "old Cuffy just got to cut de fool, you know."[41]

Quashee (Kwesi), the Akan day-name for a male born on Sunday, became the Jamaican and Anglophone Caribbean equivalent of Cuffee. In this case, not only did Quashee refer to a generic black man by the nineteenth century, but the name carried connotations of buffoonery and a clownish disposition—similar to the Sambo caricature in the United States. John Stewart, writing in *An Account of Jamaica* in the early 1800s, captured this emerging notion of Quashee as a personality type. Quashee, in Stewart's view, captured the childlike and submissive slave, with an inclination toward joviality, dancing, and other kinds of merriment. Stewart's account was among the earliest to capture in writing this new stereotype; however, Scottish philosopher and historian Thomas Carlyle greatly popularized the many manifestations of the Quashee personality type appearing in mid-nineteenth-century Anglophone literature. Like Stewart, Carlyle defined Quashee's essential personality as a "merryhearted, grinning, dancing, singing, affectionate kind of creature, with a great deal of melody and amenability in his composition." Adding to this description, he was among the first to stereotype Quashee as lazy and idle.[42] Joining this Sambo-like figure in the nineteenth-century white Jamaican imaginary was Quasheba—the Sunday-born female equivalent of Quashee—described as illiterate and foolish.[43]

Quashee and Quasheba, as catchall references for generic black men and women in the British Caribbean by the nineteenth century, represent ironic and significant linguistic turns, given the history of interactions in the Black Atlantic. Due to the peculiar Sunday religious rituals of various European nationals based in the Gold Coast, Ga- and Akan-speakers developed the unique greeting, "Yo Kwasi," as early as the seventeenth century in Accra. As mentioned earlier, this greeting—in essence—"named" all Europeans as Sunday-born due to their peculiar ways and became a catchall and a generic label for all European men.[44] The shift of this referent over the course of three centuries, from a label for all Europeans to a dismissive and diminutive meant to stereotype black men and women in Jamaica and throughout the British Caribbean, provides one of many examples of how Coromantee and its associated cultural markers and technologies radically transformed over time.

Another interpretation regarding the origin and meaning of Quashee in the white mind comes recently from Kwasi Konadu. In his contention, the specific stereotypes associated with "Quashee" point to the possibility that the word is not linked historically to the Akan day-name Kwasi. Instead, Konadu contends that the Akan word for fool, *kwasea*, is the origin of both the word and its associated stereotype.[45] Three interpretive problems trouble this conclusion. First, many of the negative characterizations associated with Quashee developed in the early years of the nineteenth century, despite the fact that the day-name was in broad circulation throughout the Western Hemisphere a century earlier. In this case, it seems plausible that the Quashee stereotype developed around an Akan day-name so ubiquitous in the Gold Coast diaspora. Second, the curious assertion that the British had a particular command of Akan language—enough to correctly use an obscure Akan word as the basis for a stereotype—seems highly suspect, especially in light of some of Konadu's arguments regarding the lack of cultural interplay and cross-fertilization between Europeans and their Akan-speaking bondspeople. Third, by linking Quashee to a real Akan word for fool, Konadu breathes life into a dangerous stereotype. Orlando Patterson began this tradition in his 1967 treatment, *The Sociology of Slavery*, when he wrote: "That Quashee existed there can be no doubt. The problem is to ascertain how real, how meaningful, this psychological complex was in the life of the slave. . . . Quashee may be said to have existed . . . as a psychological function of the real life situation of the slave."[46] John

Blassingame, responding to the reification of the Sambo stereotype by Stanley Elkins, identified a range of personality types, including Sambo, Nat, and Jack. However, in contrast with observations made by Patterson and Konadu about Quashee, Blassingame cautioned that "the legitimacy of each as a representation of typical slave behavior is limited."[47] Clearly, enslaved peoples throughout the Americas learned the necessity of donning the "mask" so eloquently described by poet Paul Lawrence Dunbar in 1896. Behind facades of smiling compliance with the hegemonic racial order, enslaved peoples successfully hid their discontent and—in the process—beguiled plantation owners and modern scholars alike.[48]

In following the interpretive lead initiated by Blassingame, we can understand the appearance of the docile and foolish Sambo stereotype in North American literature not as a reflection of a reality, but as either a goal of fearful planters or a psychological defense mechanism developed in the plantation South to explain away the real human range of behavior of the enslaved. Sambo, then, was a figment of the collective imagination of the many defenders of slavery, since no plantation would have been profitable with such characters serving as the primary labor pool. In addition, if owners imagined their "property" as capable of arson, poisoning, and bloody wrath, no slave-holding family would ever be able to sleep at night, eat the food prepared by bondspeople, or leave children in the care of enslaved women with any sense of safety or security. In similar vain, Deborah Gray White convincingly demonstrates that Mammy and Jezebel never really existed anywhere beyond the wishful thoughts of planters. Both stereotypes evolved out of a need by planters to rationalize the constant sexual exploitation of black women in the plantation U.S. South.[49]

The historiography of slave stereotypes in the antebellum United States facilitates understandings of the origin and development of the Quashee stereotype in the British Caribbean. Given the strong association between Atlantic Africans with Akan day-names and acts of violent resistance, from marronage to full-blown rebellions in the circum-Caribbean, the many Cudjoes, Cuffees, Quaws, and Quashees inhabiting the worlds of British, Dutch, and Danish slavery provided constant reminders of the mortal danger involved in slave ownership.[50] Just as slave owners in North America needed to imagine and personify happy, harmless, and loyal "darkies" in the guise of Sambo and Mammy, sugar planters and others residing in regions with large concentrations of Gold Coast Africans had a psychological imperative to transform the most dangerous among them into less threatening images. Quashee and Quasheba no longer evoked the Coromantee tropes of haughty, strong, sensible, and courageous rebels by the nineteenth century. Instead, they were consciously transformed and inverted as part of a complex ratio- nale for slavery and slaveholding by its many proponents. The existence of contented, docile, and malleable slaves like Sambo, Mammy, Quashee, and Quasheba point toward racial slavery as a humane and just system— not the exploitative hell it really was. By making Quashee and Quasheba perfect inversions of their historical Coromantee counterparts, planters in Jamaica and elsewhere symbolically "tamed" noble savages who—for two full centuries—wrought bloody havoc and destruction among them.

The fate of Coromantee as an ethnic referent followed its own con- voluted and complicated trajectory. By 1823, Coromantee resonated with some of the same meaning in Jamaica as it did during the previous cen- tury. In the words of John Stewart, "The Coromantee is . . . fierce, violent, and revengeful under injury and provocation; but hardy, laborious, and manageable under mild and just treatment." A troublesome property indeed, Coromantees were not only the "head of all insurrections" in Jamaica, but also they represented "the original parent-stock of the Ma- roons."[51] This association between Coromantees and Maroons became so close, that by the mid-nineteenth century the two labels became inter- changeable. Indeed, "Maroon" was elevated to the stature of an ethnicity or culture, and the term came to encompass many of the associations and cultural technologies once connected to the Gold Coast diaspora and the many Coromantees residing in the Americas. By the mid- to late nineteenth century, the various cognate forms deriving from Coroman- tee had lost much of their original cultural weight and meaning. In the imaginary of black and white inhabitants of the circum-Caribbean, the word began to evoke a general sense of bravery, steadfastness, austerity, and stoicism as it moved along its winding etymological and historical course. As Coromantee and its associated meanings began to fall into disuse by whites by the late nineteenth century, they became activated and mobilized in new ways by the descendants of enslaved peoples and Maroons in Jamaica, Suriname, and beyond.[52]

"Kramanti," from the late nineteenth through the early-twentieth century, became the name of a ritual play or dance and a language of secrecy among Jamaican Maroons—particularly those residing in Moore Town. Among the eastern Ndyuka Maroons in nineteenth-century Suriname, "Kumanti" referred to both a group of powerful medicine men and a specialized warrior caste.[53] Coromantee had variable meanings and uses among the Saramaka Maroons of Suriname by the twentieth century. Melville and Frances Herskovits report that "Kromanti" referred to both an all-male secret society and a "category of amulets" known collectively as *Kromanti obia*.[54] A few decades after the field work conducted by the Herskovitses, another scholar remarked that the Saramaka Maroons of Suriname gave liturgical prayers in "Kormante language, a sacred language [of the Bush Negroes] in which the Almighty God, Nana Kediapon, is invoked."[55] In addition, "Coromantee" may have been the basis for names of locations and waterways in Suriname, including Kromoti and Cromotibo.[56]

Over four centuries of continuing cultural change and ethnogenesis in the Americas, "Coromantee" and its many associations underwent radical transformations. Over time, it could refer to a place of embarkation for enslaved Gold Coast Africans, a new ethnic group in the Americas, a stoic and courageous affect, and a set of ritual and secretive practices among the descendants of maroon enclaves in Suriname and Jamaica. Despite its many variations and transmutations, the "changing same" at the core of the imaginings of Coromantee had discernible links to the seventeenth- and eighteenth-century Gold Coast and its diaspora of peoples. This continual movement in meaning, form, and function of Gold Coast diaspora ethnonyms and their associated cultural technologies implies that the linearity and finality assumed by social death, as conceived by Orlando Patterson, may not be the best way to conceptualize the dynamism of diasporic lives. While Gold Coast Africans were torn from family and familiar social structures in the process of commodification and their immersion into chattel slavery, they mobilized social and cultural scripts from their collective past as a means of social resurrection. Situated in a new set of geographies in the New World, this "rebirth" was both deeply rooted in the Gold Coast past and shaped by the American present.

FROM AMINA TO COROMANTEE—A BLACK
ATLANTIC ETHNOBIOGRAPHY

Assessing the changing meaning of Gold Coast neo-African ethnic labels in the European mind is made possible given the copious amount of materials that described the activities of these groups over the centuries throughout the Americas. Certainly, the voluminous nature of records that refer to Coromantee and (A)mina reflect the space these groups occupied in the minds of those concerned about the dangerous undertakings of rebels and maroons. In fact, trial records, confessions, and maroon treaties account for much of European and Atlantic African "testimonies" about the meanings of Coromantee and (A)mina. With this stated, those who bore personal witness to the internal workings of these ethnic formulations were few and far between. Yet, their insights reveal not only the rough outlines of Gold Coast diasporic communities, but also their interconnected nature. No one proves this more than Billy, owned by Anthony Ward in New York and the widow Ms. Langford in Antigua.[57]

Billy's Atlantic biography includes a troubled past. The July 2, 1741, New York Supreme Court trial against him included testimony linking Billy "within a few past years ... [to] two conspiracies in the West Indies, the first at St. John's, the last at Antigua, in the year 1736, where (as it was said) he became an evidence, and from thence was shipped to this city." As Billy had been accused of involvement in three concerted acts of resistance against white authorities, the New York justices "thought [it] high time to put it out of his power to do any further mischief." Sentenced to death for his involvement in the 1741 New York conspiracy, Billy was burned at the stake on Saturday, July 4.[58] Before his death, Billy exemplified the circulations of peoples and cultural technologies in the Black Atlantic and the Gold Coast diaspora. He personally transformed from an Amina to a Coromantee over the course of his brief life in the Americas and, in doing so, offered small though revealing windows into the meaning of these neo-African ethnic labels to those who embraced them.

Though it is impossible to reconstruct Billy's entire life leading up to his involvement in the 1736 Antigua conspiracy, a handful of informed extrapolations from the available data helps fill in some of the gaps. To have survived the November 1733 and May 1734 Amina takeover of Danish St. John meant that Billy was not part of the leadership core and, in all likelihood, played little more than a bit part in the whole affair. For six months, he was an "Amina"—an ethnic construction generated by a combination of Akan-, Ga-, and Adanme-speaking Gold Coast Africans exported to the Americas in the wake of the collapse of the Akwamu state in 1730. If we can assume the veracity of the revelations made to the New York Supreme Court in 1741, Billy could be counted among the 146 men and women who fought for and formed the short-lived Amina *oman* or polity. He may have been the injured young man, captured by French forces on May 9, 1734, who led investigators to a location where eleven Amina lay dead after one of many mass suicides that characterized the collapse of their attempt to construct and maintain a polity. Alternatively, Billy could have been among the fifteen rebels who managed to elude authorities and maroon hunters until August 25. Captured and transported to neighboring St. Thomas, this group reportedly suffered terrible fates; four died—perhaps by suicide—before trial, four others were to be worked to death laboring in St. Croix, and the remainder were "done to death in various ways."[59]

Somehow, Billy miraculously survived the destruction of the St. John Amina polity—only to be transported to Antigua on the eve of the Coromantee slave plot. As an Amina imported to Antigua between 1734 and 1736, Billy—owned now by the widow Ms. Langford—found a language community and familiar cultural tropes and technologies firmly established in the British Caribbean colony. One of the first people he encountered during his time with the Langfords was Robin, a fellow Gold Coast African and recruiter for Court's Coromantee army. Indeed, King Court nicknamed Robin "Quamina Jumper," an allusion to both his Akan day-name and his resemblance to a famous soldier in the employ of a Gold Coast polity. Apparently, Robin's namesake could use a cutlass so deftly as a decapitation device that he literally made men's heads "jump" off their bodies. Robin had vowed to do the same to the heads of whites once the rebellion commenced.[60] King Court's raucous "play" or coronation, in the form of an ikem dance, the presence of his braffo and other attendants, and the employment of obeah doctors instantly resonated with Billy, facilitating his rather smooth transition from an Amina to a Coromantee. Billy's own induction into the Coromantee cabal had many elements. He lived and became close friends with Robin, Coobah, and other Gold Coast Akan speakers implicated in the plot. Not only did an obeah doctor administer the "Damnation Oath" of loyalty to Billy, but he also hosted an organizing dinner and a mass loyalty oath administered to more than a dozen insurgents at his residence. Finally, Billy agreed to be an officer under King Court and "to head the Coromantees."[61]

Once the Antiguan Coromantee plot was foiled and Billy faced imminent death, he broke his oath and turned king's witness. Of the thirteen conspirators who betrayed the details of the plot, Billy offered some of the most insightful and damning descriptions of the preparations for the ikem dance and the administering of various loyalty oaths. Listed among those transported at the conclusion of the Antigua trials, Billy found himself in yet another familiar space—this time in New York City in the early months of 1737.[62] Within a five- or six-year span, he had experienced capture, enslavement, and social death in the Gold Coast; social resurrection and political life in Danish St. John as an Amina; transport to British Antigua and another social resurrection, this time as a Coromantee; and, finally, transport to British North America. Owned by Anthony Ward, Billy was immersed in familiar sights and sounds—from the first instant of his arrival. By March 1737, he may have witnessed a Pinkster festival that accompanied some of the motifs, tropes, and technologies that served as catalysts for political action throughout the Gold Coast diaspora. An anonymous white "spy" writing a serialized description of this festival in the New-York Weekly Journal observed "the Negroes divided into Companies, I suppose according to their different Nations, some dancing to the hollow Sound of a Drum. . . . The Warriors were not idle, for I saw several Companies of the Blacks, some exercising the Cudgel, and some of them small Sticks in imitation of the short Pike." While the "horrid Oaths, Imprecations, Curses," competitive dancing, drumming, and horn blowing frightened white onlookers, Billy may have taken particular comfort amid these raucous expressions, given how similar in form and function this Pinkster parade was to the ikem dance he helped stage for King Court in Antigua.[63]

During the planning of the 1741 New York slave plot, Billy participated in loyalty oaths and recruited others into the conspiracy—even to the point of admonishing reluctant recruits for their cowardice as "they had no hearts as those at Antigua." At various meetings during the early stages of the conspiracy, Billy could be found in the company of Quack (Walter), Cuffee (Philipse), Jenny (Comfort) and others known to be Coromantee. As in Antigua, Billy turned king's evidence only after he was convicted and sentenced to die. Though he betrayed his comrades and, in doing so, broke a binding loyalty oath, Billy quite ably performed Coromantee masculinity on the day of his execution. When the torch was applied to the kindling under Billy's feet, he "set his back to the stake, and raising up one of his legs, laid it upon the fire."[64]

Billy's transformation from social death in the Gold Coast to a range of ethnic landscapes in the Americas reveals some of the complexities of the varied and at times intersecting processes of ethnogenesis that continually reshaped neo-African ethnic cohorts. Just in the span of a decade, he could be identified as both Amina and Coromantee and served as a singular vector that allowed for the sharing of cultural principles across an expansive Western Hemisphere geography. His multiple social resurrections—in St. John, Antigua, and New York—prove the resilience, agency, and genius of Atlantic Africans as they participated in the creation of new worlds and performed, consciously, new identities. The many cultural technologies that Gold Coast Africans carried with them into the American diaspora—particularly those that formed key elements of the cultural geographies inhabited by Coromantees and (A)minas—become the subject of the remaining chapters.

PART 2
SOCIAL RESURRECTION
AND EMPOWERMENT

FOUR

State, Governance, and War

The warning to the Governor from Captain Cuffy of Master Barky,
Accara, likewise of Barky . . . that His Excellency with three ships
goes to Holland as quickly as possible and with the first, and if the
Governor does not . . . the Captain will come with a large number
of troops to fight . . . [we] demand that the slaves who are lower
down must not be taken with them or it will go bad for you.

CAPTAIN CUFFY, "LETTER TO GOVERNOR WOLFERT
SIMON VAN HOOGENHEIM" IN ROTH, "THE STORY
OF THE SLAVE REBELLION IN BERBICE" (1959)

King June and his retinue stood between two Black Atlantic Worlds in
1734. Four years earlier his Gold Coast home, Akwamu, was defeated by
neighboring Akyem and Akwamu's own citizens, forcing many of its
elites into exile and enslavement in the Western Hemisphere. Between
the collapse of their polity and their transformation into commodities,
the Akwamu elite indeed suffered social and political deaths. Transported in two major waves to the Danish Caribbean—115 arriving in
June 1732 on the *Countess of Laurwig*, followed by another shipment
of 242 in May 1733 on the *Laarburg Galley*—some of these men and
women had been nobles, *abirempong* (big-men and -women), *akomfo*
(priests), senior court administrators, and royal servants in Akwamu.
"King" June, also known as Jama, appears in the records of Christians-

borg Castle as a royal court official and a distinguished lieutenant of the Akwamuhene.[1] As Ray Kea notes, King June's responsibilities in the Akwamu court included a number of tasks: "He collected the monthly tribute as well as [dash] that the Danish company paid to the Akwamu sovereign; he collected fines whenever the king imposed them on the different tributary coastal towns or the Danish trading stations; he served as the king's trading agent at Christiansborg Castle. . . . Along with his civil duties as a royal revenue-collector and royal commercial agent, he served the king as a military officer."[2] War transformed him from a member of an empowered elite in the Gold Coast to a slave in the Danish Caribbean. However, King June's social and political deaths preceded a concerted effort at sociopolitical resurrection as an Amina in Danish St. John between November 1733 and May 1734.

Sold to the Danes at Christiansborg Castle in June 1732, King June's Atlantic journey ended in May 1733 with his sale to the Soedtmann sugar plantation in St. John. Perhaps owing to his past life in the Akwamu military as a commander of hundreds, King June quickly rose through the ranks of the Soedtmann plantation hierarchy and became a slave driver or foreman. Within six months of his arrival in St. John, he assumed command of a rebel cabal with a leadership core that included two Akwamu lesser nobles (Abedo and Kanta), an Akwamu prince (Aquashi), an Akwamu princess (Aquashiba), the former sovereign of the Adanme-speaking Ladoku polity near Accra (Bolombo, also known as King Clæs) and the Ladoku King's second wife (Judicia). A number of the Aminas may have been Gold Coast commoners from Akan- and Ga-speaking polities, including Cuba and Atou from the Bewerhoudstberg plantation; Coffie of the Runnels plantation; Acra (or "Accra") of the Krøyer plantation; and the two Quassis—from the Susannaberg plantation and Annaberg estate. Multiple Gold Coast ethnolinguistic groups—Ga, Adanme, and Akan—became one in this movement; under King June, they were all Aminas. Erecting a unifying neo-African ethnic banner helped smooth over former hostilities. This was a critical move, given the role the Akwamu elites played in conquering Ga and Adanme polities and enslaving their populations. The Amina revolt that began on November 23, 1733, resulted, in part, from an ethnogenesis that combined together multiple Gold Coast language cohorts and a consciousness shaped by former elites who sought to replace Danish hegemony over St. John with their own vision of a hierarchical Gold Coast *oman* or polity. Running short on ammunition and facing a coalition of Danish, English, and French forces, the rebel Aminas failed within six months in their attempt to recreate a Gold Coast state. By May 1734, King June chose to face military defeat in a way that became a hallmark of Coromantee and Amina masculinity throughout the eighteenth-century Americas. Along with three dozen of his lieutenants, he committed suicide rather than face capture, torture, and summary execution at the hands of Danish authorities.[3]

As one of the first colony-wide slave rebellions in Western Hemisphere history, the 1733–1734 Danish St. John revolt had several notable features. In their endeavors to establish an independent polity, the Amina rebels appointed royalty and sought to connect with fellow Aminas, including Akan-speaking maroons in neighboring St. Thomas and Tortola, as a means of creating a Gold Coast diaspora oman that crossed geographic boundaries in the Caribbean. Indeed, their sense of diaspora and even their understanding of be(com)ing "Amina" transcended ethnolinguistic lines while simultaneously being bounded in their minds by a Gold Coast geography. Thus, their attempt to establish an oman in St. John and possibly in St. Thomas and Tortola cannot be categorized simply as an "ethnic" or "Akan" slave rebellion, as the Amina label resulted from an ethnogenesis that encircled speakers of Ga, Adanme, and Akan.[4]

As a carryover of their elite status, comfort with hierarchical sociopolitical structures, and active support of the Atlantic slave trade, the Amina rebels resolved to enslave Atlantic Africans originating beyond the Gold Coast and to use them as a dependent labor force in the cultivation of food and cash crops. To this end, the Aminas initially divided plantation lands among themselves and preserved the sugar mills throughout St. John in the hope that, after a successful revolt, they would replace the Danes as the political and economic masters of the island. At the very minimum, they attempted to sell ten non-Aminas (that is, non-Gold Coast Africans) to Danish and English merchants during the course of the rebellion in exchange for several kegs of powder. A May 9, 1734, court deposition captures the expendability of non–Gold Coast commoners to the Aminas. An eight-year-old eyewitness to the Amina revolt and the subsequent mass suicides testified that the Aminas "murdered a Levango Negro belonging to Castan" for reasons unknown.[5] "Levango," a place-name related to the West-Central African Kongo kingdom, was an alien "other" with whom the Aminas had yet to form political, linguistic, or cultural links.[6] The alleged murder of this man demonstrates the circumscribed nature of Amina identity and Amina concepts of diaspora and inclusion in their short-lived St. John oman. The St. John revolt came at a moment when Aminas in the Danish Caribbean had not yet exchanged their country marks with either island-born creoles or Atlantic Africans from other areas. Among the Amina leadership core, their common natal origin, class status, and new sense of ethnicity mattered much more than some transcendent, ahistorical, and cultural nationalist vision of race.

The Amina revolt, then, should be understood as an anomaly in the history of slave resistance as the first and perhaps only example of an attempt at an elite or political revolution. As elites, King June and the other leaders of the Amina oman imagined a polity modeled after the top-down, hierarchical structures that represented a familiar sociopolitical geography for Gold Coast hereditary nobles; in many ways, this was less a *cultural* continuity than a continuation of elite ideas and conceptions of power and polity. Before they were "Akans" or "Aminas," the leaders of the 1733–1734 St. John revolt were an empowered economic, military, and political elite in the Gold Coast states of Akwamu, Accra, and Ladoku. Indeed, the Amina revolt represents one of the few examples of a truly "restorationist" movement as theorized by Eugene Genovese and Ray Kea, in the sense that King June and his retinue sought to recreate a "hierarchically organized, particularist vision of social order" as a "dispossessed and unfree political-military aristocracy."[7] Since most enslaved Gold Coast Africans came from commoner pasts, they did not seek to "restore" prior social or political orders in their attempts to overturn slaveocracies in the Americas. This reality raises necessary questions about the more normative experiences of former commoners exported from the Gold Coast. How were the new worlds they encountered and shaped in the Americas informed by their commoner pasts? Did commoners and peasants gravitate toward particularly nonhierarchical, egalitarian, even democratic structures in their imaginings about their post-slave status and state? Is it possible to construct an interpretation of the existence of a commoner ethos that began in the diaspora and, over time, crossed ethnolinguistic barriers? The last question has been addressed, in part, in works by John Thornton, Susan Preston Blier, T. J. Desch-Obi, and others. With these works in mind, we can theorize the creation and use of obeah, Vodun, Brer Rabbit and Ananse the Spider tales, and capoeira as part of a diasporic lingua franca, or a common tongue, of the dispossessed and dispersed in the Black Atlantic. These religious, folkloric, and martial forms crystallized commoner consciousness and became potent weapons in the hands of those seeking means to combat the new forms of subjugation encountered in the Western Hemisphere.[8]

THE ICONOGRAPHY OF POWER

The contention forwarded throughout this book is that commoner constructions of power and post-slave polity demonstrated the shaping influences of egalitarian, nonhierarchical, and democratic worldviews. Gold Coast commoners, surrounded as they were by braffos, caboceers, abirempong, awura, and ahene, understood how the powerful benefited from and participated in their debasement. The very fact that the vast majority of the enslaved were either peasants or commoners, when combined with the rigid hierarchies from the natal societies from which so many were extracted, demonstrates that slavery did not touch elites and their social lessers in the same ways. Commoners were far more vulnerable to the social dislocations, wars, and destabilizing shocks that characterized this era of human traffic. As mentioned previously, the various predations of the powerful, whether expansionist polities or sociopolitical elites involved in Atlantic commerce, had disproportionate impacts on the lower rungs of Gold Coast social orders. As Stephanie Smallwood contends, "among the likely outcomes for captives of elite status were ransom and prisoner exchange."[9] Enslaved commoners, by contrast, had very few opportunities to "redeem" loved ones or to be redeemed. Without the type of social access and protections afforded to elites, commoners could more readily become tribute slaves, unredeemed pawns, and the victims of panyarring. Likewise, the many legal measures aimed at deterring crime and maintaining the sociopolitical status quo in eighteenth-century Gold Coast states meant that judicial slavery disproportionately targeted commoners.[10] Thus, the many processes that swept up and funneled thousands toward capture, enslavement, commodification, and embarkation on European slavers were keen respecters of persons.

The new worlds encountered by commoners across the Atlantic offered new opportunities—oddly enough—for the most dispossessed to garner and take power. Part of the collective resurrection of Coromantees and (A)minas involved redefinitions of power and polity, shaped by an identifiable commoner consciousness. These redefinitions manifested themselves in many ways, across the long chronology and multiple geographies of the Gold Coast diaspora. Perhaps the most obvious and expressive were the many displays of the Gold Coast paraphernalia of power. These symbols instantly resonated with those who saw them employed in the Caribbean, South America, and North America, but it was the use of these icons in the hands of enslaved Gold Coast commoners that proved a source of inspiration.

The true brilliance, for example, of Antiguan King Court's employment of the paraphernalia of power was revealed through the many conversations between him and his lieutenants about their proper use and meaning. Those involved in the erection of the Coromantee polity in 1736 Antigua could not help but understand and embrace the image of King Court—during his coronation ceremony at Parkes' Plantation—sitting "under his canopy of state, surrounded by his great Officers." In full appreciation of the nature of the symbols that surrounded him, Court carefully prepared "badges of royalty" to be distributed among the loyal compatriots. He even devised a scheme in which his braffos and other high-ranking officials would be bequeathed plantations and lands after a successful revolution and the establishment of a decentralized Coromantee state. In the meantime, Court and his followers gave a great deal of thought to various symbols of power that would adorn the Coromantee king. The canopy, described as an "umbrella" constructed out of three-feet-long sticks, wire, and "some blew cloth and white Ozenbriggs" (or canvas), took several weeks to construct. This delay led to Court "falling out" with Emmanuel—a Portuguese-speaking slave commissioned

4.1. Man being prepared for execution with various canopies of state adorned with animal totems in the background, Asante, 1832. Source: Adams, *The Modern Voyager & Traveller*, I: front piece. Courtesy Manuscripts and Archives Division, New York Public Library, Astor, Lenox, and Tilden Foundations. Thomas E. Bowdich, *Mission from Cape Coast Castle to Ashantee* (London: Frank Cass, 1966 [1819]), between 274 and 275.

to build the all-important device. The Coromantee king insisted that a pigeon be painted on the top of the canopy—perhaps as an animal *fitiso* or totem to recognize the new Coromantee collective (see figure 4.1). Unlike the unique and otherwise fantastic or fierce beasts associated with seventeenth- and eighteenth-century animal *fitiso* in Gold Coast polities—elephants, birds of prey, bats, and leopards—Court could have found no more common an animal than a pigeon to serve as the sigil of the Antigua Coromantee state. Perhaps, then, the choice of this animal *fitiso* represents one of many manifestations of social resurrection informed by a commoner consciousness that coursed through Coromantee political movements and formations. This remade, even reborn, people were not blindly replicating symbols of political power from their natal home. With this in mind, the polities they attempted to create in the Western Hemisphere should never be described as "restorationist" since—in most cases—these visions of new diaspora states simultaneously embodied cultural continuities and decisive sociopolitical breaks.[11]

In addition to his canopy, Court displayed "a good Sabre by his Side with a red Scabbard, and appeared as King, having on a particular Cap proper to the Kings of his Country." The ornate cap was woven from green silk, embroidered with gold, with black fur and several feathers added to augment Court's regal appearance.[12] Quawcoo—an obeah doctor who played a pivotal role in the plot—showed Court "how they played with the Ikim in his Country and he had a Wooden [cutlass] to shew how they fought there . . . and blowed an Oben \i.e.\ an Elephants Tooth."[13] The *ikem*, or shield, that Court was to dance with during his coronation had a significance as both a political and martial symbol. In the course of their investigations, the various meanings of the ikem became crystal clear to the justices presiding over the 1736 Antigua conspiracy trials:

The Evidence of Witnesses and Confessions of many of the criminal *Coramantees*, make it appear to us, that it is the Custom of Africa when a *Coramantee* king has resolved upon a War with a neighbouring State, to give public Notice among his Subjects, that the *Ikem Dance* will be performed at a certain Time, and Place; and there the Prince appears in royal Habit, under an Umbrella, or Canopy of State, preceded by his Officers called *Braffo*, and his Marshal attended by his *Asseng* (or Chamberlain) and Guards, and the [Music] of his Country, with his Generals, and Chiefs about him: then he places himself upon an advanced Seat, his Generals sitting behind him upon a Bench, his Guards on each side, his *Braffo* and Marshall clearing the Circle . . . then the Drums beating the *Ikem* beat, he with an *Ikem*, i.e. (a Shield composed of Wicker-Skins, and two or three small Pieces of thin Board) upon his left Arm, and a Lance in his right hand, begins the Dance, representing the defensive Motions of the Shield, those of throwing the Lance, and the several Gestures by them used in Battle. When the Prince begins to be fatigued, the Guards run in and support him, he delivers the *Ikem* and Lance to the Person who next dances . . . the same Dance is performed by several others . . . then the Prince stepping into the Area of the Semi-circle, with his chief General, and taking a [cutlass] in his Hand, moves with a whirling Motion of his Body round about . . . then returning to the Centre of the Semi-circle with his General, makes several Flourishes with the Cutlass, gently touching with it the General's Forehead, and having at the same time the *Ikems* (the number of which is uncertain) held between his own and the other's Body, he takes an Oath (highly reverenced by the Coramantees).[14]

This oath, according to the trial justices, became a necessary step to declaring war by the "Coramantee" princes of Gold Coast polities.

Court's counterparts throughout the Gold Coast diaspora understood the meaning and use of these symbols of power. Edward Long, writing in the aftermath of the 1760 Coromantee revolt in Jamaica, mentioned a woman named Cubah who the "Coromantins of the town had raised" to the rank of royalty and named her the *"queen of Kingston."* At their secretive gatherings, Queen Cubah was known to sit "in state under a canopy, with a sort of robe on her shoulders, and a crown upon her head." The Kingston Coromantees became a cause for concern with the discovery by local authorities of an ornate wooden sword with a red feather in the hilt. According to one concerned report, this sword was used "among the Coromantins as a signal for war."[15] Another queen, the legendary Nanny of the Windward (or eastern) Jamaican Maroons, was described by a contemporary witness who may have encountered her in the 1730s as an "Obea woman" often seen in full battledress with ten knives hanging from a girdle around her waist. Captain Cuffee, one of the many leaders of Nanny Town, sported a silver-embroidered hat and a small cutlass as a means of setting himself apart from others. Both Nanny and Captain Cuffee were said to have employed the *obeng*—the Akan war horn—as a means of secret communication and to coordinate battle formations.[16]

Preceding King Court, Queen Cubah, and Nanny, King Cuffee of late seventeenth-century Barbados set the pattern that would be repeated by Coromantee royalty throughout the diaspora. Leading a group of "Cormantee or Gold Coast Negro's," Cuffee was crowned on June 12, 1675, whereupon he sat "in a Chair of State exquisitely wrought and Carved after their Mode; with Bowes and Arrowes to be likewise carried in State before his Majesty their intended King: Trumpets to be made of Elephants Teeth and Gourdes to be sounded on several Hills, to give Notice of their general Rising."[17] King Cuffee's stool—the chair carved "after their Mode"—represented an active redefinition of political power in the Gold Coast diaspora. Though no detailed descriptions exist of the means by which he became king of the Barbados Coromantee polity, we can imagine that many of the tropes and icons of Gold Coast political power were manifested during Cuffee's crowning and his elevation to a royal stool.

By appropriating the symbols of Gold Coast elites, enslaved commoners activated the ultimate social inversion associated with carnivalisque expressive play in the Black Atlantic. In this case, commoners and slaves became royalty through elaborate coronations, "plays," and processions. However, their conscious employment of a range of symbols—swords, shields, canopies, crowns, war horns, and stools of state—became the very means by which they sought to both take and redefine power. In this manner, the kind of social inversions associated with the social and political transformations of commoners into Coromantee royalty did not always function as a means of mocking elites. Speaking of nineteenth- and twentieth-century Akan mechanisms for marking the "Other" through the display of a unique iconography of power, Fritz Kramer observes that "African societies have also devised their own respective inversions and counterparts which have helped them articulate their sense of self and determine their political and ritual practices." Using inversion, Coromantees defined themselves through their appropriation of the political iconography of enemy and hostile others—in this case, the class of Atlantic African elites responsible for their enslavement and transport to the Americas. They metaphorically and literally "took" power by deploying the symbols of political elites. Donning, activating, or employing the Gold Coast paraphernalia of power were revolutionary acts that, at once, defined a newly resurrected and constituted collective, charted the rise of Coromantee and (A)mina states across the political terrain of Western Hemisphere slavery, and declared a series of wars and other destructive actions against a new set of elites—in the guise of white planters and colonial officials.[18]

The commoner consciousness that shaped Coromantee and (A)mina formations, as much as or more than a common linguistic and natal origin, manifested itself in several ways in the course of making a new political discourse in the Americas. John Thornton has theorized that former Gold Coast commoners gravitated toward "change-oriented" political concepts and structures in the making of a transnational Coromantee polity in the Americas. Among these change-oriented principles was the emphasis on the acquisition of status and title "through the possession of wealth; wealth, in turn, was the product of hard work and especially carefully managed commerce, not simply inherited or given by the state."[19] No better example of this exists than Court of the Antigua Coromantees. Though he was indeed highborn, from an influential Gold Coast family, Court's enslavement and transport at a young age effectively erased this previous status. Through dislocation and his brief, decade-long stay in the Gold Coast, Court indeed suffered social death; even fragmentary memories of his prior status would not serve him in Antigua. In the liminal space represented by New World enslavement, he had to "learn" to be(come) Coromantee and how to properly employ Gold Coast political and cultural technologies under the tutelage of community elders like Quawcoo, the old obeah doctor, and Froilus—a Coromantee carpenter.[20] In Antigua, Court's elevated rank as an adult among the enslaved was purely the result of his own efforts and talents. According to the trial justices, "His Indulgences from his Master were great, and uncommon, which gave him an Opportunity of acquiring much more Money than slaves are usually Masters of." Having, through his own devices, accumulated resources, Court chose not to hoard his "wealth" selfishly for his own purposes; instead, he shared his earnings with others by lavishing them with elaborate community dinners and plays.[21]

This egalitarian ethic shaped how Court and his followers understood their post-slave polity. While Coromantees would be at the head of the war against Antigua's white populace, they embraced both island-born creoles and "Eboes" in the planning stages—evidenced by the involvement of these groups in a number of loyalty oathing ceremonies. One enslaved man by the name of Oliver "Drank the Oath" and afterward loudly proclaimed "good blood Windward People—I am Ebo Blood and never Failed." Neither rigid ethnic hierarchies nor the use of natal origin to mark social standing played roles in how the Coromantee core in Antigua conceived of their ideal state.[22] It is the very possibility of collaborations across lines of natal origin, language, and ethnicity that pushes us beyond Thornton's analysis of the meaning of change-oriented values in the creation of a New World Coromantee nation. While Thornton emphasizes the common Gold Coast background of Coromantees in his assessment of their change-oriented principles, he does not account for their ability to incorporate creoles, other Atlantic African ethnies, and even whites in their visions of post-slave polities.[23] In the lone example of a Coromantee or (A)mina enclave shaped by "conservative" or Gold Coast elite norms, the Aminas of Danish St. John created an exclusionary oman in 1733–34 that sought to enslave Atlantic Africans who did not speak or know Akan and even went as far as to target some—including one West-Central African man—for death. With few exceptions, we can assert that a key aspect of commoner Gold Coast polities in the Americas was a greater willingness toward transethnic (and even transracial) political formations. Class and common sociopolitical backgrounds, therefore, trumped any sense of cultural nationalism and ethnic purity among the majority of Coromantee and (A)mina enclaves in the Americas.

While the Coromantees of Antigua sought to include island-born creoles and Eboes residing in the eastern portion of the island, this inclusive definition of their ethnicity and notions of a post-slave polity had parallels throughout the Western Hemisphere. The Coromantees led by Cuffee involved in the 1712 New York City revolt joined with both "Spanish Indians" and Atlantic Africans designated as "Pappa"—probably enslaved peoples originating near Popo in the Slave Coast—in their political formation.[24] Three decades later, despite being advised to only draw in their "countrymen," the Coromantee involved in the "Great Plot" in 1741 New York City sought to establish a biracial regime in which political power would be shared with disaffected whites. In the making of this polity, the Coromantee core enlisted the aid of both English- and Spanish-speaking creoles. Similar imaginings of state formations that crossed boundaries of race, ethnicity, language, and nativity could be found in colonial Louisiana, where the Mina unsuccessfully tried to incorporate Edos and Bambaras into their movement in 1791. By 1795, another Mina group in Pointe Coupee Parish formed the core of a multiethnic coalition that included creoles, Bambaras, Chambas, Congos, Ibos, and others.[25]

In addition to the issue of ethnicity and natal origin, Thornton's model also does not account for the activation of Coromantee symbols of power and the appropriation of Akan political formations and cultures. Indeed, on the surface, these actions may seem to project the kind of understanding or appreciation of royalty and polity embraced by "conservative" Gold Coast elites. I would argue however that Coromantee and (A)mina appropriations of the symbols of Gold Coast elite power were conscious and purposeful. The use of stools, canopies, crowns, and war horns served an almost ritual role as these objects became imbued with new meanings beyond their original functions. As much as flags and anthems become symbols that stir pride in nation in the modern context, the employment of Akan political iconography and paraphernalia of power became means of further crystallizing Coromantee and (A)mina identity. In the hands of former commoners in the Gold Coast diaspora, these political and martial symbols had a significance far outstripping their original uses and formed part of a new and revolutionary political discourse.

PLAYS, BALLS, AND CORONATIONS

Contemplating the dangerous combinations of Coromantees that led to a series of revolts and maroon outbreaks in Jamaica, Edward Long commented that "a particular attention should also be had to their plays, for these have always been their rendezvous for hatching plots."[26] While so-called Country Plays were by no means unique to Coromantees and (A)minas, these "great Feastings and Caballings" became central features in the formation of Gold Coast diaspora states. Country Plays, as expressions of a series of political aspirations and concepts, were far more than the externalizations of New Negro "ancestralism" as theorized by Michael Mullin. In fact, inasmuch as religion appeared in plays, it was typically relegated to the periphery. At its core, the Country Play was a political act, characterized by a series of secular rituals, serving to strengthen bonds of unity, to facilitate the planning of rebellion and war, and to become the foundation of a New World political order.[27] Through this perspective, we can better understand a range of actors and events in the Gold Coast diaspora.

When Court was "crowned King at a Play" in Antigua, uninformed white onlookers interpreted it as "an innocent play of [his] Country." Knowing that Court's industriousness had enriched him far beyond the original purchase price of an enslaved eleven-year-old, Thomas Kerby testified that Court "was incapable of any bad Design" because he was "an Elderly Distempered Fellow and had always behaved like a faithful slave and lived very well." Furthermore, the fact that Court's Country Play "was Represented before so many White People" allowed Kerby to assume that "no harm could be meant by it."[28] The dissembling and even deceptive language used to describe these events as "Plays" and their very public displays may have been akin to similar sociopolitical deployments found within Brazilian capoeira and Black Atlantic animal trickster tales. Skilled capoeristas, for example, activate a world of deception masking the lethality of this martial art. Thus, they euphemistically "play" capoeira "games" meant to deceive onlookers into a false sense of security and safety. The expressive cultural markers that surround this martial art—dance, music, and song—appear to the untrained eye and ear as more entertainment than dangerous political discourse and action. Even in the game itself, fighters often feign weakness and submission to gain a competitive or combat edge. In a similar vein, within diasporic folklore Brer Rabbit and Ananse the Spider donned masks of weakness and foolishness in masterful acts of subversion and rebellion. What seem to be innocuous folktales meant simply to entertain were keen expressions of a commoner consciousness and didactic tools fashioned to instruct the enslaved in the resistive arts of disruption, sabotage, and revolt. Both African Atlantic martial arts and animal trickster tales were consumed by white audiences and could be performed under the watchful gaze of the master class. In sum, these arts became part of a "common tongue" of the dispossessed in the Black Atlantic.[29] Plays, balls, and coronations—as political acts—can only be appreciated for their complexity and dynamism within this context.

In Antigua, court justices laid bare the designs and purposes of Country Plays during various trial confessions. In their assessment, the "chief Measures used . . . to corrupt our Slaves, were Entertainments of Dancing, Gaming, and Feasting, some of which were very expensive, always coloured by some innocent Pretence." These pretenses could include "commemorating some deceased Friend, by throwing Water on his Grave, or christening a House, or the like, according to the Negroe Customs, where they were debauch'd with Liquor, their Minds imbittered against their Masters, and against their Condition of Slavery, by strong invectives thrown out against both, and Freedom and the Possession of the Master's Estates were to be the Rewards of their Perfidy and Treachery."[30] Solidified by the ubiquitous Coromantee loyalty oath, this and other plays had mostly secular and political functions shaped by the characteristic discourse of the commoner consciousness. Even if one "pretense" for the play was to celebrate or mourn a deceased member of the slave community, the play sprang out of their collective condition in slavery and an aspiration to create a post-slave state. Indeed, a funeral served as more than a simple rationale for an inter-plantation gathering; the gravesite itself became the source of a material that shaped the one sacred dimension of Coromantee Plays, as grave dirt represented a significant component in loyalty draughts.[31]

Another example of the political dimensions of plays in the Gold Coast diaspora would be the Mina Balls in Louisiana between the 1770s and 1790s. Referred to as a "capitain" by Mina from Pointe Coupee to New Orleans and as "Coffy" by white authorities, Antonio Cofi Mina served as both leader of the Louisiana Mina and organizer of a series of balls that became a means of political consolidation. His personal background was complex and revealing. A free man by 1778, he was a shoemaker, a member of the black militia, and a Catholic. During the 1791 conspiracy trials, Cofi served as one of two official court interpreters of the Mina language—demonstrating a likely Gold or Slave Coast birth. Despite his illiteracy Cofi had mastered spoken French, as evidenced by his testimony during a 1795 court appearance in connection to an alleged involvement in the planning of a colony-wide revolt. In addition, he spoke Spanish, Louisiana creole, Catalonian, Akan, and probably some Chamba.[32] Cofi was the quintessential "Atlantic creole," with the attendant levels of linguistic and cultural dexterity necessary to escape the bonds of slavery. His cosmopolitanism and worldliness aside, Cofi defined himself as a Mina, and his political and cultural allegiances were intimately tied to this diasporic grouping in Louisiana.[33]

Since at least 1775, Cofi's Mina Balls made him one of the most recognized and influential people in the colony. Perhaps a representation of the events at a typical ball comes from the description of a festival that took place on Saturday, June 25, 1791. At this inter-plantation party, Minas congregated at the cabin of Jean-Louis—an enslaved Mina man owned by the widow Robillard. Several dozen Mina men gathered for this dance, and Jacó (or Quaco), an enslaved Mina, served as the host of the party—providing food and plenty of *aguardiente* to all present. As the host, Jacó was elected as "king" of this particular Mina Ball. Within this homosocial, all-male space, the Mina men spoke openly of waging war against the *blancos*. Caesar, an English-speaking enslaved man from Jamaica, promised to show his Mina countrymen "what the English blacks do to kill the whites"—perhaps an allusion to his own involvement in acts of violent resistance or marronage that ultimately led to his banishment to Louisiana. In support of Caesar, both Jacó and Jean-Louis talked to their Mina comrades about obtaining their freedom through rebellion. What was ostensibly a dance turned quickly into a rebel cabal, and the Minas set the night of Thursday, July 7, 1791, for the beginning of their war against their masters. Moreover, since Cofi was not mentioned in connection with this particular Mina Ball, it is likely that these gatherings were both frequent and spread across a wide geography in Louisiana. The nascent Mina polity in 1790s Louisiana was large, thoroughly organized, and equipped to communicate over vast distances at a moment's notice.[34]

Country Plays like the Mina Balls transformed over time and were superseded by other public expressions throughout the Black Atlantic. Acts of taking power through the employment of Gold Coast elite iconography and defining power through play were transformative—as a means of defining Coromantee and (A)mina political collectives in the Americas—but never static. As Coromantee and (A)mina perspectives on power and empowerment shifted over time, due to their experiences as peoples enslaved and exploited by a new set of elites, so too did the manifestations of taking and defining power. The best example of this would be the Delmina collective, which rose in rebellion and maintained an independent polity for several months in Dutch Berbice during 1763. After an initial victory by Governor Cuffy against Dutch forces in February, one report about this enclave mentioned that they "spent most of their time in revelry, debauchery and drink, dressing themselves up in the clothes which they found on plantations; over and above that, painting their faces as was their wont and imitating the planters for the rest. They had themselves rowed about in tentboats and called their wives

4.2. Representations of Jonkonnu costumes in Kingston, Jamaica, circa 1837–38. Note the European symbols of power wielded by both costumed black men—the elaborate dress and headpiece, a fan, and a whip. Source: Belisario, "Sketches of Character," in *Illustration of the Habits, Occupation, and Costume*. Courtesy of the Yale Center for British Art, Paul Mellon Collection USA/Bridgeman Images.

'madam,' sleeping in cotton hammocks fastidious in their eating and drinking."[35] The types of political and social inversions expressed in this context served both to mock European elites and to take and replicate European forms of power. The clothes, tentboats, and hammocks of the Dutch planter class, as well as their lavish consumption patterns and celebratory excesses, framed a new iconography of power for the short-lived Delmina polity. Moreover, this type of expressive inversion may have transformed into even newer modes by the late eighteenth and early nineteenth century.

Masquerades, processions, and seasonal celebrations—Mardi Gras (New Orleans), Carnival (Brazil, Trinidad and Tobago, Antigua, and St. John), Pinkster (New York), Jonkonnu (Jamaica and the Bahamas), and Big Drum (Curaçao)—may have resulted from the coming together of many separate Country Plays and the appropriation of European symbols of power (see figure 4.2). As part of a continued ethnogenesis and social resurrection, (A)minas, Congos, Bambaras, Nagos, and Eboes combined together in these spaces, engaged in competitive country dances, crowned kings and queens, and either mocked or actively contested white power. In this regard, the merging together of Country Plays within the street festivals of the circum-Caribbean and beyond may have been one of many ways that Atlantic Africans exchanged their country marks in the political and revolutionary act of becoming one people.[36]

POLITY, POWER, AND CONSCIOUSNESS

By definition, polities established by enslaved Gold Coast Africans who embraced a change-oriented ethos were more egalitarian, democratic, and nonhierarchical than, say, the 1733–34 Amina oman in Danish St. John. As a shaping influence, the commoner consciousness reflected the social and political backgrounds of the enslaved and their agency in the context of Atlantic World plantation societies. Indeed, marronage and the birth of new polities serve as prime examples of the attempt by enslaved Gold Coast Africans to recreate a portion of their Atlantic African backgrounds in the Americas. Importantly, the argument forwarded here is that neither the presence nor the structure of Gold Coast diaspora polities in the Western Hemisphere represent simple carryovers from Atlantic Africa. As much as they relied on familiar cultural technologies from their natal homes, Coromantees and (A)minas redefined a range of political and social concepts that in no way represent "continuities" or connections to their prior experiences. The true genius of their diasporic political and social reformulations was in the radical—even revolutionary—breaks from the sociopolitical realities of the seventeenth- and eighteenth-century Gold Coast. The formation of maroon states, therefore, opens useful windows into the inner social and political worlds that were characteristic parts of these inventive processes.

While maroon states in Jamaica and Suriname cannot be constructed as purely Akan-speaking, Gold Coast diaspora enclaves, historicizing some of the better-known ones reveal patterns linked to attempts to establish polities by Coromantees and (A)minas throughout the long eighteenth century. Rarely did such states come into immediate existence after a single outbreak; instead, their birth and growth came in fits and starts—often involving several different revolts and mass escapes and the eventual merging together of several groups, over time, into one. Writing in 1687, John Taylor of Jamaica noted that enslaved peoples had "severall times revolted from theire masters, rize in open rebellion, and done much mischeife, betakeing themselves to the woods and mountains" to form communities and settlements of their own.[37] More than two hundred enslaved people, mostly Coromantees, killed their owner and twelve other whites on Major Lobly's plantation in 1673 Jamaica. After securing a cache of arms and successfully repulsing a small detachment sent to recapture them, this group established a settlement in the western mountains between Clarendon, St. Elizabeth, and St. Ann's parishes. Jamaican planters in the Vere Plain of Clarendon Parish witnessed a mass conspiracy in mid-June 1683 in which 180 enslaved people on the plantation of Colonel Ivey, "most of 'em Carrammantine Negroas," elected their own king, queen, and a war captain. After the administration of a Coromantee loyalty oath, the conspirators vowed to eradicate all whites in Clarendon and beyond—until their plan was betrayed to local authorities just three days before "they were to putt this damnable disigne in practice." One of the captured conspirators conducted himself in typical Coromantee fashion during his execution: "He threw himself on his face into the midst of the fier, and never stir'd nor groan'd, but died patiently with the greates resolution imaginable."[38]

In July 1685, about 150 bondspeople simultaneously rose on several plantations in St. Catherine's Parish near Guanaboa Vale and escaped to establish a settlement in nearby mountains. Under the leadership of a Coromantee named Cuffee, the Guanaboa Maroons defeated a force of seventy soldiers and, by December 1685, they initiated a scorched earth campaign against local planters lasting another six months—setting fire to houses, cane fields, and sugar mills along a sizable swath of the parish.[39] Then, on July 29, 1690, Clarendon Parish experienced another disturbance, this time in the form of a mass revolt involving four to five hundred enslaved men and women on the Sutton plantation. After killing a white overseer and setting plantation buildings on fire, this group ransacked the stores and escaped with four cannons, dozens of firearms, and enough shot and powder to supply a small army. The Earl of Inchiquin noted the particular danger that local plantation owners were in, especially those residing in the nearby mountains, given "the great number of negroes (most of them Coramanteens), the arms, great quantity of powder and other provisions they seiz'd, with the great want of white men here." After repulsing a number of attempts to destroy their enclave, the Clarendon Coromantees established a political formation with a man named Cudjo at the head, his two real or fictive brothers—Accompong and Johnny—as the generals, and Coffy and Quaw as captains.[40]

Within a few years this Clarendon Parish group merged with the Coromantees who rebelled and left en masse from Major Lobly's plantation in 1673—an older, more firmly established maroon state residing then in Jamaica's Cockpit Country—becoming the nucleus of Jamaica's west-central or Leeward Maroons. The fact that Cudjo commanded the Leewards for about thirty years, from 1730 to the 1760s, has led one scholar to claim that this polity "established an autocratic polity cemented by kinship in the style of Asante."[41] Nothing could be further from the truth. Cudjo's long standing command of the Leewards has to be placed in context. Given the length of his reign and the claims made in contemporary records of Cudjo's involvement in the 1690 Clarendon Parish outbreak, it is entirely likely that "Cudjo" might have referred to multiple people who served as head of the Leewards. Otherwise, if the same man who led the Clarendon Coromantees also commanded the Leeward Maroons, Cudjo would have lived well into his nineties. In addition, few Asantehene would have allowed for the division of their supreme and divinely sanctioned power among a series of subcommanders, captains, and lieutenants—some of whom led their own autonomous towns and maroon enclaves. Without knowing more about the internal structure of their political formation, any statement about the autocratic and centralized structure of the Leeward Maroons is little more than interpretive speculation. Specifically, aspects of their social practices, political structures, and war aims point toward a more egalitarian and revolutionary state during their early formation.[42]

Until the Leeward Maroons formed a mature state, they externalized commoner consciousness in a number of ways. In sharp contrast with the Amina oman in Danish St. John, the Leeward Maroons sought to destroy or disrupt the local plantation economy and its associated infrastructure. The continual guerilla war they fought against the colonial establishment until 1739 had a disastrous effect on central and western Jamaica. At a cost of an estimated £240,000, the Assembly of Jamaica passed some forty-four separate acts of legislation and supported the creation of two regiments to suppress Cudjo's Leeward Maroons. Until 1738, Cudjo's aim was clearly continued social revolution. According to Bryan Edwards—an eighteenth-century Jamaican sugar planter and historical recorder of the first Maroon War—the "dastardly method of conducting the war" on the part of the Leewards included nighttime raids in which they used stealth to enter "the settlements, where they set fire to canefields and out-houses, killed all the cattle they could find, and carried the slaves into captivity." The Leewards did not envision themselves as the eventual masters of the sugar plantations nor as participants in the Atlantic World economy. Indeed, the actions of the Leewards and their predecessors from the 1680s through the 1730s "caused several plantations to be thrown up and abandoned, and prevented many valuable tracts of land from being cultivated" in and around the western and central parishes of Clarendon, St. Ann, St. Elizabeth, Westmoreland, Hanover, and St. James.[43]

Unlike their Amina counterparts in Danish St. John, who initially sought to maintain cane fields and sugar mills and to use non-Akan speakers as a dependent and enslaved labor force, the Leewards developed a social and political vision in which only the complete destruction of the plantation economy and an end to enslavement would suffice. As a direct result of this vision, the Leewards were also willing to accept and adopt non-Akan speakers as part of their collective. As mentioned in the previous chapter, the Leewards amalgamated with a group identified as being "Madagascars"—though Coromantee language, identity, and culture would continue to be rallying principles. Ethnic or linguistic difference would not become markers of inferiority for the Leewards; they embraced a broad spectrum of African peoples as part of their collective.[44] The vision of a New World political order as articulated and activated by former Atlantic African commoners had much more in common with the social revolutionaries in French Saint-Domingue who reduced to ash eight thousand sugar and coffee plantations and the richest plantation economy in the world. While Haitian leaders, especially island-born creoles like Toussaint Louverture and Jean-Jacques Dessalines, had more ambiguous relationships with slavery and plantation labor regimes, it would be the so-called Congos at the core of the movement that best represented the possibilities of commoner consciousness and social revolution.[45] The Leeward Maroons spoke the common tongue of social revolution, shared a political consciousness, and employed a similar range of cultural technologies as other former commoners and their creole descendants in the Americas.

Joining the Leeward Maroons in Jamaica were the various enclaves in the eastern portion of the island—known collectively over time as the Windward Maroons. Sourced originally by enslaved runaways owned by Spanish planters in the period before 1655, the Windwards lived in the Blue and John Crow Mountains and multiplied in the period between the 1670s and the 1730s due to successive waves of immigrant escapees who joined them. As one observer noted, the descendants of "Spanish Negros" formed a nucleus and "after many disputes and Battles with some other Gangs, incorporated and settled together in the Mountains near Port Antonio, where They made a considerable settlement, which They called Nanny Town."[46] By the 1720s the Windwards operated mainly out of Nanny Town, though the settlement itself may have been subdivided into three quarters, each named after a powerful woman—Nanny, Diana, and Molly. Just a few miles from Nanny Town stood a secondary Windward settlement known as Guy's or Gay's Town.[47] Like the Leeward Maroons, the Windwards had a decentralized structure that included a number of "captains" associated with separate towns or quarters within larger towns. Given the heterogeneous cultural and linguistic mix of peoples who helped found and maintain the Windward polity, it is notable that some of the more prominent Windward captains were Coromantees—Cuffee, Quao, Cudjoe, and Quashee (Kishee).[48] Indeed, glimpses of Windward culture gleaned from extant records—namely the presence of obeah, the effective use of the *abeng* or war horn, and even the language spoken by the Windwards—point to a Coromantee cultural provenance for this enclave.[49]

While the Leewards wreaked havoc on the western parishes in the period between the 1680s and 1730s, the Windwards joined in the carnage by the mid- to late 1680s. Plaguing the settlers and planters in northeastern Jamaica, the actions of the Windwards moved Lieutenant-Governor Hender Molesworth to request aid from the Assembly of Jamaica against their raiding parties. Having made "themselves plantations in the mountains from which they descend into the plains in great numbers for provision," the Windwards, Molesworth added, made so "much mischief" that costly military assets were deployed and kept constantly vigilant in the parishes of St. Mary, St. George, and St. Thomas. He concluded that without additional resources and the enforcement of martial law, "those of St. George's, unless relieved, are prepared to desert their settlements" due to the many "outlying and rebellious negroes."[50] This campaign by the Windwards picked up momentum as their numbers continued to swell, reaching an apex by 1702. In August of that year, Lieutenant-Governor Peter Beckford reported that the maroons "have been so bold as to come down armed and attack our settlements to Windward, and have destroyed one or two, which if not prevented would prove of fatal consequence and endanger the Island." A month later, his forces, led by Captain John King, confronted a party of three hundred Windwards lodged in a well-provisioned town hidden in the mountains. In his assessment, "they have been a great body for these ten years last past"; he hoped that the destruction of this settlement would forever pacify the Windward Maroons.[51]

By 1729, Quao—the commander of the Nanny Town Maroons—joined Cudjo and the Leewards in a decade-long struggle against British colonial rule and the plantation economy in Jamaica. The ensuing First Maroon War (1729–1739) ended with a series of treaties that represented a significant shift in the political consciousness of both maroon polities. From at least the 1680s to the 1730s, the Leewards and the Windwards were caught in existential struggles against the colonial masters of Jamaica. Their proximity to enslavement and their continuing and intermittent wars with the English colonial government created a frame within which their commoner consciousness could be fully articulated. As mature states, existing for six decades by the end of the First Maroon Wars, the Leewards and Windwards found peace, stability, and security appealing and, from that perspective, made concessions that demonstrated their transformation from revolutionary enclaves to polities principally concerned with continued survival.[52]

On March 1, 1738, the Leewards's Cudjo signed a fifteen-article peace treaty with Colonel John Guthrie on behalf of the newly appointed Governor of Jamaica, Edward Trelawny—from whom the main post-treaty Leeward settlement town would derive its new name (see figure 4.3). In exchange for the uncontested ownership of all the lands they settled and claimed—roughly 1,500 total acres—and the recognition of their freedom from bondage, Cudjo agreed to cease all hostilities and to allow any fugitives who wished to return to their owners to do so. The Articles of Pacification also stipulated how the newly-constituted "Maroons of Trelawny Town" would use their land. In Article 4, the treaty states "they shall have liberty to plant the said lands with coffee, cocoa, ginger, tobacco, and cotton" and to breed a range of livestock; but apparently Cudjo and the Leewards had no interest in supporting or participating in the sugar industry. They would also not own or employ enslaved peoples, nor would they work for whites without a written agreement spelling out compensation. In an act that completely subverted the Leeward Maroon polity as a revolutionary enclave, Cudjo also agreed to assist the colonial government against any foreign invasion, to "take, kill, suppress, or destroy" enslaved rebels, and to return all future slave fugitives back to their owners.[53]

Four years after signing the Articles of Pacification, Cudjo's pledge to assist in suppressing slave revolts was put to the test when a group of newly imported Coromantees on the plantation of a Colonel Forster near St. James Parish conspired to rebel, "to cut off all those there that were born in the woods, or came from other countries," and to kill all whites on neighboring plantations. Assuming they would receive assistance from local Coromantee maroons given their apparent linguistic and cultural ties, the St. James Parish Coromantees perhaps were surprised when the stiffest resistance they met came in the form of "Colonel" Cudjo and captains Accompong, Johnny, Cuffee, Quaco, and Quao of Trelawny Town. Some of the rebels were killed, while others were captured and returned to their plantations by the regiment of armed maroons. Cudjo went as far as to execute a handful of his own Coromantee maroons who conspired with the St. James Parish rebels. In exchange for services rendered to the crown, Colonel Cudjo, his captains, and the towns of Trelawny and Accompong received several cows, an annual al-

4.3. Colonel John Guthrie and the Leewards's Cudjo before the March 1, 1738, peace agreement. Source: Dallas, *History of the Maroons* 1: facing title page. Courtesy of the Manuscripts, Archives, and Rare Books Division, Schomburg Center for Research in Black Culture, New York Public Library, Astor, Lenox, and Tilden Foundations.

lowance of clothes, and the freedom of one Molly—a girl "nearly related to colonel Cudjoe."[54] By helping crush this burgeoning rebel movement, Cudjo and the Trelawny Town Maroons signaled their transformation from social revolutionaries into instruments of social control.

On July 23, 1739, Quao of the Windward Maroons signed a similar treaty with British colonial forces—in effect ending the First Maroon War. In exchange for recognition of their partial sovereignty, the Windwards agreed to cease their aggressions and to actively assist the colonial regime against rebel and runway enslaved peoples. They also located their new settlements in two new towns—Moore Town and Charles Town. Ratified by the Assembly of Jamaica in early 1740, Quao's treaty mirrored Cudjo's in a number of ways.[55] While both can be seen as acts that subjugated and transformed sovereign polities into military and political extensions of the colonial regime, this construction tends to erode the many and complicated layers of human agency that frame these agreements. After sixty years of existence, both the Windward and Leeward Maroon enclaves had become mature polities that developed new guiding principles—based in self-interest and survival—far removed from the commoner consciousness that undergirded their rise and that sustained them beginning in the 1680s. The agreements signed and consecrated by Quao and Cudjo represented the actions of war-weary states and statesmen who sued for peace as assurance of their continued existence. Like cultures and peoples, polities—even ones that began as revolutionary states—do not remain static; the consciousness that gave birth to the Trelawny Town and Accompong Town Leewards and the Moore Town and Charles Town Windwards proved the continual movement, circulations, and motion in the Gold Coast diaspora.

Though the two principal Jamaican Maroon polities transitioned into agents of colonial repression, the spirit of social revolution and commoner consciousness did not die. Tackey's 1760 revolt represents one of the best articulations of polity and war in Jamaica, as shaped by the Gold Coast diaspora commoner consciousness, in the period between the First and Second Maroon Wars. With Tackey as leader, this articulation of commoner consciousness was not complete, however. Jamaica's Tackey shared a number of traits with his Antiguan Coromantee counterpart and namesake. Claimed to be a "Koromantyn" and a "chief in

Guiney," Jamaica's Tackey may have been a former Ga-speaking royal originally from Accra. Unlike Antigua's Tackey—who arrived in the Americas at a young age—the Tackey heading the Jamaican Coromantees in 1760 was likely an adult with full memory of his former status and rank. This may have blunted some of the edge of the social revolution he led.[56] Set to start in St. Mary's Parish because, as Long states, "it abounded with their countrymen," the planned revolt was to be an island-wide affair. After a successful revolution, the post-slavery polity imagined by Tackey and others would be devoid of whites—who were slated for complete extirpation. In a revealing twist, the Coromantees allegedly planned on "the enslaving of all such Negroes as might refuse to join them." While little corroboration for this idea can be found in other extant records, perhaps Tackey's royal lineage and his fresh memories of having retainers and slaves and subjugating a range of others in the Gold Coast allowed for this Coromantee polity to embrace the continuation of human bondage.[57]

After the death of all whites and the enslavement of noncompliant blacks, the Coromantees planned to divide Jamaica "into small principalities in the African mode; to be distributed among their leaders and head men."[58] The division of power into such small increments was not necessarily in the "African mode" as represented by many eighteenth-century Gold Coast polities, where, with the notable exception of the coastal coalition of Fante states, centralized political authority and hereditary elites held sway.[59] Indeed, the "polity" they sought to establish would not be one sovereign entity but rather a series of independent provinces bound together by political alliances reflecting their adoption of a non-elite worldview. Moreover, the clearest manifestation of the commoner consciousness in this movement was the actual commencement of their war against the slaveocracy. The outbreak began on Easter Day, April 7, 1760, when scores of rebels from the Trinity, Frontier, and Heywood Hall plantations shouted the "Koromantyn yell of war," attacked Port Maria, and seized forty muskets and four barrels of gunpowder. As a critical part of their "bloody business," the Coromantees under Tackey's lead torched cane fields, sugar mills, and plantation buildings at Heywood Hall and ransacked neighboring Esher plantation—where they killed the overseer. With fire and blood, Tackey's Coromantees—if not Tackey himself—sought to clear the slate, making the world anew, devoid of the physical mechanisms of Atlantic commerce and labor exploitation. Sugar was as much their enemy as white colonial authorities, and the Coromantees were determined to destroy the economic structures that resulted in their enslavement and shipment to Jamaica.[60]

The 1760s represented a reignition of the spirit of revolt in the Dutch colonies in the Americas, and the South American colony of Berbice was no exception. Led initially by Governor or Captain Cuffy, the Delminas of Berbice rose in rebellion on February 27, 1763. With a strong and determined Delmina core, the polity that this group sought to establish would be a diverse, multiethnic, and even multiracial construct including creoles, enslaved West-Central Africans (Angolans), mutinied mercenaries from Suriname, and a group known as the Guangos.[61] Though reportedly born in Atlantic Africa, Cuffy was highly acculturated, having been transported to Berbice at a very young age. On the Lelienburg plantation he became a house servant before being trained as a cooper. Even his mode of operation, as head of the Delmina cabal, demonstrated an affinity for—or at least a facility with—Dutch culture. In attempting to negotiate a treaty with the Governor of Berbice, Wolfert Simon Van Hoogenheim, Cuffy sent letters written by a series of "secretaries" in perfect Dutch. Before his death by suicide, Cuffy had created a decentralized command structure in which he served as governor and several subordinates were appointed as captains, including Accara and Atta "and other negroes as officers to serve under them." Like so many other attempts at social revolution by Coromantees and (A)minas, the Delminas of Berbice spread devastation in their wake, particularly targeting cane fields and the associated apparatus of sugar production. According to one report, "the rebels had already spread themselves over all the plantations above [Fort Nassau] and everywhere had been playing sad havoc in a terrible manner, destroying and devastating everything by fire." Though the attempt to create a Delmina polity ultimately failed, the actions of Cuffy, Accara, Atta and others proved the continuation of the commoner consciousness and a social and political life that existed beyond social death.[62]

The concessions and agreements made by Jamaican Maroon polities in the 1730s were representative of phenomena across the Western

Hemisphere. No better example of this exists than the September 19, 1762, treaty signed by the Saramaka Maroons in Dutch Suriname. Like other maroon polities, the Saramaka community developed in fits and starts, aggregating slowly over time as the result of revolts and waves of runaways. When the region was under the sway of the English, settlers and planters witnessed a series of raids between 1667 and 1680 by a group of maroons under the leadership of a Coromantee named Jermes. Having established a fortified settlement in the Para region, this group became the first of many maroon enclaves in Suriname.[63]

By 1702, the number of fugitives living in the Para region was estimated to be between five and six thousand. These numbers continued to swell in ensuing decades. In 1738, "Coromantins" on the Pereyra Plantation in Sarua rose in mass, killed their Jewish owner, and temporarily escaped into the nearby wilderness before forty-seven were taken prisoner by two groups of citizen volunteers. By the early decades of the eighteenth century, two maroon polities—Saramaka and Ndjuka—had made the colony a "theater of perpetual war" and had become everpresent threats to sugar planters and a colonial economy that had shifted to Dutch control. An abortive military expedition sent against the Saramaka Maroons in 1749 forced the Dutch to attempt a diplomatic solution in the form of the 1762 "Treaty with the Bush Negroes of Upper Saramacca and Suriname."[64]

Contained within the fifteen articles of this treaty was a familiar blueprint. Though the Saramaka represented a multiethnic construction, at their core were a number of Coromantees and others with Akan day-names, including Coffy, Quakoe Eija, Quakoe Quamina, and Cojo. Consecrated by an oath "in their manner," this treaty stipulated the end of all hostilities and recognized the Saramaka as free persons with full rights to the lands they inhabited. In exchange for recognizing the sovereignty of their polity, the Saramaka agreed to "return without exception all slaves who have deserted to them since the peace negotiations" and "in case of mutiny by slaves or of foreign enemies, they shall immediately give all assistance."[65] Like the Leewards and Windwards of Jamaica, the Saramaka made a counterrevolutionary turn in their quest to maintain a sovereign state. These acts of accommodation, in which rebellious enclaves shaped by a Black Atlantic commoner consciousness

4.4. An armed Coromantyn ranger or maroon hunter in Suriname, 1770s.
Source: Stedman, *Narrative, of a Five Years' Expedition* 2: opposite 87. Courtesy
of the Manuscripts, Archives, and Rare Books Division, Schomburg Center for
Research in Black Culture, New York Public Library, Astor, Lenox, and Tilden
Foundations.

shifted into accomplices of colonial enterprises, marked a new political terrain in the complicated and fluid worlds inhabited by peoples in the Gold Coast diaspora.

Maroon polities in Jamaica and Suriname serve as political middle grounds between the Aminas of Danish St. John and the many other Coromantees and (A)minas who participated in attempts at social revolution. Representing many of the values of Gold Coast elites, the St. John Aminas sought to maintain cane fields, sugar mills, and sugar production with the plan to employ non–Gold Coast Africans as a dependent and enslaved labor force. Theirs was the only movement in the history of slave resistance in the Americas that can be defined as restorationist. The former royals and elites who comprised the St. John Amina collective sought to restore a lost polity—complete with its rigid hierarchies and corporatist social structures. Their version of social resurrection was more akin to the social and political lives they left behind in the Gold Coast.

On the other hand, the many Gold Coast diaspora social revolutionaries influenced by commoner consciousness—including maroon polities during their earlier phases—literally burned the apparatuses of labor exploitation and enslavement. Their social and political vision can be measured by the hundreds of acres of cane field and dozens of sugar mills and plantations turned to ashes in their wake. In addition, these social revolutionaries sought to avoid direct involvements in Atlantic commerce and embraced the elusive goals of abolition and liberty for all (or most). They imagined decentralized and inclusive post-slave polities that were multiethnic, even multiracial in specific cases. In short, their ideal post-slave states and political formations differed significantly from eighteenth-century Gold Coast polities.

Between these two radically different political poles, mature maroon polities signed treaties that established their territorial base and political sovereignty while fully recognizing the legitimacy of slavery. In making these concessions, maroon polities and their leaders became more than just accomplices of colonial slaveocracies; they actively and forcibly put down slave rebellions and plots or returned runaways to their owners. Even so, maroon polities avoided cultivating cash crops for Atlantic commerce and, for the most part, prohibited slavery within their boundaries. The long and ambiguous history of Jamaica's maroon polities demonstrates, in part, the ability of those who achieved the goals of freedom and sovereignty to suppress the spirit of social revolution and commoner consciousness for the sake of their own survival. These enclaves and their inhabitants swiveled constantly between resistance, accommodation, and counterrevolution. Even within this broad and ambivalent range of possibility, commoner consciousness and change-oriented principles factored into the political agency of many Gold Coast Africans and their American-born descendants.

FIVE

Obeah, Oaths, and Ancestral Spirits

Among their other superstitions also, must not be omitted their
mode of administering an oath of secrecy or purgation.—Human
blood, and earth taken from the grave of some near relation,
are mixed with water, and given to the party to be sworn.

BRYAN EDWARDS, *THE HISTORY, CIVIL AND COMMERCIAL,*
OF THE BRITISH COLONIES IN THE WEST INDIES (1783)

The dead, and communication with the dead, play traditionally
a large part in Atlantic religions. Wherever West African beliefs
have survived in the New World, this place of the dead has been
maintained. . . . the power of the dead to help or harm is common
tenant even among those who have discarded hoodoo.

ZORA NEALE HURSTON, "HOODOO IN AMERICA" (1931)

Like his Antigua Coromantee comrade Billy, Sam Hector found himself a member of multiple Gold Coast diasporic enclaves in his Black
Atlantic sojourn. Listed as "Byam's Quaw" in a 1736 inventory of captured insurgents slated for transport from Antigua, Sam Hector was
banished to the Danish Virgin Islands in April 1737. Upon arrival, he
became the "property" of Pieter Heyliger of St. Croix—where he resided
and toiled until his execution in 1759. In the course of the intervening
decades, he transformed himself from Coromantee traitor to Amina

commander—even in the ironic and simultaneous process of becoming an acculturated Atlantic creole. In this movement across geographic spaces and between political and cultural poles, Sam Hector witnessed and personally activated a range of spiritual technologies that proved powerful inducements in the rebellious designs of Coromantees and (A)minas in the circum-Caribbean and beyond.[1]

As a young man of about eighteen years, Sam Hector, then known as Quaw, turned king's witness, providing evidence against Court's Antigua Coromantees and his own father, "Old Cormante" Tom (Byam). During his December 10, 1736, trial, Quaw confessed his guilt and from then on was "made use of as a Witness by the Present Justices" in giving details about the plot and implicating a range of co-conspirators. Despite claims made later by court justices in Danish St. Croix, Quaw's confession to the Antigua court did not lead directly to his father's arrest and execution. Coromantee Tom took flight shortly after the revelation of the plot to local authorities in Antigua and, despite a series of rewards offered for his capture, he successfully eluded the dragnet through at least early 1737. Indeed, no extant records point to his capture or death. According to court officials, Tom "had great Influence over the slaves" and had a number of Coromantees who claimed to be under his command. As a result, his disappearance created a great deal of concern given the fears and real possibilities of Tom's involvement in a local maroon community or another planned uprising against the Antigua slaveocracy.[2] Moreover, Tom's "great Influence" meant that his son, Quaw, had first-hand knowledge of the inner workings of, and motivations for, the 1736 conspiracy.

In addition to being Tom's son, Quaw's understanding of the Coromantee language—an amalgam of Akan, Ga, and Adanme—granted him access to and insights about the plot that very few had. In his testimony against Johnno (Warner), Quaw described a planning feast organized by Secundi at Ned William's plantation at which Tomboy—the island-born co-leader of the 1736 Antigua plot—"Drank to Johnno in Wine that Looked Muddy" due to the fact that "the Oath Ingredients were in it." This was the so-called "Damnation Oath" that Coromantee, Eboe, and island-born creole alike used as a binding and supposedly inviolable pact to protect the secrecy of the plan and to carry through with their war against their white masters. The oathing ingredients, carried later in a vial by Johnno after his initiation into the rebel cabal, contained a range of substances believed to have sufficient spiritual force to kill, damn, or confuse those who broke their vows. As Quaw clarified later in the trial against his namesake, Quao (Oliver), the oath drink that Johnno and many others took on the night of the feast contained "Rum, with Grave Dirt in it"—a fact he could recall because he understood the discussions surrounding the oath between several men who spoke of it in Coromantee. For this particular feast, Johnno and Secundi "went Down to a Silk Cotton Tree to the Grave of Secundo's Sister Cicile and talked at the Grave, about a Quarter of an hour, then they returned to Secundo's house, Secundo bringing up some of the grave Dirt in his hand; he put some of it in a Glass, and then poured Rum on it out of a Bottle and Drank the Damnation Oath to Johnno."[3] Evoking a Coromantee ancestor—in this case Secundi's sister—and securing dirt from her grave site for use in an oath drink were key aspects of the secrecy contracts forged between the Antigua conspirators in 1736. Quaw's intimate knowledge of the damnation oath and the ingredients of the oath draught—facilitated by his command of the Coromantee language—became critical for him later during his time in Danish St. Croix.

Quaw also bore witness to the powerful role of obeah as inspirational tool and spiritual technology in the Antigua plot. He likely knew (Governor William Mathew's) Caesar and Coromantee Quawcoo—obeah-men King Court personally enlisted into the movement. Indeed, Quawcoo orchestrated an elaborate ceremony in honor of Secundi in the weeks following betrayal of the plot and the executions of the conspiracy's two principal leaders—King Court and Tomboy. Quaw may have been one of the participants who witnessed this loyalty oath ceremony in which the rebels appointed Secundi as their new commander. In his trial testimony (Colonel Frye's) Quamina reveals,

> I saw this Obey Man at Secundi's House after I waked at Midnight, I found him and Hunts Cuffee there. Secundi gave him a [coin], a Bottle of Rum and a Dominique Cock and Quawcoo put Obey made of Sheeps Skin upon the ground, upon and about the bottle of Rum, and the [chicken] upon the bottle, Then took the Cock, cut open his Mouth, and one of his Toes, and so poured the Cocks blood Over all the Obey, and then Rub'd

Secundi's forehead with the Cocks bloody Toe, Then took the Bottle and poured Some Rum upon the Obey, Drank a Dram, and gave it to Secundi and made Secundi Sware not to Discover his Name. Secundi Pledged him and Swore not to Discover his name to anybody. Secundi then Asked him when he must begin to Rise. Quawcoo took a String ty'd knots in it, and told him not to be in a hurry, for that he would give him Notice when to Rise and all Should go well and that as he tyed those knots so the Bacararas should become Arrant fools and have their Mouths Stoped, and their hands tyed that they should not Discover the Negro's Designs.[4]

As diviner, oracle, and military advisor to Secundi, Coromantee Quawcoo played a familiar set of roles for those living in Gold Coast diaspora communities. His example would not be forgotten by Quaw during his banishment to Danish St. Croix.

In the time between his exile from British Antigua to becoming the "drive wheel" of the 1759 Amina plot in the Danish Virgin Islands, Quaw—now Sam Hector—went through a series of radical transformations. According to various descriptions of him, Sam Hector "had a good deal of native ability, could both read and write, [had] 'higher sentiments' than are ordinarily found in a Negro, and an ambition that led him—as he has himself said and other Negroes in the plot have testified—to be ashamed to associate with others of his own color." Furthermore, he may have been a practicing Christian by the time of the Amina plot, and the apparent rejection of his Akan day-name by 1759 points toward a decided move away from connections to Gold Coast cultural geographies. Despite the assumed distance he may have had from the enslaved masses and his own Gold Coast past, Sam Hector grew into a natural leader and "was to have the direction and supreme command (during) the time of the rebellion." After the war was over and the St. Croix Amina polity established, Sam Hector would share power over the island with Prince Quakoe and a free black creole named William Davis.[5]

Sam Hector's past as someone who "was always practiced in the art" of rebellion made him particularly formidable to Danish colonial authorities. His memory and activation of the Coromantee and (A)mina resistive arts in St. Croix meant a life beyond his supposed social death—Sam Hector's Atlantic journey was punctuated, as it were, by more than one social resurrection. Like the Coromantees of Antigua, the St. Croix

Aminas used an elaborate oathing ceremony as the basis for their conspiracy. Described in detail by Prince Quakoe in his trial confession, the loyalty oath began when conspirators cut their own fingers and then "mixed the blood with earth and water, and drank it with the assurance that they would not confess to the conspiracy no matter what pain they were subjected to." Later, William Davis's wife explained to court officials that the earth used for the oath drink had special properties, as "the most binding oath that a Negro could take, was when he took earth from a dead Negro's grave, mixed it with water, and drank it."[6]

While the activation of the "Damnation Oath," including the use of grave dirt, bound the Amina conspirators to their Gold Coast and diasporic ancestors, perhaps it was their faith in transplanted spiritual notions that allowed them to lay violent hands on themselves when the plans were revealed to local authorities. After one of the principal leaders, the creole William Davis, was taken by authorities and examined on December 12, 1759, he violated the terms of the oath he had made by divulging details about the plot and the names of fellow conspirators. By the next morning he had slashed his own throat, despite the fact that his hands had been securely bound. Officials at the fort where William was held found him in time to staunch the bleeding and dress his wound. As a principal in the rebel plan, they wanted him to reveal as much as possible about the plot before his banishment or execution. By the following night, however, William tore through his bandages, once again ripping open the gaping wound in his neck. On the morning of December 14, authorities discovered his lifeless body in a pool of blood. His suicide may have been testament to his faith in the Amina expression—summarized by a former governor of the Danish West Indies—"When I die, I shall return to my own land." Links between suicide and transmigration became ubiquitous features in the resistive arts mastered by so many in the Gold Coast diaspora. However, as an island-born creole, William's "own land" was St. Croix, not a particular locale in Atlantic Africa. In his case, and perhaps others throughout the Americas, suicide held the potential of transforming him into an ancestral spirit to be activated by the living in their designs against colonial regimes and slaveholders. Perhaps Sam Hector contemplated similar thoughts of spiritual ascension. After being convicted of criminal conspiracy, he was sentenced to a slow death by gibbeting. Placed in an iron cage, elevated several feet off the ground, and denied water and food, Sam Hector lingered on death's edge for forty-two hours. It may have been thoughts of a triumphant return to his Gold Coast home or his impending transformation into a wrathful ancestral spirit in St. Croix that provided him with some measure of comfort as he awaited passage from this world to the next.[7]

Across the various spaces in which he found himself, Sam Hector (or Quaw) personally witnessed or activated the compelling power of obeah, blood oaths, and transmigration. As spiritual technologies and weapons in the Coromantee and (A)mina arsenal, they each represented a different aspect of the commoner consciousness that shaped so much of the Gold Coast diaspora. I argue that obeah was the quintessential marker of this consciousness in the Gold Coast as its Akan-speaking cognate form, bayi, did not have state sanction and was defined by the elites of many polities as anti-social and anti-state witchcraft. As a potentially dangerous and empowering concept, bayi was actively repressed and its practitioners became the targets of a range of state-sanctioned reprisals. In this sense, bayi and its diasporic expression, obeah (or *abroykire* bayi), were the natural purview of subordinated peoples on both sides of the Black Atlantic. Indeed, the very fact that obeah may have developed out of a generative fusion between Akan bayi, Igbo *dibia*, and other Atlantic African belief systems implies that like other spiritual and expressive forms in the Black Atlantic, this esoteric practice and resistive art formed a critical part of the "common tongue" spoken by the enslaved and dispossessed in the Western Hemisphere. Similar to Vodun, capoeira, plays, and animal trickster tales, obeah allowed for the expression of discontent that transcended ethnic and linguistic boundaries and helped facilitate social revolution in the Americas.

Blood oaths, on the other hand, functioned as critical mechanisms of Gold Coast polities in the form of inviolable military and political pacts with ancestral spirits, state oracles, or deities. Their appropriation and invocation by enslaved commoners throughout the Gold Coast diaspora exemplify new sociopolitical formations and visions. Given the associations and links between play, coronations, and loyalty oaths, the activation of these concepts in the same or overlapping spaces reinforces the notion that they were part of the process of taking or defining political power by former peasants and commoners. While the form of the blood oath mirrors similar binding contracts in Gold Coast polities, at least one unique Western Hemisphere addition (e.g., grave dirt) implies that Coromantees and (A)minas reformulated and redefined the meanings and metaphors associated with loyalty oaths. Grave dirt as a diasporic trope for the continuing role and power of the ancestors within the earthly (and diasporic) realm would find a range of expressions in the cultural practices of peoples across the Americas.

Lastly, this chapter interprets suicide (or suicidal action), stoicism in the face of torture and death, and belief in transmigration as another set of weapons in the hands of enslaved Gold Coast commoners. While obeah and blood oaths embodied the activation of ritual, political, and martial powers, suicide gave the enslaved and dispossessed command over their very souls upon death's approach. Embracing notions of spiritual immortality and the circularity of life both emboldened believers and may explain their pain tolerance, fearlessness, and seeming disregard for their mortality. The destruction of earthly bonds and the release of the spirit to its destiny may have been welcome thoughts to those facing a lifetime of bondage in a strange and hostile land. Death, even by suicide, hastened transmigration and allowed for those who believed to "reshuffle the deck" with the liberatory potential of being reborn as free people in Atlantic Africa. Another possibility, explored in this chapter, is that enslaved rebels facing death did so with the belief that they would be transformed into empowered ancestors with the ability to continue the fight against slavery in the Americas. Even in failing to create new Coromantee or (A)mina states, rebels could return to the land of their ancestors or become activated—as ancestors themselves—by the living as the ultimate acts of resistance to slaveocracies and colonial governments. The belief in the transmigration of souls became a potent weapon in the hands of the dispossessed in the Black Atlantic.

Combined, obeah, loyalty oaths, and transmigration became—in the words of James Scott—"weapons of the weak" in the Americas and represented cultural (re)inventions by the Coromantees and (A)minas who deployed them.[8] These spiritual tools and technologies helped them make sense of the new worlds around them and enabled them to mount effective resistance movements—at times against insurmountable odds.

Moreover, the ubiquitous presence of these technologies in the Gold Coast diaspora provides some of the best evidence that social death was simply a phase or waypoint in the process of social resurrection. The ability of Coromantees and (A)minas to fashion new lives in the Americas and to connect with forces energized and activated by ancestral spirits implies simultaneous disconnection from and connection to the Gold Coast past. At the very same time they were (re)inventing themselves and becoming new peoples, their new identities and concepts of a post-slave state were framed by the ancestral realm.

THEORIZING OBEAH SORCERY AND
COROMANTEE OATHS IN THE AMERICAS

Abroykire bayi, literally "foreign witchcraft" in Akan-Twi, became a persuasive force wielded by Coromantees and (A)minas in their visions of freedom and new political formations in the Americas. In the Gold Coast, bayi was suppressed by state actors and elites and, in some cases, became the basis upon which people were enslaved, sold to Europeans, and shipped to distant lands across the horizon.[9] The case of an unnamed man—a former Akan- and English-speaking trader—onboard the ship *Brooks* in 1783 or 1784 proves instructive. Originating from Saltpan, a Fante-speaking town in the central Gold Coast, this trader found himself in conflict with the caboceer or town headman who, in turn, accused the man, his wife, two daughters, and mother of witchcraft. After a summary trial, they were all convicted of bayi, enslaved, and embarked on the *Brooks* on their way to a life of bondage in Kingston, Jamaica. His ability to speak English, as evidenced by the trader's accounts of his enslavement to the ship's crew, points to his direct involvement in the Atlantic slave trade. Perhaps in these moments of reflection onboard the *Brooks,* the trader came to understand the irony of his predicament. While none of the family were likely abayifo (obayifo, singular), or bayi witches, this form of judicial enslavement represented one of many active pipelines feeding the outbound transatlantic slave trade from the Gold Coast.[10]

As a trader, this unnamed man may have been interpreted by the town caboceer as a threat to the hereditary, established, and empowered Gold Coast *ancien régime.* As mentioned in the first chapter, caboceers could be military or political officeholders, and many were agents actively engaged in Atlantic commerce. By definition, however, caboceers were hereditary nobles whose power and domain were defined by the stools they occupied. The unnamed trader, however, did not occupy a hereditary stool. Instead, he accumulated wealth through hard work, singular effort, or the ever-expanding possibilities resulting from Atlantic commerce. New means of generating wealth and even entrepreneurship in later periods of Gold Coast history became rationales for Akan-speaking states to erect anti-witchcraft shrines (*abosom-brafo*) and for states to target for political or social reprisals those who climbed the socioeconomic ladder in the course of becoming a new class of wealthy elites.[11] As summarized by Meera Venkatachalam, in the late nineteenth-century Akan forest belt, "the introduction of cash cropping and integration into the broader colonial economy led to rapid social change resulting in the emergence of new wealthy elites. These elites challenged established social hierarchies and transformed the very structure of society. The success of these *nouveaux riches* raised suspicions that they used witchcraft to restrict the reproductive ability and success of others."[12] A similar transformation occurred in the decades after the Gold Coast became a net exporter of slaves. The new resources and commercial possibilities circulating in the southern Gold Coast by the late seventeenth century allowed for a small handful to experience rapid upward social mobility without depending upon an inherited status. The resulting tensions between these "Atlantic entrepreneurs" linked to new revenue streams generated by overseas commerce and the older, hereditary nobility led to accusations of witchcraft—a cycle that has been repeated in the Gold Coast and Ghana in several successive waves since the late-eighteenth century.[13]

While witchcraft accusations reflected concerns about unbridled upward social mobility, another fear associated with local bayi was that it represented destabilizing anti-social, anti-state, or even revolutionary forces.[14] By its very nature, bayi democratized spiritual empowerment; commoner and noble alike could be born with the special connections to the ancestral and spirit realm that could lead one on the path to becoming an obayifo. They could be born misshapen, deformed, with a caul or veil of skin covering their faces, or in some other distinctive way. Obayifo could also be an inheritable title, from father to son or mother to daughter.[15] While the children of elites might be funneled into state-sanctioned and -sponsored priest- and priestess-hoods—*akomfo* or *abosomfo*—commoners lacked this type of access, and many rural hamlets and villages developed a range of ritual specialists, including healers, diviners, and midwives. Unlike their state-sanctioned counterparts, these local and non-elite ritualists did not operate from oracles or shrines and inhabited a nebulous social space. Collectively, they engaged in a type of altruistic spiritual banditry that channeled, redirected, or redistributed power for the benefit of the various have-nots in Gold Coast societies. By definition, abayifo and other non-elite ritualists mastered a form of spiritual and political malfeasance by claiming power beyond the watchful eye and control of state actors.[16] Swept up into the many streams and tributaries that channeled the continuous outflow of peoples and cultural technologies across the Atlantic, this caste of ritual specialists became one of the most critical components in the development of the commoner consciousness in the Americas.

Instead of being understood as an anti-social ritual practice in the Americas, obeah became normative and quotidian as enslaved rebels employed it frequently in their quests to create new political and social orders. Its centrality among maroon political formations and its activation by rebels in Suriname, Jamaica, Antigua, and Barbados helped further crystallize Gold Coast diaspora identities. At the same time, obeah compelled the continuing transformation of Coromantee and (A)mina ethnicities into more inclusive formations in their political thrust and appeal.[17] Beyond the realm of the resistive arts, obeah became embedded in the everyday lives of the enslaved in the British and Dutch circum-Caribbean and beyond (see figure 5.1). At times, it could be employed by the enslaved against one another. Thomas Walduck observed, for example: "That one Negro can bewitch another (Obia as they call it) . . . is beyond doubt, by sending an unaccountable pain in different parts of their body, lameness, madness, loss of speech, lose the use of all their limbs without any paine."[18] Also, obeah could be activated by colonial authorities and plantation owners as a mechanism of social control. Even with these exceptions in mind, the practice never lost its revolutionary potential. Like other African Atlantic religious and spiritual systems, it could be a catalyst—as opposed to an opiate—for the enslaved masses

5.1. Trinidad Obeah-man conducting an oathing ceremony on suspected thieves, circa 1820s. Source: Bridgens, *West India Scenery,* plate 21.

in inspiring social revolution and wars against Western Hemisphere slaveocracies.[19]

The true power of obeah was in its exponential reach. Just one obay-ifo transplanted to a single locale in the Americas could inspire generations of belief. A 1678 survey of the enslaved population of St. Kitts conducted by French Jesuit Jean Mongin showed, for example, twenty-six alleged and self-admitted "sorcerers" among roughly 2,400 people. The one percent of those variably referred to as sorcerers, obeah doctors, or conjurers was all that was needed to sustain belief.[20] Indeed, the physical presence of abayifo was not required for the associated belief systems to take root in diasporic soil. Many Atlantic Africans carried memories of such ritual specialists with them through the Middle Passage, and this could facilitate the reemergence of associated practices in the Americas. Unlike akomfo and other state-sanctioned Gold Coast ritualists who relied on shrines, oracles, and deities and a more systematized ritual structure to engage their craft and develop new initiates, bayi did not depend upon a pantheon of gods. Instead, this was a decentralized practice. Shrines, temples, and other places of worship did not play a role in bayi; indeed, "worship" and other forms of public expression were virtually nonexistent in either bayi or obeah. Belief in the power of the obeah doctor to reach beyond the material plane in order to engage and activate the extraordinary was all that was needed for obeah to have any effect. In this case, obeah never relied upon conversion or the creation of large pools of adherents or congregants. Obeah doctors, similar to their obayifo counterparts in the Gold Coast, served in mercenary roles—employed only when there was need. Maintaining individual "clients" as opposed to masses of adherents may have helped to keep this practice clandestine, pushed to the margins and into the shadows of diasporic communities where it could be safely harbored.[21]

Obeah, as manifested in the Americas, was not sustained solely as a result of the influx of Gold Coast Africans. Instead, it represented, potentially, a confluence of Atlantic African peoples, cultures, and spiritual technologies. Proof of this appears in a range of sources and recent historical interpretations. In a letter to James Petiver—Apothecary and Fellow of the Royal Society—Thomas Walduck provided several details about obeah in Barbados. Among his most insightful statements was an observation in which he reports, "No Negro that was born in Barbados can doe [obeah], only those that are brought from the Coast of Africa and Chiefly the *Calarmale* Negros."[22] "Calarmale," a probable corruption of "Calabari," refers to Igbo-speakers and a range of others from Calabar and the Bight of Biafra.[23] Given the domination of Gold Coast Africans in Barbadian import estimates in the first decade of the eighteenth century and the growing concerns about the Coromantees residing there since the discovery of the 1675 slave plot, the omission of any reference to the Gold Coast and its diaspora of peoples in this correspondence is more than curious.

More recently, Douglas Chambers, Jerome Handler, and Kenneth Bilby have theorized either an Igbo origin to, or a significant Igbo dimension in, the ritual formulation that became obeah in the British Caribbean. In part, their evidentiary base includes the Walduck letter and a etymological assessment of the similarities between obeah and a ritual practice centered around healing among twentieth-century speakers of Efik and Igbo—*dibia*.[24] In this regard, obeah may have been the result of a cultural "negotiation" between the many cast out from Gold Coast and Bight of Biafra embarkation ports to meet and become part of communities in the British colonies in the Americas. Similar formulations and negotiations between multiple Atlantic African groups may have been behind Saint-Domingue Vodun, Brazilian Candomblé, and Cuban Regla de Ocha (or Santería)—concepts that drew upon spiritual technologies carried by Kongo Christians and devotees of Edo, Fon, and Yoruba pantheons, divination systems, and cosmologies.[25]

Like other diasporic cultural forms, obeah was particularly malleable and plastic, and this may have been at the core of its ability to reach across lines of ethnic and linguistic divide. With this said, obeah may not have been simultaneously born in the Gold Coast and the Biafran interior—as argued by others. Nor was it simply a "catchall" term or a practice devoid of connections to specific Atlantic African cultural geographies.[26] Instead, I contend that Gold Coast bayi served as a base around which a range of Atlantic African spiritual concepts became intertwined and entangled—resulting in different variants of obeah coming to fruition throughout the Americas. This allows, for example, obeah to exist in regions or colonies in which imports from the Bight of Biafra were few or relatively nonexistent. It also provides space for a range of Atlantic Africans to embrace and find resonances within obeah—despite its ostensibly Gold Coast origins. Though it may have had a wide variety of manifestations across both space and time, the enslaved—creole and Atlantic African alike—could interpret, use, and be empowered by obeah in similar fashion. While it may have had Gold Coast origins, its amorphous structure allowed many other Atlantic African groups to latch on to and activate obeah, as its forms and basic principles would have been familiar to people from a wide range of backgrounds. This broader historical foundation—which decouples the growth or practice of obeah from a particular ethnolinguistic enclave in the Americas— may open new interpretive possibilities. In this sense, obeah had Gold Coast foundations, but the continuation of the practice in the Americas did not rely solely upon the continual importation or even the presence of enslaved Gold Coast Africans. If obeah doctors could originate from a range of speech communities or neo-African ethnic groups, then certain

Black Atlantic ritual specialists linked to British or Dutch Caribbean origins—Salem's Tituba (Barbados) and Saint-Domingue's Boukman (Jamaica)—can be reframed as practitioners of obeah. In this light, we can better understand an observation made by a visitor to Barbados in 1710: "Most people in the West Indies are given to the observation of Dreams & Omens, by their conversation with Negros or the Indians, and some of the Negros are a sort of Magicians and I have seen surprising things done by them."[27] Conjure, obeah, hoodoo, and other spiritual concepts not linked to particular pantheons of Atlantic African deities can be understood as dimensions of a common set of concerns about the past, hopes for the future, and present fears shared by many in the Black Atlantic.

This reframing of obeah as part of a broader interpretation of cultural transformation is far from novel. In his 1903 anthology, *The Negro Church*, W. E. B. Du Bois includes a chapter titled "Obeah Sorcery"; he contends the practice was one of many manifestations of "the Negro Church" in the Americas. Echoing sentiments articulated in *Souls of Black Folk*, Du Bois added that these religions were among the "only social institutions of the Negroes which started in the African forest and survived slavery; under the leadership of [the] priest or medicine man . . . the Church preserved in itself the remnants of African tribal life."[28] Referred to more obliquely in *Souls of Black Folk* as "the heathenism of the Gold Coast," obeah and similar practices became embedded within the expressive cultures associated with the black church and determined, for Du Bois, the "pythian madness," "demoniac possession," and "frenzied shouting" at the core of "the most vital part of the history of the Negro in America."[29] Indeed, Du Bois had in mind the Jamaican obeah-man when he claimed that the "Priest or Medicine-man" appeared early on plantations throughout the Americas "and found his function as the healer of the sick, the interpreter of the Unknown, the comforter of the sorrowing, the supernatural avenger of wrong, and the one who rudely but picturesquely expressed the longing, disappointment, and resentment of a stolen and oppressed people. Thus, as bard, physician, judge, and priest, within the narrow limits allowed by the slave system, rose the Negro preacher, and under him the first Afro-American institution, the Negro church."[30] When this section of *Souls* is read through the optic of Du Bois's discussions in *The Negro Church*, it becomes clear that much of his theoretic framing of the internal workings of black religion came out of his research on African Atlantic spiritual systems in the eighteenth-century British Caribbean. In fact, the principal source from which Du Bois derived his assessments about obeah and obeah doctors was Bryan Edwards, the Jamaican slave-owner and sugar planter who penned a 1783 work titled *The History, Civil and Commercial of the British West Indies*. Working through the details of Tackey's 1760 Coromantee war in Jamaica, in which obeah played a central role, Edwards recorded information derived from the interrogation of a captured Coromantee obeah-man.[31] In the hands of Du Bois, the historical examples of obeah in the Caribbean become a way of theorizing the cultural transformations that undergird key institutions in African-American life.

The spiritual practices and concerns that gave rise to obeah in the eighteenth-century circum-Caribbean formed part of a continuum of experiences for the enslaved that were coded and embedded with generative cultural and sociopolitical materials. More than simply representing "remnants" of a generic African "tribal life," the origins of obeah point to specific Atlantic African language cohorts, cultural technologies, and sociopolitical spheres. From a Gold Coast foundation, the practice spread and became activated by many others in the Americas. As "spiritual technologies," they allowed for the activation and deployment of powerful forces in the hands of the dispossessed and enslaved who used them as the basis for social revolution and rebellion. The practice and activation of obeah—part of the Coromantee resistive arts in the Americas—represent far more than "degraded" and "exaggerated form[s] of witchcraft and medicine," "heathen rites," or "degenerated" African religious systems as articulated by Du Bois.[32] As Du Bois himself hints, but does not fully articulate, these resistive arts and cultural technologies were key in the processes of generating new social institutions, new cultural expressions, indeed new peoples in the Black Atlantic.

While Gold Coast Africans were separated from family and familiar social structures in the process of commodification, they mobilized social and cultural scripts from their collective past as a means of social resurrection. Situated in a new set of geographies in the New World, this "rebirth" was both deeply rooted in the Gold Coast past and shaped by the American present. One example of this social resurrection or rebirth would be the events surrounding the July 1685 revolt in Guanaboa, Jamaica. Led by a Coromantee named Cuffee, some 150 rose on the estate of the Widow Grey, stealing firearms and killing one man. During the early hours of the revolt, the Coromantee rebels were forced to retire and later retreat, "having lost one of their conjurors, on whom they chiefly depended." Though no extant records link the unnamed conjuror specifically to obeah, his involvement in a Coromantee rebellion and their reliance on his abilities to aid them in insurrection point in useful directions.[33]

British Jamaica quickly became a kind of cultural epicenter for obeah in the Americas by the first few decades of the eighteenth century. Given the continued circulations of peoples and ideas in the eighteenth-century Western Hemisphere, it is entirely likely that Barbados, Jamaica, and Antigua helped disseminate obeah throughout the Caribbean and beyond. Indeed, banishments in the wake of rebellions and conspiracies provided a multitude of human vectors—like Antigua's Billy and Sam Hector—who carried the concept (and the word) with them to their new homes. The shift in focus to Jamaica in the spiritual geography of obeah was likely due to the presence and activities of the Leeward and Windward Maroons. Apparently, the practice of obeah was sheltered and given renewed life within these rebel communities. The types of entangled cultural practices that became characteristic of Jamaican Maroon enclaves served as the perfect climate for the growth and further elaboration of practices associated with obeah. During the course of the First Maroon War, a series of skirmishes between July and August 1735 resulted in the capture of a maroon "who was discovered to be one of their Obia men or conjurers." After he was taken, this obeah-man had a quick trial and execution. Clearly his banishment to another colony would not put an end to the continuous threat represented by obeah.[34] Despite his death, the Leewards continued to be inspired by obeah-men, a fact that points to the presence of many others within their enclave who claimed control over spiritual and ancestral powers.

A contemporary witness who visited the Leewards after the signing of the 1738 Articles of Pacification remarked, "They have not the least idea of a Diety" and "They were very superstitious having during their State of Actual Rebellion, a Person whom they called Obea Man whom they greatly revered, his Words Carried the Force of an Oracle with them, being Consulted on every Occasion." This observer goes on to note that the Leewards' faith in their obeah-man had waned in the handful of years before his visit. Apparently, this obeah-man had prophesized that one of their previous towns could be neither detected nor attacked by whites, yet "the falseness of it" was proven when—during the course of the First Maroon War—British forces assaulted this town and burned many houses to the ground. Indeed, it was the destruction of this principal Leeward town that would lead to the creation of Trelawny Town—the residence of a sizable number of Leeward Maroons until the Second Maroon War of 1795–96.[35]

Even when the powers proclaimed by obeah-doctors seemingly failed, this did not dislodge from the masses of enslaved people the belief in a world beyond the material realm. On this note, Thomas Thistlewood, the notorious Jamaican overseer, recorded an entry on January 6, 1754, about a "noted Obia man" named Jinney Quashe "pretending to pull bones, &c. out of several of our Negroes for which they was to give him money." When he was "discovered by them to be a cheat," they threatened him and chased him away from the plantation.[36] As Douglas Hall states, even discovery of the ineffectiveness of obeah could be explained away. He notes that if an obeah doctor was set to protect a "charmed person from death, and if death should come it would signify the weakness or unworthiness of the charmed rather than of the charm."[37] While impostors may be discovered or weak leaders exposed due to their lack of faith, the one thing that remained constant was the potential and power of obeah.

In the case of Antigua, both obeah and Coromantee loyalty oaths became organizing principles in the commission of the island-wide conspiracy in 1736. King Court's own Coromantee "apprenticeship," as mentioned previously, came under one of the principal obeah-men involved in the conspiracy—Quawcoo. Feared and highly respected by fellow conspirators, Quawcoo's very presence could cause "a great Consternation at the Sight of the Obey Man." Though the records do not reveal whether the Coromantee obeah doctors created charms, poisons, or powders, we do know that Quawcoo created a ritual object—known in the records as an "Obey"—made of sheepskin, upon which he poured animal blood and other substances. This ritual object, resembling in all aspects a Gold Coast *sumán*, became the center of Quawcoo's spiritual powers and his ability to consecrate oaths. In addition, both Quawcoo and John Obia orchestrated a series of oathing ceremonies over the course of several months leading up to and beyond the intended outbreak of violence. Trial justices often measured the guilt of those alleged to have some involvement in the conspiracy by the number of oathing ceremonies they attended. In the aftermath of the trials, court justices wrote that "the Oath of Secrecy and Fidelity, had been taken both by Court and Tomboy, and almost every one of the first twelve, and by everyone that was since condemned and executed, or stands recommended for Banishment."[38] This use of the Damnation Oath as a litmus test of guilt and complicity is clear in the trials of the brothers Benjamin and Billy Johnson—free island-born creoles implicated by at least four others as being "very deeply concerned in the plot." Benjamin Johnson was accused of taking the Damnation Oath—including rum, grave dirt, and blood—"twice to destroy the Christians" despite his own "constant attendance at church for a year past." Billy apparently exceeded his brother: "at one of the conspirator's feasts he drank the damnation health twice in one day and a single evidence proves his drinking of it a third time at another place." Billy went so far as to take the oath on a fourth occasion, this time administered by John Obia.[39]

The fact that the Antiguan Coromantees and creoles chose funerals as the occasions for many of their oathing ceremonies is indicative of the power the ancestral realm represented in the minds of the enslaved. Funerals gave the conspirators a practical reason to gather and have a feast; they also provided the enslaved with both a key substance for their loyalty draughts in grave dirt and an immediate connection to ancestral forces to help bind their oaths. It is clear from the very nature of the oath that the actual "Damnation" would be caused by ancestral spirits. In the evidence presented against Mingo, the court noted that an oathing ceremony conducted at Secundo's house included a "Creed Oath in a Glass of Rum and Dirt of a Grave, which Mingo and the Rest took; a Glass in one hand and the Other upon the Cock tyed upon the Table, the Oath in these Words—Damnation to the failers in the intended Insurrection."[40] Bryan Edwards of Jamaica explains further that oath takers or those forced to submit to an oath test must consume a concoction of human blood, grave dirt, and water and do so "with an imprecation, that it may cause the belly to burst, and the bones to rot" upon violation of the terms of the oath or "if the truth be not spoken."[41] Charles Leslie of Barbados, reflecting on a visit to Jamaica in the 1730s, noted that after items were found to be stolen on a plantation, "they have a solemn kind of Oath, which the eldest Negro always administers, and which by them is accounted so sacred." After arranging themselves at a gravesite, "one of them opens a Grave" and "the Priest, takes a little of the earth, and puts into every one of the Mouths; they say, that if any has been guilty, their Belly swells, and occasions their Death."[42] Whether damnation, confusion, or death resulted from breaking an oath or being dishonest, the spirits of departed friends or relatives would be the agents of vengeance and punishment.

While similar oaths, known as "eating fetish," became important tools for Gold Coast polities, merchants, and militaries, grave dirt as an ingredient of an oath draught seems to be a unique New World adaptation and may have been borrowed from other Atlantic African cohorts.[43] Whereas local or state deities, oracles, and bossum guaranteed oaths in the Gold Coast, Gold Coast diaspora loyalty oaths—shaped as they were by democratizing concerns and a commoner consciousness—were secured by spiritual forces to which everyone had direct access or connection—ancestral spirits. Unlike deities, the power of the ancestors did not need to be mediated through oracles, priests, or priestesses and, as a result, their protective or harmful influences could be activated by a much wider range of specialists and practitioners. Within this interpretive frame, the spiritual and even social meaning of the graveyard and grave dirt, or "goopher dust," as a component in oath drinks can be realized more fully.[44] It would be, as Zora Neale Hurston intimates, the ancestors and not concerns about death that shaped so much of what was and what became hoodoo, obeah, conjure, and other forms of "Negro magic" in the Americas.[45]

Tackey's 1760 war in Jamaica mirrored many of the aspects of the 1736 Antigua conspiracy, particularly in the employment of obeah and loyalty oaths. The use of these Coromantee spiritual technologies forged group unity during the planning phases and served as vectors of the collective wrath of the aggrieved and enslaved. Du Bois's own theories about the transformation of black religion and the black church were undergirded by the testimony from an obeah-man captured in St. Mary's Parish during a routine security check. As described by Edward Long, this obeah doctor was "a famous obeiah man or priest, much respected among his countrymen." Indeed, Long goes on to add that this man

> was an old Coromantin, who, with others of his profession, had been chief in counseling and instigating the credulous herd, to whom these priests administered a powder, which, being rubbed on their bodies, was to make them invulnerable: they persuaded them into a belief that Tacky, their generalissmo in the woods, could not possibly be hurt by the white men, for that he caught all the bullets fired at him in his hand, and hurled them back with destruction to his foes. This old impostor was caught whilst he was tricked up with all his feathers, teeth, and other implements of magic.[46]

For future purposes, it would be the "implements of magic" and claims of otherworldly communication by obeah doctors that concerned Jamaican authorities as much as anything else connected to the 1760 revolt. In the aftermath of Tackey's war, on December 18, 1760, the Assembly of Jamaica made obeah illegal and its practice a crime punishable by death or banishment from the colony by legislative act. They specifically banned the various implements associated with the practice, including "Blood, Feathers, Parrots Beaks, Dogs Teeth, Alligators Teeth, Broken Bottles, Grave Dirt, Rum, Eggshells." In addition, they voiced concerns over "the many Mischiefs that may hereafter arise from the wicked Art of Negroes going under the appeallation of Obeah Men and Women," particularly because these ritual specialists could convince others of their powers through "pretending to have Communication with the Devil and other evil spirits."[47]

What the members of the Jamaica Assembly failed or refused to understand was that practitioners of obeah never claimed to be in contact with diabolical forces or entities. Reading obeah through the optic of eighteenth-century English witchcraft, colonial officials interpreted any claim of otherworldly contact as communication with the Devil and his agents. From the perspective of obeah doctors and their many supplicants, clients, and believers, spirit represented a neutral power that could be activated and used for good or evil. Moreover, ancestral spirit, in particular, was one of the most potent forces in their arsenal in the continuing struggle against what they perceived to be the true evils—colonial administrators and the planter elite.

The continuing power of the ancestral realm found expression in Jamaica just five years after the execution by hanging of the captured Coromantee obeah doctor mentioned by Edward Long. Those who survived the 1760–61 court proceedings met with other conspirators in 1765 to wage a renewed war against Jamaica's planters. Apparently, many were still bound in common cause through a Coromantee loyalty oath administered initially in 1760. With rum as the base of the oath drink, the Coromantees involved in the 1760 plot added "some gunpowder and dirt taken from a grave" in addition to blood from the arm of each conspirator. After some additional preparations, this concoction was consumed by each confederate before they vowed to aid Tackey in his 1760 war. For those involved in this 1760 oath, it represented a binding enough pact between each other and with their ancestors for them to risk another attempt at revolt five years later in 1765.[48] We can imagine that the 1765 conspirators renewed their vows and brought into their cabal new recruits who submitted to similar Coromantee loyalty oaths.

As weapons of the weak and Gold Coast diaspora spiritual technologies, obeah and blood oaths became powerful inducements in attempts at social revolution and the construction of post-slave polities. In both the Gold Coast and the Americas, bayi and its cognate forms were commoner appropriations of power and means of empowerment. Blood oaths, on the other hand, were vehicles of state power in the Gold Coast and became the principal means by which economic, political, and military elites could "sign" contracts, make alliances, or guarantee arrangements across vast distances. In the hands of former commoners from the Gold Coast, blood oaths became essential and even signal markers of Coromantee resistance in the circum-Caribbean. By making a suppressed activity normative—in the case of obeah—and inverting Akan loyalty oaths—elite mechanisms—into tools and weapons of the oppressed, peoples who defined themselves as Coromantees and (A)minas in the Americas laid the foundation for new social and politi-

cal visions around which others could rally. The "mysterious Obi worship with its barbarous rites, spells, and blood-sacrifice," to borrow the
phrasing of Du Bois, indeed became the "centre of Negro group life"—
serving as one of many spurs to the cultural transmutations that created
African American peoples throughout the Western Hemisphere.[49]

SPARTAN FORTITUDE, SUICIDE, AND TRANSMIGRATION

In his 1783 historical account about the British Caribbean, planter Bryan
Edwards spent a considerable amount of attention on Coromantee behavioral traits—especially as they relate to the warrior-like disposition
of so many Gold Coast diaspora men. Reflecting on the then long history of Coromantee rebelliousness and even contemporary examples of
their general recalcitrance, he repeated what—by that time—had become standard fare in considerations of this difficult people. He noted,
for example, "The courage or unconcern which the people of this country manifest at the approach of death" and how it results from "their
national manners, wars and superstitions, which are all, in the highest
degree, savage and sanguinary."[50] In this particularly insightful passage, Edwards had his finger on the interpretive pulse of the foundation
for Coromantee courage and perhaps pain tolerance. First, many Gold
Coast men captured, enslaved, and transported to the Americas may
have served in armies or asafo companies, and this probably factors into
their courage in the face of death. Second, a strong belief in transmigration, the immortality of the human soul, and the transformation of the
deceased into powerful ancestral spirits who could be activated through
obeah—the supposed Coromantee "superstitions"—might lead to people
having less concern about their fleshly bonds to the material plane.

The alleged martial aptitude of Coromantees and (A)minas alone
would not sufficiently explain the many examples of their pain tolerance
and fearlessness. As Edwards adds, "This contempt of death, or indifference about life, they bring with them to the West Indies." Observing the
same traits among children brought from the Gold Coast led Edwards
to assume that it was a natural inclination or endowment. Their "evident
superiority, both in hardiness of frame, and vigour of mind, over all

the young people of the same age imported from other parts of Africa," proved to him that Coromantees were quite different from others. To support this claim, he gives the story of the branding of "ten Kormantyn boys, and the like number of Eboes" no older than twelve or thirteen years of age. When the first youngster—a stout Eboe boy, received his "mark," Edwards notes that "he screamed dreadfully, while his companions of the same nation manifested strong emotions of sympathetic terror." In stark contrast, the "Koromantyn boys" laughed at the Eboes and "coming forward of their own accord, offered their bosoms undauntedly to the brand" which they all took without flinching.[51]

Far more grisly scenes than the one offered by Edwards occurred throughout the circum-Caribbean in connection to the executions and public torture of Coromantee or (A)mina rebels, runaways, and maroons. Their Spartan fortitude was to be tested far too often.[52] In the aftermath of the 1760 Jamaica revolt, court justices tried and sentenced one Coromantee rebel to be burned alive as a part of a public spectacle to quash the spirit of insurrection. Chained to an iron stake and forced to sit on the ground, the unnamed rebel had a torch applied to his feet and legs. Neither flinching nor uttering a moan, he endured "his legs reduced to ashes with the utmost firmness and composure." When one of his arms managed to get loose, he threw a lit brand in the face of his executioner. Two other men, sentenced to execution by gibbeting, "never uttered the least complaint except only of cold in the night, but diverted themselves all day long in discourse with their countrymen." They both "laughed immoderately," according to an eyewitness just a day before one of the Coromantee men died in his sleep.[53]

John Gabriel Stedman's five years in Dutch Suriname, beginning February 1773, left a remarkable impression on him. His reflections on this experience deepen our understandings of the links between Coromantee fortitude and their belief in transmigration. Despite attempts at pacification through treaty between 1760 and 1762, several new maroon enclaves in the colony began assaulting plantations and colonists living near the Cottica and Commewijne rivers. This wave of attacks, including the destruction of plantations and the capture of colonial military outposts, led to an increasing number of military expeditions launched by Dutch States-General and Governor Jan Nepveu between 1768 and 1772. During this period, two of the larger rebellious maroon settlements—Boni's Maroons and Kormantin Kodjo's Maroons—conducted a multifront war against the Dutch that would last until 1777. With the colonial economy failing and hundreds of enslaved people streaming into the new maroon settlements, Governor Nepveu made a request for the importation and use of professionally trained soldiers from Europe, with the first groups arriving by spring 1772.[54]

Among the soldiers requested by Suriname's governor, Stedman was involved in a handful of mostly uneventful campaigns against the maroons during the later portion of the First Boni-Maroon War (1768–1777).[55] His most compelling encounters with "Rebel Negroes" came as the result of watching the torture and execution of captured maroons. Though "hurt by the cruelty" of the horrible burnings and dismemberments he witnessed, Stedman expressed a measure of surprise "at the intrepidity with which the Negroes bore their punishment." On May 21, 1773, seven captured maroons were tortured and executed at Fortress Zeelandia. Though we know little about their ethnic backgrounds, we can say for certain that many of Kodjo's Maroons—including his brother Kwaw—were Coromantees, mixed with a number of Atlantic Africans from Sierra Leone and Senegambia, the so-called Gangu. Many other maroons, including Boni, were classified as "bush creoles" or people born in Suriname within an existing maroon enclave. Even in this case, Coromantee culture and norms shaped some of the core principles held dear by a wide range of Suriname's rebel maroon groups. In any event, the captured rebels Stedman wrote about performed Coromantee masculinity in ways repeated in the Americas since the late seventeenth century. One captive, broken on the rack, suffered "under the most excruciating torments, through which he manfully went without heaving a sigh or complaining." Another, sentenced to death by hanging, "gave a hearty laugh of contempt at the magistrates who attended the execution."[56]

The executions clearly wore on Stedman to the degree that he had to be consoled by another onlooker. This "decent-looking man" told the newcomer "there can be nothing more common in this colony" than the vile tortures Stedman had just seen. He then proceeded to tell Stedman of a few executions he had personally witnessed:

5.2. The breaking of Neptune, a free black carpenter in Suriname who was tortured and allowed to die slowly as punishment for theft. During his hours of torment, he issued no groan, sigh, or complaint, but told two jokes to the white onlookers, 1770s. Source: Stedman, *Narrative, of a Five Years' Expedition* 2: facing 296. Courtesy of the General Research and Reference Division, Schomburg Center for Research in Black Culture, New York Public Library, Astor, Lenox, and Tilden Foundations.

I saw a black man hanged alive by the ribs, between which an incision was first made with a knife, and then an iron hook clinched with a chain. In this manner he kept alive three days, hanging with his head and feet downwards.... Notwithstanding all this, he never complained and even upbraided a Negro for crying while he was flogged below the gallows, by calling out to him "You man? Da boy fasi." (Are you a man? You behave like a boy.")....Another Negro (said he) I have seen quartered alive and, after four strong horses were fastened to his legs and arms, and after having had iron sprigs driven home underneath every one of his nails, on his hands and feet, without a motion he first asked a dram and then bid them pull away, without a groan.[57]

Perhaps for men tortured in such ways, death's embrace was not to be feared. For those who believed in the transmigration of souls, death offered a renewed opportunity for not just escape—but either a fresh start in the lands of their ancestors or transformation into wrathful spirits whose powers could be activated by the living (see figure 5.2).

Transmigration of souls was not just a spiritual concept carried to the Americas by Gold Coast Africans alone. Writing in the late 1730s about his visit to Jamaica, Charles Leslie of Barbados added to a familiar formula: "'Tis indeed surprising to see with what Courage and Intrepidity some of them will meet their Fate, and be merry in their last Moments; they are quite transported to think their Slavery is near an End, and that they shall revisit their happy native Shores, and see their old Friends and Acquaintance." Indeed, they meet death without lament or sorry, "but with a great deal of Joy . . . firmly believing [they are] gone home, and happy."[58] C. G. A. Oldendorp, a Moravian missionary living in the Danish Virgin Islands between 1767 and 1768, reports: "The doctrine of the migration of souls from one body to another is widely accepted by the Karabari and by several other black nations." Upon death, the soul is "reincarnated in the infant born most immediately after his demise."[59] Indeed, in mortuary practices, beliefs in transmigration, and the activation of the ancestral realm for earthly purposes, Orlando Patterson aptly notes, "There is a striking uniformity in the death customs of West African [peoples]."[60] While it may be impossible to fully disaggregate the practices and beliefs of Gold Coast Africans from this cultural formulation, perhaps the martial backgrounds of many of the men who found themselves in diaspora led to some uniquely Coromantee and (A)mina manifestations of these concepts.[61]

The combination of belief in transmigration and recent training in the arts of war may explain why so many Gold Coast Africans became involved in conspiracies, revolts, and maroon enclaves. Certainly, an outcome of this combination was a proclivity toward suicide—a trait normally associated with Eboes and others from the Bight of Biafra. While Eboes had a reputation for being melancholy and timid and were thus seen as prone to self-destruction by British Caribbean planters, in Patterson's view "the evidence suggests that the highly desired Gold Coast Slaves had an even greater record of suicide for the opposite reason, namely, their intractability and stubborn refusal to accept their status as slaves."[62] Several mass suicides involving Coromantees and (A)minas throughout the Americas provides a body of evidence to undergird this conclusion. Six committed suicide in the aftermath of the 1712 New York City revolt. Some thirty-six Aminas, including most of the leadership core, killed themselves when their polity was crushed in Danish St. John in May 1734. Mass suicides followed in the wake of the 1760 Jamaica revolt in the parishes of Westmoreland, St. James, and St. Mary—the latter including the suicide of twenty-five rebels in one instance. The suicides of prominent leaders marked the 1759 Danish St. Croix rebellion and the 1763 Berbice revolt. Five Coromantees hanged themselves after a failed rebellion in the British Caribbean island of Tobago in 1770.[63]

While many previous studies have drawn links between transmigration and suicide, the many examples assessed above—when placed within a broader context of the mortuary beliefs of Coromantees and (A)minas—point in another, generative direction.[64] Instead of interpreting suicide as a means by which vanquished rebels, captured runaways, and defeated maroons could "return home" to the lands of their forebears, I argue that at least in some cases, self-destruction may have been seen as an act of empowerment and as a means of further resistance in the here and now. Upon the approach of death, Coromantees and (A)minas faced transformation from defeated slaves and maroons into empowered ancestors who could provide further assistance in the fight against the forces of oppression. Their laughter and even joviality in the face of excruciating tortures were not because they looked forward to a homecoming back in the Gold Coast. Instead, their intrepidity and courage (the famed Spartan fortitude of Coromantees and (A)minas, along with their propensity to commit suicide when all seemed lost) may have been due to an unfaltering faith in their abilities to continue fighting—as wrathful ancestral spirits. A glimpse of this possibility is mentioned by Stedman, who notes that "Negroes" he encountered in Suriname had a full and complete trust in their vision of the afterlife. In his words, they had no "fear of death, confident they will see some of their friends and relations again in another world, but not that if they die abroad they will rise in their own country."[65] Spiritual transmigration for them ended when they joined other friends and relatives in the ancestral realm. Released from their mortal bonds and activated by grave dirt taken from places of their interment, Coromantee and (A)mina ancestral spirits may have been understood by the living to be the most potent weapons in the arsenals of Gold Coast Africans and their diasporic descendants.

SIX

Women, Regeneration, and Power

Sound the abeng,
Make ready the lowland raids.
Slaughter the English enemies
On lowland plains . . .
Victoriously we return
Oh chieftaness of the Mountain Passes.

MARGUERITE CURTIN, "NANNY," IN GOTTLIEB,
THE MOTHER OF US ALL (2000)

Clara's Atlantic journey from the Gold Coast to Jamaica involved a rather ironic and dramatic personal transformation. As she related when interviewed by planter Bryan Edwards sometime between 1787 and 1793, she came from a small rural hamlet not far from Fante-speaking Anomabu in the central coast. Her parents and eight siblings were all slaves belonging to a "great man" named Anamoa. Given the multigenerational nature of their enslavement, they may have been war captives. Indeed, their master, Anamoa, may have been the ohene or warlord responsible for their capture and transformation into slaves. Their master's untimely death precipitated the sale of Clara, two of her siblings, and several others to local merchants to cover his many debts. This separation from her parents and most of her siblings represented the second social death Clara suffered in her short life; she would undergo a few more over the course of coming months. She and her two brothers found themselves onboard an English slaver, disembarking in Jamaica by late 1784. We know little of their Atlantic journey other than the fact that Edwards purchased all three after 1787 and they joined a sizable contingent of "Koromantyn Negroes" on his holdings. The twenty others formerly owned by Anamoa who went unsold, including most of Clara's immediate family, suffered far worse fortunes than shipment to the Western Hemisphere. Of their fate, Clara reported to Edwards all the "others were killed" at their master's funeral.[1]

In offering some explanation for Clara's account, Edwards noted that "his" Koromantyns informed him "that whenever a considerable man expires, several of his wives, and a great number of his slaves, are sacrificed at his funeral." "This is done," he continues, "say they that he may be properly attended in the next world. This circumstance has been confirmed to me by every Gold Coast Negro that I have interrogated on the subject, and I have enquired of many."[2] In the course of his interview of Clara, Edwards asked her "which country she liked best, Jamaica or Guiney?" The question itself reveals much about his intentions and ulterior motives. A staunch opponent of the abolitionist movement, Edwards served on the Assembly of Jamaica, where he helped reform and further tighten the island's slave codes in 1787 and delivered a fierce antiabolitionist presentation in 1789 that was later published in London. By 1791, he joined a mission from Jamaica to deliver arms, food, and other provisions to the French in Saint Domingue seeking to quash the burgeoning revolution that had just started. The following year, he visited England in an attempt to further solidify support for Jamaica's planters and to more directly attack abolitionists. In this context the question he asked Clara was far from innocuous, and the inclusion of this "interrogation" in his book may have been little more than a move to provide further support for slavery's many apologists.[3]

Edwards's motivations aside, Clara's alleged answer to his query proved to be revealing. In his words, she claimed "that Jamaica was the better country, '*for that people were not killed there, as in Guiney, at the funeral of their masters.*'"[4] A decade later in Barbados, a similar "interrogation" took place with a far different outcome. When John Ford sat down to record biographical information from Ashy "of the Fantee tribe," we do not know if he had any motives other than to present this story to a broader public. Probably a slaveholder residing in Barbados, little else is known about Ford as he does not appear in surviving records. In her recounting of the past, Ashy immediately began with her present: "Ah! Massah dis country here dat you call Babadus, um no good—um no good Massah." She offered this statement despite the fact that, like Clara in Jamaica before her, Ashy also noted the cruel fate that awaited Gold Coast slaves and servants who had the misfortune of living long enough to see their masters die. She struck a familiar chord by stating, "And Massah if any of our Grandee people die, den all de head of his servants is cut off, and bury in de same place wid him, but if dey run away and stay long time when dey come back dey no hurtee dem." She also detailed the story of a servant sacrificed to the sky god in order to insure the end of a lengthy drought. Despite the sharp socioeconomic and political divides that made the Gold Coast have-nots expendable in the eyes of elites, Ashy concluded in the manner she began her tale, emphasizing, "Massah my country is a boon (good) country, a boon country massah, no like yours."[5]

Between the stories of Clara and Ashy, we arrive at the fact that Atlantic Africans carried with them distinct memories of their immediate past into the new societies they inhabited in the Americas. In these particular cases, the reflections offered by Clara and Ashy of the stark social and political hierarchies at play in the Gold Coast provides a background against which they offer comparative assessments—both positive and negative—of their bondage in the British Caribbean. A critical component to this equation was their keen understanding of the differential treatment accorded social lessers, particularly women, in the Gold Coast. When we note that most enslaved peoples kept for local labor needs in the Gold Coast—and throughout Atlantic Africa—were indeed women, then the stories about the mortuary slayings of the wives and servants of "grandees," "great men," and ahene take on added significance.[6] In short, any assessment of the differential, abusive, and even inhumane treatment of social lessers in the Gold Coast has to include gender as a critical dimension.

Read another way, the insights given by Clara and Ashy also reflect class attitudes about the past and present. Clara, a slave in the Gold Coast who may have been born into that status, saw little of a redeeming nature in her past—instead observing that Jamaica was a comparatively better place to live. In Ashy's story, her past status as a free woman shapes her decidedly negative assessment of Barbados and her yearning for a return home.[7] Both of these Gold Coast women, transported to the British Caribbean to live in servitude, remembered Atlantic Africa—albeit in contrasting ways—and these memories provide frameworks against which we can assess transformations and intersections of gender and class in the Gold Coast diaspora.

If slaves and peasants were at the bottom of corporatist and hierarchically structured polities in the Gold Coast, then women in these categories sometimes occupied the lowest possible rank and status. Their valuation, judged as a combination of their productive and reproductive capabilities, made them more attractive for Gold Coast slave markets but did not result in measurable increases in their social, economic, or political roles and standing. Throughout Atlantic Africa, most slaves were women; as Claire Robertson notes, "Most pawns were girls whose labor paid the interest of their fathers' or other male relatives' debts."[8] While some women in the diverse class of free commoners had a measure of power in the Gold Coast, even they were pawns and political dependents of nobles and other elites who relied upon their labor and revenue generation to define, take, and retain power. In the seventeenth and eighteenth century Gold Coast, political offices or stools monopolized by elite men depended on the collection of levies in specie and kind, as well as the mobilization of a range of labor services from a sizable class of commoners. The structure of corporatist Gold Coast polities allowed spaces for empowered women as market sellers, low-ranking priestesses, healers, and midwives to become commercial, religious, or social agents. However, local markets, shrines, and clinics represented spheres of power for women that were—by their very nature—highly provincial and circumscribed. All commoners—men and women—were one misfortune away from becoming the retainers or, worse, slaves of office- and stool-holding elites. Moreover, it was the product of the collective labor of commoners that undergirded a range of political offices (and, thus political power) to which these social lessers had no real access, and which they had no real possibility of holding.[9]

Even the wives of elites and nobles might become tools of a peculiar productive mode. The role, for example, of "planted wives" in creating a new range of crime and creative mechanisms for forcing men into debt ultimately fed outbound streams of enslaved peoples. In discussing the Akwamu ahene, Reindorf explains: "Another source of wealth for the king arose from the fines he demanded from people who had criminal connection with any of the many wives he had married in every town and village, leaving these women free with a view of getting people into trouble."[10] Johannes Rask notes that if a free man "transgresses" against a wealthy man's wife, "he was to pay the woman's husband as many *bendas* of gold, to the value that her husband demands."[11] Debt generated by planted wives created a cycle in which adulterers, unable to immediately pay their debts, could pawn their own daughters or wives to avoid further repercussions, including their own enslavement. Within this framework, some of these daughters, wives, and philandering husbands were then sold to European merchants and transported across the Atlantic. In sum, the internal valuation of women in the Gold Coast needs to be measured against the expendability of the lives (and bodies) of the servants and wives of elites and of non-elite women.

In terms of the excesses of Gold Coast ahene in defining women as tools of exploitation, we are reminded of the entreaties made by Asantehene Osei Bonsu to Joseph Dupuis—British envoy and consul in Kumasi beginning in 1820. Desperate to reopen the transatlantic slave trade and the enormous revenues it could generate for the Asante kingdom, Bonsu offered the British envoy and his delegation prisoners from his conquest of Gaman. Among the ten thousand Gaman war captives Bonsu promised, he planned to set aside for Dupuis several "fine handsome girls and women to give his captains" and stated that he could "send him great numbers."[12] Scenarios like this were repeated throughout Gold Coast history. Expansionist polities—from Akwamu to Asante—and the many wars that followed in their wake reduced free women to war captives, and even their "absorption" and "assimilation" into the homes of their conquerors were euphemisms for systematic rape and concubinage. The processes by which captive women joined new familial structures were preceded by social disruptions akin to a type of death. They were then "married" into polygamous family units of a conquering state and expected to generate offspring for husbands that represented a class of elites responsible for the destruction of their natal homes and the forced break-up of their original families.[13]

While we must be careful not to reify eighteenth-century justifications for the slave trade and enslavement devised by the many apologists for these dehumanizing systems, the biographies of Clara and Ashy force a few interconnected queries about the comparative valuation and role of women in Atlantic Africa and the Americas. Systematic rape, labor exploitation, and a demographic circumstance in which British Caribbean planters preferred to save money by continually importing new slaves as opposed to investing in the health and upkeep of the ones already laboring for them create doubts in the veracity of the claim made by Clara that Jamaica was, indeed, better than the Gold Coast. However, we cannot ignore the fate of her family and, by extension, the fate of a wider range of women in the Gold Coast who had, simultaneously, high value and limited opportunity. As mentioned in chapter 1, the invisibility of empowered and powerful women in the seventeenth- and eighteenth-century Gold Coast—particularly as political figures—necessitates reassessments of gender and the roles of women in this context.

As part of this reassessment, this chapter analyzes a discernable evolution in the ideas about womanhood and power in the Gold Coast diaspora, with particular emphases on political, martial, and spiritual leadership in maroon and slave communities, as well as a range of new egalitarian norms for sexuality. Cubah, the "Queen of Kingston," played a central role as a political symbol—complete with a crown, canopy, and a sword of state—in the 1760 Coromantee plot in Jamaica. In addition, the histories, fictions, and traditions regarding "Grandy Nanny," a martial, political, and spiritual leader of the Nanny Town Maroons of Jamaica, reinforces the notion that Coromantee and (A)mina women experienced a revolution in their social and political value as an ironic result of their enslavement and transportation to the Americas. In this sense, their high valuation may have been matched by expanded opportunities and the ability to be more fully articulated historical agents. They used their enhanced valuation to serve as community leaders, spiritualists, healers, and warriors—in ways decidedly different from slave, peasant, and commoner counterparts in the Gold Coast. Furthermore,

Jamaican maroon communities developed radical or revolutionary new protocols and norms for community and familial roles. In developing a series of complicated social mores and even connubial contracts with provisions for offspring, sexual access, and marital conflict resolution, maroons created sharp breaks from the Gold Coast past in their New World present. While these evolving norms may have been cultural reactions to the unique demographic circumstances in the Americas and within maroon polities, the changing sexual norms and creation of new social and gender rules demonstrate active reevaluations and reformulations of patterns discussed in the first two chapters of the book. In sum, Coromantee and (A)mina women inhabited realms of political, martial, spiritual, and social power within and beyond their communities that represented new conceptualizations of normative gender roles and womanhood in the Gold Coast diaspora.

QUEENS, RITUAL SPECIALISTS, AND WARRIORS

Sitting under her royal canopy, with a robe, a crown, and a wooden sword of state, Queen Cubah of Kingston, Jamaica, must have been an impressive sight to behold for the many Coromantees living in and around the bustling city. Though her story amounts to little more than a fragmentary historical record at best, we can extrapolate from the two brief extant accounts to reveal larger truths about her role and importance. After discovery of the sword of state in Kingston, local officials conducted an investigation leading to the discovery that "Coromantins of that town had raised one Cubah, a female slave belonging to a Jewess, to the rank of royalty, and dubbed her *queen*." This discovery, occurring as it did in the midst of island-wide disturbances in 1760, led authorities to immediately assume the sword of state "was used among the Coromantins as a signal for war" and that the newly appointed "queen of Kingston" had some role to play in Tackey's War. Queen Cubah was seized from the estate of the widow Rachel Cohen, tried, and sentenced to banishment.[14]

Loaded onto the schooner *Mary*—captained by John Swain—the queen of Kingston was to be transported to Spanish Cuba to live a life of exile and laborious toil, probably on a sugar plantation. This may have been viewed as a fate worse than death. Not only did Cubah face transportation to a region without large contingents of Gold Coast Africans and their diasporic, creole-born descendants, but also she would be forced to make the difficult transition from urban servitude to rural slavery. Shortly after disembarkation, Queen Cubah somehow convinced James Daniel—commander of the sloop *Catherine*—to take her back to Jamaica. Upon her request, Daniel indeed returned her, landing in the Leeward portion of the island at Crooke-Cove in Hanover Parish.[15] There Cubah found safe harbor for several weeks—probably among fellow Coromantees—on the plantation of James Crooke. But there she was discovered and captured by James Dawes, and the Assembly of Jamaica ordered Cubah to "be sent in safe custody to the said town of Kingston, to be dealt with pursuant to the laws" of Jamaica.[16] In all likelihood, given her history of recalcitrance, officials in Kingston ordered and carried out her execution.

Whether or not Queen Cubah played a role in the various conspiracies and revolts that convulsed Jamaica in 1760 may not matter as much as the meaning of her presence among the Kingston Coromantees. No records exist detailing her coronation nor the means by which she became a Coromantee regent. However, her elevation to royal status represents a break from a Gold Coast political culture in which notable queens or queen-mothers were few and far between in the seventeenth or eighteenth centuries. I argue that this was partly a function of a remarkably patriarchal Gold Coast elite culture—despite the well-documented matrilineal structures that determined rules of inheritance and political succession. As expendable servants, pawned girls, captured women transformed into concubines, or the "planted" wives of elite men, Gold Coast women representing many social ranks were relegated to constant subordination to the interests of powerful men. Slavery in the Americas, however, represented a social leveling of sorts that replaced old hierarchies and social norms with newer social and political visions. In this case talent and ability trumped heredity, and a new set of viable leaders emerged in this dynamic process. Queen Cubah's elevation and her ability to negotiate with a white ship captain for her safe return to Jamaica—in the midst of island-wide revolts and disturbances—point to an innate charisma and strength of conviction desperately needed in

New World slave communities.[17] Indeed, the role she assumed may have been prefigured by the most famous Coromantee woman in the history of the Americas—Queen Nanny.

Folkloric traditions in Jamaica shape a great deal regarding imaginings of Nanny and her role among the Windward Maroons. Lively stories about her ability to use her buttocks to absorb bullets and cannonballs, only to return them—with force—to her enemies imply that the common "Mother" of all maroons may have existed more as folk legend than the real co-regent of Nanny Town. Mention of Nanny, or women assumed to be her, can be found in only a handful of extent written sources. Even these records do little to reveal useful biographical details.[18] She appears as "the rebels old obeah woman" in the March 1733 minutes of the Assembly of Jamaica. In this case, Nanny was recorded as deceased, the result of the work of a man named Cuffee (William) who reportedly killed her and assisted in the destruction and occupation of Nanny Town.[19] By January 1735, another incarnation of Nanny executed three captured white soldiers during the continuation of the First Maroon War. An eyewitness named Cupid, an Ebo man who "escaped" from the Windwards to report on their activities to local authorities, noted that Nanny was among a leadership core that included Nanny's unnamed husband, Scipio, Cesar, and Adubah. Cupid deemed Nanny's husband a "greater man" than Adou—a military commander among the Windwards—though he "never went in their Battles."[20]

By 1739, Philip Thicknesse described an "old Hagg" and "Obea woman" who wielded a significant amount of political power during his visit to a Windward Maroon settlement on the eve of the peace treaty. In the presence of Captain Quao, Thicknesse requested knowledge about the fate of a previous treaty delegation sent by Governor Edward Trelawny to the Windwards. This delegation, led by British envoy, Laird of Laharets, had met with Quao and informed him of the treaty signed by Colonel Cudjo of the Leeward Maroons in an attempt to induce the Windward leader to agree to a similar peace accord. Quao told Thicknesse, "When I consulted our *Obea woman*, she opposed the measure, and said, *him bring becara* [whites] *for take the town, so cut him head off*." On her orders, Laird and the others accompanying him were killed. Afterward, the grisly reminders of this action were evident to Thicknesse,

who saw that Laird's lower jawbone had been transformed into an ornament for an obeng and that the teeth of his men became adornments for
the anklets and bracelets worn by the town's obeah-women. Based on
the many daggers in sheaths the principal obeah-woman had on a girdle
encircling her waist, Thicknesse concluded that she served as the town's
executioner—imagining that her knives "had been plunged in human
flesh and blood" on previous occasions.[21] Though he never refers to this
woman as the legendary Queen Nanny, her political power, the mention by Quao of her connection to obeah, and her role as executioner of
white captives or visitors combine to link the "old Hagg" in Thicknesse's
description to the Nanny appearing in the earlier two records.

Whether Nanny was, in reality, one person or many different women
who assumed "Nanny" as a title may never be known. Either as a name
or title, Nanny may derive from nana—an Akan reverential title used for
political or spiritual leaders. Even her title as "queen" of the Windwards
or Nanny Town resulted from honorifics added to her legend by the
descendants of Jamaica's Moore Town Maroons well after her death. No
extant source accorded the historical Nanny the royal title of queen, and
even among maroons she is variably recognized as either "Grandy" or
Granny Nanny. Assuming "Nanny" refers to a central political and ritual
leader among the Windwards in the period between 1723 to 1740, her dual
roles reflect radical transformations in the stature of women in the Gold
Coast diaspora. Revered enough as a leader by a large community of
followers, Nanny as a political figure was formidable and imposing. The
place named for her, Nanny Town, served as the military and political
capital of the Windward Maroons until its destruction in 1734. Given
their guile, guerilla tactics, and elusiveness, one has to wonder if both
the town and its powerful woman leader borrowed their names from
"Nanni" or Ananse, the trickster spider who used wit and cunning—at
least in the diasporic renditions of these Gold Coast folktales—to vanquish a range of foes.[22]

Nanny clearly contested for power, on a seemingly equal basis, with
the headmen and captains of the Windwards. For example, Captain
Quao consulted with her about the possibility of peace with British colonial officials, and, according to his statements to Thicknesse, Nanny had
little trust for whites and went as far as to execute the earlier delegation

sent to broker a peace treaty. In all likelihood, even during and after the visit made by Thicknesse, Nanny continued to doubt the entreaties of the British. Indeed, the Articles of Pacification make no mention of Nanny and only include the name of Captain Quao as the Windward leader, with his successors listed as "Thomboy, Apong, Blackweel, and Clath."[23] Nanny led a group of former Windwards the following year to create an independent settlement near Moore Town, even naming it New Nanny Town. A land patent issued on August 14, 1740, by Governor Edward Trelawny granted "said Nanny and the people residing with her and other heirs . . . a certain parcel of land containing five hundred acres in the parish of Portland branching north south and east on Kingsland."[24]

The 1740 land patent for what became New Nanny Town represented something different from, yet parallel to, the Articles signed by Quao in July 1739. In exchange for a yearly rent of "one pound and ten pence current money of Jamaica," as well as assurance that Nanny and the residents of this settlement would be ready to put down "any insurrection, mutiny, rebellion, or invasion," they would be allowed to live in relative peace. They were spared from some of the more restrictive aspects of the Articles of Pacification signed by Captain Quao—including prohibitions against executing prisoners and selling "stock or provisions" in nearby towns without a license. Nanny's followers, by contrast, would be under the jurisdiction of the terms of the land patent and the Act for Effectually Settling the Parish of Portland passed by the Assembly of Jamaica in March 1737.[25] The "old" Nanny Town had ceased to exist by the time the Articles of Pacification were enacted with the Windwards, who opted instead to name their principal settlement Moore Town. The idea that Nanny survived the war and used the land grant to create a separate town is supported by a maroon oral tradition that details a "Woman's Town," inhabited primarily by women and children and under a different jurisdiction than Moore Town. Whether this Woman's Town and New Nanny Town were the same settlement remains a mystery. At some point after 1740, however, this independent town established by Nanny, along with all or most of its inhabitants, merged with Moore Town.[26]

The political power wielded by Nanny found its source in her command over esoteric forces. As a ritual specialist, she could inspire and compel her followers to feats that exceeded their physical limitations.

In fact, I contend that her combined duties as obeah-woman and executioner went hand-in-hand. As conduits of vitality and community and cultural life, women who served as ritual specialists in the African diaspora were the natural gatekeepers between the spiritual and material planes. In a literal sense, they gave or facilitated birth and, in doing so, eased the transmigration of souls or the resurrection of ancestral spirits. In a more abstract way, ritual specialists—particularly midwives, root doctors, and healers—could facilitate the passage of souls between this realm and the next. The spiritual beliefs and knowledge of the Atlantic African pharmacopoeia that they carried into New World slavery granted a range of ritual specialists the ability to create "cures" for pregnancy (e.g., abortifacients), to manufacture lethal poisons, to assist with the delivery of healthy babies, and to the heal the wounded.[27] This is precisely where Nanny stood among her followers—a gatekeeper with supreme mastery over life or death. This role served as the foundation for her immense value among maroons and for the political or judicial power to execute white captives without permission from the men who led the Windwards.

Women like Nanny, both within and beyond maroon enclaves in the Americas, commanded a seemingly paradoxical range of life-giving generative powers and destructive forces, which further augmented their political potential. Indeed, no single concept embodies this more than the cultivation of cassava or manioc in the Caribbean and South America. Cassava farming, processing, and food preparation—defined as "women's work" throughout Atlantic Africa and in a range of diasporic communities—provided one of many sources of food calories for enslaved laborers and maroons. In addition, the preparation of cassava as a life-sustaining food involved the extraction of large amounts of hydrocyanide from the starchy tuber before it could be processed into flour or bread. In small doses—for example, the amount ingested when chewing sticks from a cassava shrub—hydrocyanide poison became an abortion agent among enslaved women in the Americas. When used in higher concentrations, most abortifacients could be transformed into poisons with sufficient toxicity to kill able-bodied adults. Cassava thus joined a range of abortifacients-turned-poisons employed throughout the Black Atlantic, including cotton seed oil, green pineapple, rue, pennyroyal, cedar berries, dogwood root, cocklebur root, wild tansy, and water germander. The use of these plants, herbs, and seeds in the creation of abortifacients and lethal toxins represents a realm of ethnobotanical knowledge monopolized by enslaved and maroon women.[28] Though not as vital for maroon women, the ability to produce abortifacients by free and enslaved women represented the potential of gynecological resistance and means of achieving contraception, reduced fertility, and even sterility. The demographic pressures all maroon enclaves faced meant that controlling or deterring reproductive capacity was, in and of itself, a political act and a potential source of political power.[29] Additionally, the obvious military applications for lethal poisons elevated women politically and further enhanced their centrality among maroons.

Midwives and obeah-women—ritual specialists and gatekeepers between the realms—served complementary roles to healers. By producing poisons and easing childbirth, obeah-women and midwives became critical in the ability of maroon enclaves to facilitate both war and regeneration. Healers, likewise, activated their knowledge of Atlantic African and American pharmacopeia to sustain life in the midst of warfare, brutal plantation regimes, and disease ecologies that included a range of debilitating and lethal afflictions. For inhabitants of maroon enclaves and plantations alike, constant cycles of triage, intervention, and recovery became quotidian aspects of life. From broken bones and gashes suffered on the field of battle to deep lacerations caused by the overseer's scourge, healers applied salves and herbal poultices to help mend broken black bodies.[30] Together, obeah-women, midwives, and healers should be understood as political agents who protected, regenerated, and sustained the "body politic" of maroon enclaves and plantation communities. In this sense, Nanny's mastery over life and death, and her role as gatekeeper between the two realms, was replicated by a much larger range of women ritual specialists in the Americas. The presence of these women across Western Hemisphere societies validates the existence of transgenerational and even transnational female knowledge networks assessed in the works of Deborah Gray White, Barbara Bush, Michael Gomez, and Margaret Washington.[31]

The powers Nanny had over life and death became further elaborated over the nineteenth and twentieth centuries in the folkloric traditions of the descendants of the Windward Maroons. Among their many oral traditions, Jamaican maroons developed an origins story in which two sisters—Nanny and Sekesu—represent the mothers of all Jamaicans. Both were captured in the Gold Coast and brought to Jamaica onboard the same ship. Nanny, however, immediately escaped into the wilderness to found Nanny Town. From her secluded mountain abode, she used guerilla warfare and raised an entire generation of warriors to destabilize the Jamaican slaveocracy and British colonial government. As her heirs, the Moore Town Maroons understand themselves as Nanny's *yoyo*, or progeny, and Nanny represents both a common ancestress and the blood connection between all maroons. Her sister, Sekesu, on the other hand, never escaped bondage and—according to this tradition—she became the mother of all plantation slaves. While both sisters were born in the Gold Coast, they eventually seeded the creation of a new, national identity as the mothers of all modern Afro-Jamaicans.[32] In the long memory represented by these maroon traditions, this particular story of Afro-Jamaican ethnogenesis may represent—in allegorical form—the process by which Coromantees, Eboes, Congos, and both "bush" and plantation creoles exchanged their country marks in becoming one people.

Moore Town Maroons and their descendants credit Nanny not only with founding the earliest maroon settlements, but also with developing ingenious methods for their continued existence and growth. For example, one tradition tells how of a beleaguered Queen Nanny who, after suffering a series of devastating defeats, was distraught that her followers did not have sufficient stores of food to survive. Visited by ancestral spirits in her sleep, Nanny gained renewed courage and discovered magical pumpkin seeds that the ancestors had apparently placed in her pocket. For several years, these pumpkins bore fruit and sustained the maroons; even now, one of the regions near old Nanny Town is still called Pumpkin Hill.[33] Other folklore traditions that center on Nanny refer to some combination of her ritual or martial expertise. Her ability, in maroon oral tradition, to catch and repel bullets with her buttocks elevated her beyond Colonel Cudjo of the Leewards. According to a nineteenth-century chief of the Moore Town Maroons: "Nanny had more science in fighting than even Cudgoe. . . . After the signing of the treaty, Nanny say that she show them science. She told fifty soldiers to load their guns and then to fire on her. She fold back her hands between her legs and catches the fifty shots. This was called Nantucompong, Nanny takes her back to catch the balls."[34] In addition to the story of Nantucompong, maroon oral traditions recount Nanny's masterful ability to employ the abeng as a means of communication and deception and to use a magical pot to rain boiling water on the heads of enemy soldiers. In combination, these traditions all highlight Nanny as progenitor, protector, and sustainer of the maroons—reflecting, again, the historical roles played by women like her in a wider range of maroon and plantation societies.[35]

In serving the vital function of ritual specialist for the Windwards, Nanny had a number of unnamed acolytes under her supervision who may have received formal training from their leader. During his 1739 visit to the Windwards, Thicknesse specifically noted the presence of "Obea women" who wore ankle and wrist bracelets adorned with the teeth of enemy soldiers.[36] Indeed, given the pattern of naming Nanny Town after a principal obeah-woman, I conjecture that the town's other two quarters or subdivisions—Diana and Molly—may have been named after other prominent and powerful ritual specialists.[37] One of these women or another obeah-woman may have been the person reportedly killed by (William's) Cuffee in a March 1733 British assault on Nanny Town.[38]

While no extant records exist in Jamaica further detailing the specific activities of these and other obeah-women within maroon enclaves, examples from Suriname provide useful and generative insights. J. C. Dörig, a white visitor to the Saramaka Maroon community from October 1762 to March 1763, relates an incident in which he was approached by "an old Negro woman, entirely painted white, with a slave plantation sabre or machete in her hand, holding it diagonally over the other arm, going up and down and making a lot of noise, babbling in her language."[39] Though Dörig offers no further description of this scene, the fact that it occurred on the eve of the 1762 Treaty with the Bush Negroes of Upper Saramacca and Suriname signals the possibility that this mysterious woman—probably in touch with ancestral spirits given the color of her body paint—used her threatening actions to lodge protest against both the treaty negotiations and the presence of white men among the Saramaka.[40]

The presence of women as politically empowered ritual specialists among Suriname's maroon enclaves finds additional corroboration in Stedman's *Narrative of a Five Years' Expedition*. In discussing spiritualists holding "high reverence" for silk cotton trees and selling "*obias,* or amulets," he includes a detailed description of their role in both slave and maroon communities:

> Nor are a kind of *Sibyls* wanting among them, who deal in oracles; these sage matrons dancing and whirling round in the middle of an audience, till they absolutely froth at the mouth and drop down in the middle of them. Whatever she says to be done during this fit of madness is sacredly performed by the surrounding multitude, which makes these meetings exceedingly dangerous among the slaves, who are often told to murder their masters or desert to the woods, and on which account the excessiveness of this piece of fanaticism is forbidden in the Colony of Surinam, on pain of the most rigorous punishment. Yet it is often put in execution in private places and is very common among the [Ndjuka] and Saramaka Negroes, where captains Friderici and Van Geurike told me they saw it performed.[41]

While the "Sibyls" and "sage matrons" noted by Stedman were probably devotees of Mami Wata, a serpent-wielding water goddess in the form of a mermaid, this syncretic and highly malleable African Atlantic and diaspora religious expression involved a number of ritual practices that paralleled obeah (see figure 6.1).[42] Like Nanny of the Jamaican Windwards, these devotees of Mami Wata used their connections to the world beyond as a means of political empowerment in the here and now, compelling others to engage in acts of violent resistance. Those who could claim direct contact with ancestors or Atlantic Africa deities occupied pivotal political spaces that allowed them to shape slave and maroon enclaves in immeasurable ways.

While women acted as ritual specialists in the Gold Coast context, playing roles in the affairs of rural hamlets and villages, they did not have the same social stature and political voice as the priestess and other ritual specialists in Western Hemisphere societies. No figure as striking as Nanny, for example, appears in the annals of Gold Coast history until Yaa Asantewaa, who led a military campaign against British imperialism at the turn of the twentieth century. To be clear, my assessment does not contend that capture, enslavement, and transport to the Americas determined the elevation of Gold Coast women. Instead, it was the very fact that—in the absence of Gold Coast elites—enslaved men and women who carried with them and further articulated the commoner consciousness had a unique opportunity to build their new communities

6.1. Mami Wata priestess in Suriname performing a healing ritual, 1831.
Source: Benoit, *Voyage à Surinam,* plate 17, figure 36.

from the ground up. By concentrating the population of commoners, racial slavery created the conditions for the emergence of radical new social forms. The realities of Western Hemisphere slavery encouraged the employment of these social forms as modes of resistance and new strategies for survival. This afforded them the chance to disrupt hierarchical social and political structures seen as normative in the Gold Coast. In this process of social leveling and political reinvention, a radical new vision of the role and status of women became part of a generative core in Gold Coast diaspora formations. While Nanny, Diana, and Molly may not have been queens, they wielded political power, swayed men and women alike to follow them, and commanded respect and authority in ways that represent a revolutionary break from the Gold Coast past.[43]

Maroon women, in particular, represented a new definition of womanhood for the untold thousands exiled from the Gold Coast. While their roles as healers, obayifo, and midwives did not represent new formulations, the fact that their access to and connections with the ancestral realm granted them a political voice can be understood as an "Americanism"—an addition to African Atlantic cultural matrices spawned in the sociopolitical geography of Western Hemisphere slavery. Nanny, Diana, Molly, and many other women shared in the new possibilities represented by marronage as well as the attendant dangers. From one description, it is clear that women served as auxiliaries to maroon raiding parties and would "help carry off the spoil," serve as lookouts who would torch houses on the approach of enemies, or directly engage attacking parties when needed.[44] Though little else has been uncovered about their roles as soldiers or their martial aptitude, maroon women faced the same excruciating tortures and executions as their male counterparts upon capture by colonial authorities. A communiqué from a member of the Assembly of Jamaica, a Mr. Edlyne, to the assembly speaker illustrates this point. In his message, Edlyne noted the several rewards for "rebel negroes" that had been issued by 1733, including "ten pounds per head for every rebellious negro man, eight pounds for every rebellious woman, and four pounds for every rebellious boy and girl under the age of ten years, that should be killed or taken alive."[45]

In keeping with the Spartan fortitude associated with Coromantees and (A)minas, maroon women could exhibit the same resolution and intrepidity. In this regard, Stedman detailed the fate of eleven captured rebels after a 1730 uprising in Dutch Suriname. Of the six women captured in this group, he notes they were all "broken alive upon the rack, and two girls were decapitated, through which tortures they went without uttering a sigh."[46] In addition, women were among those involved in mass suicides at the end of failed Coromantee and (A)mina revolts and conspiracies. The strength of spirit, fortitude, and pain tolerance at the core of Gold Coast diaspora constructions of masculinity shaped a new form of womanhood for Coromantee and (A)mina women. They too faced breaking, burning, and gibbeting without complaint, in anticipation of becoming empowered ancestors.[47] Their warrior spirits indeed survived within the many maroon and slave enclaves shaped by Gold Coast diaspora concepts of martial valor, courage, and resilience.

VALUE AND REGENERATION WITHIN MAROON FORMATIONS

Given the demographic equation operative throughout the transatlantic slave trade, practically every colony—with the exception of Barbados—

imported more Atlantic African men than women. This demographic disparity explains the sexual imbalance in slave societies. When coupled with high mortality and low rates of fertility, enslaved peoples in the circum-Caribbean were not a self-reproducing population for the majority of the history of the slave trade. These matters became further augmented within maroon enclaves.[48] The natural outcome of the lack of women within maroon formations shaped some of their war aims in Jamaica, Suriname, and beyond—particularly the focus on raiding slave plantations to liberate enslaved women. One report noted, "In all plunderings they were Industrious in procuring Negro Women, Girls, and Female Children."[49] Accordingly, enslaved and maroon women were highly valued; their presence meant the possibility of families, offspring, and new generations of maroon fighters and ritual experts. This runs counter to the claims made by Bryan Edwards, who noted that the Trelawny Town Maroons often treated women and girls with great contempt:

> The labours of the field, however, such as they were (as well as every other species of drudgery), were performed by the women . . . the Maroons, like all other savage nations, regarded their wives as so many beasts of burthen; and felt no more concern at the loss of one of them, than a white planter would have felt at the loss of a bullock. . . . This spirit of brutality which the Maroons always displayed towards their wives, extended in some degree to their children. The paternal authority was at all times most harshly exerted; but more especially towards the females. . . . Nothing can more strikingly demonstrate the forlorn and abject condition of the young women among the Maroons, than the circumstances which every gentleman, who has visited them on festive occasions, or for the gratification of curiosity, knows to be true, the offering their own daughters, by the first men among them, to their visitors; and bringing the poor girls forward, with or without their consent, for the purpose of prostitution.[50]

Writing in 1796 and relying upon the accounts of others who visited various maroon enclaves in Jamaica, Edwards conveyed his clear disdain for the maroons while misunderstanding some of the inner workings of their communities.

Rather than being used as "beasts of burden," maroon women engaged in agricultural pursuits much in the same way as their Atlantic African and enslaved or free circum-Caribbean counterparts. The many provisioning grounds and public markets controlled by women of color throughout the British Caribbean demonstrate their agency in the productive processes that undergirded informal economies, highlighting an innate entrepreneurial spirit. In this context, the provisioning ground and the public market were domains of empowerment, not debasement, for women. As cultivators, market sellers, and higglers they contributed to family and community economies while carving out a measure of independent social and economic space from men.[51] Given the terms of the Articles of Pacification signed by both the Leewards and Windwards, maroon women could apply for licenses in order to sell their "Hogs, Fowls, and any other kind of Stock or Provisions" at public markets.[52] Their involvement in local, informal economies and their particular gender-based division of labor, far from representing the oppression of maroon women, reflected key roles they shared in sustaining these enclaves. In the oral traditions of the Moore Town Maroons, Nanny's ability to grow pumpkins using magical seeds given to her by the ancestors serves as a metaphor for perseverance and survival—not laborious drudgery and slavish duty to men. As such, "Queen" Nanny and other maroon women like her were held in high regard and not despised as expendable beasts of burden as Edwards claims.

Moreover, the notion given voice by Edwards that maroon men "felt no more concern at the loss" of a woman makes little sense, given the significant risks taken in liberating women from plantations and the lengths to which they worked to protect women and children.[53] A range of contemporaries of Edwards noted, for example, that maroons created sexually segregated towns for the protection of maroon women and children during times of war. Indeed, this becomes one of the best examples demonstrating the differential valuation of women—in the eyes of community leaders—in maroon political formations and Gold Coast polities.[54] Women may have been expendable in the eyes of Gold Coast elites in ways that they simply could not be among maroons and others in the Americas. However, their roles and status among maroons did not result simply from demographic or reproductive necessity. These factors may have contributed to their collective value and importance, but I contend that commoner consciousness helped define a new womanhood in which Coromantee, (A)mina, and maroon women could more readily elevate to community, ritual, and economic leadership. While patriarchal norms still prevailed—particularly within maroon enclaves—the consciousness that served as a shaping influence for New World ethnic formations allowed for the existence of empowered political, spiritual, and economic domains for women.

With the above in mind, it is the range of comments made by Edwards about maroon family formations, connubial relationships, and sexuality that prove the most problematic. A witness who visited the Trelawny Town Maroons in the 1740s recounts a set of interesting observations regarding their ideas about family and connubial relations. While this visitor penned his December 20, 1743, letter a half century before the statements made by Edwards, he had the vantage of personally witnessing what he saw and heard. In this account, he notes:

> Each man is allowed as many Wive's as He can Maintain and should any of their Women be catched Playing loose with another Man, they are never Angry, and far from giving them Correction; on the Contrary, the Husband agrees with the Galant, alternately to enjoy the woman, the former three days and Nights and the latter two: Nay further should any Man incline to share a Wife with a Husband, on Application, 'tis allowed under the aforementioned Regulation; and let which of them get the child the first Man Fathers all, and this for no other Reason, than an Encrease of Children to keep up their Gangs; fearing the Incapacity of One Man with One Woman.[55]

This description implies a radically different understanding of normative family structures and values than those prevailing elsewhere in the eighteenth century. This view among the Trelawny Maroons of monogamous relationships as an "Incapacity" and the decision making ability of women to choose sexual partners, or "play loose," without repercussion or correction demonstrates that the new Gold Coast diaspora womanhood—alluded to earlier—had a range of manifestations within maroon social orders and family concepts.

Barbara Kopytoff has argued that these connubial contracts among the Trelawny Town Maroons represented a response to their inability to replenish their numbers through natural reproduction and a "system of sexual rights in women which included the granting and sharing of these rights by men."[56] This approach, however, ignores the fact that these connubial contracts vested the power of certain decisions with maroon women, who were free to "play loose" and, in essence, have more than one husband. While polyandry may have been a natural outcome of having so few women within maroon polities, this example of the Trelawny Town Maroons represents a complete inversion of social, family, and marital norms operative in eighteenth-century Atlantic Africa.[57] Within the Gold Coast, polygynous families headed by an elite man were the only polygamous family formations present. Polyandry in the Gold Coast and, more broadly, Atlantic Africa would have been practically impossible.

The presence of polyandry within patrilineal and patriarchal maroon formations represents one of the most radical (re)formulations in the Gold Coast diaspora. Rigid, hierarchical, and elite male-dominated societies lacked the type of social flexibility that would have allowed this type of maroon family structure to thrive. While demographic conditions in the eighteenth-century Gold Coast and the Gold Coast diaspora in the Americas were vastly different, this alone does not explain the social rigidity preventing the emergence of polyandrous family formations among Akan-, Ga-, Adanme-, and Ewe-speaking peoples. Even matrilineal, matrifocal, and matrilocal forms at the core of Akan-speaking societies could not facilitate the creation of more flexible family structures. Polyandry, as a possibility for new families forming in the Gold Coast diaspora, should be understood as a revolutionary disjuncture from the past in the process of shaping a viable present and future.

The democratic and egalitarian principles undergirding the commoner consciousness allowed for a series of transformations that were, in essence, miniature social revolutions within Gold Coast diaspora communities. Former commoners took power, using the emblems and icons of Gold Coast and European elite political cultures as means of transforming the world around them. Obeah-doctors, men and women, used their connections to Atlantic African and diaspora ancestors to generate the spiritual resources necessary to wage wars against planters and the forces of colonial governments. Finally, women found multiple avenues to empowerment—political, ritual, martial, economic, and social—to overturn assumptions about gender and to forge a new sense of womanhood in the Gold Coast diaspora. Far more significant than their failures and successes in creating New World polities was that they managed to create New World peoples whose revolutionary consciousness evolved into core principles at the heart of African American cultures throughout the Caribbean, and beyond.

Postscript

Chattel slavery did not have the power to fully vanquish the enslaved—turning them into a collection of Sambos, Mammys, Quashees, and Quashebas. The best proof of this can be found within the corpus of Ananse the Spider tales collected in Jamaica and Suriname. As folk hero, rebel, and didactic metaphor, Ananse's continuous existence in the long memory of Gold Coast diaspora communities demonstrates the many inadequacies of social death as a theoretical frame in understanding the fate of Atlantic Africans and their creole kin in Western Hemisphere slavery. The processes of capture, commodification, and transport, as well as the transitions into chattel slavery, did not form a linear historical trajectory from fully articulated Atlantic African "lives" to the flattened potentialities and personalities of the socially dead.[1] At best, social death was a temporal waypoint preceding liminality and, later, the resurrection of reinvented peoples in the Americas. The vibrant traditions associated with Ananse support the notion that Gold Coast diaspora peoples and their American-born descendants achieved afterlives beyond social death.

As one of many cultural technologies transported to the Americas by enslaved Gold Coast Africans, Ananse stories became a key dimension of the commoner consciousness developed by Coromantees and (A)minas. Beyond serving as counter-hegemonic discourse, these folktales also played roles in the continual transformations from ethnicity to race in the Black Atlantic. Embedded within Ananse stories lie clues to how Eboes, Congos, and others negotiated with and joined Coromantees and (A)minas to form new transethnic constructions that resembled racial and, later, national identities. Though peoples from a range of Atlantic African regional diasporas helped shape these processes, Coromantee and (A)mina icons, cultural technologies, and ancestors were at the heart of new concepts of identity. ·

Though the first recorded Western Hemisphere Ananse Spider tales can be tracked to early twentieth-century collections, this trickster appeared in other ways across the historical terrain of the Gold Coast diaspora. The infamous Jamaican overseer Thomas Thistlewood, for example, first noted hearing "Coromantee stories" in May 1751. A connoisseur of various "Negro Diversions," Thistlewood detailed one such Coromantee tale titled "How the Crab Got Its Shell"—one of the first transcriptions of an Atlantic African animal story. In the version told to him by an enslaved island-born creole named Phibbah, an elderly woman refused to give her granddaughter food until she could ascertain the grandmother's "true" African name. After some trial and error, the granddaughter cleverly queried a nearby crab, who revealed the six words constituting her elder's original name. In the story, the granddaughter saved herself from starvation by using quick wit and ingenuity. Later, upon discovery of the informant, the grandmother hurled a calabash gourd at the crab in anger. The gourd stuck to the crab's back and became its "shell" from that point forward.[2] Though Ananse does not appear in this particular Coromantee story, the idea at the core of this didactic tale—using wit to attend to the material deprivations of chattel slavery—draws it into the cultural orbit of other trickster folk traditions found throughout the Atlantic African diaspora.[3]

In subsequent years, Thistlewood would encounter other forms of Coromantee stories. From September 17 to 27, 1768, two enslaved Coromantee women—Vine and Abba—revealed to him a number of "Nancy stories," which Thistlewood found "entertaining enough."[4] Innocuous and harmless to the untrained ears of eighteenth-century white listeners, Ananse and other Coromantee tales could be disseminated and consumed in ways that imply that they formed part of a hidden transcript—similar to country "plays" in the Anglophone Caribbean and capoeira "games" in Brazil. While James Scott allows for aspects of hidden transcripts to occur away from the watchful eyes of the powerful, the mocking and vengeance expressed in slave folklore and other forms were embedded in public performances—though coded and buried under layers of multiple meaning. Ananse, then, could "entertain" an overseer as brutal as Thistlewood in eighteenth-century Jamaica while offering a culturally coded and, therefore, "safe" means of relaying discontent and counter-hegemonic discourse.[5]

Thistlewood, however, never revealed the content of the Nancy stories with which Vine and Abba amused him. Likewise, Jamaican planter Matthew Lewis heard a number of "Nancy stories" between 1815 and 1818 but neglected to transcribe a single one.[6] Both Thistlewood and Lewis considered the stories they heard harmless and unremarkable because enslaved storytellers successfully masked the didactic and counter-hegemonic content. We are left, therefore, to conjecture about the embedded meanings and messages contained within Ananse Spider tales in the eighteenth and nineteenth centuries. It would not be until the dawn of the twentieth century that a few dozen Ananse Spider stories appeared in print in a range of venues. Then, in 1904, Walter Jekyll—an English-born writer who spent thirty-four years in Jamaica—published the first book-length collection of Jamaican folklore which included fifty-one Ananse stories and songs. Jekyll's 1904 collection opens a small window into the worlds of the descendants of Jamaican slaves and maroons and, perhaps, creates glimpses of the prior content of Ananse Spider stories.[7]

In the earliest Ananse stories collected and published, we get a strong sense of transformative cultural processes and a political discourse shaped by commoner consciousness. In one Jamaican tale collected by Jekyll, Ananse encounters a king's eldest daughter, whose name, Yung-kyum-pyung, is a clear reference to the Akan sky god—rendered as "Yancúmpong" or "Jancómpon" in early-modern Gold Coast travel accounts.[8] In the story, Ananse has to learn the names of all three of the king's daughters in order to claim the king's throne. He crafts an ornate basket, leaves it for them to discover, and hides under their house to eavesdrop on their conversation. Eventually, all three marvel at the gift and, unwittingly, sing out each other's names in delight. After revealing all three of their names, Ananse claims the king's throne and marries the youngest daughter—Eggie Law.[9] By the 1890s, the Gold Coast was but a distant memory to many Jamaicans; this may explain, in part, the "demotion" of the Akan sky god from omnipotent creator to the name of an insignificant daughter of a king and a minor refrain in an Ananse

Spider song. Another possibility is that Jancómpon could not make the journey to the Americas with Gold Coast Africans as they tended to latch on to more egalitarian ritual practices associated with their commoner ancestors—bayi and the production of sumán.[10]

While Ananse was decoupled from the Akan sky god in the Americas, he had other spiritual connections that proved the transethnic appeal of this trickster. Jekyll recounts a tale titled "Sea-Mahmy" in which Ananse seeks to outwit Blackbird and gain access to his "feeding tree" in the midst of a famine. Since the feeding tree is located on an island in the middle of a sea, Ananse tricks Blackbird into giving him feathers so he can take wing and fly to the food. After eating his fill and becoming too laden to fly back to the mainland, Ananse sinks into the sea, where he receives assistance from his "cousin," Sea-Mahmy.[11] Depicted in the tale as a mermaid who commands sea creatures, Sea-Mahmy bears strong resemblance to Mami Wata—the pan-African water goddess whose worship extends from modern-day Senegal to Tanzania and across the Atlantic to Suriname, Jamaica, and Brazil. Belief in Mami Wata spread throughout the Black Atlantic as a consequence of long-standing cultural cross-fertilizations between a range of Europeans and Atlantic Africans during the eras of Atlantic commerce and European imperialism.[12] Perhaps, then, it is fitting that Ananse found kinship with such a transethnic, transnational, inclusive, and fluid goddess as this link mirrored the kind of processes historically shaping and connecting peoples throughout the Black Atlantic.

In addition to Mami Wata and a version of Jancómpon, Ananse encountered another spiritual force in his Jamaican adventures—Brother Death. In the version of the story recounted by Jekyll, Ananse schemes to take all of Death's food, in part by marrying his daughter to Brother Death. After claiming Death's stores of meat and vegetables, Ananse discovers to his horror that Brother Death has killed and dismembered his daughter. Death eventually corners Ananse and his wife and two boys in their house in retaliation for the confiscation of his food. As all four hang from the rafters of the house to avoid Brother Death, Ananse's wife and children fall and are captured, one by one. When Ananse is the last one left, he strikes a bargain with Death. He convinces Death that he will drop from the rafters, but only after Brother Death fetches a barrel of flour to cushion Ananse's fall. Unbeknownst to Brother Death, the barrel he retrieves contains quicklime, a highly caustic chemical compound. When Ananse jumps, he falls on Death's head forcing it into the barrel of quicklime. With Brother Death blinded and incapacitated, Ananse frees his family and they all escape from the house.[13]

While Ananse duped and defeated a series of powerful foes in these early stories—Tiger, Snake, the Devil, and the King—his conquest over Death was the most resounding.[14] Ananse's defeat of Death serves as a metaphor for the survival of Coromantees and (A)minas in chattel slavery and beyond. Indeed, they achieved a semblance of immortality within the national consciousness of modern-day states in the circum-Caribbean. Nothing attests to this phenomenon better than the 1763 Monument in Georgetown, Guyana. A towering bronze sculpture erected in 1976, this monument dedicated to Captain Cuffy—commander of the Delmina during the 1763 Berbice rebellion—stands now as a symbol of courage and national sovereignty. As mentioned in chapter 4, Cuffy transformed himself from house servant to rebel captain and led a multilingual army of hundreds in a four-month campaign to establish a sovereign state in the Dutch colony. Modern Guyanese remember Cuffy not simply as a Delmina or a slave rebel, but as a founding national hero. Celebrated in Guyana and beyond, Cuffy joins Nanny, Jamaica's Tacky, Tacky Court (Antigua), and Quamina Gladstone (Guyana)—co-leader of an 1823 slave revolt in British Demerara—as part of a pantheon of Coromantees and (A)minas recognized as national heroes throughout the circum-Caribbean. Memorialized at national monuments and murals, on currency, and in reggae anthems, Coromantee and (A)mina revolutionaries not only defied death but also spurred the rise of new national identities in the postcolonial era. In the midst of their independence movements, Jamaicans, Antiguans, and Guyanese consciously replaced European colonial founding fathers with a new set of iconic national champions that epitomized the struggle against white hegemonic rule in earlier eras. In the process of forging postcolonial national identities, Coromantee and (A)mina forbears became metaphors for perseverance, survival, and triumph.[15] Even now, they live on in the popular memory, folklore, and national consciousness of communities in far-flung reaches of the Black Atlantic—from Suriname and Jamaica to Nova Scotia and Sierra Leone.[16]

NOTES

Introduction

1. "Discharge of Private Don Juan, July 10, 1846," in War Office, Royal Hospital Chelsea: Soldiers Service Documents (1760–1854) (hereafter WO), 97/1159/61, National Archives, Kew, UK; Riley, *Poverty and Life Expectancy*, 23–24.

2. "Discharge of Private Don Juan, July 10, 1846," WO, 97/1159/61. A detailed discussion of "Coromantee" behavioral performances appears in chapter 3. For seventeenth-, eighteenth-, and nineteenth-century insights, see "Governor Jonathan Atkins to Colonial Secretary Joseph Williamson, Oct. 3, 1675," in Headlam, *Calendar of State Papers, Colonial Series, America and West Indies* (hereafter *CSPC*), IX:294; "Governor Christopher Codrington to the English Board of Trade, Dec. 30, 1701," in *CSPC*, XIX:720–721; Snelgrave, *New Account*, 168–174, 184; "A History of Sugar Cane," 487; Long, *History of Jamaica*, II:403–404; Peytraud, *L'Esclavage aux Antilles Françaises*, 89; Edwards, *History, Civil and Commercial*, IV:266–268, 272–276, 278–279, 293; Phillippo, *Jamaica*, 386; "Glimpses of the Western Indies," in *The Monthly Christian Spectator, 1851–1859*, vol. IV, 370.

3. Caulfield, *100 Years' History*, 45–53; Reindorf, *History of the Gold Coast*, 191–192.

4. Caulfield, *100 Years' History*, 53–70.

5. "Discharge of Private Don Juan, July 10, 1846," WO, 97/1159/61.

6. Chambers, "Ethnicity in the Diaspora," 31–32; Behn, *Oroonoko*, xvii–xix, xxi, 12–14, 76; Beach, "Behn's Oroonoko," 216–217.

7. While "(A)mina" in this book includes the Amina of the Danish Virgin Islands, the Delmina of Dutch Berbice (in modern-day Guyana), and the Mina of Spanish and French Louisiana, this term does not encompass the Mina of Portuguese Brazil. "Mina" has a complicated and convoluted history in the Lusophone world. As early as the sixteenth century, Mina had ambiguous ethnolinguistic or regional connotations and was employed as an occupational label to describe Atlantic Africans from Greater Senegambia and the Gold Coast skilled at gold mining. By the eighteenth century in Brazil, Mina denoted mostly speakers of Ewe, Aja, and Fon originating from the Slave Coast. Mina, thus, never had a stable ethnolinguistic or regional association when employed in early-modern Brazil. In sum, the

Brazilian Mina and the (A)mina discussed in this book have little to no connection. See G. M. Hall, *Slavery and African Ethnicities*, 36–37, 47, 67, 112–119; G. M. Hall, "African Ethnicities and the Meanings of 'Mina,'" in Lovejoy and Trotman, *Trans-Atlantic Dimensions of Ethnicity*, 65–78; Law, "Ethnicities of Enslaved Africans," 247–267; Sweet, *Recreating Africa*, 3; Curto and Lovejoy, *Enslaving Connections*, 12, 98–99, 151; Hawthorne, *From Africa to Brazil*, 3, 44, 181, 251.

8. J. Thornton, "War, the State, and Religious Norms in 'Coromantee' Thought: The Ideology of an African American Nation," in St. George, *Possible Pasts*, 196–198; J. Thornton, *Warfare in Atlantic Africa*, 142–143; Rebecca Shumway, *Fante*, 40–51, 101; Kea, *Settlements, Trade, and Polities*, 286; Kea, "'When I Die, I Shall Return to My Own Land': An 'Amina' Slave Rebellion in the Danish West Indies, 1733–1734," in Hunwick and Lawler, *Cloth of Many Coloured Silks*, 174–180; Wood, *Black Majority*, 126–127.

9. Mehta, "Sparta in the Enlightenment," 1–3. The best example of the transformation of Coromantee identity would be the modern conflation of "Coromantee" with "Maroon" in Jamaica and Suriname. Indeed, in Guyana and Jamaica people continue to revere "Coromantee" or (A)mina maroons and rebels as national heroes—with a range of historical monuments, place names, and other memorials. See Kopytoff, "Development of Jamaican Maroon Ethnicity," 33–50; Alleyne and Hall-Alleyne, "Language Maintenance and Language Death," 55–57; Dunham, *Katherine Dunham's Journey*, 44.

10. Fort Kormantse, now Fort Amsterdam, shared its name with the Fante-speaking towns—Upper and Lower Kormantse—from 1598 to 1665. Built originally by the Dutch as one of their principal factories in the Gold Coast, the fort was captured by the British in 1645. Fort Kormantse changed hands again, in 1665, during the Anglo-Dutch War; the Dutch renamed it Fort New Amsterdam, perhaps in response to having "lost" New Amsterdam to the British in North America. In the modern orthography, the fort is known simply as Fort Amsterdam. Agorsah, "Archaeology and Resistance History," 178–180.

11. In addition to Don Juan, records exist for at least one other man in the 2nd West India Regiment—Sergeant Edward Confoo—who claimed to be born in Coromantee either shortly before or after the passage of the 1807 Slave Trade Act. Discharged on May 11, 1852, in Trinidad, Edward Confoo—like Don Juan six years earlier—chose to settle in Jamaica for his retirement. "Discharge of Sergeant Edward Confoo, May 11, 1852," WO, 97/1156/195; Adderley, *New Negroes from Africa*, 1–4, 95, 127–129, 230.

12. Gomez, *Exchanging Our Country Marks*, 39–40; Sidbury and Cañizares-Esguerra, "Mapping Ethnogenesis," 186–189; Hartman, *Lose Your Mother*, 102–104.

13. Hartman, *Lose Your Mother*, 103.

14. Chambers, "Ethnicity in the Diaspora," 27–29; Sidbury and Cañizares-Esguerra, "Mapping Ethnogenesis," 186.

15. Gomez, *Exchanging Our Country Marks*, 71–72, 82–87; Diouf, *Servants of Allah*, 3, 10–11, 92–93, 97–106.

16. Kea, "An 'Amina' Slave Rebellion," 167–169, 175–180; Hartman, *Lose Your Mother*, 91–94; J. Thornton, *Warfare in Atlantic Africa*, 142–143.

17. An example of this would be *bayi* and other forms of anti-social spiritual power defined as "witchcraft" in the Gold Coast as early as the seventeenth century. Unlike state sanctioned and appointed priesthoods, bayi—from which *obeah* receives some of its etymological and cultural origin—was a particularly non-elite or subaltern means of spiritual empowerment in the Gold Coast. As such, bayi practitioners—by their very existence—acted against the interests of polities and often became the targets of urban elites and slave traffickers. Instead of being understood as an anti-social ritual practice in the Americas, obeah became normative as enslaved rebels employed it in their quests to create new political and social orders. Its centrality among maroons and its activation by rebels in Suriname, Jamaica, Antigua, and Barbados are assessed, at length, in chapter 4. For a parallel treatment of obeah, see J. Thornton, "Coromantees," 161–178.

18. Smallwood, *Saltwater Slavery*, 195; V. Brown, *Reaper's Garden*, 5–12, 58.

19. See V. Brown, "Social Death and Political Life," 1231–1249; Beach, "Behn's Oroonoko," 217–218.

20. Patterson, *Slavery and Social Death*, 38–40.

21. Berlin, "From Creole to African," 508; Lovejoy, "African Diaspora," 7; V. Brown, "Social Death and Political Life," 1231–1249; Diptee, *From Africa to Jamaica*, 6, 79–80; Sweet, "Defying Social Death" 251–272.

22. J. Thornton, *Africa and Africans*; Gomez, *Exchanging Our Country Marks*; Palmer, "Modern African Diaspora," 27–32. For works on ethnic, linguistic, religious, and geographic Atlantic African diasporas, see Diouf, *Servants of Allah*; Carney, *Black Rice*; Mann and Bay, *Rethinking the African Diaspora*; Heywood, *Central Africans*; Sweet, *Recreating Africa*; Lovejoy and Trotman, *Trans-Atlantic Dimensions of Ethnicity*; Falola and Childs, *Yoruba Diaspora*; Chambers, *Murder at Montpelier*; Hall, *Slavery and African Ethnicities*; Young, *Rituals of Resistance*; Byrd, *Captives and Voyagers*; Hawthorne, *From Africa to Brazil*; Diptee, *From Africa to Jamaica*; Ferreira, *Cross-Cultural Exchange*; R. M. Brown, *African-Atlantic Cultures*; Parés, *The Formation of Candomble*.

23. A handful of articles and book chapters focusing on the Gold Coast or "Akan" diaspora in the Americas appeared before the publication of the book-length works by Smallwood and Brown. See Schuler, "Akan Slave Rebellions," 8–29; J. Thornton, "Coromantees," 161–178; J. Thornton, "War, the State, and Religious Norms," 181–200; Chambers, "Ethnicity in the Diaspora," 25–39.

24. Smallwood, *Saltwater Slavery*, 52–64, 106, 118–120, 167, 189, 191–196. Smallwood mentions Coromantees twice in the entire book.

25. Brown, *Reaper's Garden*, 127.

26. Ibid., 7–8, 64–69, 73, 127, 134, 136–150, 212–213.

27. Ibid., 7–8, 29–31, 261.

28. Northrup, "Igbo and Myth Igbo," 3.

29. Konadu, *Akan Diaspora*, 4, 17, 44–48, 54, 95, 102, 146, 202–235; Northrup, "Igbo and Myth Igbo," 1–6, 18.

30. Konadu, *Akan Diaspora*, 5, 6–10, 13–15, 24, 113–114, 122–123, 130, 146.

31. Among historians, Paul Lovejoy first employed this turn of phrase in 1997. See Lovejoy, "African Diaspora," 7.

32. Brown, *Reaper's Garden*, 255–261; Sweet, *Recreating Africa*, 7.

33. Mann, "Shifting Paradigms," 5. For varying expressions of this concept, see Palmer, "Modern African Diaspora," 30; J. Thornton, "Stono Rebellion," 1101–1102; J. Thornton, *Africa and Africans*, 5–6; Gomez, "Muslims in Early America," 672; Lovejoy, "African Diaspora," 6–8; Lovejoy, "Identifying Enslaved Africans in the African Diaspora," in Lovejoy, *Identity in the Shadow*, 1–4; Hall, *Slavery and African Ethnicities*, xiii–xvii, 50–52; Law, "Meanings of 'Mina' (Again)," 248.

34. Palmer, "Modern African Diaspora," 30.

35. Ferreira, *Cross-Cultural Exchange*, 240–241, 245.

36. Wilks, *Forests of Gold*, 92–93; Kea, *Settlements, Trade, and Polities*, 292–320; Meillassoux, *Anthropology of Slavery*, 35–36; Eltis, *Rise of African Slavery*, 109–110; Bailey, *African Voices*, 61–63.

37. Painter, *Soul Murder and Slavery*, 7–8.

38. Austen, "Slave Trade as History," 239; Frey and Wood, "Introduction," in Frey and Wood, *From Slavery to Emancipation*, 3–4; Genovese, *From Rebellion to Revolution*, xix, 90–96, 121–125, 134–135; Mullin, *Africa in America*, 5–6, 218–219; Dubois, *Avengers of the New World*, 105.

39. Hartman, *Scenes of Subjection*, 115–124.

1. Gold Coast Backgrounds

1. Lovejoy, "The African Diaspora," 6–8; Mann, "Shifting Paradigms," 5.

2. For example, Konadu defines "Akan" culture as "the composite culture designed by West African forest settlers between the Komóe and Volta rivers to the edge of the forest. . . ." This region, as defined by Konadu, includes and encompasses Ga-, Adanme-, and Ewe-speaking peoples and polities—among others. This sweeping approach, which not only sees Akan culture as genetic, homogeneous, and timeless but also ignores other ethnolinguistic groups in the Gold Coast is representative of larger historiographic trends. See Konadu, *Akan Diaspora*, 17. For a critique and corrective to this approach, see Shumway, *Fante*, 17–21; Parker, *Making the Town*, xxiv–xxviii.

3. Shumway, *Fante*, 8–9; Morgan, "Cultural Implications," 131–132, 135–137; Smallwood, *Saltwater Slavery*, 24–25, 96–97. Stephanie Smallwood specifically dates the Asante dominance in Gold Coast Atlantic commerce to the first decade of the eighteenth century. Though noting that the lack of documentary material makes it impossible to accurately "map those historically shifting contours in detail," Smallwood follows this discussion with analyses of the diverse ethnic composition and the "socioethnic" landscape of the Gold Coast diaspora. See Smallwood, *Saltwater Slavery*, 96–97.

4. Mann, "Shifting Paradigms," 16.

5. Shumway, *Fante*, 9, 23–24; Kea, *Settlements, Trade, and Polities*, 1; Fynn, *Asante and Its Neighbours*, 1–2; Reindorf, *History of the Gold Coast*, 17.

6. Rømer, *Reliable Account*, 16–17; Ellis, *Tshi-Speaking Peoples*, 1–3; Kea, *Settlements, Trade, and Polities*, 1–3; Buah, *History of Ghana*, 1–3; Philip D. Curtin, "'The White Man's Grave,'" 95.

7. Kea, *Settlements, Trade, and Polities*, 2-7, 11-14; Chouin and Decorse, "Prelude to the Atlantic Trade," 123-125, 129, 138, 142-145; Klein, "Toward a New Understanding," 248-253, 263; Wilks, *Forests of Gold*, 64-72, 92-97.

8. Klein, "Toward a New Understanding," 260-262; Wilks, "Slavery and Akan Origins?" 661; "Wilhelm Johann Müller's Description of the Fetu Country, 1662-9," in Jones, *German Sources*, 134, 137, 138-141; Rømer, *Reliable Account*, 17-19, 115-116.

9. Kea, *Settlements, Trade, and Polities*, 2, 4; Fynn, *Asante and Its Neighbours*, 2, 4; J. M. Stewart, "Akan History," 54-58; Painter, "Guang and West African Historical Reconstruction," 58-66; Manoukian, *Akan and Ga-Adangme Peoples*, 9; Konadu, *Akan Diaspora*.

10. Parker, *Making the Town*, xxvi; Shumway, *Fante*, 3, 7-9, 15.

11. Meyerowitz, *Akan Traditions of Origin*, 95; Boahen, "Origins of the Akan," 9; Fynn, *Asante and Its Neighbours*, 27-29.

12. Bosman, *New and Accurate Description*, 123; Wilks, *One Nation, Many Histories*, 15-18; Klein, "Toward a New Understanding," 254; Merrick Posnansky, "Prelude to Akan Civilisation," in Schildkrout and Gelber, *The Golden Stool*, 15; Dickson, *Historical Geography of Ghana*, 24.

13. Anquandah, *Rediscovering Ghana's Past*, 126-127; Boahen, "Origins of the Akan," 4-7; Balmer, *History of the Akan Peoples*, 26-31; Meyerowitz, *Akan Traditions of Origin*, 33-35, 63-64, 74; Danquah, "Culture of Akan," 360, 363; Wilks, *Forests of Gold*, 64-66; Gocking, *History of Ghana*, 21.

14. Reindorf, *History of the Gold Coast*, 48; Daaku, *Oral Traditions of Adanse*, i-ii, 1, 3-4, 6; Dickson, *Historical Geography of Ghana*, 22-26; Meyerowitz, *Akan Traditions of Origin*, 95, 130; Boahen, "Origins of the Akan," 9; Fynn, *Asante and Its Neighbours*, 27-29; Vivian, "Recent Excavations of Adansemanso," 37-41; Shumway, *Fante*, 37-40. For seventeenth- and eighteenth-century political maps of the Gold Coast and their uses, see Kea, *Settlements, Trade, and Polities*, 23-32.

15. Reindorf, *History of the Gold Coast*, 24; Manoukian, *Akan and Ga-Adangme Peoples*, 66; Henderson-Quartey, *The Ga of Ghana*, 19; Parker, *Making the Town*, 2, 6.

16. Reindorf, *History of the Gold Coast*, 21, 25, 42; Manoukian, *Akan and Ga-Adangme Peoples*, 66-69; Henderson-Quartey, *The Ga of Ghana*, 20, 39-43, 49; Parker, *Making the Town*, 8-9; Stewart, "Akan History," 54-58.

17. Reindorf, *History of the Gold Coast*, 21, 47-48; Henderson-Quartey, *The Ga of Ghana*, 42; Manoukian, *Akan and Ga-Adangme Peoples*, 66.

18. Akyeampong, *Between the Sea and the Lagoon*, 1-7; Greene, *Gender, Ethnicity, and Social Change*, 20-26; Greene, "The Anlo-Ewe," 1-8; Greene, "Social Change," 70-72.

19. Greene, "The Anlo-Ewe," 23-36; Manoukian, *Ewe-Speaking People*, 12; Bailey, *African Voices*, 28-33.

20. Greene, "The Anlo-Ewe," 37-42; Manoukin, *The Ewe-Speaking People*, 11-13.

21. Bailey, *African Voices*, 1, 69-70; Smallwood, *Saltwater Slavery*, 87; J. Thornton, *Africa and Africans*, 192-194; Law, *Slave Coast of West Africa*, 156-166; "Resolutions of the Director-General and Council at Elmina, 18 February 1692," in Van Dantzig, *Dutch Documents*, I:36; "Hortogh to Pranger, 31 October 1730," in Van Dantzig, *Dutch Documents*, II:165; "Copy of Letter Relating to Sloop *Elizabeth* Sent

to Mr. Edward Chester at Antegua, April 1713," in Treasury Records, Records of the Company of Royal Adventurers of England Trading with Africa and Successors (hereafter, T70), National Archives, Kew, T70/3, ff. 25–26.

22. Wilks, *One Nation, Many Histories*, 14.

23. Shumway, *Fante*, 132–153.

24. One of the best examples of the latter would be the transformation of Ananse the trickster spider from fool to rebel and Ananse stories becoming didactic tales of social change and revolution.

25. Gocking, *History of Ghana*, 8–10.

26. Daaku, *Oral Traditions of Adanse*, i; Daaku, "Pre-Asante States," 10–13; Fynn, *Asante and Its Neighbours*, 19; Kea, *Settlements, Trade, and Polities*, 1, 5–8; J. Thornton, *Africa and Africans*, 74–76.

27. Kea, *Settlements, Trade, and Polities*, 19, 28–37, 52, 57, 64–73, 90–94, 97–104, 112–129; "Müller's Description of the Fetu Country, 1662–9," in Jones, *German Sources*, 181–184.

28. "Samuel Brun's Voyages of 1611–20," in Jones, *German Sources*, 88; Rømer, *Reliable Account*, 141–156; Sarpong, *Sacred Stools of the Akan*, 26–27; "Müller's Description of the Fetu Country, 1662–9," in Jones, *German Sources*, 168, 186, 194–195; "Report by Jac. Van den Broucke & Nic. Du Bois on Their Voyage to Aquamboe, 27 March 1703," in Van Dantzig, *Dutch Documents*, I:41; Barbot, *Coasts of North and South Guinea*, in *A Collection of Voyages and Travels*, III:263; Hair, Jones, and Law, *Barbot on Guinea*, II:599–600; Ross,"Iconography of Asante Sword Ornaments," 16–20; McCaskie, "Accumulation of Wealth and Belief," 26–29.

29. "Agreement between Willem de la Palma in the Name of Their Highmightinesses of the States-General of the United Netherlands as Well as Their General Chartered West Indian Company on the Coast of Africa on the One Side, with Aquando, King of Aquamboe as Well as His Councillors and Principal Chiefs on the Other," in Van Dantzig, *Dutch Documents*, I:62.

30. Shumway, *Fante*, 100–104, 111, 114, 117–124, 129–131; T. C. McCaskie, "Nananom Mpow of Mankessim: An Essay in Fante History," in Henige and McCaskie, *West African Economic and Social History*, 136; Kea, *Settlements, Trade, and Polities*, 127–128; "Müller's Description of the Fetu Country, 1662–9," in Jones, *German Sources*, 181–187; Barbot, *Coasts of North and South Guinea*, III:290; "Treaty between the Kingdom of Fetu, the King of Denmark and the Danish Africa Company, 20 December 1659," in Justesen, *Danish Sources*, 8–9, 9n23; Hair, Jones, and Law, *Barbot on Guinea*, II:597, 603n; "Letter from the Directory General, 18 June 1689," in Van Dantzig, *Dutch Documents*, I:59.

31. Barbot, *Coasts of North and South Guinea*, III:290–291; "Report by Jac. Van den Broucke & Nic. Du Bois on Their Voyage to Aquamboe, 27 March 1703," in Van Dantzig, *Dutch Documents*, I:59.

32. "Müller's Description of the Fetu Country, 1662–9," in Jones, *German Sources*, 145–146, 169; Barbot, *Coasts of North and South Guinea*, III:290; Reindorf, *History of the Gold Coast*, 27.

33. Rømer, *Reliable Account*, 78–79, 97–98; de Marees, *Historical Account of the Gold Kingdom*, 167–170, 248; "Treaty with Three Caboceers of Cape Three Points, 16

May 1681," in Jones, *Brandenburg Sources*, 17–18. Barbot uses "Braffo" and "Caboceer" interchangeably. See Barbot, *Coasts of North and South Guinea*, III:295, 299.

34. Shumway, *Fante*, 41, 129–131; Kea, *Settlements, Trade, and Polities*, 98–100, 113–125; de Marees, *Historical Account of the Gold Kingdom*, 96; "Andreas Josua Ulsheimer's Voyage of 1603–4," in Jones, *German Sources*, 30; "Müller's Description of the Fetu Country, 1662–9," in Jones, *German Sources*, 187.

35. Reindorf, *History of the Gold Coast*, 71, 83; Atkins, *Voyage to Guinea*, 188; "John Hippisley, Cape Coast Castle, 13 July 1766," T70/31; "John Roberts and Council, Cape Coast Castle, 8 October 1780," T70/32.

36. Shumway, *Fante*, 117; Morgan, *Laboring Women*, 12–49; Snelgrave, *A New Account*, 3–4; de Marees, *Historical Account of the Gold Kingdom*, 22–24, 36–39; "Otto Friedrich Von Der Groeben's Account of His Voyage to Guinea, 1682–83," in Jones, *Brandenburg Sources*, 25; "Müller's Description of the Fetu Country, 1662–9," in Jones, *German Sources*, 182–183, 298. For assessments of the colonial-era gaze and women of color, see Hunt and Lessard, *Women and the Colonial Gaze*.

37. Miller, "Nzinga of Matamba," 201–216; J. Thornton, "Legitimacy and Political Power," 25–40; J. Thornton, *Africa and Africans*, 240; Bay, "Belief, Legitimacy and the Kpojito," 9–16, 16n59; Bay, *Wives of the Leopard*, 71–80; Law, "Dahomey and the Slave Trade," 248n72; Alpern, "Origins of the Amazons," 16–20.

38. Manoukian, *Akan and Ga-Adangme Peoples*, 39; Rattray, *Ashanti*, 19–21; Agnes Akosua Aidoo, "Asante Queen Mothers in Government and Politics in the Nineteenth Century," in Steady, *Black Woman Cross-Culturally*, 65–77; Kwame Arhin, "The Political and Military Roles of Akan Women," in Oppong, *Female and Male in West Africa*, 91–98; Akyeampong and Obeng, "Spirituality, Gender, and Power," 488–508.

39. Kea, *Settlements, Trade, and Polities*, 26–28; Daaku and Van Dantzig, "Map of the Regions," opposite 70; Affrifah, *Akyem Factor*, 10; Fynn, *Asante and Its Neighbours*, 3–4.

40. Fynn, *Asante and Its Neighbours*, 3, 19; Wilks, "Rise of the Akwamu Empire," 99; Daaku and Van Dantzig," Map of the Regions," opposite 70; Reindorf, *History of the Gold Coast*, 60–61.

41. Wilks, "Note on Twifo and Akwamu," 215–217; Reindorf, *History of the Gold Coast*, 60–63; Buah, *History of Ghana*, 9, 19–20, 22; Wilks, "Rise of the Akwamu Empire," 100. Perhaps the most famous instance of this "ritual" was the vassalage and service of Osei Tutu, the founder of the Asante Union, to the court of Denkyira. After serving in Denkyira's military, Tutu would return to Kumasi, garner and consolidate political authority, and lead Asante's military to defeat Denkyira in 1701.

42. Wilks, "Rise of the Akwamu Empire," 102; Parker, *Making the Town*, 10–12; Barbot, *Coasts of North and South Guinea*, V:185.

43. Rømer, *Reliable Account*, 116–119; Reindorf, *History of the Gold Coast*, 24–34. Since Akwamuhene Ansa Sasraku did not die until 1689 and was succeeded by a dual regency, the version of events as recounted by Rømer seems questionable. See Henderson-Quartey, *The Ga of Ghana*, 178–181.

44. Wilks, "Rise of the Akwamu Empire," 106–111; Barbot, *Coasts of North and South Guinea*, IV:322, V:182; Greene, "The Anlo-Ewe," 85; "William Pley, James

Fort, Accra, 13 August 1681," in Law, *The English in West Africa*, I:164; "W. De la Palma to Assembly of Ten, Elmina, 26 June 1702," in Van Dantzig, *Dutch Documents*, I:48; Bosman, *New and Accurate Description*, 61.

45. Rask, *Brief and Truthful Description*, 18; Tilleman, *Short and Simple Account*, 16n144.

46. Barbot, *Coasts of North and South Guinea*, V:185; Hair, Jones, and Law, *Barbot on Guinea*, II:437–438, 450n.

47. Wilks, "Rise of the Akwamu Empire," 112–113, 116–117, 124–125; Rask, *Brief and Truthful Description*, 116, 164.

48. Kea, "Akwamu-Anlo Relations," 29, 33; Greene, "The Anlo-Ewe," 82–88; Wilks, "Rise of the Akwamu Empire," 129–130; Rask, *Brief and Truthful Description*, 116–117, 119–120, 122.

49. Kea, *Settlements, Trade, and Polities*, 27; Affrifah, *Akyem Factor*, 6–13; Fynn, *Asante and Its Neighbours*, 20–21; Reindorf, *History of the Gold Coast*, 61–62; Addo-Fening, "The Akim or Achim," 1–3; Boahen, "Arcany or Accany or Arcania," 105–106. Given the considerable historiographic debate about the meaning of "Akanni," "Acanij," or "Arcany," a reasonable supposition holds that the references could refer to a number of different polities, state actors, or unaffiliated commercial entities. In a 1679 letter to the Assembly of Ten, Dutch factor Heerman Abramsz notes "Behind [Etsii] lies the great country of Accaniën, which is portioned in three main-parts: to the North of, or in the interior of Elmina the Akkanists are called Crysakeese, in the interior North of Cormantyn are the Cocoriteese and behind [Accra] are the Akimse Akkanists." "Great Acanny" was associated with Akyem since at least Propheet's 1629 map and became "Akimse Akkani" fifty years later when Abramsz penned his letter. In general, this region refers to what later became Akyem Abuakwa. "Acanni," "Acanij," or "Little Accany" probably refers to the Assin state. Finally, the "Akani" may have been a group of merchants living in towns near the Pra and Ofin rivers and who formed a commercial association. See "Heerman Abramsz to Assembly of Ten, 23 November 1679," in Van Dantzig, *Dutch Documents*, I:5; Kea, *Settlements, Trade, and Polities*, 248–255; Shumway, *Fante*, 37–40, 174n79–n84.

50. "Michael Hemmersam's Description of the Gold Coast, 1639–45," in Jones, *German Sources*, 97, 105; Bosman, *New and Accurate Description*, 68.

51. Rask, *Brief and Truthful Description*, 116.

52. Daaku and Van Dantzig, "Map of the Regions," opposite 70; Barbot, *Coasts of North and South Guinea*, V:188. In this case, Barbot probably used Bosman's account, though he may have witnessed Akyem's growing regional influence. See Law, "Jean Barbot as a Source," 155–157; Fage, "'Good Red Herring,'" 315–320; Hair, Jones, and Law, *Barbot on Guinea*, I:xix–lvi; II:439.

53. Bosman, *New and Accurate Description*, 57, 61; Barbot, *Coasts of North and South Guinea*, V:182; Reindorf, *History of the Gold Coast*, 61; "Resolutions of the Director-General and Council at Elmina, 10 March 1700," in Van Dantzig, *Dutch Documents*, I:43; Wilks, "Rise of the Akwamu Empire," 123.

54. "Resolutions of the Director-General and Council at Elmina, 10 March 1700," in Van Dantzig, *Dutch Documents*, I:41, 43; "Van Sevenhuysen to Assembly of Ten, Elmina, 8 May 1699," in Van Dantzig, *Dutch Documents*, I:44.

55. Barbot, *Coasts of North and South Guinea*, III:294; Addo-Fening, "The Akim or Achim," 2–3; Wilks, "Rise of the Akwamu Empire," 117–118.

56. "Willem de la Palma to Presidial Chamber, 10 October 1703," in Van Dantzig, *Dutch Documents*, I:64. Rømer, in the employ of the Danish West India and Guinea Company, later criticized the Dutch for assuming such lofty titles as "Director-General" or "Council of the North and South Coast of Africa" noting that "such meaningless titles are the product of their imaginations, since in reality they have no more say over the Negroes than we do, that is, only as far as their shot can reach." See Rømer, *Reliable Account*, 44.

57. "Willem de la Palma to Assembly of Ten, 31 August 1704," in Van Dantzig, *Dutch Documents*, I:67.

58. Bosman, *New and Accurate Description*, 68; Reindorf, *History of the Gold Coast*, 65–66; Fynn, *Asante and Its Neighbours*, 20–21; Fynn, "Asante and Akyem Relations," 63–66. Reindorf's account of the 1717 Asante-Akyem war and its immediate aftermath includes a number of flawed historical details.

59. Fynn, "Asante and Akyem Relations," 66–67; Wilks, "Rise of the Akwamu Empire," 132; Fynn, *Asante and Its Neighbours*, 74–77.

60. Law, *The English in West Africa, 1681–1683*, I:99; Smallwood, *Saltwater Slavery*, 24.

61. Barbot, *Coasts of North and South Guinea*, III:189; Bosman, *New and Accurate Description*, 63–65, 73–74; Reindorf, *History of the Gold Coast*, 49; McCaskie, "Denkyira in the Making of Asante," 1, 11; "William De la Palma to Assembly of Ten, 31 August 1704," in Van Dantzig, *Dutch Documents*, I:67, 69.

62. Kumah, "Rise and Fall of the Kingdom," 34–35; Bosman, *New and Accurate Description*, 63; Reindorf, *History of the Gold Coast*, 49–50; Fynn, *Asante and Its Neighbours*, 21–22.

63. Fynn, *Asante and Its Neighbours*, 22; Kumah, "Rise and Fall of the Kingdom," 35; McCaskie, "Denkyira in the Making of Asante," 1–2; "Resolutions of the Director-General and Council at Elmina, 10 March 1700," in Van Dantzig, *Dutch Documents*, I:42; "Van Sevenhuysen to Assembly of Ten, Elmina, 21 June 1700," in Van Dantzig, *Dutch Documents*, I:46.

64. McCaskie, "Denkyira in the Making of Asante," 2–3; Fynn, *Asante and Its Neighbours*, 29–31.

65. Fynn, *Asante and Its Neighbours*, 29–30; Reindorf, *History of the Gold Coast*, 52–53; McCaskie, "Komfo Anokye of Asante," 315–339.

66. "Van Sevenhuysen to Assembly of Ten, Elmina, 30 May 1701," in Van Dantzig, *Dutch Documents*, I:46.

67. Fynn, *Asante and Its Neighbours*, 31–33; McCaskie, "Denkyira in the Making of Asante," 2–3.

68. Akyeampong and Obeng, "Spirituality, Gender, and Power," 495; Wilks, *Asante in the Nineteenth Century*, 112.

69. Akyeampong and Obeng, "Spirituality, Gender, and Power," 494–495; McCaskie, "Denkyira in the Making of Asante," 10; Fynn, *Asante and Its Neighbours*, 37–40; Fynn, "Asante and Akyem Relations," 59–60; Reindorf, *History of the Gold Coast*, 53–54; "Van Sevenhuysen to Assembly of Ten, Elmina, 16 November 1701," in Van Dantzig, *Dutch Documents*, I:48.

70. Fynn, "Asante and Akyem Relations," 60, 63–66; Fynn, *Asante and Its Neighbours*, 43, 45–51, 58, 60, 61–81; Reindorf, *History of the Gold Coast*, 85.

71. Rømer, *Reliable Account*, 136–137; Fynn, *Asante and Its Neighbours*, 69–71.

72. Fynn, *Asante and Its Neighbours*, 61–81.

73. Shumway, *Fante*, 9, 13, 28, 42; Daaku and Van Dantzig, "Map of the Regions," opposite 70; Fynn, *Asante and Its Neighbours*, 3.

74. Daaku and Van Dantzig, "Map of the Regions," opposite 70; Shumway, *Fante*, 31–32, 42–47; Law, "The Komenda Wars," 134–136; Bosman, *New and Accurate Description*, 26–41.

75. Shumway, *Fante*, 88.

76. Ibid., 89, 93–101, 106.

77. Ibid., 132–153.

78. Ibid., 144.

79. Shumway, *Fante*, 134–144; Holsey, *Routes of Remembrance*, 89–95; Fynn, "Nanaom Pow of the Fante," 54–59; T.C. McCaskie, "Nananom Mpow of Mankessem: An Essay in Fante History," in Henige and McCaskie, *West African Economic and Social History*, 133–150.

2. Making the Gold Coast Diaspora

1. Cugoano, *Thoughts and Sentiments*, x, 12–16, 153n19.

2. Ibid., 14–16, 27–28.

3. Ibid., 15.

4. Ibid., 16–17, 143.

5. The temporal scope of this chapter corresponds to the focus, in the second part of the book, on the formation of the Gold Coast diaspora in the Americas from the 1680s to the 1760s—with references to the 1770s and 1790s.

6. *Voyages: The Trans-Atlantic Slave Trade Database*, http://www.slavevoyages .org/tast/database/search.faces (accessed April 12, 2014).

7. Manning, *Slavery and African Life*, 65–66.

8. G. M. Hall, *Slavery and African Ethnicities*, 106–107, 110–111; Lovejoy, *Transformations in Slavery*, 55–56; Smallwood, *Saltwater Slavery*, 118; Shumway, *Fante*, 133; J. Thornton, "The Coromantees," 164–166; Gomez, *Exchanging Our Country Marks*, 105.

9. Mintz and Price, *Birth of African-American Culture*, 10–11.

10. de Marees, *Historical Account of the Gold Kingdom*, 35.

11. "Müller's Description of the Fetu Country, 1662-9," in Jones, *German Sources*, 155. Jean Barbot provides a similar account based on his experience in the late 1670s and early 1680s, though it may have been derivative of earlier sources. See Barbot, *Coasts of North and South Guinea*, III:257; Bosman, *New and Accurate Description*, 107–108.

12. The 1980s and 1990s African American take on this handshake was a relatively recent appropriation started by black fraternities and not a long-standing cultural continuity from Atlantic West Africa. See L. Green, *African American English*, 145.

13. "Müller's Description of the Fetu Country, 1662–9," in Jones, *German Sources*, 183; Rømer, *Reliable Account*, 32–33, 164–165; de Marees, *Historical Account of the Gold Kingdom*, 47–50, 91, 96. In polities in the central coast, a viador was a court office-holder who served variably as a treasurer (specifically of a King's personal gold) or manager of the personal affairs of an ohene.

14. de Marees, *Historical Account of the Gold Kingdom*, 48–49.

15. Snelgrave, *A New Account*, unpaginated introduction.

16. Hair, *Founding of the Castelo*, 8; "The Foundation of the Castle and City of São Jorge Da Mina, 1482," in Newitt, *The Portuguese in West Africa*, 90–95; Holsey, "'Watch the Waves of the Sea,'" 83–84.

17. For assessments of Atlantic creoles in the Gold Coast, see Berlin, "From Creole to African," 256–264. James Sweet offers a poignant and effective counterbalance to the Eurocentric tendencies among modern historians. See his commentary in Sweet, *Domingos Álvares*, 4–6.

18. de Marees, *Historical Account of the Gold Kingdom*, 10.

19. Ibid., 78–85.

20. "Samuel Brun's Voyages of 1611–1620," in Jones, *German Sources*, 44, 67.

21. Mintz and Price, *Birth of African-American Culture*, 20.

22. For the extensive Akan vocabularies compiled by de Marees and Müller, see de Marees, *Historical Account of the Gold Kingdom*, 246–259; "Müller's Description of the Fetu Country, 1662–9," in Jones, *German Sources*, 269–326. Practically every word in both vocabularies have Akan origins.

23. Barbot, *Coasts of North and South Guinea*, III:321.

24. Bosman, *New and Accurate Description*, 112.

25. Rask, *Brief and Truthful Description*, 111.

26. Ibid., 126.

27. Ibid., 126; Bosman, *New and Accurate Description*, 112.

28. Kpobi, *Saga of a Slave*, 21–26, 64–65; Truteneau, *Introduction to the Fante and Accra (Gaji) Languages*, 59–66; J. Thornton, "The Coromantees," 164.

29. J. Thornton, "The Coromantees," 165.

30. Rask, *Brief and Truthful Description*, 9–10, 126–131. The seventeenth- and eighteenth-century coastal Akan equivalents for these words are: tobacco pipe (*aubuà* or *aibiboa*), knife (*dareba* or *dáda-ba*), ear (*asso, asschaba,* or *assouba*), nose (*egwinni* or *och-huen*), mouth (*anom, annú,* or *annon*), head (*eteri, etyr,* or *itery*). See de Marees, *Historical Account of the Gold Kingdom*, 251, 254; "Müller's Description of the Fetu Country, 1662–9," in Jones, *German Sources*, 281, 282, 302, 305; Barbot, *Coasts of North and South Guinea*, IV:417–419.

31. Rømer, *Reliable Account*, 99–100. The first appearance of this greeting appears in de Marees's 1602 account. Such an early reference means that this practice likely began in response to the Sunday rituals initiated by the Portuguese in the Gold Coast. See de Marees, *Historical Account of the Gold Kingdom*, 249.

32. T. Thompson, *Account of Two Missionary Voyages*, 70; Reese, "'Sheep in the Jaws,'" 348–372.

33. Parker, *Making the Town*, xiii–xv; Henderson-Quartey, *The Ga of Ghana*, 42–47; Akyeampong, *Between the Sea and the Lagoon*, xi–xii.

34. Rømer, *Reliable Account*, 23–24.

35. Rømer, *Reliable Account*, xi, xiv–xv, 23–24; "Resolutions of the Director-General and Council at Elmina, 7 August 1684," in Van Dantzig, *Dutch Documents*, I:29.

36. Reindorf, *History of the Gold Coast*, 40; Perbi, *History of Indigenous Slavery*, 24–25; J. Thornton, *Africa and Africans*, 96; Parker, *Making the Town*, 12–17; Henderson-Quartey, *The Ga of Ghana*, 86, 169–175. Interestingly, the current residents of Ngleshie Alata and Osu Alata are now recognized as part of Ga-speaking stool territories.

37. J. Thornton, *Africa and Africans*, 185–186.

38. Rømer, *Reliable Account*, 98–100; Quartey-Papafio, "Use of Names among the Gãs," 170–171, 178–181. By the twentieth century, Ewe-speakers as far east as Togo and Benin adopted the Akan day-naming scheme. See Paul Agbedor and Assiba Johnson, "Naming Practices," in Lawrance, *Handbook of Eweland*, 162–165.

39. Isert, *Journey to Guinea*, 175–176.

40. Bosman, *New and Accurate Description*, 178.

41. West India Company Letter, 18 March 1748 in Furley Collection, Balme Library, University of Ghana, Legon (hereafter Furley Collection), Dutch Records, N46; West India Company Letter, February 1748, Furley Collection, Dutch Records, N46; West India Company Letter from Cormantyn to Elmina, 26 November 1769, Furley Collection, Dutch Records, N55; Odotei, "History of Ga," 248–249, 258–259; Henderson-Quartey, *The Ga of Ghana*, 86–87; Perbi, *History of Indigenous Slavery*, 25.

42. Odotei, "The History of Ga," 259. The adoption of this Akan day-name was perhaps because of the similarity between his original name (Ojo) and Cudjo.

43. Rømer, *Reliable Account*, 78.

44. Here, "tradition" is not meant to convey a static or even ahistorical conceptualization of cultural practices. Indeed, the continual changes within Gold Coast folkloric "traditions" become evident in the later portions of this book. Instead, I employ here and later an operational definition culled from Sally and Richard Price's appropriation of the "changing same"—a phrase coined by Amiri Baraka. In this sense, "tradition" embodies both a set of relatively stable core principles (continuity) and shifting boundaries and parameters that adjust to changing circumstances and times (change). More recently, T. J. Desch-Obi has defined what he calls "living tradition" as cultural forms that continue to change "to new realities but does so in accordance with an enduring central paradigm." See S. Price and R. Price, *Maroon Arts*, 277–283, 308; Baraka, *Black Music*, 180–212; T. J. Desch-Obi, *Fighting for Honor*, 205–206; Vansina, *Paths in the Rainforests*, 258–260; Hobsbawm and Ranger, *Invention of Tradition*.

45. Rømer, *Reliable Account*, 80; Rask, *Brief and Truthful Description*, 77.

46. "Johann Peter Oettinger's Account of His Voyage to Guinea," in Jones, *Brandenburg Sources*, 193.

47. "Müller's Description of the Fetu Country, 1662–9," in Jones, *German Sources*, 178.

48. Truteneau, *Introduction to the Fante and Accra (Gãfi) Languages*, 11–12.

49. de Marees, *Historical Account of the Gold Kingdom*, 73.

50. Barbot, *Coasts of North and South Guinea*, IV:418.

51. T. Thompson, *Account of Two Missionary Voyages*, 44.

52. Rømer, *Reliable Account*, 80n10; Rask, *Brief and Truthful Description*, 77n53; J. Thornton, "The Coromantees," 167.

53. Rømer, *Reliable Account*, 78–79, 95.

54. The notion that dismemberment disrupts spiritual ascension or transmigration was a ubiquitous concept in the worldviews of Gold Coast Africans in the diaspora. European knowledge of this idea led to postmortem beheadings and other bodily mutilations of rebels, runaways, and those seeking escape from toil by suicide. See V. Brown, *Reaper's Garden*, 134–135; V. Brown, "Spiritual Terror and Sacred Authority," 24–53.

55. Rask, *Brief and Truthful Description*, 141–142; Bosman, *New and Accurate Description*, 222–224.

56. Rømer, *A Reliable Account*, 106–108. This could be due to how Rømer read or interpreted Okpoti's statements.

57. Konadu, *Akan Diaspora*, 23. Some of the best examples of European and Christian interpenetrations in Akan and other Gold Coast religions would be the use of schnapps, gin, rum, or brandy as ritual fluids in Akan libations and other religious ceremonies; the spiritual connotations associated with white (pure and good) and black (unclean and evil); European-imported horsetails as spiritual items associated with priests and royal courts; the image of a horned and hoofed Devil or Satan figure serving as the embodiment of evil; and perhaps even the notion of Jancómpon as a sky god presiding over heaven. Certainly, the Ga-speakers' practice of circumcision is likely linked to Islamic influences from as early as the twelfth or thirteenth century. The denial of the cultural plasticity of coastal Atlantic African peoples by Konadu is astounding given the weight of the evidence. See van den Bersselaar, *King of Drinks*, 1–4; Akyeampong, "Ahenfo Nsa (The 'Drink of Kings'): Dutch Schnapps and Ritual," in van Kessel, *Merchants, Missionaries and Migrants*, 50–54; Hagan, "Akan Colour Symbolism," 8–13; Rømer, *A Reliable Account*, 80–81, 85; "Müller's Description of the Fetu Country, 1662-9," in Jones, *German Sources*, 158, 176–177, 179; de Marees, *Historical Account of the Gold Kingdom*, 73n15, 169.

58. Bosman, *New and Accurate Description*, 300.

59. Rømer, *Reliable Account*, 80.

60. Ibid., 80–83.

61. Bosman, *New and Accurate Description*, 135, 217.

62. "Johann Peter Oettinger's Account of His Voyage to Guinea," in Jones, *Brandenburg Sources*, 193; Rask, *Brief and Truthful Description*, 77.

63. Bosman, *New and Accurate Description*, 123–124, 222; de Marees, *Historical Account of the Gold Kingdom*, 67–74; "Müller's Description of the Fetu Country, 1662-9," in Jones, *German Sources*, 118–119, 158–163. *Fetisso* comes from the Portuguese word *feitiço*, meaning magic or artificial (as in "fake"), and is also the source of the English "fetish." This broad category encompasses lesser deities and even ancestral spirits, personal charms and talismans, and a more quotidian notion of spiritual causality that ironically borders on scientific rationality—especially

in reference to "eating fetish" and its physical effects. See Jones, *Brandenburg Sources*, 314.

64. "Müller's Description of the Fetu Country, 1662–9," in Jones, *German Sources*, 158–159, 162–166, 170–173; Barbot, *Coasts of North and South Guinea*, III:244; Rask, *Brief and Truthful Description*, 78; J. Thornton, "War, the State, and Religious Norms," 191–192.

65. "Müller's Description of the Fetu Country, 1662–9," in Jones, *German Sources*, 171.

66. J. Thornton, "War, the State, and Religious Norms," 191–194. Thornton contends that "sumang" represented a change-oriented principal carried by those from commoner backgrounds to the Americas. Though most of his analysis on this point is sound, the only quibble I have is with his claim that obeah is derived "from the Akan word for witchcraft, *obayi*. . . ." As I argue in chapter 5, obeah in the Americas has one spiritual-etymological root in Akan-speaking bayi, but it also was the perfect example of intra-African creolization, sharing origins (both spiritual and etymological) with Igbo-speaking concepts related to *dibia*. With significant numbers of Akan-speakers from the Gold Coast and Igbo-speakers and others from the Bight of Biafra arriving in the eighteenth-century British Caribbean, obeah may have resulted from a set of cultural negotiations between the two sizable import groups. See Chambers, "'My Own Nation,'" 74, 82–84, 88–90; Handler and Bilby, "Early Use and Origin of the Term 'Obeah,'" 87–100; Rucker, *River Flows On*, 220n82.

67. Paul Nugent, "A Regional Melting Pot: The Ewe and Their Neighbours in the Ghana-Togo Borderlands," in Lawrance, *The Ewe of Togo and Benin*, 30–31; Greene, *History of the Anlo-Ewe*, 33–34, 41–42; Akyeampong, *Between the Sea and the Lagoon*, 41–43.

68. Parker, *Making the Town*, 14, 16, 18–19, 22; Henderson-Quartey, *The Ga of Ghana*, 75; Reindorf, *History of the Gold Coast*, 98, 102–104, 111–112, 114, 130.

69. Reindorf, *History of the Gold Coast*, 98. This change was temporary as Ga-speakers in Accra reverted back to a patrilineal descent system at some point during the late nineteenth to early twentieth century. From this perspective, the Ga replication of Akan descent patterns relates directly to their political subjugation by Akwamu, Akyem, and Asante. See Perbi, *History of Indigenous Slavery*, 111; Greene, *Gender, Ethnicity, and Social Change*, 33–35.

70. Reindorf, *History of the Gold Coast*, 111–115.

71. de Marees, *Historical Account of the Gold Kingdom*, 69.

72. Rømer, *Reliable Account*, 100n77, 100–103; "Treaty between the Kingdom of Fetu, the King of Denmark and the Danish Africa Company, 20 December 1659," in Justesen, *Danish Sources*, 9, 9n26; "Müller's Description of the Fetu Country, 1662–9," in Jones, *German Sources*, 174–176; Barbot, *Coasts of North and South Guinea*, IV:572; Bosman, *New and Accurate Description*, 149–151; Rask, *Brief and Truthful Description*, 180–183; Isert, *Journey to Guinea*, 129–130; Reindorf, *History of the Gold Coast*, 117, 124.

73. de Marees, *Historical Account of the Gold Kingdom*, 20; Rømer, *Reliable Account*, 101; "Johan Nieman's Letter from Gross-Friedrichsburg, 8 March 1684,"

in Jones, *Brandenburg Sources*, 88. In the case mentioned by de Marees, the oathing test involved a suspected cheating spouse forced to eat salt placed on top of a "conjuration of her Idol or Fetissos." If the spouse was indeed guilty of infidelity, "her Fetisso will kill her for taking a false oath." In Rømer's case, a suspected thief is forced to eat a crumb of bread from a "fetish" made from "a stuffed snake skin, without head or tail, but in their stead, the hair from an elephant's tail, or a cow's tail or wolf's tail, mingled with feathers from a cock." Upon eating the bread placed on top of the ritual object, the suspected thief states "If I have stolen this or that, then let the fetish kill me." Verification that these ritual objects were likely sumán comes from Müller who notes "the Fetu Blacks swear an oath by their *summàn* or fitiso." See "Müller's Description of the Fetu Country, 1662–9," in Jones, *German Sources*, 175.

74. Müller's Description of the Fetu Country, 1662–9," in Jones, *German Sources*, 174.

75. Reindorf, *History of the Gold Coast*, 117.

76. Müller's Description of the Fetu Country, 1662–9," in Jones, *German Sources*, 174–176; "Otto Friedrich Von Der Groeben's Account of His Voyage to Guinea, 1682–1683," in Jones, *Brandenburg Sources*, 51; "Treaty with Three Caboceers of Cape Three Points, 16 May 1681," in Jones, *Brandenburg Sources*, 18; "Treaty with 24 Caboceers of Akwida, 24 February 1684," in Jones, *Brandenburg Sources*, 84; Rask, *Brief and Truthful Description*, 136; Reindorf, *History of the Gold Coast*, 116–117.

77. Bosman, *New and Accurate Description*, 125.

78. Rask, *Brief and Truthful Description*, 136.

79. In the neighboring Slave Coast, the act of "drinking *vodun*" appears frequently in travel accounts as a useful parallel to "eating fetish" in the Gold Coast. Jean Barbot, for example, describes an oathing ceremony in 1680s Whydah in which participants consumed a mixture of earth and blood. Another description from the 1710s involved a water-based drink infused with sacrificial ashes. Given the significant commercial and political ties between the Gold and Slave Coasts, these oathing ceremonies may have had a common, but unknowable, source. See Law, *Slave Coast of West Africa*, 114–115.

80. Konadu, *Akan Diaspora*, 4–5.

81. "Müller's Description of the Fetu Country, 1662–9," in Jones, *German Sources*, 218; Rømer, *A Reliable Account*, 87, 87n34, 100; Rask, *A Brief and Truthful Description*, 106, 107; Henderson-Quartey, *The Ga of Ghana*, 42–47, 58, 61; Parker, *Making the Town*, 7.

82. Akyeampong, *Between the Sea and the Lagoon*, 36; Greene, *Gender, Ethnicity, and Social Change*, 1, 26–27; Kraamer, "Ghanaian Interweaving," 36–53.

83. V. Brown, *Reaper's Garden*, 7–8.

84. *Genuine Narrative*, 2–9; Gaspar, *Bondsmen and Rebels*, 227–254.

85. P. Morgan, "Cultural Implications," 141.

86. Northrup, "Igbo and Myth Igbo," 18.

87. Sidbury and Cañizares-Esguerra, "Mapping Ethnogenesis," 186.

88. Bosman, *New and Accurate Description*, 112–113; Kea, *Settlements, Trade, and Polities*, 105–108; Perbi, *History of Indigenous Slavery*, 116–117.

89. Kea, *Settlements, Trade, and Polities*, 105.

90. Ibid., 104–105; Meredith, *An Account of the Gold Coast of Africa*, 144.

91. Kea, *Settlements, Trade, and Polities*, 106–107.

92. Mintz and Price, *Birth of African American Culture*, 43–44; Rediker, *Slave Ship*, 303–306.

93. See G. M. Hall, *Slavery and African Ethnicities*, 80–100; Gomez, *Exchanging Our Country Marks*, 90–105; Washington [Creel], *A Peculiar People*; Fields-Black, *Deep Roots*; Barry, *Senegambia*; Carney, *Black Rice*.

94. P. Morgan, "Cultural Implications," 129, 132; J. Miller, *Way of Death*, 141–153, 189–203, 226; J. Miller, "The Numbers, Origins, and Destinations of Slaves in the Eighteenth Century Angolan Slave Trade," in Inikori and Engerman, *Atlantic Slave Trade*, 78–89, 104–110; G. M. Hall, *Slavery and African Ethnicities*, 144, 149–157, 159–164.

95. G. M. Hall, *Slavery and African Ethnicities*, 102–105; Shumway, *Fante*, 33–37; Smallwood, *Saltwater Slavery*, 16–20.

96. Shumway, *Fante*, 9, 42–43, 47–51; Smallwood, *Saltwater Slavery*, 29–32.

97. Shumway, *Fante*, 9.

98. Holsey, *Routes of Remembrance*, 40–41, 81–102; Rediker, *Slave Ship*, 272, 334; Hartman, *Lose Your Mother*, 86–87, 157–161, 245. *Donkor* seems to refer more specifically to enslaved Tchamba-speakers from the northern Gold Coast.

99. Quoted in Hartman, *Lose Your Mother*, 158.

100. Chambers, "Ethnicity in the Diaspora," 25–26, 34n5; *Voyages: The Trans-Atlantic Slave Trade Database*.

101. Shumway, *Fante*, 48–51.

102. G. M. Hall, *Slavery and African Ethnicities*, 56–57, 66, 68, 70–71, 110–111; Smallwood, *Saltwater Slavery*, 9–10, 166–176.

103. *Voyages: The Trans-Atlantic Slave Trade Database*; Smallwood, *Saltwater Slavery*, 9–10.

104. *Voyages: The Trans-Atlantic Slave Trade Database*; Smallwood, *Saltwater Slavery*, 187–189. In sum, some slavers recorded as embarking their human cargo in the Slave Coast actually began the Atlantic African portion of their journeys in the Gold Coast. Given the Ewe presence in a range of Slave Coast polities and the Ga-speaking population at Little Popo, we may conclude that an additional portion of the Slave Coast commerce involved people familiar with Akan language and cultures.

105. G. M. Hall, *Slavery and African Ethnicities*, 136; Burnard and Morgan, "Dynamics of the Slave Market," 205–207, 209, 210, 215–216; *Voyages: The Trans-Atlantic Slave Trade Database*; Patterson, *Sociology of Slavery*, 134, 137–138; Littlefield, *Rice and Slaves*, 11; Eltis, "Volume and Structure," 36–37, 40, 46. For a fuller assessment of British asiento traffic to the Spanish Americas, see Palmer, *Human Cargoes*.

106. P. Morgan, "Cultural Implications," 133; Postma, *The Dutch*, 47–55, 168–169, 226; Green-Pederson, " Scope and Structure," 149–197; Westergaard, *Danish West Indies*, 145–150.

107. Byrd, *Captives and Voyagers*, 21–26, 38, 53–55; G. M. Hall, *Slavery and African Ethnicities*, 139–140, 144, 149; Michael Gomez, "A Quality of Anguish: The Igbo Response to Enslavement in America," in Lovejoy and Trotman, *Trans-Atlantic*

Dimensions, 82–95; Herbert S. Klein and Stanley Engerman, "Long-Term Trends in African Mortality in the Transatlantic Slave Trade," in Eltis and Richards, *Routes to Slavery*, 44; J. Miller, *Way of Death*, 140–141, 314, 322–323; Joseph C. Miller, "Central Africa during the Era of the Slave Trade c. 1490s–1850s," in Heywood, *Central Africans and Cultural Transformations*, 54–56; P. Morgan, "Cultural Implications," 129; Smallwood, *Saltwater Slavery*, 137.

108. Shumway, *Fante*, 56–61.

109. Perbi, *History of Indigenous Slavery*, 55; Kea, "Amina Slave Rebellion," 167; Kea, *Settlements, Trade, and Polities*, 162; Ray A. Kea, "'I Am Here to Plunder on the General Road': Bandits and Banditry in the Pre-Nineteenth-Century Gold Coast," in Crummey, *Banditry, Rebellion, and Social Protest*, 126–127. Rømer, *Reliable Account*, 121–122, 131–132. Kea postulates that "siccading" or "sika-den" can be roughly translated as "black gold" in Akan-Twi. More than likely, sika-den was a local idiomatic expression—possibly of Portuguese creole origin—referring to the ability of these paramilitary bands to generate gold revenues from their commercial activities with Europeans. Eighteenth-century reference to the term appears only in Rømer's account; he translates siccadinger as "crafty man"—a description of someone akin to a grifter or con artist.

110. Kea, "I Am Here to Plunder," 110–111; Shumway, *Fante*, 59–61; "Director-General to the Council, 4 April 1710," in Van Dantzig, *Dutch Documents*, II:101.

3. Slavery, Ethnogenesis, and Social Resurrection

1. "Report of the Justices Appointed to Inquire into the Conspiracy of the Negroes at Antigua, December 20, 1736," CO 152/22, W94, National Archives, Kew, UK (hereafter "Report of the Justices," CO 152/22); *Genuine Narrative*, 3–4, 8; Parker, *Making the Town*, 50, 54–57, 102–103; Henderson-Quartey, *The Ga of Ghana*, 90–91, 268–270; Reindorf, *History of the Gold Coast*, 105–107. By the early nineteenth century, the *Gamantse* (or kings of Ga-speaking Accra) began to use the title *Takyi* to reflect their status. Thus, a long line of Ga rulers adopted this custom, including Taki Kome, Taki Tawia, Taki Obili, and Taki Yaoboi. The origins of the adoption of this practice are, perhaps, unknowable as is the etymology of the word itself. Given the fact that early Ga-speaking government in Accra was a theocracy ruled by priest-kings, the conquest by a series of Akan-speaking polities introduced new forms of government and new titles for court officials. The title *Takyi* may have had Akan origins, entering Ga as one of many cultural interventions resulting from the conquest of Accra in 1681. Konadu takes great liberties with the Antigua court record when he claims that Court's name was "Kwaku Takyi" based on the reference to "Coquo Tackey" in the Coromantee chant. In every instance in the trial records, Tackey is translated as "king"; this is thus a title and not a personal name. Also, the Antigua court translated *Coquo* to mean "great," and so the word clearly was not, as Konadu contends, a version of the Akan day-name Kwaku. Given the large number of Quaccos (or Quawccos) appearing in the Antigua conspiracy trial records, it would seem quite odd that this sort of misspelling would occur. See Konadu, *Akan Diaspora*, 137–138; "A List of Slaves Executed for the Late Conspiracy, December 15,

1736" and "A List of Negroes Proposed to be Banished, December 15, 1736" in *Genuine Narrative*, 21, 23.

2. *Genuine Narrative*, 4–7; "Report of the Justices," CO 152/22; "Council Minutes, January 24, 1737," CO 9/10; "Assembly Minutes, January 24, 1737," CO 9/12; Gaspar, *Bondmen and Rebels*, 249–254.

3. "Report of the Justices," CO 152/22; "Council Minutes, January 12, 1737," CO 9/10; *Genuine Narrative*, 13; Gaspar, *Bondmen and Rebels*, 246–247; Gaspar, "Antigua Slave Conspiracy of 1736," 322; J. Thornton, "The Coromantees," 170; Rucker, "Conjure, Magic, and Power," 84–90.

4. "Report of the Justices," CO 152/22; "Council Minutes, January 12, 1737" and "Tryal of Jack a Coromantee Field Slave belonging to Colonel Cochran, December 3, 1736," CO 9/10; *Genuine Narrative*, 9, 13; Oldendorp, *History of the Mission*, 203; R. Price and S. Price, *Stedman's Surinam*, 260; "Müller's Description of the Fetu Country, 1662–9," in Jones, *German Sources*, 281, 299; de Marees, *Historical Account of the Gold Kingdom*, 253, 254, 257; Barbot, *Coasts of North and South Guinea*, IV:418. Müller's vocabulary also includes "brafu" (army commander) and "ockim" (shield). See Müller, "Description of the Fetu Country, 1662–9," in Jones, *German Sources*, 318.

5. "Report of the Justices," CO 152/22; "Council Minutes, January 12, 1737" and "Tryal of Tom, a Field Negro of Edward Otto's, November 24, 1736," CO 9/10; *Genuine Narrative*, 3–13, 20–24; Handler and Bilby, "Early Use and Origin of the Term 'Obeah,'" 88–91; Gaspar, *Bondmen and Rebels*, 240–241, 242–245; J. Thornton, "The Coromantees," 170–172.

6. T. Davis, *A Rumor of Revolt*, 12–13; *Minutes of the Common Council of the City of New York, 1675–1776*; *New York Weekly Journal*, March 23 and June 8, 1741, IV:56, 82–82; V:22.

7. T. Davis, *New York Conspiracy*, 159–161; Clarke, "Negro Plot of 1741," 169. This particular meeting and the oathing ceremony find corroboration in the confessions of Jack Sleydall, Cajoe Gomez, William Kane, Pedro De Peyster, and Cato Shurmur. See T. Davis, *New York Conspiracy*, 164–165, 238, 249–251, 252–253, 285.

8. T. Davis, *New York Conspiracy*, 239.

9. Ibid., 468–473, appendix, "List of Negroes Committed on Account of the Conspiracy"; Rucker, *'River Flows On,'* 79–83; Rucker "'Only Draw in Your Countrymen,'" 102–108.

10. Agorsah, "Archaeology and Resistance History," 185–186; Davidson, *African Slave Trade*, 72; Schuler, "Ethnic Slave Rebellions," 375; Herskovits, *Myth of the Negro Past*, 35; Kea, *Settlements, Trade, and Polities*, 15, 69, 147; Davies, *Royal African Company*, 9, 40, 42, 265.

11. For the varying meanings and ethnolinguistic associations of Mina in Brazil, see G. M. Hall, *Slavery and African Ethnicities*, 36–37, 47, 67, 112–119; G. M. Hall, "African Ethnicities and the Meanings of 'Mina,'" in Lovejoy and Trotman, *Trans-Atlantic Dimension of Ethnicity*, 65–78; Law, "Ethnicities of Enslaved Africans," 247–267; Curto and Lovejoy, *Enslaving Connections*, 12, 98–99, 151; Hawthorne, *From Africa to Brazil*, 3, 44, 181, 251.

12. See, for example, Schuler, "Akan Slave Rebellions," 9–10; Schuler, "Ethnic Slave Rebellions," 375–376; Patterson, "Slavery and Slave Revolts," 289–335; Eugene

Genovese, *From Rebellion to Revolution*, 19, 28–30, 36, 99–100; Mullin, *Africa in America*, 14, 269–271.

13. Mullin, *Africa in America*, 131, 254; Long, *History of Jamaica*, II:457–462.

14. G. M. Hall, *Africans in Colonial Louisiana*, 319–320; G. M. Hall, "African Ethnicities and the Meanings of 'Mina,'" in Lovejoy and Trotman, *Trans-Atlantic Dimension of Ethnicity*, 65–66, 74.

15. See Siguret, "Esclaves d'Indigoteries," 224–225; "Testimonio del Proceso Criminal de los Negros Rebueltos de Este Puesto contra los Blancos de decho Puesto Junio 1792," folios 39r, 43r, 44v, 47v–102r (hereafter "Testimonios"), Gwendolyn Midlo Hall Papers (hereafter Hall Papers), Amistad Research Center, Tulane University; Ulysses S. Ricard, Jr., "The Pointe Coupee Slave Conspiracy of 1791," 14, Hall Papers; Jack D. L. Holmes, "Abortive Slave Revolt," 359–361; "Pointe Coupee Conspiracy Trial Testimony, 1795," Hall Papers; G. M. Hall, "The 1795 Slave Conspiracy in Pointe Coupee," 8, Hall Papers; G. M. Hall, *Africans in Colonial Louisiana*, 284, 321, 364–365.

16. For a similar interpretation, see Sidbury and Cañizares-Esguerra, "Mapping Ethnogenesis," 185–191.

17. See Kiyaga-Mulindwa, "The 'Akan' Problem," 503–506; J. Thornton, "The Coromantee," 164–165.

18. Roth, "Slave Rebellion in Berbice, Parts I–VII"; Velzing, "Berbice Slave Revolt," 2–13; Benjamin, "Origins of the Berbice Slave Revolt," 2–9; Blair, "Wolfert Simon van Hoogenheim," 56–76.

19. "Testimonios," folios 1r–105r, Hall Papers; Ricard, "Pointe Coupee Slave Conspiracy," 5–11, Hall Papers; G. M. Hall, *Africans in Colonial Louisiana*, 319–331.

20. "Testimonios," folio 9r, Hall Papers; Ricard, "The Pointe Coupee Slave Conspiracy," 8, Hall Papers.

21. Ricard, "Pointe Coupee Slave Conspiracy," 8, 11–13, Hall Papers; "Pointe Coupee Conspiracy Trial Testimony, 1795," Hall Papers; G. M. Hall, "The 1795 Slave Conspiracy in Pointe Coupee," 1–10, Hall Papers.

22. Stuckey, *Slave Culture*, 4–5; Mintz and Price, *Birth of African-American Culture*, 42–49. Stuckey states, explicitly, that "slave ships were the first real incubators of slave unity across cultural lines, fostering resistance thousands of miles before the shores of the new land appeared." See Stuckey, *Slave Culture*, 4.

23. See Miller, *Way of Death*, 66–67; Hartman, *Lose Your Mother*, 68–69.

24. Agorsah, "Archaeology and Resistance History," 178–180; Schaffer and Agorsah, "Bioarchaeological Analysis," 2, 8–9; Agorsah and Butler, "Archaeological," 2–6; Behn, *Oroonoko*, xxi–xxiv; Joanna Lipking, "Confusing Matters: Searching the Backgrounds of Oroonoko," in Todd, *Aphra Behn Studies*, 259–281.

25. de Marees, *Historical Account of the Gold Kingdom*, 7, 84n; "Samuel Brun's Voyages of 1611–1620," in Jones, *German Sources*, 65; Hair, Jones, and Law, *Barbot on Guinea*, II:416–418; "Correspondence of Edwyn Steed and Stephen Gascoigne of Barbados to Cape Coast Castle, 1 July 1686," in Law, *The English in West Africa, 1685–1688*, no. 974:417; "Correspondence of John Browne to Annamaboe, 24 April 1697," in Law, *The English in West Africa, 1691–1699*, no. 863, 354n189; "Muller's Description of the Fetu Country, 1662–1669," in Jones, *German Sources*, 172n146.

26. At least by 1625, Cormantin was noted to be "under the King of Foetui." Purchas, *Hakluytus Posthumus,* II:946.

27. "Samuel Brun's Voyages of 1611–1620," in Jones, *German Sources,* 92–93; Shumway, *Fante,* 89, 93–101, 106; Chambers, "Ethnicity in Diaspora," 32; Konadu, *Akan Diaspora,* 60–61; Reindorf, *History of the Gold Coast,* 67; Fynn, *Asante and Its Neighbours,* 48–49; H. U. E. Thoden van Velzen, "Dangerous Ancestors: Ambivalent Visions of Eighteenth- and Nineteenth-Century Leaders of the Eastern Maroons of Suriname," in Palmié, *Slave Cultures,* 126–127. Chambers misreads, significantly, the assessment by Van Velzen. Instead of discussing "Kromanti" among the Saramaka Maroons, Van Velzen's focus is on what he terms "Kumanti"—a sacred knowledge monopolized by medicine men among the Ndyuka Maroons in late eighteenth-century Suriname.

28. Craton, *Testing the Chains,* 108–109; Dunn, *Sugar and Slaves,* 257–258; Handler, "Slave Revolts and Conspiracies," 13–19; "Governor Jonathan Atkins to Sir Joseph Williamson, 3 October 1675," *CSPC,* no. 690 (and CO 1/35); *Great Newes from the Barbadoes,* 9–12; "Minutes of the Assembly of Barbadoes, 23–25 November 1675," *CSPC,* no. 712; Kea, "An Amina Slave Rebellion," 159–160.

29. Henry Drax, "Instructions for the Management of Drax-Hall and the Irish-Hope Plantations, 1670–1682," in Belgrove, *Treatise,* 67; "Correspondence of Edwyn Steed and Stephen Gascoigne of Barbados to Cape Coast Castle, 1 July 1686," in Law, *The English in West Africa,* no. 974, 416–417.

30. "Account of the Supply of Barbadoes with Negro Servants, Addressed to the African Company by Edwyn Stede, 28 February 1693," Harley MSS, British Library, folio 7310; Craton, *Testing the Chains,* 25; Thomas Phillips, "A Journal of a Voyage Made in the Hannibal of London, ann. 1693, 1694, from England to Barbadoes," in *Collection of Voyages and Travels,* IV:214.

31. "Governor Codrington to the Council of Trade and Plantations, 30 December 1701," in *CSPC,* vol. 19, no. 1132.

32. Snelgrave, *New Account,* 162–185; Phillips, *American Negro Slavery,* 36–37.

33. Edwards, *History, Civil and Commercial,* II:70, 74; Schuler, "Akan Slave Rebellions," 11.

34. Long, *History of Jamaica,* II:470–471.

35. Ibid., 472–475.

36. Le Page, *Jamaican Creole,* 97–98; Dallas, *History of the Maroons,* I:31–33.

37. Sharpe, "Negro Plot of 1712," 162–163; Boston *News-Letter,* April 7–14, 1712; J. Thornton, "The Coromantees," 165–166.

38. Kea, "An Amina Slave Rebellion," 160, 169, 175–176; Hartman, *Lose Your Mother,* 91–94; J. Thornton, *Warfare in Atlantic Africa,* 142–143; Pannet, *Report on the Execrable Conspiracy,* 12–14, 17–18; Low and Valls, *St. John Backtime,* 9, 11; Oldendorp, *History of the Mission,* 236; J. L. Anderson, *Night of the Silent Drums,* 62–63, 70, 71, 100–101, 116, 163, 168, 259–260, 272–273, 277, 403–405.

39. Hart, *Slaves Who Abolished Slavery,* 15, 155n1; Edwards, *History, Civil and Commercial,* II:75, 78.

40. J. Thornton, "On the Trail of Voodoo," 261–278.

41. Stephens, *High Life in New York,* 82, 181; Sheila Walker, "Everyday Africa in New Jersey: Wonderings and Wanderings in the African Diaspora," in Walker,

African Roots/American Cultures, 53; Mencken, "Designations for Colored Folks," 173; Sterling Stuckey, "The Skies of Consciousness: African Dance at Pinkster in New York, 1750–1840," in Stuckey, *Going Through the Storm,* 58; Pollard, *Black Diamonds,* 1; Stowe, *Minister's Wooing,* 110–111; Hurston, *Dust Tracks on a Road,* 221, 233. Pinkster, the Dutch celebration of the Pentecost or Whitsunday, began as a three- or four-day holiday in New Netherland and New York until the mid-nineteenth century. Enslaved peoples appropriated the public parade at an early point and, in many ways, made it their own.

42. Patterson, *Sociology of Slavery,* 174–181; Stewart, *Account of Jamaica,* 234–235; Cumming, *Carlyle Encyclopedia,* 386–387; Carlyle, *Occasional Discourse,* 13–15, 37–38.

43. Alexander, *Transatlantic Sketches,* I:95; *Antigua and the Antiguans,* II:125.

44. Craton, *Testing the Chains,* 57; de Marees, *Historical Account of the Gold Kingdom,* 249; Rømer, *Reliable Account,* 99–100.

45. Konadu, *Akan Diaspora in the Americas,* 266n40.

46. Patterson, *Sociology of Slavery,* 178.

47. Blassingame, *Slave Community,* 141.

48. "We Wear the Mask," in Dunbar, *Selected Poems,* 17; Hartman, *Scenes of Subjection,* 8.

49. Hartman, *Scenes of Subjection,* 4–8; White, *Ar'n't I a Woman?,* 27–61.

50. Patterson, *Sociology of Slavery,* 174–181.

51. John Stewart, *State of the Island of Jamaica,* 250–251.

52. Kopytoff, "Development of Jamaican Maroon Ethnicity," 40–42; Kenneth Bilby, "Maroon Culture as a Distinct Variant of Jamaican Culture," in Agorsah, *Maroon Heritage,* 72–85; Chambers, "Ethnicity in the Diaspora," 32–33; DjeDje, "Remembering Kojo," 67–112.

53. Agorsah and Butler, "Archaeological Investigation," 4–5; Dalby, "Ashanti Survivals," 31–51; Kuss, *Music in Latin America,* 328–329; Bilby, "Kromanti Dance," 54–55; Bilby, "How the Ýolder Headsý Talk," 37–88.

54. M. and F. Herskovits, *Rebel Destiny,* 316, 350.

55. De Groot, "Bush Negro Chiefs," 392.

56. Van Velzen, "Dangerous Ancestors," in Palmié, *Slave Cultures,* 126–127.

57. Davis, *New York Conspiracy,* 265–266, 322, 463; "Report of the Justices," CO 152/22; "Witnesses to be sent off," in *Genuine Narrative,* 2; "Council Minutes, November 8, 1736," CO 9/10; "A List of Negroes that were Evidences, May 27, 1737" CO 152/23, X7: 34.

58. Davis, *New York Conspiracy,* 265–266, 322, 463.

59. Pannet, *Report on the Execrable Conspiracy,* 7; Westergard, *Danish West Indies,* 174–176.

60. "Tryal of Ms. Langford's Robin a Caromantee, November 13, 1736," CO 9/10.

61. Ibid.; *Genuine Narrative,* 12–14.

62. "Tryal of Ned Chester, a Mullatto Carpenter belonging to Cesar Rodney, November 26, 1736," "Tryal of Froilus Commonly Called Yabby a Cormante Carpenter belonging to the Estate of Thomas Freeman, December 10, 1736," and "Tryal of Quawcoo an Old Oby Man, Physician, and Cormantee belonging to Mr. William Hunt, December 11, 1736," CO 9/10; "Report of the Justices," CO 152/22; "Witnesses

to be sent off" in *Genuine Narrative,* 2; "Council Minutes, November 8, 1736," CO 9/10; "A List of Negroes that were Evidences, May 27, 1737," CO 152/23, x.7: 34.

63. *New-York Weekly Journal,* March 7, 14, and 21, 1737.

64. Davis, *New York Conspiracy,* 212, 225, 277–278, 239, 322, 463–464.

4. State, Governance, and War

1. Kea, "An Amina Slave Rebellion," 167–169, 175–180; J. Thornton, *Warfare in Atlantic Africa,* 142–143; Westergaard, *Danish West Indies,* 21, 40n.

2. Kea, "An Amina Slave Rebellion," 177.

3. Kea, "An Amina Slave Rebellion," 160, 169, 175–176; Hartman, *Lose Your Mother,* 91–94; J. Thornton, *Warfare in Atlantic Africa,* 142–143; Fynn, *Asante and Its Neighbours,* 21; Shumway, *The Fante,* 37, 58; Pannet, *Report on the Execrable Conspiracy,* 12–14, 17–18; Low and Valls, *St. John Backtime,* 9, 11; Oldendorp, *History of the Mission,* 236; Anderson, *Night of the Silent Drums,* 62–63, 70, 71, 100–101, 116, 163, 168, 259–260, 272–273, 277, 403–405.

4. Pannet, *Report on the Execrable Conspiracy,* 1, 8, 17; Schuler, "Ethnic Slave Rebellions," 375, 378–381.

5. Caron and Highfield, *French Intervention,* 34, 41–49; Kea, "An Amina Slave Rebellion," 159, 182–184, 187; Low and Valls, *St. John Backtime,* 11; Pannet, *Report on the Execrable Conspiracy,* 7–8, 17. Three decades following the failed Amina revolt, Akwamu elites still lived in the Danish St. John, St. Croix, and St. Thomas. During his March 1767–October 1769 mission to the Danish Caribbean, Christian Georg Andreas Oldendorp interviewed three former members of the Akwamu elite: "One of these, formerly a rich merchant and slave-hunter. . . . The other was a brother of the king, and the third had command over three thousand men in the army of a vassal king, his close relative." Using a range of archival sources in Denmark in preparation for writing his fictionalized account of the 1733–34 rebellion, John Anderson estimates that St. John, at the time of the Amina revolt, had "four African princes serving as slaves . . . a least fifty lesser noblemen, and one African king." See Oldendorp, *History of the Mission,* xvii, 162–163; Anderson, *Night of the Silent Drums,* 60.

6. "Levango" could also be a reference to the Portuguese city of Luanda in Angola. See Oldendorp, *History of the Mission,* 168.

7. The first quotation is from Eugene Genovese; see *From Rebellion to Revolution,* xviii–xxii, 38, 49, 82–85, 91–92. The second is from Ray Kea; see "An Amina Slave Rebellion," 160–162, 183, 189. This critique of the 1733–34 Amina revolt as a restorationist movement is repeated by Saidiya Hartman, who fails to cite either Genovese or Kea. See Hartman, *Lose Your Mother,* 91–93, 246n.

8. See Rucker, *River Flows On,* 204–206; J. Thornton, "War, the State, and Religious Norms in 'Coromantee' Thought," in St. George, *Possible Pasts,* 181–200; Blier, *African Vodun;* T. J. Desch-Obi, *Fighting for Honor.*

9. Smallwood, *Saltwater Slavery,* 27.

10. J. Thornton, "War, the State, and Religious Norms in 'Coromantee' Thought," in St. George, *Possible Pasts,* 187, 190–193, 196; Shumway, *Fante,* 58; Kea, *Settlements,*

Trade, and Polities, 57–61, 295–313; Kea, *Cultural and Social History,* 417–418, 437; Diptee, *From Africa to Jamaica,* 63. Rediker, *Slave Ship,* 101.

11. "The Examination of Emanuel, A Portuguese Negro Slave belonging to Mr. Edward Gregory, October 15, 1736," CO 9/10.

12. *Genuine Narrative,* 8.

13. "Trial of Froilus Commonly Called Yabby, A Cormantee Carpenter belonging to the Estate of Thomas Freeman, December 10, 1736" and "Tryal of Quawcoo an Old Oby Man, Physician, and Cormantee belonging to Mr. William Hunt, December 9, 1736," CO 9/10; *Genuine Narrative,* 7–9. "Obeng" or *abeng* is an Akan word for a type of trumpet made from a hollowed-out animal tusk or horn. See de Marees, *Historical Account of the Gold Kingdom,* 253; "Müller's Description of the Fetu Country, 1662–9," in Jones, *German Sources,* 304; Barbot, *Coasts of North and South Guinea,* IV:420.

14. *Genuine Narrative,* 6–7; "Report of the Justices," CO 152/22.

15. Long, *History of Jamaica,* II:455–456; "Assembly Minutes, December 5, 1760," *Journals of the Assembly of Jamaica,* V:233.

16. Thicknesse, *Memoirs and Anecdotes,* 64, 74–78; Gottlieb, *"Mother of Us All,"* 23–27; Patterson, "Slavery and Slave Revolts," 302–303; Robinson, *Fighting Maroons,* 53–54; "Governor Hunter to the Council of Trade and Plantations: Further Examination of Sarra, alias Ned, Taken by Order of H.E., October 1, 1733," in *CSPC,* vol. 40, no. 358 (also CO 137/21, 42). It is entirely likely that this unnamed woman was not Queen Nanny and that Nanny never existed as a historical figure.

17. *Great Newes from the Barbadoes,* 9–10.

18. Crichlow and Armstrong, "Carnival Praxis," 400–401, 404; Kramer, *Red Fez,* 2.

19. J. Thornton, "War, the State, and Religious Norms in 'Coromantee' Thought," in St. George, *Possible Pasts,* 185, 193, 195–200.

20. "Trial of Froilus Commonly Called Yabby, A Cormantee Carpenter belonging to the Estate of Thomas Freeman, December 10, 1736" and "Tryal of Quawcoo an Old Oby Man, Physician, and Cormantee belonging to Mr. William Hunt, December 9, 1736," CO 9/10.

21. *Genuine Narrative,* 4–6.

22. "Tryal of Primus, an Ebo field Negro belonging to Peter Brown, December 13, 1736," and "Tryal of London, a Creole Slave belonging to the Estate of John Goble, December 3, 1736," and "Tryal of Jack a Creole Carpenter and belonging to Old Thomas Elmos, December 7, 1736," CO 9/10; "Evidence against Billy and Benjamin Johnson, November 8, 1736," CO 152/23; *Genuine Narrative,* 3–5, 15. The mention of "Windward People" in the Antigua trial records is slightly confusing, as it is seemingly used in reference to an ethnic group—of which the "Ebo" were a major portion. In this case, "Windward" refers to a general location in Antigua and not a place of origin (e.g., the Windward Coast or the Ivory Coast) in Atlantic Africa.

23. Thornton, "War, the State, and Religious Norms in 'Coromantee' Thought," in St. George, *Possible Pasts,* 187.

24. *Boston News-Letter,* April 7–14, 1712; Sharpe, "Negro Plot of 1712," 162–163.

25. Ricard, "Pointe Coupee Slave Conspiracy," 5–11, Hall Papers; G. M. Hall, *Africans in Colonial Louisiana,* 316–374.

26. Long, *History of Jamaica*, II:472.

27. *Genuine Narrative*, 10; J. Thornton, "The Coromantees," 169–170; Mullin, *Africa in America*, 67–68, 72–73.

28. "The Substance of the Information given by Robert Arbuthnot, Esq. to the General Council of the Discoverys He Had Made of the Dangerous Designs and Behaviours of the Slaves, October 15, 1736," CO 9/10.

29. See Lewis, *Ring of Liberation*; Desch-Obi, *Fighting for Honor*; Roberts, *From Trickster to Badman*; Stuckey, "Through the Prism of Folklore," 417–437.

30. *Genuine Narrative*, 5–6; "Report of the Justices," CO 152/22.

31. Mullin, *Africa in America*, 67.

32. G. M. Hall, *Africans in Colonial Louisiana*, 331–332; "Carondelet to Luis de las Casas, June 16, 1795," Dispatches of the Spanish Governors of Louisiana, El Baron of Carondelet 1793–1796 (IX) [Library of Congress, Facsimiles from Archivo General de Indies], Bundle 1445 B; Letter #691, Amistad Research Center, Tulane University, Special Collections.

33. See Berlin, "From Creole to African," 253–268, 282–288.

34. Ricard, "Pointe Coupee Slave Conspiracy," 5–7, G. M. Hall, *Africans in Colonial Louisiana*, 320; Hall Papers; "Testimonios," folios 13v, 28v–29r, 42r–48v.

35. Roth, "Slave Rebellion in Berbice," II:39; VI:61.

36. See Elizabeth W. Kiddy, "Who is the King of Congo? A New Look at African and Afro-Brazilian Kings in Brazil," in Heywood, *Central Africans*, 153–182; Kiddy, "Ethnic and Racial Identity," 221–252; Sterling Stuckey, "The Skies of Consciousness: African Dance at Pinkster in New York, 1750–1840," in Stuckey, *Going Through the Storm*, 53–82; Burton, *Afro-Creole*; Johnson, "New Orleans's Congo Square," 117–157; Donaldson, "Window on Slave Culture," 63–72.

37. Buisseret, *Jamaica in 1687*, 274–275; "History of the Revolted Negroes in Jamaica" in "Account of the Maroons, and Papers Respecting the Rebellion of the Negroes, 1733–1739," C. E. Long Papers, Additional Manuscripts, 12431, British Library. Regarding the incremental and uneven growth of maroon communities, the anonymous writer of this history of Jamaican slave revolts notes "They likewise associated themselves with some of those small Bodies, follow'd the same Customs, and abated of their Severity to those, who deserted and came to join them. Hence arose the other Great Gang, which Consisted of the Descendants of the Spanish Negro's who . . . were joined by divers small Bodies, and after many disputes and Battles with some other Gangs, incorporated and settled together in the Mountains."

38. "History of the Revolted Negroes in Jamaica," Long Papers, Add. Manuscripts, 12431; Knight, "Political History of Jamaica," Long Papers, Add. Manuscripts, 12419; Buisseret, *Jamaica in 1687*, 275–276;

39. "History of the Revolted Negroes in Jamaica," Long Papers, Add. Manuscripts, 12431; "Minutes of a Council of War held at Jamaica, August 1, 1685," *CSPC*, vol. 12, no. 299; "Lieutenant-Governor Molesworth to William Blathwayt, August 29, 1685," *CSPC*, vol. 12, no. 339 (also CO 138/5); "Minutes of Council of Jamaica, November 5, 1685," *CSPC*, vol. 12, no. 445; "Minutes of Council of Jamaica, April 8, 1686," *CSPC*, vol. 12, no. 623.

40. Patterson, "Slavery and Slave Revolts," 299–302; Craton, *Testing the Chains*, 75–79; Dallas, *History of the Maroons*, I:26, 30–34; "History of the Revolted Negroes

in Jamaica," Long Papers, Add. Manuscripts, 12431; Knight, "History of Jamaica," Long Papers, Add. Manuscripts, 1241 9; "Earl of Inchiquin to the Committee, Jamaica, August 31, 1690," CO 138/7.

41. Craton, *Testing the Chains*, 77–78, 353–354n24.

42. Ibid., 353–354n24.

43. Edwards, *History, Civil and Commercial*, I:525–535.

44. Dallas, *History of the Maroons*, I:31–33; Knight, "History of Jamaica," Long Papers, Add. Manuscripts, 12419. Knight adds some additional details regarding this amalgamation of the Madagascars within the Coromantee collective, hinting at the fact that this process was marked by confrontation and violence. In this regard, he notes, "These, two Parties, after many disputes, and bloody battles wherein a great Number were slain on both Sides and among others the Madagascar Captain, joined and incorporated themselves. Hence arose that great Body of Negro's, near Deans Valley in St. Elizabeth's now under the Command of Captn. Cudjo."

45. David Geggus, "The Haitian Revolution" in Knight and Palmer, *The Modern Caribbean*, 21, 24, 29–44; Fick, *The Making of Haiti*, 109, 169–173; Dubois, *Avengers of the New World*, 108–109, 160, 171–176, 193, 247, 294–296; Dubois and Garrigus, *Slave Revolution in the Caribbean*, 13, 36–37, 86–88, 90. Indeed, a direct link between Jamaica and the 1791 Haitian Revolution came in the guise of Boukman Dutty—the man responsible for the Vodun ceremony at Bois-Caïman that sparked the movement against the French. According to a number of records, Boukman originated in Jamaica and may have been either a Muslim or an obeah-doctor before his transport to and arrival in Haiti on the eve of the revolution. See Diouf, *Servants of Allah*, 153; Dubois, *Avengers of the New World*, 101.

46. Kopytoff, "Early Political Development," 290; Dallas, *History of the Maroons*, I:25–28; "Minutes of Council of Jamaica: Petition of the Parish of St. George, September 16, 1686," in *CSPC*, vol. 12, no. 869; "History of the Revolted Negroes in Jamaica," Long Papers, Add. Manuscripts, 12431.

47. "Christopher Allen's Journal, March 1732," CO 137/54, folio 52; Kopytoff, "Early Political Development," 298.

48. "Governor Hunter to the Council of Trade and Plantations: Further Examination of Sarra, alias Ned, Taken by Order of H.E., October 1, 1733," in *CSPC*, vol. 40, no. 358; Craton, *Testing the Chains*, 81; Patterson, "Slavery and Slave Revolts," 302n52.

49. Thicknesse, *Memoirs and Anecdotes*, 64, 73–78; Patterson, "Slavery and Slave Revolts," 302–303; "Governor Hunter to the Council of Trade and Plantations: Further Examination of Sarra, alias Ned, Taken by Order of H.E., October 1, 1733," in *CSPC*, vol. 40, no. 358; Dalby, "Ashanti Survivals," 31–51.

50. "Lieutenant-Governor Molesworth to William Blathwayt, September 28, 1686," in *CSPC*, vol. 12, no. 883; "Lieutenant-Governor Molesworth to William Blathwayt, November 1, 1686," in *CSPC*, vol. 12, no. 965.

51. "Lt.-Governor Beckford to the Council of Trade and Plantations, August 25, 1702," in *CSPC*, vol. 20, no. 912; "Journal of the Assembly of Jamaica: Miscellaneous Messages from the Governor, September 29, 1703," in *CSPC*, vol. 21, no. 1107; "Lt.-Gov. Beckford to the Earl of Nottingham, September 22, 1702," in *CSPC*, vol. 20, no.

980; "History of the Revolted Negroes in Jamaica," Long Papers, Add. Manuscripts, 12431.

52. Patterson, "Slavery and Slave Revolts," 303–311; Edwards, *History, Civil and Commercial*, I:530–535.

53. Craton, *Testing the Chains*, 88–91; Patterson, "Slavery and Slave Revolts," 311–312; "History of the Revolted Negroes in Jamaica," Long Papers, Add. Manuscripts, 12431; Dallas, *History of the Maroons*, I:56, 58–65, 79–84, 97, 105–107; Twentieth-century descendants of the Leeward Maroons, known now as the Accompong Maroons, claim that this treaty was consecrated by a blood oath. No extant written records validates this claim, though it would not be beyond the realm of possibility. See Bilby, "Swearing by the Past," 658–659; Campbell, *Maroons of Jamaica*, 115.

54. Dallas, *History of the Maroons*, I:61–63, 102–103; "Mr. Fuller's Report to the Speaker of the Assembly, May 1, 1742," *Journals of the Assembly of Jamaica*, III:594. Trelawny Maroons played a small role in helping quash Tackey's 1760 rebellion. Ironically, it would be the Trelawny Leewards who initiated and waged the Second Maroon War between July 1795 and March 1796. See Long, *History of Jamaica*, II:452–455; Craton, *Testing the Chains*, 92, 211–223.

55. Craton, *Testing the Chains*, 91–92; Dallas, *History of the Maroons*, I:73, 75–77; "Assembly Minutes, April 16 and March 18, 1740," *Journals of the Assembly of Jamaica*, III:505, 513; "History of the Revolted Negroes in Jamaica," Long Papers, Add. Manuscripts, 12431.

56. Long, *History of Jamaica*, II:447–470; Edwards, *History, Civil and Commercial*, II:75–76. Edwards specifically notes that the majority of those involved in the revolt were "Gold Coast Negroes newly imported"—increasing the likelihood that Tackey had been a royal as an adult. In addition, no records exist regarding his Jamaican background and the first mention of him, historically, was as the leader of the Coromantee rebels.

57. Long, *History of Jamaica*, II:447; Kea, *Settlements, Trade, and Polities*, 97–108.

58. Long, *History of Jamaica*, II:447.

59. Kea, *Settlements, Trade, and Polities*, 112–121; Shumway, *Fante*, 88, 93–104.

60. Craton, *Testing the Chains*, 129; Edwards, *History, Civil and Commercial*, II:75–78; Long, *History of Jamaica*, II:448–452.

61. Roth, "Slave Rebellion in Berbice," I:41; Velzing, "Berbice Slave Revolt," 2–13; Blair, "Wolfert Simon van Hoogenheim," 63–66; Schuler, "Akan Slave Rebellions," 20. Schuler links the Guango, convincingly, to a band of West-Central African mercenaries known as the Imbangala. "Guango" is very similar to a place name (the Kwango River) were the Imbangala were known to operate. Also, in both West-Central Africa and among the Delmina rebels in Berbice, the so-called Guango were feared and reviled for their alleged taste for human flesh. See J. Thornton, "African Experience," 422, 425–427; J. Thornton, "Resurrection for the Jaga," 223–226.

62. Roth, "Slave Rebellion in Berbice," II:38–39. In an interesting twist, Accara reportedly volunteered to hunt down the remaining Delminas after the rebellion ended and was later transported to Suriname. More than a decade after his arrival, he encountered and worked with John Gabriel Stedman in his expedition against

the Saramaka Maroons. Stedman notes that on February 19, 1775, Accara "discovered an old decrepit slave called Paulus, belonging to this estate, to be his brother, whom he treated with much kindness, the same being both surprising and affecting." See Schuler, *Akan Slave Rebellions*, 19; R. Price and S. Price, *Stedman's Surinam*, 17, 137, 227.

63. R. Price, *To Slay the Hydra*, 3–12, 159; R. Price, *The Guiana Maroons*, 19; Marcus and Chyet, *Historical Essay*, 57–58.

64. Marcus and Chyet, *Historical Essay*, 67–73, 86; Price, *To Slay the Hydra*, 12, 16–18, 21–23.

65. Price, *To Slay the Hydra*, 159–165.

5. Obeah, Oaths, and Ancestral Spirits

1. *A Genuine Narrative*, 22; "Justices to William Mathew, Captain General and Governor in Chief of the Leeward Islands, December 15, 1736," CO 9/10; "Council Minutes: List of Forty-five Banishments with Eight Evidences, March 1737," CO 9/11 (ff. 50–51); Westergaard, "Account of the Negro Rebellion on St. Croix," 55–56; Caron and Highfield, *French Intervention*, 55n13. The fact that "Aminas" resided in eighteenth-century St. Croix finds corroboration in records kept by the Danish West Indies Company in Christiansted. A roster of "Company" slaves employed to labor in public works projects from 1740 to 1755 includes a large number claimed to be Aminas, including: Acra, Adu, Cuffee, Juaw (Quaw), Josie (Osei), Quaco, four Quashis, and Quamina. See George Tyson, "Contributions of Africans," 6.

2. "Council Minutes: List of Forty-five Banishments with Eight Evidences, March 1737," CO 9/11 (ff. 50–51); "Tryal of Quaw son of Old Cormante Tom belonging to the Estate of Edward Byam, December 10, 1736," CO 9/10; "Report of the Justices," CO 152/22; Westergaard, "Account of the Negro Rebellion," 55; Gaspar, *Bondmen and Rebels*, 34; *Genuine Narrative*, 15, 22.

3. "Evidence against Warner's Johnno, a Cooper belonging to Folly's Plantation, January 21, 1737," CO 9/11 (ff. 10–11); "Evidence against Colonel Luca's Cesar, a Driver, January 20, 1737," CO 9/11 (ff. 10); "Evidence against Oliver's Quao, January 21, 1737," CO 9/11 (ff. 12).

4. "Tryal of Quawcoo an Old Oby Man, Physician, and Cormantee belonging to Mr. William Hunt, December 9, 1736," CO 9/10.

5. Westergaard, "Account of the Negro Rebellion," 55–56, 58; N. Hall, *Slave Society*, 71; Oldendorp, *History of the Mission*, 508, 523.

6. Westergaard, "Account of the Negro Rebellion," 55, 57.

7. Westergaard, "Account of the Negro Rebellion," 54–55, 57, 58, 59; Kea, "An Amina Slave Rebellion," 159–160; Caron and Highfield, *French Intervention*, 55n13.

8. Scott, *Weapons of the Weak*.

9. Greene, *Sacred Sites*, 112; H. W. Debrunner, *Witchcraft in Ghana*, 1.

10. Rediker, *Slave Ship*, 17–18. The trader did not survive the passage to the New World, attempting suicide twice by clawing open wounds in his neck with his own fingernails. The unnamed trader finally succeeded in ending his life through a prolonged hunger strike.

11. Rediker, *Slave Ship*, 17–18; Kea, *Settlements, Trade, and Polities*, 97–99; Bosman, *New and Accurate Description*, 164–165; J. Thornton, "War, the State, and Religious Norms in 'Coromantee' Thought," in St. George, *Possible Pasts*, 184–185, 189; Parish, "Anti-witchcraft Shrines," 19; Debrunner, *Witchcraft in Ghana*, 105–111. Debrunner, in particular, links the ebbs in anti-witchcraft to times of economic prosperity in the twentieth century. He notes: "Roughly speaking, there have been three main crests in the waves of anti-witchcraft shrines: before 1912, between 1924 and the economic crisis, and in and after World War II. At each of these times the influx of foreign ideas was particularly strong and the country had something of an economic boom."

12. Venkatachalam, "Between the Devil and the Cross," 56.

13. J. Thornton, "War, the State, and Religious Norms in 'Coromantee' Thought," in St. George, *Possible Pasts*, 186–187; McCaskie, "Anti-Witchcraft Cults," 125–126; Greene, *Sacred Sites*, 136–137; Austen, "Slave Trade as History," 238–240; Parish, "From the Body to the Wallet," 487–488. The recent "Sakawa Boys" phenomenon represents the latest iteration of this concept. These young men in Ghana use internet scams to generate large pools of cash that they spend lavishly on cars, jewelry, and clothing. Supposedly, they mix bayi with a command of cyber technology and, for this reason, have been linked to Ghanaian witchcraft since the earliest reports about their activities. Indeed, it is their use and embrace of witchcraft—not necessarily their international cybercrimes ring—that has garnered much of the local news coverage and attention in Ghana. See Warner, "Understanding Cyber-Crime," 736; Eshun, "Socio-Religious Implication."

14. Shaw, *Memories of the Slave Trade*, 221.

15. Patterson, *Sociology of Slavery*, 189; Oldendorp, *History of the Mission*, 192.

16. Debrunner, *Witchcraft in Ghana*, 29–30.

17. For a parallel treatment of obeah, see J. Thornton, "The Coromantees," 161–178.

18. "Thomas Walduck to James Petiver, Apothecary and Fellow of the Royal Society in Aldergate, (no date)," Sloan MSS, 2302, British Library.

19. V. Brown, "Spiritual Terror and Sacred Authority: The Power of the Supernatural in Jamaican Slave Society," in Baptist and Camp, *New Studies in the History of American Slavery*, 182, 195–198; Rucker, "Conjure, Magic, and Power," 86–94.

20. J. Thornton, *Africa and Africans*, 264. More than a century later, obeah was a widespread practice in British St. Kitts and throughout the Leeward Islands. In 1788, a representative from St. Kitts testified in Parliament that obeah was used "for the protection of their persons and provision grounds, hogs, poultry, etc. and often imagine they are obeahed or bewitched.... they sometimes operate extraordinary cures in diseases which have baffled the skill of regular practitioners and more especially in foul sores and ulcers." See Bilby and Handler, "Obeah: Healing and Protection," 158.

21. Olmos and Paravisini-Gebert, *Sacred Possessions*, 6–8; Olmos, Murphy, and Paravisini-Gebert, *Creole Religions*, 132–136; Hedrick and Stephens, *It's a Natural Fact*, 2, 5–9, 30; Poole, *Beneficent Bee*, II:229–230, Obeah Folder, Barbados Museum and Historical Society, St. Michael, Barbados (hereafter BMHS); "Tales of Old Bar-

bados," 177–178, Obeah Folder, BMHS; Edward A. Stoute, "The 'Obeah' Doctor," *Advocate Magazine* (Sunday, January 5, 1976), Obeah Folder, BMHS.

22. "Thomas Walduck to James Petiver, Apothecary and Fellow of the Royal Society in Aldergate, (no date)," Sloane MSS, 2302, British Library. Emphasis added.

23. For the various renderings of Calabari, including "Kalabari," "Karabari," "Carabalí," "Caravali," see Oldendorp, *History of the Mission,* 166; Chambers, "Ethnicity in the Diaspora," 28; Paul Lovejoy, "Ethnic Designations of the Slave Trade," in Lovejoy and Trotman, *Atlantic Dimensions of Ethnicity,* 17; Northrup, "Igbo and Myth Igbo," 7–10. In a statement about the Calabar interior that reads eerily similarly to Equiano's narrative, Oldendorp notes that his interview of five Kalabaris, "a cheerful and hearty people," detailed that "they had lived very far from the sea and that a great river ran through their land." Oldendorp later notes that the "Ibo" are the neighbors of the "Kalabari," but that they "speak a common language"—implying that they spoke mutually intelligible languages (or a common lingua franca) or that these groups were the result of an ethnogenesis similar to the one that produced Coromantees and Aminas.

24. Chambers, "'My Own Nation,'" 82–83, 84, 88–90; Handler and Bilby, "Early Use and Origin of the Term 'Obeah,'" 87–100; Williams, *Voodoos and Obeahs,* 136; Patterson, *Sociology of Slavery,* 185n6; Johnston, *The Negro in the New World,* 253n1.

25. As perhaps no surprise, the Bight of Benin and West-Central Africa combined to contribute overwhelming percentages of enslaved imports disembarked from identifiable Atlantic African ports in Saint-Domingue (24% and 46%), Bahia, Brazil (56% and 35%), and Cuba (14% and 29%). The Cuban import estimates for West-Central African disembarkations are artificially low since the eighteenth-century asiento traffic from the British Caribbean to the Spanish Caribbean and mainland colonies may not be accounted for in the slave trade dataset. See *Voyages: The Trans-Atlantic Slave Trade Database;* Palmer, *Human Cargoes,* 7, 28; Eltis, "Volume and Structure," 36–40.

26. Paton, "Witchcraft, Poison, Law," 326n1; V. Brown, *Reaper's Garden,* 145.

27. "Letters from Barbados, November 24, 1710," Sloane MSS, 2302, British Library.

28. Du Bois, *Negro Church,* 5–6.

29. Du Bois, *Souls of Black Folk,* 149–150.

30. Ibid., 152.

31. Edwards, *History, Civil and Commercial,* II:306–307.

32. Du Bois, *Negro Church,* 6.

33. "Lieutenant-Governor Molesworth to William Blathwayt, August 29, 1685," in *CSPC,* vol. 12, no. 339 (also CO 138/5); "History of the Revolted Negroes in Jamaica," Long Papers, Add. Manuscripts, 12431; "Minutes of a Council of War held at Jamaica, August 1, 1685," *CSPC,* vol. 12, no. 299.

34. "President Ayscough to the Duke of Newcastle, August 16, 1735," *CSPC,* vol. 42, no. 73.

35. "Lewis to James Knight, December 20, 1743," Long Papers, Add. Manuscripts, 12431, 99–100.

36. D. Hall, *In Miserable Slavery,* 61. The description of the "powers" of this doctor parallels information contained in a letter by Thomas Walduck to James Petiver:

"Have knowne upon Negros complaining that they are bewitched, an Obia Negro hath taken out of their eye bones, shells out of their thighs, pieces of iron out of their belleys, and such odd things out of other parts that I have admired at it, but by what legerdemain I could never discover, having been careful to search them before." See "Thomas Walduck to James Petiver, Apothecary and Fellow of the Royal Society in Aldergate, (no date)," Sloane MSS, 2302, British Library.

37. D. Hall, *In Miserable Slavery*, 93.

38. "Tryal of Quawcoo an Old Oby Man, Physician, and Cormantee belonging to Mr. William Hunt, December 9, 1736," CO 9/10; "Report of the Justices," 152/22, W94; *A Genuine Narrative*, 5–6, 12–13, 15, 19; Schuler, "Akan Slave Rebellions," 21.

39. "Governor William Mathew to Alured People, May 11, 1737," *CSPC*, vol. 43, no. 287; "Governor William Mathew to the Lords of Trade, May 11, 1737," CO 152/23, x2; "Some Reasons Humbly Offered for Consideration for Stoping the Further Execution of Slaves Concern'd in the Barbarous Conspiracy, January 17, 1737," CO 9/10.

40. "Governor William Mathew to Alured People, May 11, 1737," *CSPC*, vol. 43, no. 287; *Genuine Narrative*, 13; "Tryal of Monk's Mingo, November 15, 1736," CO 9/10.

41. Edwards, *History, Civil and Commercial*, II:86.

42. Leslie, *New History of Jamaica*, 308.

43. Müller's Description of the Fetu Country, 1662–9," in Jones, *German Sources*, 174–176; "Otto Friedrich Von Der Groeben's Account of His Voyage to Guinea, 1682–1683," in Jones, *Brandenburg Sources*, 51; Rask, *Brief and Truthful Description*, 136.

44. Whitten, "Contemporary Patterns of Malign Occultism," 314; J. E. Anderson, *Conjure in African American Society*, 36–39, 101, 105; Chireau, *Black Magic*, 48, 62. Chireau notes specifically that "The gravel and earth gathered from the surfaces of cemetery graves and stone markers, sometimes called 'goopher dust,' was a near-universal element in the pharmacopoeia of African American supernaturalism."

45. Hurston, "Hoodoo in America," 319.

46. Long, *History of Jamaica*, II:451–452.

47. "An Act to Remedy the Evils Arising from Irregular Assemblies of Slaves . . . and for Preventing the Practice of Obeah . . . and to Prevent Any Captain, Master, or Supercargo of Any Vessel Bringing back Slaves Transported off the Island, Jamaica, December 18, 1760," CO 139/21.

48. Gardner, *History of Jamaica*, 141; "Assembly Minutes, June 25, 1765," *Journals of the Assembly of Jamaica*, V:592–596.

49. Du Bois, *Souls of Black Folk*, 153; Craton, *Testing the Chains*, 46.

50. Edwards, *History, Civil and Commercial*, II:80.

51. Ibid., II:83.

52. Phillips, *American Negro Slavery*, 42.

53. Edwards, *History, Civil and Commercial*, II:79.

54. R. Price and S. Price, *Stedman's Surinam*, xix–xxii; Hoogbergen, *Boni Maroon Wars*, 52–104.

55. Hoogbergen, *Boni Maroon Wars*, 83.

56. R. Price and S. Price, *Stedman's Surinam*, 50–51; Hoogbergen, *Boni Maroon Wars*, 70, 83, 91; Hoogbergen, "Aluku," 187, 190, 192. Other notable Coromantee and

bush creole maroons during the First Boni-Maroon War include Kwamina Adjubi (leader of Ndjuka Maroons), Kwami (leader of the Patamacca Maroons), and Kwasi (leader of Meulwijk Maroons).

57. R. Price and S. Price, *Stedman's Surinam*, 51.

58. Leslie, *New History of Jamaica*, 307–308.

59. Oldendorp, *History of the Mission*, 199.

60. Patterson, *Sociology of Slavery*, 196.

61. J. Thornton, "War, the State, and Religious Norms in 'Coromantee' Thought," in St. George, *Possible Pasts*, 196–197.

62. Bush, *Slave Women in Caribbean Society*, 46; Patterson, *Sociology of Slavery*, 64. For assessments linking Eboes and others from Biafra to suicide, see Peytraud, *L'Esclavage aux Antilles Françaises*, 89; Gomez, *Exchanging Our Country Marks*, 116–120, 127–128, 131; Littlefield, *Rice and Slaves*, 10, 13.

63. Rucker, *River Flows On*, 27; Schuler, *Akan Slave Rebellions*, 15, 19, 23; Kea, "An Amina Slave Rebellion," 187; Long, *The History of Jamaica*, II:454–455, 457–458, 461; Patterson, *Sociology of Slavery*, 264–265; Craton, *Testing the Chains*, 155.

64. Mullin, *Africa in America*, 69.

65. R. Price and S. Price, *Stedman's Surinam*, 262.

6. Women, Regeneration, and Power

1. Edwards, *History, Civil and Commercial*, II:80–81; Olwyn M. Blouet, "Bryan Edwards, F.R.S.," 217–222.

2. Edwards, *History, Civil and Commercial*, II:80–82. In terms of his "interrogations," Edwards provides information from another Coromantee named Cudjoe to corroborate Clara's story. According to his account, Cudjoe was born in "the kingdom of Asiantee, the king or chieftain of which country was named Poco [Opoku Ware]," around the 1750s. He notes specifically that "when the king or any considerable man dies, a great number of his slaves are sacrificed at his tomb." The Asantehene immediately preceding Opoku Ware died and, in Cudjoe's recounting, "one hundred people were slaughtered on that occasion." Much of Cudjoe's story fits with what we know about Asante history, with one exception. Asantehene Opoku Ware's immediate predecessor was not himself an Asantehene; rather he was Mamponghene Amainampon appointed as king-regent of Asante to serve as executive administrator from 1717 to 1720. Also, the practice of mortuary slayings at state funerals in Asante and other Akan polities finds corroboration in a wide range of sources. See Boahen, Akyeampong, Lawler, McCaskie, and Wilks, *History of Ashanti Kings*, 123; Wilks, *Forests of Gold*, 215–240; Ivor Wilks, "Asante: Human Sacrifice," 443–452; Oldendorp, *History of the Mission*, 184; R. Price and S. Price, *Stedman's Surinam*, 269.

3. Edwards, *History, Civil and Commercial*, II:80–81; Blouet, "Bryan Edwards, F.R.S.," 218; Diptee, *From Africa to Jamaica*, 17–18.

4. Edwards, *History, Civil and Commercial*, II:81.

5. "Two Narratives of Slave Women, 1799, Written down by John Ford, Barbados," Ms. Eng. Misc. b. 4, 50–51, Boldleian Library, Oxford University; Handler, "Life Stories of Enslaved Africans," 137–138n13. Her use of "boon" to mean "good"

demonstrates further, as mentioned in chapter 2 the interpenetrations of Portuguese in the coastal dialects of peoples living in the Gold Coast. This was particularly the case with Fante, which combined Akan, Portuguese creole, and other languages together in becoming a regional lingua franca and a key element in Fante ethnogenesis.

6. Oldendorp, *History of the Mission*, 184. Oldendorp reports, "Immediately after the death of a king of the Amina nation, the life of his number one wife is taken. Moreover the arms and legs of his primary servant are broken during the course of his funeral, and they are placed in this miserable condition in the spacious tomb" to slowly die. After the next king is chosen, the occasion is celebrated "by shedding the blood of a hundred innocent people before his tomb."

7. "Two Narratives of Slave Women," Ms. Eng. Misc. b. 4, 51, Boldleian Library. In the longer version of her autobiographical account, she clearly notes that in cases of a drought in her country, the grandees would purchase a black sheep and "one big negur man" to be sacrificed to the "one big Blackee Man de same dat you call God." Given her more cavalier attitude about ritual and mortuary sacrifice, we can assume that she may have been a woman of some social standing in the central Gold Coast.

8. Smallwood, *Saltwater Slavery*, 83; Perbi, *Indigenous Slavery in Ghana*, 43; Claire Robertson, "Africa into the Americas? Slavery and Women, the Family, and the Gender Division of Labor," in Gaspar and Hine, *More Than Chattel*, 6; Lovejoy and Richardson, "Pawnship in Western Africa," 73–75.

9. Kea, *Settlements, Trade, and Polities*, 106–108.

10. Reindorf, *History of the Gold Coast*, 71.

11. Rask, *Brief and Truthful Description*, 103. For other examples of using "planted wives" to generate revenue, see "Müller's Description of the Fetu Country, 1662–9," in Jones, *German Sources*, 189–190; Bosman, *New and Accurate Description*, 200–202, 211–215; Romer, *Reliable Account*, 124n53. Luring men into debt, pawnship, or slavery through the use of planted wives is mentioned by Rømer as well. He observes:

> The King of [Akwamu] and his Big Men also want to live off the public, and they accomplished this in the following way. To every town they took some women, three or four, according to the size of the town, and settled them there. Then every year the men travelled around and had these women eat fetish to reveal who had touched them. The women admitted this quite willingly, since they received part of the fine, and unless their friends ransomed them the gallants had to be sold as slaves. These [methods] were also employed by the Akim kings, and anyone who was on the Coast during that time knows what great numbers of merchants ran after Bang, the King of Akim, with their trade-goods when he made his annual tour.

See Rømer, *Reliable Account*, 124.

12. Wilks, "Human Sacrifice or Capital Punishment?," 452; Dupuis, *Journal of a Residence in Ashantee*, 162–164.

13. Smallwood, *Saltwater Slavery*, 27.

14. Long, *History of Jamaica*, II:455; "Assembly Minutes, December 5, 1760," *Journals of the Assembly of Jamaica*, V:233; "Assembly Minutes, December 10, 1760," *Journals of the Assembly of Jamaica*, V:240.

15. Long, *The History of Jamaica*, II:455–456; "Assembly Minutes, December 5, 1760," *Journals of the Assembly of Jamaica*, V:233; "Assembly Minutes, December 10, 1760," *Journals of the Assembly of Jamaica*, V:240.

16. "Assembly Minutes, December 10, 1760," *Journals of the Assembly of Jamaica*, V:240; "An Act to . . . Prevent Any Captain, Master, or Supercargo of Any Vessel Bringing back Slaves Transported off the Island, Jamaica, December 18, 1760," CO 139/21. A number of recent scholars claim that Queen Cubah was immediately executed upon discovery in Hanover Parish, despite the fact that she was in custody for at least five days before transport back to Kingston to await trial. See Craton, *Testing the Chains*, 360n15; Dadzie, "Searching for the Invisible Woman," 32; Bush, *Slave Women in Caribbean Society*, 72.

17. The Jamaican Assembly was so concerned about her ability to influence a white ship captain that it enacted a "penalty on masters of vessels bringing back transported slaves" of at least £100 and six months imprisonment. See "An Act to . . . Prevent Any Captain, Master, or Supercargo of Any Vessel Bringing back Slaves Transported off the Island, Jamaica, December 18, 1760," CO 139/21; "Assembly Minutes, December 18, 1760 and April 4, 1761," *Journals of the Assembly of Jamaica*, V:248, 257.

18. Craton, *Testing the Chains*, 81–82; Gottlieb, *Mother of Us All*, 22–41.

19. "Assembly Minutes, March 29–30, 1733," *Journals of the Assembly of Jamaica*, III:121.

20. "Bryan Roark Report of an Ebo Named Cupid Belonging to Samuel Taylor, January 31, 1734," CO 137/21, ff. 207 (also "Information by an Ebo Named Cupid Escaped from the Rebels, January 31, 1735," *CSPC*, vol. 41, no. 484). The version of the account appearing in *CSPC* omits the reference to the fact that Nanny ordered and carried out the executions. Also, this citation is often muddled by others who have rendered Adou as Nanny's husband and the statement from Cupid as a claim that Nanny was a "greater man" than her husband. See Gottlieb, *Mother of Us All*, 24; Campbell, *Maroons of Jamaica*, 177.

21. Thicknesse, *Memoirs and Anecdotes*, 73–75; Dallas, *History of the Maroons*, I:73–74.

22. Craton, *Testing the Chains*, 81–82; Patterson, "Slavery and Slave Revolts," 302; Gottlieb, *Mother of Us All*, 23–24; Dalby, "Ashanti Survivals," 48. For a seventeenth-century Gold Coast rendering of Ananse as "Nanni," see Rømer, *Reliable Account*, 80–83.

23. Dallas, *History of the Maroons*, I:73, 75–77; "History of the Revolted Negroes in Jamaica," Long Papers, Add. Manuscripts, 12431, British Library.

24. "Appendix A: Land Patent to Nanny, 1740," in Gottlieb, *Mother of Us All*, 95–97; "Assembly Minutes, May 27, 1740," *Journals of the Assembly of Jamaica*, III:537.

25. "Appendix A: Land Patent to Nanny, 1740," in Gottlieb, *Mother of Us All*, 95–97; Dallas, *History of the Maroons*, I:73, 75–77; "Assembly Minutes, March 18 and May 27, 1740," *Journals of the Assembly of Jamaica*, III:505, 537.

26. Kenneth Bilby and Filomina Chioma Steady, "Black Women and Survival: A Maroon Case," in Steady, *Black Woman Cross-Culturally*, 455; Mathurin, *Rebel*

Woman, 37; Kopytoff, "Early Political Development," 299; Brathwaite, *Nanny, Sam Sharpe, and the Struggle*, 12.

27. Barbara Bush, "Hard Labor: Women, Childbirth, and Resistance in British Caribbean Societies," in Gaspar and Hine, *More Than Chattel*, 204–206; Fett, *Working Cures*, 38–39; T. H. Smith, *Conjuring Culture*.

28. Carney and Rosomoff, *In the Shadow of Slavery*, 54, 110–111, 178; F. C. Knight, *Working the Diaspora*, 43–44; Dadzie, "Searching for the Invisible Woman," 29–30; R. Price and S. Price, *Stedman's Surinam*, 68; Fett, *Working Cures*, 65; S. Price and R. Price, *Maroon Arts*, 20–21, 29, 36; Grimé, *Ethno-Botany of the Black Americans*, 122; J. H. Morgan, "Causes of the Production of Abortion," 117–123. The destructive potential of cassava was recognized and, perhaps, feared by colonial authorities throughout the Americas. Despite the importance of cassava (or "bammy") to the diet of Jamaica's maroons, neither the Windward nor Leeward pacification treaties mentioned it as among the crops "they shall have liberty to plant" on their lands. A century after both maroon treaties, Dr. Michael Clare—a Jamaican physician—told a parliamentary committee that midwives administered wild cassava to enslaved women, which he described as "a drastic of the most violent kind" when used as an abortion agent. See Dallas, *History of the Maroons*, I:60; Edwards, *History, Civil and Commercial*, I:530–535; Dadzie, "Searching for the Invisible Woman," 29.

29. Barbara Bush, "Hard Labor: Women, Childbirth, and Resistance in British Caribbean Societies," in Gaspar and Hine, *More Than Chattel*, 204–206. Even as late as the 1930s, the Djuka Maroons of Surinam employed herbal "cures for pregnancy." See Kahn, *Djuka*, 127–128.

30. Bush, *Slave Women in Caribbean Society*, 154–156; Dadzie, "Searching for the Invisible Woman," 29.

31. White, *Ar'n't I a Woman?*, 124–125, 128–136; Barbara Bush, "Hard Labor: Women, Childbirth, and Resistance in British Caribbean Societies," in Gaspar and Hine, *More Than Chattel*, 206; Gomez, *Exchanging Our Country Marks*, 94–100; Creel, *A Peculiar People*, 2, 47, 285; Georgia Writer's Project, *Drums and Shadows*, 65–66.

32. Gottlieb, *Mother of Us All*, 61–62; Kenneth Bilby and Filomina Chioma Steady, "Black Women and Survival: A Maroon Case," in Steady, *Black Woman Cross-Culturally*, 458, 461–462; Dalby, "Ashanti Survivals," 49–50.

33. Kenneth Bilby and Filomina Chioma Steady, "Black Women and Survival: A Maroon Case," in Steady, *Black Woman Cross-Culturally*, 458.

34. Quoted in Mathurin, *Rebel Woman*, 36.

35. Gottlieb, *Mother of Us All*, 44–51, 66; Kenneth Bilby and Filomina Chioma Steady, "Black Women and Survival: A Maroon Case," in Steady, *Black Woman Cross-Culturally*, 459; Mathurin, *Rebel Woman*, 36.

36. Thicknesse, *Memoirs and Anecdotes*, 73.

37. "Christopher Allen's Journal, March 1732," CO 137/54, folio 52.

38. "Assembly Minutes, March 29–30, 1733," *Journals of the Assembly of Jamaica*, III:121.

39. Price, *To Slay the Hydra*, 171, 239n5. Using kaolin or white chalk as facial paint, by the late nineteenth to the early twentieth centuries, was associated with Gold Coast ritual specialists possessed by an ancestral spirit or otherwise engaged with the spirit realm. The color white, in the complex (and ever shifting) Akan

color symbolism scheme, could mean victory or spiritual purity. Also, white is the color of the Akan gods. See Beckwith, Fisher, and Fitzgerald, *Painted Bodies*, 282; Hagan, "A Note on Akan Colour Symbolism," 8; R. S. Rattray, *Religion and Art in Ashanti* (Oxford: Clarendon Press, 1927), 165–169.

40. R. Price, *To Slay the Hydra*, 159–165.

41. R. Price and S. Price, *Stedman's Surinam*, 263.

42. Van Stipriaan, "Watramama/Mami Wata," 323–337; Drewal, *Sacred Waters*; Kramer, *Red Fez*, 226–239. Stedman specifically adds: "This is here called *winty play*, or the dance of the mermaid, and takes its origin from time immemorial, the classic authors making frequent mention of this unaccountable practice." In addition, he claims these women had the power to call or conjure serpents and the snakes would "twine and wreathe about their arms, neck, and breast." See R. Price and S. Price, *Stedman's Surinam*, 263–264.

43. Kopytoff, "Early Political Development," 300, 301.

44. "Confession Made by Scyrus, a Negro Belonging to Mr. George Taylor, August 25, 1733," *CSPC*, vol. 40, no. 320.

45. "Assembly Minutes, March 29, 1733," *Journals of the Assembly of Jamaica*, III:121.

46. R. Price and S. Price, *Stedman's Surinam*, 26.

47. Schuler, *Akan Slave Rebellions*, 15, 19, 23; Kea, "An Amina Slave Rebellion, 187; Long, *History of Jamaica*, II:454–455, 457–458, 461; Patterson, *Sociology of Slavery*, 264–265; Craton, *Testing the Chains*, 155.

48. Kopytoff, "Early Political Development," 288.

49. "History of the Revolted Negroes in Jamaica," Long Papers, Add. Manuscripts, 12431, British Library.

50. Edwards, *History of the British West Indies*, I:540–541.

51. Bush, *Slave Women in Caribbean Society*, 46–50; Kopytoff, "Early Political Development," 297; "History of the Revolted Negroes in Jamaica," Long Papers, Add. Manuscripts, 12431, British Library.

52. "History of the Revolted Negroes in Jamaica," Long Papers, Add. Manuscripts, 12431, British Library; "Assembly Minutes, March 18, 1740," *Journals of the Assembly of Jamaica*, III:505.

53. Edwards, *History of the British West Indies*, I:540.

54. Patterson, "Slavery and Slave Revolts," 303; Kenneth Bilby and Filomina Chioma Steady, "Black Women and Survival: A Maroon Case," in Steady, *Black Woman Cross-Culturally*, 455–456; "Confession Made by Scyrus, a Negro Belonging to Mr. George Taylor, August 25, 1733," *CSPC*, vol. 40, no. 320; *Journals of the Assembly of Jamaica*, III:62.

55. "Lewis to James Knight, December 20, 1743," Long Papers, Add. Manuscripts, 12431, 99–100, British Library.

56. Kopytoff, "Early Political Development," 303–304. The comparative, Atlantic African background is mostly missing from Kopytoff's analysis, though she does cite two article-length studies of twentieth century polygamous societies in Nigeria: M. Smith, "Secondary Marriage in Northern Nigeria," 298–323; and Sangree, "Secondary Marriage and Tribal Solidarity," 1234–1243.

57. Kenneth Bilby and Filomina Chioma Steady, "Black Women and Survival: A Maroon Case," in Steady, *Black Woman Cross-Culturally*, 457.

Postscript

1. Patterson, *Sociology of Slavery*, 174–181; Patterson, *Slavery and Social Death*, 91; N. Painter, *Soul Murder and Slavery*, 7–8; Hartman, *Scenes of Subjection*, 8; M'Baye, *Trickster Comes West*, 196; Marshall, "Anansi Tactics," 143.

2. Morgan, "Slaves and Livestock," 70; Marshall, "Anansi Tactics," 149n10; D. Hall, *In Miserable Slavery*, 12.

3. Marshall, "Anansi Tactics," 126–127, 128, 138; M'Baye, *Trickster Comes West*, 16–17; Roberts, *From Trickster to Badman*, 23–24; Rucker, *River Flows On*, 204–206. In versions of this story recorded in the early twentieth century, the granddaughter is actually Ananse in disguise.

4. D. Hall, *In Miserable Slavery*, 160.

5. J. Scott, *Domination and the Arts of Resistance*, 1–12, 45–47.

6. Lewis, *Matthew Lewis*, 194, 253–254.

7. Marshall, "Anansi Tactics," 133; Jekyll, *Jamaican Song and Story*, liii.

8. Jekyll, *Jamaican Song and Story*, 11–13; Rømer, *Reliable Account*, 80; Rask, *Brief and Truthful Description*, 77; T. Thompson, *Two Missionary Voyages*, 44; Truteneau, *Christian Protten's 1764 Introduction*, 11–12.

9. Jekyll, *Jamaican Song and Story*, 11–13.

10. Herskovits notes a reference to the Akan sky god in his ethnography of the Saramaka Maroons of Suriname. In this instance, "Nyankompon" is the source of "the great healing spirit" consulted by "those who call the gods and speak to the ancestors and who, surpassing all else in wisdom, know how to control *obia*." See M. Herskovits and F. Herskovits, *Rebel Destiny*, 25, 352.

11. Jekyll, *Jamaican Song and Story*, 124–126.

12. Van Stipriaan, "Watramama/Mami Wata," 323–337; Kramer, *Red Fez*, 226–239; Drewal, "Performing the Other," 160–162, 165.

13. Jekyll, *Jamaican Song and Story*, 31–34.

14. *Ibid.*, 7–10, 11–13, 44–45, 78, 136–137.

15. L. Brown, "Monuments to Freedom," 106; Zips, *Black Rebels*, 154–155; David Lambert, "'Part of the Blood and Dream,'" 353–354, 366; A. Thompson, "Symbolic Legacies of Slavery," 193, 197–203, 205, 208; Shepherd, "From 'Numbered Notations,'" 214–216; "Tacky a Hero, Maroons Traitors," *The Gleaner* (Jamaica), October 18, 2013; "Trekking for Tacky," *Jamaica Observer*, July 23, 2012.

16. In the aftermath of Jamaica's Second Maroon War (1795–1796), British colonial officials first exiled the Trelawny Town Maroons to Nova Scotia, followed by resettling them in Sierra Leone in 1800. In both locales, "Coromantee" practices such as obeah, day-naming, plays, and Ananse Spider tales became representative aspects of Jamaican Maroon cultures in exile. In Sierra Leone, Jamaican Coromantee or Maroon culture became one of three principal foundations for the development of Krio (or Creole) culture. See Grant, *Maroons in Nova Scotia*; 66–67; Campbell, *Back to Africa* (Africa World Press, 1993); Dallas, *History of the Maroons*, II:232–289; C. Magbaily Fyle, "The Yoruba Diaspora in Sierra Leone's Krio Society," in Falola and Childs, *Yoruba Diaspora*, 366–382.

BIBLIOGRAPHY

ABBREVIATIONS

BMHS   Barbados Museum and History Society
CO   Colonial Office
CSPC   Calendar of State Papers: Colonial Series
T70   Treasury Records, Records of the Company of
    Royal Adventurers of England
WO   War Office

UNPUBLISHED ARCHIVAL SOURCES

Barbados

Barbados Museum and Historical Society
    Obeah Folder

England

British Library
    C. E. Long Papers
    Harley MSS
    Sloane MSS
National Archives, Kew (PRO)
    Colonial Office Records
    Treasury Records, 1660–1833
    War Office Records, 1732–1868
Lambeth Palace Library
    Society for the Propagation of the Gospel Correspondence, 1711–undated
    Society for the Propagation of the Gospel Minutes, 1711–1712, 1740–1744
Bodleian Library, Oxford University
    Rawlinson MSS
    "Two Narratives by Female Slaves at Barbados, Written down by John Ford, 1799"

Ghana

Balme Library, University of Ghana, Legon
    Furley Collection
        Board of Trades and Plantations, 1749–1753
        Danish Records (D 2)
        Dutch Records (N 1–8, 19, 29, 40, 44, 46–47, 55)
        Dutch Records, Tribal States (N 37–38)
        English Records (E 4, 8–11, 23–4, 26)

United States

Louisiana

Amistad Research Center, Tulane University
    Gwendolyn Midlo Hall Papers
    African Nations of Slaves in Records of the
        Superior Council of Louisiana, 1729–1752
    Hall, "The 1795 Slave Conspiracy in Pointe Coupee"
    Pointe Coupee Conspiracy Trial Testimony, 1795
    Ulysses S. Ricard, "The Pointe Coupee Slave Conspiracy of 1791"
    "Testimony of the Criminal Process of the Rebel Blacks of [Pointe Coupee]
        against the Whites of Said Post, June 1792"
Howard-Tilton Memorial Library, Tulane University
    Dispatches of the Spanish Governors of Louisiana, 1766–1796
Pointe Coupee Parish Courthouse
    "Procès Contre les Esclaves du Poste de Pointe Coupée."
        Original Acts, May 4–29, 1795

New York

New York City Municipal Archives
    Minute Book of the Court of General Sessions, 1705–1714
    Minutes of the Court of Quarter and General Sessions,
        begun August 7th Anno 1694
New-York Historical Society, New York City
    Horsmanden Papers, 1714–1747
    Parish Transcripts of Material on Slavery in the
        Public Record Office in London, 1690–1750

PUBLISHED PRIMARY SOURCES

Adams, William. *The Modern Voyager & Traveller through Europe, Asia, Africa, & America.* 4 vols. London: H. Fisher, Son, and P. Jackson, 1833.

Alexander, James Edward. *Transatlantic Sketches, Comprising Visits to the Most Interesting Scenes in North and South America, and the West Indies: With Notes on Negro Slavery and Canadian Emigration.* London: R. Bentley, 1833.

Aljoe, Nicole N. *Creole Testimonies: Slave Narratives from the British West Indies, 1709–1838*. New York: Palgrave Macmillan, 2012.

Antigua and the Antiguans: A Full Account of the Colony and Its Inhabitants from the Time of the Caribs. London: Saunders and Otley, 1844.

Atkins, John. *A Voyage to Guinea, Brasil, and the West-Indies in His Majesty's Ships the Swallow and Weymouth*. London: Ward and Chandler, 1737.

Barbot, Jean. *A Description of the Coasts of North and South Guinea*, in *A Collection of Voyages and Travels*. London: Henry Lintot and John Osborn, 1744.

Behn, Aphra. *Oroonoko*. New York: Penguin Books, 2003 [1688].

Belgrove, William, ed. *A Treatise upon Husbandry and Planting*. Boston: D. Fowle, 1755.

Belisario, Isaac Mendes. *Illustration of the Habits, Occupation, and Costume of the Negro Population, in the Island of Jamaica: Drawn after Nature, and in Lithography*. Kingston, Jamaica: Published by the artist, at his residence, 1837–1838.

Benoit, Pierre Jacques. *Voyage á Surinam; Description des Possessions Néerlandaises dans la Guyane*. Brussels, Belgium: Société des Beaux-arts, 1839.

Bosman, Willem. *A New and Accurate Description of the Coast of Guinea: Divided into the Gold, the Slave, and the Ivory Coasts*. 2nd ed.. London: Knapton, Midwinter, Lintot, Strahan, Round, and Bell, 1721.

Bowdich, Thomas E. *Mission from Cape Coast to Ashantee*. London: Frank Cass, 1966 [1819].

Bridgens, Richard. *West India Scenery with Illustrations of Negro Character, the Process of Making Sugar, &C. from Sketches Taken during a Voyage to and Residence of Seven Years in, the Island of Trinidad*. London: R. Jennings, 1836.

Buisseret, David, ed. *Jamaica in 1687: The Taylor Manuscript at the National Library of Jamaica*. Kingston, Jamaica: University of West Indies Press, 2008.

Carlyle, Thomas. *Occasional Discourse on the Nigger Question*. London: Thomas Bosworth: 1853.

Caron, Aimery P., and Arnold R. Highfield, eds. *The French Intervention in the St. John Revolt of 1733–34*. Christiansted, St. Croix: Bureau of Libraries, Museums, and Archaeological Services, Dept. of Conservation and Cultural Affairs, 1981.

Carson, Patricia, ed., *Materials for West African History in the Archives of Belgium and Holland*. London: Athlone Press, 1962.

Caulfield, Colonel J. E. *100 Years' History of the 2nd West India Regiment, 1795–1898*. London: Forster Groom, 1889.

Christaller, Johann Gottlieb. *A Grammar of the Asante and Fante Language, Called Tshi (Chwee, Twi) Based on the Akuapem Dialect with Reference to the Other (Akan and Fante) Dialects*. Ridgewood, NJ: Gregg Press, 1964 [1875].

A Collection of Voyages and Travels. London: Henry Lintot and John Osborn, 1732.

Crooks, John Joseph. *Records Relating to the Gold Coast Settlements from 1750 to 1874*. London: Frank Cass, 1973.

Cruickshank, Brodie. *Eighteen Years on the Gold Coast*. London: Frank Cass, 1966 [1853].

Cugoano, Quobna Ottobah. *Thoughts and Sentiments on the Evil of Slavery*. Edited by Vincent Carretta. New York: Penguin Books, 1999 [1787].

Curtin, Philip D., ed. *Africa Remembered: Narratives by West Africans from the Era of the Slave Trade*. Madison: University of Wisconsin Press, 1967.

Cuvier, Georges. *The Animal Kingdom Arranged in Conformity with Its Organiza-tion* (London: G. B. Whittaker, 1827).

Daaku, K. Y., ed. *Oral Traditions of Adanse*. Legon, Ghana: Institute of African Studies, 1969.

———, ed. *Oral Traditions of Assin-Twifo*. Legon, Ghana: Institute of African Stud-ies, 1969.

———, ed. *Oral Traditions of Denkyira*. Legon, Ghana: Institute of African Studies, 1970.

Daaku, K. Y., and Albert Van Dantzig, trans. and eds. "Map of the Regions of the Gold Coast of Guinea." *Ghana Notes and Queries* 9 (1966): opposite 70.

Dallas, Robert Charles. *The History of the Maroons from Their Origin to the Es-tablishment of Their Chief Tribe at Sierra Leone*. Vols. 1 and 2. London: T. N. Longman and O. Rees, 1975 [1803].

Dapper, D. Olfert. *Description de l'Afrique: Naukeurige beschrijvinge der Afri-kaensche Eylanden*. Amsterdam: Wolfgang, Waesberge, Boom & Van Some-ren, 1686.

Davis, Thomas J., ed. *The New York Conspiracy by Daniel Horsmanden*. Boston: Beacon Press, 1971.

de Marees, Pieter. *Description and Historical Account of the Gold Kingdom of Guinea (1602)*. Edited and translated by Albert Van Dantzig and Adam Jones. Oxford: Oxford University Press, 1987 [1602].

Donnan, Elizabeth, ed. *Documents Illustrative of the History of the Slave Trade to America*. Vols. 1–3. Washington, DC: Carnegie Institution of Washington, 1931–1933.

Doortmont, Michel R., and Jinna Smit, eds. *Sources for the Mutual History of Gha-na and the Netherlands: An Annotated Guide to the Dutch Archives Relating to Ghana and West Africa in the Nationaal Archief, 1593–1960s*. Boston: Brill, 2007.

Dubois, Laurent, and John D. Garrigus, eds. *Slave Revolution in the Caribbean, 1789–1804: A Brief History with Documents*. Boston: Bedford/St. Martin's, 2006.

Dupuis, Joseph. *Journal of a Residence in Ashantee, Comprising Notes and Re-searches Relative to the Gold Coast, and the Interior of Western Africa . . .* Lon-don: H. Colburn, 1824.

Edwards, Bryan. *The History, Civil and Commercial, of the British Colonies in the West Indies*. London: G. and W. B. Whitaker, 1819 [1783].

Ellis, A. B. *The Tshi-Speaking Peoples of the Gold Coast of West Africa: Their Reli-gion, Manners, Customs, Laws, Language, Etc.* London: Chapman and Hall, 1887.

Finlason, William Francis. *The History of the Jamaica Case: Being an Account, Founded Upon Official Documents, of the Rebellion of the Negroes in Jamaica*. London: Chapman and Hall, 1869.

Fynn, John Kofi, ed. *Oral Traditions of Fante States: Edina (Elmina)*. Legon, Ghana: Institute of African Studies, 1974.

———, ed. *Oral Traditions of Sefwi: Ahnwiaso and Bekwai*. Legon, Ghana: Institute of African Studies, 1974.

Gardner, William James. *A History of Jamaica from Its Discovery by Christopher Columbus to the Present Time*. London: Elliot Stock, 1878.

A Genuine Narrative of the Intended Conspiracy of the Negros at Antigua. New York: Arno Press, 1972 [1737].

Great Newes from the Barbadoes, or, A True and Faithful Account of the Grand Conspiracy of the Negroes against the English and the Happy Discovery of the Same: With the Number of Those That Were Burned Alive, Beheaded, and Otherwise Executed for Their Horrid Crimes. London: L. Curtis, 1676.

Green, John, ed. *A New General Collection of Voyages and Travels*. Vol. 2. London: Thomas Astley, 1745–47.

Green, Lisa J. *African American English: A Linguistic Introduction*. New York: Cambridge University Press, 2002.

Hair, Paul, Adam Jones, and Robin Law, eds. *Barbot on Guinea: The Writings of Jean Barbot on West Africa, 1678–1712*. Vols. 1 and 2. London: The Hakluyt Society, 1992.

Hall, Douglas, ed. *In Miserable Slavery: Thomas Thistlewood in Jamaica, 1750–1786*. Mona, Jamaica: University of the West Indies Press, 1999.

Handler, Jerome S. *A Guide to Source Materials for the Study of Barbados History, 1627–1834*. New Castle, DE: Oak Knoll Press, 2002.

Headlam, Cecil, ed. *Calendar of State Papers, Colonial Series, America and the West Indies, 1700*. Vol. 18. London: His Majesty's Stationery Office, 1910. Humphreys, David. *An Account of the Endeavours Used by the Society for the Propagation of the Gospel in Foreign Parts, to Instruct the Negroe Slaves in New York; Together with Two of Bp. Gibson's Letters on That Subject; Being an Extract from Dr. Humphrey's Historical Account of the Incorporated Society for the Propagation of the Gospel in Foreign Parts, from its Foundation to the Year 1728*. London: Society for the Propagation of the Gospel in Foreign Parts, 1830.

Isert, Paul Erdmann. *Journey to Guinea and the Caribbean Islands of Columbia (1788)*. Translated and edited by Selena Axelrod Winsnes. Legon-Accra, Ghana: Sub-Saharan Publishers, 2007 [1788].

Jekyll, Walter. *Jamaican Song and Story: Annancy Stories, Digging Sings, Ring Tunes, and Dancing Tunes*. London: David Nutt, 1907 [1904].

Jones, Adam, ed. *German Sources for West African History, 1599–1669*. Wiesbaden: Franz Steiner Verlag, 1983.

———, ed. *Brandenburg Sources for West African History, 1680–1700*. Stuttgart: Franz Steiner Verlag, 1985.

Journals of the Assembly of Jamaica, Vols. 2–3, 5.

Justesen, Ole, ed. *Danish Sources for the History of Ghana, 1657–1754*. Vols. 1 and 2. Copenhagen: Det Kongelige Danske Videnskabernes Selskab, 2005.

Law, Robin, ed. *The English in West Africa 1681–1683: The Local Correspondence of the Royal African Company of England 1681–1699*. Part 1. New York: Oxford University Press, 1997.

———, ed. *The English in West Africa, 1685–1688: The Local Correspondence of the Royal African Company of England 1681–1699*. Part 2. New York: Oxford University Press, 2001.

——, ed. *The English in West Africa, 1691–1699: The Local Correspondence of the Royal African Company of England 1681–1699.* Part 3. New York: Oxford University Press, 2006.

Leslie, Charles. *A New History of Jamaica, from the Earliest Accounts, to the Taking of Porto Bello by Vice-Admiral Vernon: In Thirteen Letters from a Gentleman to His Friend . . .* London: J. Hodges, 1740.

The Letters and Papers of Cadwallader Colden. Vol. 2. New York: New-York Historical Society, 1918.

Lewis, Matthew G. *Matthew Lewis: Journal of a West India Proprietor.* Oxford, UK: Oxford University Press, 1999.

Long, Edward. *The History of Jamaica: Reflections on Its Situations, Settlements, Inhabitants, Climate, Products, Commerce, Laws and Government.* Vols. 1–3. Montreal: McGill-Queen's University Press, 2002 [1774].

Low, Ruth Hull, and Rafael Valls, eds. *St. John Backtime: Eyewitness Accounts from 1718 to 1956.* St. John: Eden Hill Press, 1985.

Minutes of the Common Council of the City of New York, 1675–1776. Vols. 3–5. New York: Dodd, Mead, 1905.

The Monthly Christian Spectator, 1851–1859. Vol. 4. London: William Freeman, 1854.

Morgan, John H. "An Essay on the Causes of the Production of Abortion among Our Negro Population." *Nashville Journal of Medicine and Surgery* 19 (1860): 117–123.

Newitt, Malyn, ed. *The Portuguese in West Africa, 1415–1670: A Documentary History.* New York: Cambridge University Press, 2010.

O'Callaghan, E. B., ed. *Laws of His Majesties Colony of New York As They Were Enacted by the Governor, Council and General Assembly in Divers Sessions, the First of Which Began April 9th, 1691.* Albany: Weed, Parsons, and Company, 1849.

——, ed. *Documents Relative to the Colonial History of the State of New York.* Vols. 1–5. Albany: Weed, Parsons, and Company, 1853–1858.

——, ed. *Calendar of Historical Manuscripts in the Office of the Secretary of State.* Vols. 1 and 2. Albany: Weed, Parsons, and Company, 1865–1866.

——, ed. *Voyage of the Slavers St. John and Arms of Amsterdam.* Albany: J. Munsell, 1867.

Oldendorp, C. G. A. *History of the Mission of the Evangelical Brethren on the Caribbean Islands of St. Thomas, St. Croix, and St. John.* Edited by Johann Jakob Bossard. Ann Arbor: Karoma, 1987 [1770].

Pannet, Pierre J. *Report on the Execrable Conspiracy Carried out by the Amina Negroes on the Danish Island of St. Jan in America 1733.* Christiansted, St. Croix: Artilles Press, 1984 [1733].

Peytraud, Lucien Pierre. *Esclavage aux Antilles Françaises avant 1789.* Cambridge, UK: Cambridge University Press, 2011 [1789].

Phillippo, James M. *Jamaica: Its Past and Present State.* Philadelphia: J. M. Campbell, 1843.

Pollard, Edward Alfred. *Black Diamonds Gathered in the Darkey Homes of the South.* New York: Negro Universities Press, 1968 [1859].

Poole, Robert. *The Beneficent Bee or, Traveller's Companion: Containing Each Day's Observation, in a Voyage from London, to Gibraltar, Barbadoes, Antigua, Barbuda . . . Containing a Summary Account of the Said Places, Their Inhabitants, Product, Money, Customs . . .* London: E. Duncomb, 1753.

Porch, Francis Peyre. *Resources of the Southern Fields and Forests, Medical, Economical and Agricultural.* Charleston: Walker, Evans, and Cogwell, 1869.

Price, Richard, ed. *To Slay the Hydra: Dutch Colonial Perspectives on the Saramaka Wars.* Ann Arbor: Karoma Press, 1983.

———. *Stedman's Surinam: Life in an Eighteenth-Century Slave Society* [an abridged, modernized edition of John Gabriel Stedman, *Narrative of a Five Years' Expedition against the Revolted Negroes of Surinam,* 1796]. Baltimore: Johns Hopkins University Press, 1992.

Purchas, Samuel. *Hakluytus Posthumus or Purchase His Pilgrimes: Contayning a History of the World in Sea Voyages and Lande Travells by Englishmen and Others.* Glasgow: MacLehose, 1905 [1625].

Rask, Johannes. *A Brief and Truthful Description of a Journey to and from Guinea, 1708–1713.* Translated by Selena Axelrod Winsnes. Accra, Ghana: Sub-Saharan Publishers, 2009 [1754].

Reindorf, Carl C. *History of the Gold Coast and Asante.* Accra: Ghana Universities Press, 2007 [1895].

Rømer, Ludewig Ferdinand. *A Reliable Account of the Coast of Guinea (1760).* Translated and edited by Selena Axelrod Winsnes. Oxford: Oxford University Press, 2000 [1760].

Roth, Walter. "The Story of the Slave Rebellion in Berbice 1762: Translated from J. J. Hartsinck's 'Beschryving Van Guiana Etc.'" *Journal of the British Museum and Zoo of the Royal Agricultural and Commercial Society* 20–27 (1958–1960): Parts I–VII.

The Royal African, or, Memoirs of the Young Prince of Annamaboe Comprehending a Distinct Account of His Country and Family. Woodbridge, CT: Research Publications, 1982.

Sainsbury, W. Noel, ed. *Calendar of State Papers Colonial Series, America and West Indies, 1675–1676 and Addenda 1574–1674.* Vol. 9. London: Her Majesty's Stationery Office, 1893.

Sharpe, John. "The Negro Plot of 1712." *New York Genealogical and Biographical Record* 21 (1890): 162–163.

———. "Journal of Reverend Sharpe." *Pennsylvania Magazine* 40 (1916): 412–425.

Snelgrave, William. *A New Account of Some Parts of Guinea and the Slave Trade.* London: Frank Cass, 1971 [1734].

Stedman, John Gabriel. *Narrative of a Five Years Expedition against the Revolted Negroes of Surinam.* Baltimore: Johns Hopkins University Press, 1988 [1790].

Stephens, Ann S. *High Life in New York.* New York: Bunce and Bro., 1854.

Stewart, John. *An Account of Jamaica, and Its Inhabitants.* London: Longman, Hurst, Rees, and Orme, 1808.

———. *A View of the Past and Present State of the Island of Jamaica; With Remarks on the Moral and Physical Condition of the Slaves, and on the Abolition of Slavery in the Colonies.* New York: Negro Universities Press, 1969 [1823].

Stokes, Isaac Newton Phelps, ed. *The Iconography of Manhattan Island, 1498–1909.* Vol. 4. New York: Arno Press, 1967.

Stowe, Harriet Beecher. *The Minister's Wooing.* Ridgewood, NJ: Gregg Press, 1968 [1859].

Thicknesse, Philip. *Memoirs and Anecdotes of Philip Thicknesse, Late Lieutenant Governor of Land Guard Fort, and Unfortunately Father to George Touchet, Baron Audley.* Dublin: Graisberry and Campbell, 1790.

Thompson, Stanbury, ed. *The Journal of John Gabriel Stedman (1744–1797), Soldier and Author, Including an Authentic Account of His Expedition to Surinam, in 1772.* London: Mitre Press, 1962.

Thompson, Thomas. *An Account of Two Missionary Voyages by the Appointment of the Society for the Propagation of the Gospel in Foreign Parts: The One to New Jersey in North America, the Other from America to the Coast of Guiney.* London: J. Oliver for Benjamin Dod, at the Bible and Key in Ave-Mary-Lane, near St. Paul's, 1758.

Tilleman, Erik. *A Short and Simple Account of the Country Guinea and its Nature 1697.* Madison: University of Wisconsin Press, 1994.

Truteneau, H. Max, ed. *Christian Protten's 1764 Introduction to the Fante and Accra (Gafi) Languages.* London: Afro-Presse, 1971.

Van Dantzig, Albert, ed. *Dutch Documents Relating to the Gold Coast and Slave Coast (Coast of Guinea), 1680–1740: Translations of Letters and Papers Collected in the Algemeen Rijks Archief (ARA), State Archives of the Netherlands at the Hague.* 2 vols. Legon: University of Ghana, 1971.

Zabin, Serena R., ed. *The New York Conspiracy Trials of 1741: Daniel Horsmanden's Journal of the Proceedings, with Related Documents.* Boston: Bedford/St. Martin's, 2004.

SECONDARY SOURCES

Adderley, Rosanne Marion. "New Negroes from Africa": Slave Trade Abolition and Free African Settlement in the Nineteenth-Century Caribbean. Bloomington: Indiana University Press, 2006.

Addo-Fening, R. "The Akim or Achim in the 17th and 18th Century Historical Contexts; Who Were They?" *Research Review* 4 (1988): 1–15.

Affrifah, Kofi. *The Akyem Factor in Ghana's History, 1700–1875.* Accra: Ghana Universities Press, 2000.

Agorsah, E. Kofi. "Archaeology and Resistance History in the Caribbean." *African Archaeological Review* 11 (1993): 175–195.

———. *Maroon Heritage : Archaeological, Ethnographic, and Historical Perspectives.* Kingston, Jamaica: Canoe Press, 1994.

Agorsah, E. Kofi, and Thomas Butler. "Archaeological Investigation of Historic Kormantse, Ghana: Cultural Identities." *African Diaspora Archaeology Newsletter* (September 2008): 1–22.

Akyeampong, Emmanuel. *Between the Sea and the Lagoon: An Eco-Social History of the Anlo of Southeastern Ghana c. 1850 to Recent Times*. Athens: Ohio University Press, 2001.

Akyeampong, Emmanuel, and Pashington Obeng. "Spirituality, Gender, and Power in Asante History." *International Journal of African Historical Studies* 28 (1995): 488–508.

Alleyne, Mervyn C., and Beverley Hall-Alleyne. "Language Maintenance and Language Death in the Caribbean." *Caribbean Quarterly* 28 (1982): 52–59.

Alpern, Stanley B. "On the Origins of the Amazons of Dahomey." *History in Africa* 25 (1998): 9–25.

Anderson, Jeffrey E. *Conjure in African American Society*. Baton Rouge: Louisiana State University Press, 2005.

Anderson, John L. *Night of the Silent Drums*. New York: Charles Scribner's Sons, 1975.

Anquandah, James. *Rediscovering Ghana's Past*. Harlow, UK: Longman Group, 1982.

Anstey, Roger. "The British Slave Trade 1751–1807: A Comment." *Journal of African History* 17 (1976): 606–607.

Armah, Ayi Kwei. *Two Thousand Seasons*. Portsmouth, NH: Heinemann, 1973.

Austen, Ralph A. "The Slave Trade as History and Memory: Confrontation of Slaving Voyage Documents and Communal Traditions." *William and Mary Quarterly* 58 (2001): 229–244.

Bailey, Anne. *African Voices of the Atlantic Slave Trade: Beyond the Silence and the Shame*. Boston: Beacon Press, 2005.

Balmer, W. T. *A History of the Akan Peoples of the Gold Coast*. London: Atlantic Press, 1926.

Baptist, Edward, and Stephanie Camp, eds. *New Studies in the History of American Slavery*. Athens: University of Georgia Press, 2006.

Baraka, Amiri. *Black Music*. New York: W. Morrow, 1967.

Barima, Kofi Royston. "Without Treaty: Runaways and Maroons in Jamaica, the Foundation of Opposition to the State." Ph.D. diss., Howard University, 2009.

Barry, Boubacar. *Senegambia and the Atlantic Slave Trade*. Cambridge, UK: Cambridge University Press, 1998.

Bascom, William. *Continuity and Change in African Cultures*. Chicago: University of Chicago Press, 1959.

———. *African Folktales in the New World*. Bloomington: Indiana University Press, 1992.

Bay, Edna G. "Belief, Legitimacy and the Kpojito: An Institutional History of the 'Queen Mother' in Precolonial Dahomey." *Journal of African History* 36 (1995): 1–27.

———. *Wives of the Leopard: Gender, Politics, and Culture in the Kingdom of Dahomey*. Charlottesville: University of Virginia Press, 1998.

Beach, Adam R. "Behn's Oroonoko, the Gold Coast, and Slavery in the Early-Modern Atlantic World." *Studies in Eighteenth Century Culture* 39 (2010): 215–233.

Beckles, Hilary McD. *Natural Rebels: A Social History of Enslaved Women in Barbados*. New Brunswick: Rutgers University Press, 1989.

Beckwith, Carol, Angela Fisher, and Mary Anne Fitzgerald, eds. *Painted Bodies: African Body Painting, Tattoos, and Scarification.* New York: Rizzoli, 2012.

Beckwith, Martha Warren. *Black Roadways: A Study of Jamaican Folk Life.* New York: Negro Universities Press, 1969.

———. *Jamaica Anansi Stories.* New York: G. E. Stechert, 1969.

Bell, Hesketh. *Obeah: Witchcraft in the West Indies.* Westport, CT: Negro Universities Press, 1970.

Bellegarde-Smith, Patrick, ed. *Fragments of Bone: Neo-African Religions in a New World.* Urbana: University of Illinois Press, 2005.

Benjamin, Ansa J. "The Origins of the Berbice Slave Revolt of 1763." *History Gazette* 30 (1991): 2–9.

Berlin, Ira. "From Creole to African: Atlantic Creoles and the Origins of African-American Society in Mainland North America." *William and Mary Quarterly* 53 (1996): 251–288.

———. *Many Thousands Gone: The First Two Centuries of Slavery in North America.* Cambridge, MA: Belknap Press, 1998.

———. *Generations of Captivity: A History of African-American Slaves.* Cambridge, MA: Belknap Press, 2004.

Bilby, Kenneth M. "The Kromanti Dance of the Windward Maroons of Jamaica." *New West Indian Guide* 55 (1981): 52–101.

———. "How the Ỳolder Headsý Talk: A Jamaican Maroon Spirit Possession Language and Its Relationship to the Creoles of Suriname and Sierra Leone." *New West Indian Guide* 57 (1983): 37–88.

———. "'Two Sister Pikni': A Historical Tradition of Dual Ethnogenesis in Eastern Jamaica." *Caribbean Quarterly* 30 (1984): 10–25.

———. "Swearing by the Past, Swearing to the Future: Sacred Oaths, Alliances, and Treaties Among the Guianese and Jamaican Maroons." *Ethnohistory* 44 (1997): 655–689.

Bilby, Kenneth M., and Jerome S. Handler. "Obeah: Healing and Protection in West Indian Slave Life." *Journal of Caribbean History* 38 (2004): 153–183.

Bilby, Kenneth M., and Kevin A. Yelvington. *True-born Maroons.* Gainesville: University Press of Florida, 2005.

Blair, Barbara. "Wolfert Simon van Hoogenheim in the Berbice Slave Revolt of 1763–1764." *Bijdragen tot de Taal-, Land- en Volkenkunde* 140 (1984): 56–76.

Blakey, Michael. "The New York Burial Ground Project: An Examination of Enslaved Lives, A Construction of Ancestral Ties." *Transforming Archaeology: Journal of the Association of Black Anthropologists* 7 (1998): 53–58.

Blassingame, John W. *The Slave Community: Plantation Life in the Antebellum South.* New York: Oxford University Press, 1972.

Blier, Suzanne Preston. *African Vodun: Art, Psychology, and Power.* Chicago: University of Chicago Press, 1995.

Blouet, Olwyn M. "Bryan Edwards, F. R. S., 1743–1800." *Notes and Records of the Royal Society of London* 54 (2000): 215–222.

Boahen, Adu. "The Origins of the Akan." *Ghana Notes and Queries* 9 (1966): 3–10.

———. "Arcany or Accany or Arcania and the Accanists of the Sixteenth and Seventeenth Centuries' European Records." *Transactions of the Historical Society of Ghana* 14 (1973): 105–112.

Boahen, Adu, Emmanuel Akyeampong, Nancy Lawler, T. C. McCaskie, and Ivor Wilks, eds. *The History of Ashanti Kings and the Whole Country Itself and Other Writings.* Oxford: Oxford University Press, 2003.

Boxer, Charles R. *The Dutch Seaborne Empire, 1600–1800.* New York: Oxford University Press, 1965.

Brathwaite, Edward Kamau. *Nanny, Sam Sharpe, and the Struggle for People's Liberation.* Kingston, Jamaica: Agency for Public Information, 1977.

Brown, Christopher Leslie, and Philip D. Morgan, eds. *Arming Slaves: From Classical Times to the Modern Age.* New Haven: Yale University Press, 2006.

Brown, Laurence. "Monuments to Freedom, Monuments to Nation: The Politics of Emancipation and Remembrance in the Eastern Caribbean." *Slavery and Abolition* 23 (2002): 93–116.

Brown, Ras Michael. *African-Atlantic Cultures and the South Carolina Lowcountry.* New York: Cambridge University Press, 2012.

Brown, Soi-Daniel W. "From the Tongues of Africa: A Partial Translation of Oldendorp's Interviews." *Plantation Society in the Americas* 2 (1983): 37–61.

Brown, Vincent. "Spiritual Terror and Sacred Authority in Jamaican Slave Society." *Slavery and Abolition* 24 (2003): 24–53.

———. *The Reaper's Garden: Death and Power in the World of Atlantic Slavery.* Cambridge, MA: Harvard University Press, 2008.

———. "Social Death and Political Life in the Study of Slavery." *American Historical Review* 114 (2009): 1231–1249.

Browne, Randy M. "The 'Bad Business' of Obeah: Power, Authority, and the Politics of Slave Culture in the British Caribbean." *William and Mary Quarterly* 68 (2011): 451–480.

Bruce-Myers, J. M. "The Origin of the Gãs." *Journal of the Royal African Society* 27 (1928): 167–173.

Bryant, Sherwin K., Rachel Sarah O'Toole, and Ben Vinson, eds. *Africans to Spanish America: Expanding the Diaspora.* Urbana: University of Illinois Press, 2012.

Buah, F. K. *A History of Ghana.* Oxford: Macmillan, 1998 [1980].

Buckridge, Steve O. *The Language of Dress: Resistance and Accommodation in Jamaica, 1750–1890.* Kingston: University of the West Indies Press, 2004.

Burnard, Trevor. "Slave Naming Patterns: Onomastics and the Taxonomy of Race in Eighteenth-Century Jamaica." *Journal of Interdisciplinary History* 31 (2001): 325–346.

Burnard, Trevor, and Kenneth Morgan. "The Dynamics of the Slave Market and Slave Purchasing Patterns in Jamaica, 1655–1788." *William and Mary Quarterly* 58 (2001): 205–228.

Burton, Richard D. E. *Afro-Creole: Power, Opposition, and Play in the Caribbean.* Ithaca: Cornell University Press, 1997.

Bush, Barbara. *Slave Women in Caribbean Society, 1650–1838.* Bloomington: University of Indiana Press, 1990.

Byfield, Judith A., LaRay Denzer, and Anthea Morrison, eds. *Gendering the African Diaspora: Women, Culture, and Historical Change in the Caribbean and Nigerian Hinterland*. Bloomington: Indiana University Press, 2010.

Byrd, Alexander X. *Captives and Voyagers: Black Migrants across the Eighteenth-Century British Atlantic World*. Baton Rouge: Louisiana State University Press, 2008.

Campbell, Mavis, C. *The Maroons of Jamaica, 1655–1796*. Trenton, NJ: Africa World Press, 1990.

———. *Back to Africa: George Ross and the Maroons: From Nova Scotia to Sierra Leone*. Trenton, NJ: Africa World Press, 1993.

Carey, Bev. *The Maroon Story: The Authentic and Original History of the Maroons in the History of Jamaica, 1490–1880*. Gordon Town, Jamaica: Agouti Press, 1997.

Carney, Judith Ann. *Black Rice: The African Origins of Rice Cultivation in the Americas*. Cambridge, MA: Harvard University Press, 2001.

Carney, Judith Ann, and Richard Nicholas Rosomoff. *In the Shadow of Slavery: Africa's Botanical Legacy in the Atlantic World*. Berkeley: University of California Press, 2009.

Caron, Peter. "'Of a Nation Which Others Do Not Understand': Bambara Slaves and African Ethnicity in Colonial Louisiana, 1718–60." *Slavery and Abolition* 18 (1997): 98–121.

Catron, John William. "Across the Great Water: Religion and Diaspora in the Black Atlantic." Ph.D. diss., University of Florida, 2008.

Chambers, Douglas B. "'My Own Nation': Igbo Exiles in the Diaspora." *Slavery and Abolition* 18 (1997): 72–97.

———. "Ethnicity in the Diaspora: The Slave-Trade and the Creation of African 'Nations' in the Americas." *Slavery and Abolition* 22 (2001): 25–39.

———. *Murder at Montpelier: Igbo Africans in Virginia*. Jackson: University Press of Mississippi, 2005.

Chireau, Yvonne P. *Black Magic: Religion and African American Conjuring Tradition*. Berkeley: University of California Press, 2003.

Chivallon, Christine. "Can One Diaspora Hide Another? Differing Interpretations of Black Culture in the Americas." *Social and Economic Studies* 54 (2005): 71–105.

Chouin, Gérard, and Christopher Decorse. "Prelude to the Atlantic Trade: New Perspectives on Southern Ghana's Pre-Atlantic History (800–1500)." *Journal of African History* 51 (2010): 123–145.

Christaller, Johann G. *A Grammar of the Asante and Fante Language Called Tshi [Chwee, Twi]: Based on the Akuapem Dialect, with Reference to the Other (Akan and Fante) Dialects*. Ridgewood, NJ: Gregg Press, 1964.

Clair, William St. *The Door of No Return: The History of Cape Coast Castle and the Atlantic Slave Trade*. New York: Bluebridge, 2009.

Clarke, T. Wood. "Negro Plot of 1741." *New York History Quarterly* 25 (1944): 167–181.

Costa, Emilia Viotti da. *Crowns of Glory, Tears of Blood: The Demerara Slave Rebellion of 1823*. New York: Oxford University Press, 1997.

Craton, Michael. *Testing the Chains: Resistance to Slavery in the British West Indies.* Ithaca: Cornell University Press, 1982.

———. *Empire, Enslavement and Freedom in the Caribbean.* Princeton: Ian Randle, 1997.

Creel, Margaret Washington. *A Peculiar People: Slave Religion and Community-Culture Among the Gullahs.* New York: New York University Press, 1988.

Crichlow, Michaeline A., and Piers Armstrong. "Carnival Praxis, Carnivalesque Strategies and Atlantic Interstices." *Social Identities* 16 (2010): 399–414.

Crummey, Donald, ed. *Banditry, Rebellion, and Social Protest in Africa.* Portsmouth, NH: Heinemann, 1986.

Cumming, Mark, ed. *The Carlyle Encyclopedia.* Madison: Fairleigh Dickinson University Press, 2004.

Curtin, Philip. *Two Jamaicas: The Role of Ideas in a Tropical Colony, 1830–1865.* Westport, CT: Greenwood Press, 1955.

———. "'The White Man's Grave': Image and Reality, 1780–1850." *Journal of British Studies* 1 (1961): 94–110.

———. *The Atlantic Slave Trade: A Census.* Madison: University of Wisconsin Press, 1969.

Curto, Jose C., and Paul E. Lovejoy, eds. *Enslaving Connections: Changing Cultures of Africa and Brazil during the Era of Slavery.* Amherst, NY: Humanity Books, 2004.

Daaku, Kwame Yeboa. "Pre-Asante States." *Ghana Notes and Queries* 9 (1966): 10–13.

———. *Trade and Politics on the Gold Coast, 1600–1720: A Study of the African Reaction to European Trade.* Oxford: Oxford University Press, 1970.

———. "Aspects of Precolonial Akan Economy." *International Journal of African Historical Studies* 5 (1972): 235–247.

Dadzie, Stella. "Searching for the Invisible Woman: Slavery and Resistance in Jamaica." *Race and Class* 32 (1990): 21–38.

Dalby, David. "Ashanti Survivals in the Language and Traditions of the Windward Maroons of Jamaica." *African Language Studies* 12 (1971): 31–51.

Danquah, J. B. "The Culture of Akan." *Africa: Journal of the International African Institute* 22 (1952): 360–366.

Davidson, Basil. *The African Slave Trade.* Boston: Little, Brown, 1980.

Davies, K. G. *The Royal African Company.* New York: Athenaeum, 1970.

Davis, Darién J. *Beyond Slavery: The Multilayered Legacy of Africans in Latin America and the Caribbean.* Lanham, MD: Rowman and Littlefield, 2006.

Davis, Thomas J. "The New York Slave Conspiracy of 1741 as Black Protest." *Journal of Negro History* 56 (1971): 17–30.

———. *A Rumor of Revolt: The "Great Negro Plot" in Colonial New York.* Amherst: University of Massachusetts Press, 1985.

de Barros, Juanita, Audra Diptee, and David Vincent Trotman, eds. *Beyond Fragmentation: Perspectives on Caribbean History.* Princeton, NJ: M. Wiener, 2006.

Debrunner, H. W. *Witchcraft in Ghana: A Study on the Belief in Destructive Witches and Its Effect on the Akan Tribes.* Kumasi, Ghana: Presbyterian Book Depot, 1959.

DeCamp, David. "African Day-Names in Jamaica." *Language* 43 (1967): 139–149.

DeCorse, Christopher. "Culture Contact, Continuity and Change on the Gold Coast, A.D. 1400–1900." *African Archaeological Review* 10 (1992): 163–196.

———. "The Danes on the Gold Coast: Culture Change and the European Presence." *African Archaeological Review* 11 (1993): 149–173.

———. *An Archaeology of Elmina: Africans and Europeans on the Gold Coast, 1400–1900.* Washington, D.C: Smithsonian Institution Press, 2001.

Desch-Obi, T. J. *Fighting for Honor: The History of African Martial Art Traditions in the Atlantic World.* Columbia: University of South Carolina Press, 2008.

Dickson, Kwamina B. "Trade Patterns in Ghana at the Beginning of the Eighteenth Century." *Geographical Review* 56 (1966): 417–431.

———. *A Historical Geography of Ghana.* Cambridge, UK: Cambridge University Press, 1969.

Diouf, Sylviane A. *Servants of Allah: African Muslims Enslaved in the Americas.* New York: New York University Press, 1998.

———, ed. *Fighting the Slave Trade: West African Strategies.* Athens: Ohio University Press, 2003.

Diptee, Audra A. *From Africa to Jamaica: The Making of an Atlantic Slave Society, 1775–1807.* Gainesville: University Press of Florida, 2010.

DjeDje, Jacqueline Cogdell. "Remembering Kojo: History, Music, and Gender in the January Sixth Celebration of the Jamaican Accompong Maroons." *Black Music Research Journal* 18 (1998): 67–112.

Donaldson, Gary A. "A Window on Slave Culture: Dances at Congo Square in New Orleans, 1800–1862." *Journal of Negro History* 69 (1984): 63–72.

Drewal, Henry John. "Performing the Other: Mami Wata Worship in Africa." *Drama Review* 32 (1988): 160–185.

———, ed. *Sacred Waters: Arts for Mami Wata and Other Divinities in Africa and the Diaspora.* Bloomington: Indiana University Press, 2008.

Dubois, Laurent. *Avengers of the New World: The Story of the Haitian Revolution.* Cambridge, MA: Belknap Press, 2005.

———. "On the History of the Jamaican Maroons." *Journal of African American History* 93 (2008): 64–69.

Du Bois, W. E. B., ed. *The Negro Church: Report of a Social Study Made under the Direction of Atlanta University; Together with the Proceedings of the Eighth Conference for the Study of the Negro Problems, Held at Atlanta University, May 26th, 1903.* Atlanta: Atlanta University Press, 1903.

———. *The Souls of Black Folk.* Boston: Bedford Books, 1997 [1903].

Duffy, James. *Portuguese Africa.* Cambridge, MA: Harvard University Press, 1961.

Dunbar, Paul Laurence. *Selected Poems.* New York: Penguin Books, 2004.

Dunham, Katherine. *Katherine Dunham's Journey to Accompong.* Westport, CT: Negro Universities Press, 1971.

Dunn, Richard S. *Sugar and Slaves: The Rise of the Planter Class in the English West Indies, 1624–1713.* Chapel Hill: University of North Carolina Press, 1972.

Egerton, Douglas. *He Shall Go Out Free: The Lives of Denmark Vesey.* Madison: Madison House, 1999.

Eltis, David. *The Rise of African Slavery in the Americas*. Cambridge, UK: Cambridge University Press, 2000.

———. "The Volume and Structure of the Transatlantic Slave Trade: A Reassessment." *William and Mary Quarterly* 58 (2001): 17–46.

Eltis, David, Stephen Behrendt, David Richardson, and Herbert Klein, eds., *The Trans-Atlantic Slave Trade: A Database on CD-ROM*. Cambridge, UK: Cambridge University Press, 1999.

Eltis, David, and David Richardson, eds. *Routes to Slavery: Direction, Ethnicity and Mortality in the Transatlantic Slave Trade*. London: Routledge, 1997.

Eshun, Edwin Kwame. "Socio-Religious Implication of the Practice of 'Sakawa' among the Youth in Ghana." Ph.D. diss., University of Oslo, 2010.

Fage, J.D. "'Good Red Herring': The Definitive Barbot." *Journal of African History* 34 (1993): 315–320.

Falola, Toyin, and Matt D. Childs, eds. *The Yoruba Diaspora in the Atlantic World*. Bloomington: Indiana University Press, 2004.

Falola, Toyin, and Akinwumi Ogundiran, eds. *Archaeology of Atlantic Africa and the African Diaspora*. Bloomington: Indiana University Press, 2007.

Feinberg, Harvey M. "Africans and Europeans in West Africa: Elminans and Dutchmen on the Gold Coast During the Eighteenth Century." *Transactions of the American Philosophical Society* 79 (1989): 1–186.

Feinberg, Harvey M., and William Smith. "An Eighteenth-Century Case of Plagiarism: William Smith's 'A New Voyage to Guinea.'" *History in Africa* 6 (1979): 45–50.

Ferreira, Roquinaldo Amaral. *Cross-Cultural Exchange in the Atlantic World: Angola and Brazil during the Era of the Slave Trade*. New York: Cambridge University Press, 2012.

Fett, Sharla. *Working Cures: Healing, Health, and Power on Southern Slave Plantations*. Chapel Hill: University of North Carolina Press, 2002.

Fick, Carolyn. *The Making of Haiti: The Saint Domingue Revolution from Below*. Knoxville: University of Tennessee Press, 1990.

Fields-Black, Edda L. *Deep Roots: Rice Farmers in West Africa and the African Diaspora*. Bloomington: Indiana University Press, 2008.

Foote, Thelma Wills. "'Some Hard Usage': The New York City Slave Revolt." *New York Folklore* 28 (2001): 147–159.

———. *Black and White Manhattan: The History of Racial Formation in Colonial New York City*. New York: Oxford University Press, 2004.

Frey, Sylvia R., and Betty Wood, eds. *From Slavery to Emancipation in the Atlantic World*. London: Frank Cass, 1999.

Fynn, J. K. *Asante and Its Neighbours, 1700–1807*. London: Longman Group, 1971.

———. "Asante and Akyem Relations, 1700–1831." *Research Review* 9 (1972): 58–81.

———. "The Nanaom Pow of the Fante: Myth and Reality." *Sankofa: Legon Journal of Archaeological and Historical Studies* 2 (1976): 54–59.

Galenson, David W. "The Atlantic Slave Trade and the Barbados Market, 1673–1723." *Journal of Economic History* 42 (1982): 491–511.

Garrigus, John D., and Christopher Morris, eds. *Assumed Identities: The Meanings of Race in the Atlantic World.* College Station: Texas A&M University Press, 2010.

Gaspar, David Barry. "The Antigua Slave Conspiracy of 1736: A Case Study of the Origins of Collective Resistance." *William and Mary Quarterly* 35 (1978): 308–323.

——. *Bondmen and Rebels: A Study of Master-Slave Relations in Antigua.* Durham: Duke University Press, 1985.

Gaspar, David Barry, and Darlene Clark Hine, eds. *More Than Chattel: Black Women and Slavery in the Americas.* Bloomington: Indiana University Press, 1996.

Geggus, David. "Jamaica and the Saint Domingue Slave Revolt, 1791–1793." *The Americas* 38 (1981): 219–233.

——. "The Enigma of Jamaica in the 1790s: New Light on the Causes of Slave Rebellions." *William and Mary Quarterly* 44 (1987): 274–299.

——. "Sex Ratio, Age and Ethnicity in the Atlantic Slave Trade: Data from French Shipping and Plantation Records." *Journal of African History* 30 (1989): 23–44.

——. "The French Slave Trade: An Overview." *William and Mary Quarterly* 58 (2001): 119–138.

Gemery, H. A., and Jan S. Hogendorn, eds. *Uncommon Market: Essays in the Economic History of the Atlantic Slave Trade.* New York: Academic Press, 1979.

Genovese, Eugene. *From Rebellion to Revolution: Afro-American Slave Revolts in the Making of the Modern World.* Baton Rouge: Louisiana State University Press, 1979.

Georgia Writers' Project. *Drums and Shadows: Survival Studies among the Georgia Coastal Negroes.* Athens: University of Georgia Press, 1986 [1940].

Gilroy, Paul. *The Black Atlantic: Modernity and Double-Consciousness.* Cambridge, UK: Harvard University Press, 1993.

Gocking, Roger. *The History of Ghana.* Westport, CT: Greenwood Press, 2005.

Gomez, Michael. "Muslims in Early America." *Journal of Southern History* 60 (1994): 671–710.

——. *Exchanging Our Country Marks: The Transformation of African Identities in the Colonial and Antebellum South.* Chapel Hill: University of North Carolina Press, 1998.

——. "African Identity and Slavery in America." *Radical History Review* 75 (1999): 111–120.

——, ed. *Diasporic Africa: A Reader.* New York: New York University Press, 2006.

Gottlieb, Karla. *"The Mother of Us All": A History of Queen Nanny, Leader of the Windward Jamaican Maroons.* Trenton, NJ: Africa World Press, 2000.

Grant, John N. *The Maroons in Nova Scotia.* Halifax, Nova Scotia: Formac, 2002.

Green, Lisa J. *African American English: A Linguistic Introduction.* New York: Cambridge University Press, 2002.

Green, Toby. *The Rise of the Trans-Atlantic Slave Trade in Western Africa, 1300–1589.* Cambridge, UK: Cambridge University Press, 2011.

Green-Pederson, Svend E. "The Scope and Structure of the Danish Negro Slave Trade." *Scandinavian Economic History Review* 19 (1971): 149–197.

Greene, Sandra. "The Anlo-Ewe: Their Economy, Society and External Relations in the Eighteenth Century." Ph.D. diss., Northwestern University, 1981.

———. "Land, Lineage and Clan in Early Anlo." *Africa: Journal of the International African Institute* 51 (1981): 451–464.

———. "The Past and Present of an Anlo-Ewe Oral Tradition." *History in Africa* 12 (1985): 73–87.

———. "Social Change in Eighteenth-Century Anlo: The Role of Technology, Markets and Military Conflict." *Africa: Journal of the International African Institute* 58 (1988), 70–86.

———. *Gender, Ethnicity, and Social Change on the Upper Slave Coast: A History of the Anlo-Ewe.* Portsmouth, NH: Heinemann, 1996.

———. "Sacred Terrain: Religion, Politics and Place in the History of Anloga (Ghana)." *International Journal of African Historical Studies* 30 (1997): 1–22.

———. *Sacred Sites and the Colonial Encounter: A History of Meaning and Memory in Ghana.* Bloomington: Indiana University Press, 2002.

Griffith, R. Marie, and Barbara Dianne Savage, eds. *Women and Religion in the African Diaspora: Knowledge, Power, and Performance.* Baltimore: Johns Hopkins University Press, 2006.

Grimé, William. *Ethno-Botany of the Black Americans.* Algonac, MI: Reference Publications, 1979.

Gyekye, Kwame. *An Essay on African Philosophical Thought: The Akan Conceptual Scheme.* New York: Cambridge University Press, 1987.

Haenger, Peter. *Slaves and Slave Holders on the Gold Coast: Towards an Understanding of Social Bondage in West Africa.* Basel, Switzerland: P. Schlettwein, 2000.

Hagan, G. P. "A Note on Akan Colour Symbolism." *Research Review* 7 (1970): 8–13.

Hair, P. E. H. *The Founding of the Castelo de Sao Jorge da Mina: An Analysis of Sources.* Madison: University of Wisconsin Press, 1994.

———. *Africa Encountered : European Contacts and Evidence, 1450–1700.* Brookfield, VT: Variorum, 1997.

Hall, Gwendolyn Midlo. *Africans in Colonial Louisiana: The Development of Afro-Creole Culture in the Eighteenth Century.* Baton Rouge: Louisiana State University Press, 1995.

———. *Databases for the Study of Afro-Louisiana History and Genealogy 1699–1860: Computerized Information from Original Manuscript Sources.* Baton Rouge: Louisiana State University Press, 2000.

———. *Slavery and African Ethnicities in the Americas: Restoring the Links.* Chapel Hill: University of North Carolina Press, 2005.

Hall, Neville A. T. *Slave Society in the Danish West Indies: St. Thomas, St. John and St. Croix.* Mona, Jamaica: University of the West Indies Press, 1992.

Handler, Jerome S. "Slave Revolts and Conspiracies in Seventeenth-Century Barbados." *New West Indian Guide* 56 (1982): 5–43.

———. "Life Stories of Enslaved Africans in Barbados." *Slavery and Abolition* 19 (1998): 129–141.

———. "Slave Medicine and Obeah in Barbados, Circa 1650 to 1834." *New West Indian Guide* 74 (2000): 57–90.

————. *The Unappropriated People: Freedmen in the Slave Society of Barbados.* Kingston, Jamaica: University of the West Indies Press, 2009.

Handler, Jerome S., and Kenneth M. Bilby. "On the Early Use and Origin of the Term 'Obeah' in Barbados and the Anglophone Caribbean." *Slavery and Abolition* 22 (2001): 87–100.

Handler, Jerome S., and JoAnn Jacoby. "Slave Names and Naming in Barbados, 1650–1830." *William and Mary Quarterly* 53 (1996): 685–728.

Hansen, Joyce, and Gary McGowan. *Breaking Ground Breaking Silence: The Story of New York's African Burial Ground.* New York: Henry Holt, 1998.

Hanserd, Robert. "The Gold Coast, Jamaica and New York: Akan Ideas of Freedom in the Afro-Atlantic during the Eighteenth Century." Ph.D. diss., Northern Illinois University, 2011.

Harms, Robert. *The Diligent: A Voyage through the Worlds of the Slave Trade.* New York: Basic Books, 2003.

Hart, Richard. *Slaves Who Abolished Slavery.* Kingston, Jamaica: University of the West Indies Press, 2002.

Hartman, Saidiya V. *Scenes of Subjection: Terror, Slavery, and Self-Making in Nineteenth-Century America.* New York: Oxford University Press, 1997.

————. *Lose Your Mother: A Journey along the Atlantic Slave Route.* New York: Farrar, Straus, and Giroux, 2007.

Hawthorne, Walter. *From Africa to Brazil: Culture, Identity, and an Atlantic Slave Trade, 1600–1830.* Cambridge, UK: Cambridge University Press, 2010.

Hedrick, Basil C., and Jeanette E. Stephens. *It's A Natural Fact: Obeah in the Bahamas.* Greeley: University of Northern Colorado, Museum of Anthropology Miscellaneous Series no. 39, 1977.

Henderson-Quartey, David K. *The Ga of Ghana: History and Culture of a West African People.* London: Book-in-Hand, 2001.

Henige, David. "Akan Stool Succession under Colonial Rule: Continuity or Change?" *Journal of African History* 16 (1975): 285–301.

————. "John Kabes of Komenda: An Early African Entrepreneur and State Builder." *Journal of African History* 18 (1977): 1–19.

Henige, David, and T. C. McCaskie, eds. *West African Economic and Social History: Studies in Memory of Marion Johnson.* Madison: University of Wisconsin Press, 1990.

Herskovits, Melville. *The Myth of The Negro Past.* Boston: Beacon Press, 1990 [1941].

Herskovits, Melville, and Frances Herskovits. *Rebel Destiny: Among the Bush Negroes of Dutch Guiana.* New York: Whittlesey House, 1934.

————. *Suriname Folklore.* New York: AMS Press, 1969.

Heuman, Gad, ed. *Out of the House of Bondage: Runaways, Resistance and Marronage in Africa and the New World.* London: Frank Cass, 1986.

Heywood, Linda M., ed. *Central Africans and Cultural Transformations in the American Diaspora.* Cambridge, UK: Cambridge University Press, 2002.

Highfield, Arnold R., and Vladimir Barac. *History of the Mission of the Evangelical Brethren on the Caribbean Islands of St. Thomas, St. Croix, and St. John.* Edited by Johann Jakob Bossard. Ann Arbor: Karoma, 1987.

Hill, Jonathan David. *History, Power, and Identity: Ethnogenesis in the Americas, 1492–1992*. Iowa City: University of Iowa Press, 1996.

Hobsbawm, E. J., and T. O. Ranger, eds. *The Invention of Tradition*. Cambridge, UK: Cambridge University Press, 1983.

Hogg, Donald W. "Magic and 'Science' in Jamaica." *Caribbean Studies* 1 (1961): 1–5.

Holmes, Jack D. L. "The Abortive Slave Revolt at Pointe Coupee, Louisiana, 1795." *Louisiana History* 11 (1970): 341–362.

Holsey, Bayo. *Routes of Remembrance: Refashioning the Slave Trade in Ghana*. Chicago: University Of Chicago Press, 2008.

———. "'Watch the Waves of the Sea': Literacy, Feedback, and the European Encounter in Elmina." *History in Africa* 38 (2011): 79–101.

Hoogbergen, Wim. "Aluku." *New West Indian Guide* 63 (1989): 175–198.

———. *The Boni Maroon Wars in Suriname*. Leiden: Brill, 1990.

Hunt, Tamara L., and Micheline R. Lessard, eds. *Women and the Colonial Gaze*. New York: New York University Press, 2002.

Hunwick, John, and Nancy Lawler, eds. *The Cloth of Many Coloured Silks: Papers on History and Society Ghanaian and Islamic in Honor of Ivor Wilks*. Evanston: Northwestern University Press, 1996.

Hurston, Zora Neale. "Hoodoo in America." *Journal of American Folklore* 44 (1931): 318–417.

———. *Dust Tracks on a Road: An Autobiography*. Urbana: University of Illinois Press, 1984 [1942]).

Ingersoll, Thomas N. "The Slave Trade and the Ethnic Diversity of Louisiana's Slave Community." *Louisiana History* 37 (1996): 133–161.

Inikori, Joseph E., and Stanley L. Engerman, eds. *The Atlantic Slave Trade: Effects on Economies, Societies and Peoples in Africa, the Americas, and Europe*. Durham: Duke University Press, 1992.

Jacobs, Jaap. *The Colony of New Netherland: A Dutch Settlement in Seventeenth-Century America*. Ithaca: Cornell University Press, 2009.

Jamieson, Ross. "Material Culture and Social Death: African-American Burial Practices." *Historical Archaeology* 29 (1995): 39–58.

Jenkins, Ray. "Impeachable Source? On the Use of the Second Edition of Reindorf's 'History' as a Primary Source for the Study of Ghanaian History." *History in Africa* 4 (1977): 123–147.

Johnson, Jerah. "New Orleans's Congo Square: An Urban Setting for Early Afro-American Culture Formation." *Louisiana History* 32 (1991): 117–157.

Johnston, Harry Hamilton. *The Negro in the New World*. New York: Johnson Reprint, 1969.

Jones, Adam, and Marion Johnson. "Slaves from the Windward Coast." *Journal of African History* 21 (1980): 17–34.

Kahn, Morton C. *Djuka: The Bush Negroes of Dutch Guiana*. New York: Viking, 1931.

Kaufman, Edward, ed. *Reclaiming Our Past, Honoring Our Ancestors: New York's 18th Century African Burial Ground and the Memorial Competition*. New York: African Burial Ground Coalition, 1994.

Kea, Ray A. "Akwamu-Anlo Relations, c. 1750–1813." *Transactions of the Historical Society of Ghana* 10 (1969): 29–63.

——. "Firearms and Warfare on the Gold and Slave Coasts from the Sixteenth to the Nineteenth Centuries." *Journal of African History* 12 (1971): 185–213.

——. *Settlements, Trade, and Polities in the Seventeenth-Century Gold Coast.* Baltimore: Johns Hopkins University Press, 1982.

——. *A Cultural and Social History of Ghana from the Seventeenth to the Nineteenth Century.* Lewiston, NY: Edwin Mellen Press, 2012.

Kiddy, Elizabeth W. "Ethnic and Racial Identity in the Brotherhoods of the Rosary of Minas Gerais, 1700–1830." *The Americas* 56 (1999): 221–252.

Kilson, Martin, and Robert Rotberg, eds. *The African Diaspora: Interpretive Essays.* Cambridge, MA: Harvard University Press, 1976.

Kiyaga-Mulindwa, D. "The 'Akan' Problem." *Current Anthropology* 21 (1980): 503–506.

Klein, A. Norman. "Slavery and Akan Origins?" *Ethnohistory* 41 (1994): 627–656.

——. "Reply to Wilks's Commentary on 'Slavery and Akan Origins?'" *Ethnohistory* 41 (1994): 666–667.

——. "Toward a New Understanding of Akan Origins." *Africa: Journal of the International African Institute* 66 (1996): 248–273.

Klingler, Thomas A. *If I Could Turn My Tongue Like That: The Creole Language of Pointe Coupee Parish, Louisiana.* Baton Rouge: Louisiana State University Press, 2003.

Knight, Franklin W., and Colin A. Palmer, eds. *The Modern Caribbean.* Chapel Hill: University of North Carolina Press, 1989.

Knight, Frederick C. *Working the Diaspora: The Impact of African Labor on the Anglo-American World, 1650–1850.* New York: New York University Press, 2010.

Konadu, Kwasi. *The Akan Diaspora in the Americas.* New York: Oxford University Press, 2010.

Kopytoff, Barbara Klamon. "Jamaican Maroon Political Organization: The Effects of the Treaties." *Social and Economic Studies* 25 (1976): 87–105.

——. "The Development of Jamaican Maroon Ethnicity." *Caribbean Quarterly* 22 (1976): 33–50.

——. "The Early Political Development of Jamaican Maroon Societies." *William and Mary Quarterly* 35 (1978): 287–307.

——. "Religious Change Among the Jamaican Maroons: The Ascendance of the Christian God within a Traditional Cosmology." *Journal of Social History* 20 (1987): 463–484.

Kpobi, David Nii Anum. *Saga of a Slave: Jacobus Capitein of Holland and Elmina.* Legon, Ghana: Cootek, 2001.

Kraamer, Malika. "Ghanaian Interweaving in the Nineteenth Century: A New Perspective on Ewe and Asante Textile History." *African Arts* 39 (2006): 36–53.

Kramer, Fritz. *The Red Fez: Art and Spirit Possession in Africa.* London: Verso, 1993.

Kumah, J. K. "The Rise and Fall of the Kingdom of Denkyira." *Ghana Notes and Queries* 9 (1966): 33–35.

Kuss, Malena. *Music in Latin America and the Caribbean: Performing the Caribbean Experience.* Austin: University of Texas Press, 2007.

La Roche, Cheryl, and Michael Blakey. "Seizing Intellectual Power: The Dialogue at the New York African Burial Ground." *Historical Archaeology* 31 (1997): 84–106.

Lambert, David. "'Part of the Blood and Dream': Surrogation, Memory, and the National Hero in the Postcolonial Caribbean." *Patterns of Prejudice* 41 (2007): 345–371.

Landers, Jane G. *Atlantic Creoles in the Age of Revolutions.* Cambridge, MA: Harvard University Press, 2010.

Law, Robin. "Jean Barbot as a Source for the Slave Coast of West Africa." *History in Africa* 9 (1982): 155–173.

——. "Dahomey and the Slave Trade: Reflections on the Historiography of the Rise of Dahomey." *Journal of African History* 27 (1986): 237–267.

——. "Ideologies of Royal Power: The Dissolution and Reconstruction of Political Authority on the 'Slave Coast,' 1680–1750." *Africa: Journal of the International African Institute* 57 (1987): 321–344.

——. *The Slave Coast of West Africa, 1550–1750: The Impact of the Atlantic Slave Trade on an African Society.* Oxford: Oxford University Press, 1991.

——. *Ouidah: The Social History of a West African Slaving Port 1727–1892.* Athens: Ohio University Press, 2004.

——. "Ethnicities of Enslaved Africans in the Diaspora: On the Meanings of 'Mina' (Again)." *History in Africa* 32 (2005): 247–267.

——. "The Komenda Wars, 1694–1700: A Revised Narrative." *History in Africa* 34 (2007): 133–168.

Law, Robin, and Kristin Mann. "West Africa in the Atlantic Community: The Case of the Slave Coast." *William and Mary Quarterly* 56 (1999): 307–334.

Lawrance, Benjamin, ed. *A Handbook of Eweland: The Ewe of Togo and Benin.* Accra: Woeli Publishing Services, 2005.

Lawrence, A. W. *Trade Castles and Forts of West Africa.* Stanford: Stanford University Press, 1964.

Le Page, R. B. *Jamaican Creole: An Historical Introduction to Jamaican Creole.* New York: St. Martin's Press, 1960.

Lepore, Jill. *New York Burning: Liberty, Slavery, and Conspiracy in Eighteenth-Century Manhattan.* New York: Alfred A. Knopf, 2005.

Levine, Lawrence W. *Black Culture and Black Consciousness: Afro-American Folk Thought from Slavery to Freedom.* New York: Oxford University Press, 1977.

Lewis, John Lowell. *Ring of Liberation: Deceptive Discourse in Brazilian Capoeira.* Chicago: University of Chicago Press, 1992.

Lewis, Lucy. "Ethnicity and Nation-building: The Surinamese Experience." *Caribbean Quarterly* 40 (1994): 72–83.

Lindsay, Lisa A., ed. *Captives as Commodities: The Transatlantic Slave Trade.* Upper Saddle River, NJ: Pearson Prentice Hall, 2008.

Linebaugh, Peter, and Marcus Rediker. *The Many-Headed Hydra: Sailors, Slaves, Commoners, and the Hidden History of the Revolutionary Atlantic.* Boston: Beacon Press, 2001.

Littlefield, Daniel. *Rice and Slaves: Ethnicity and the Slave Trade in Colonial South Carolina.* Baton Rouge: Louisiana State University, 1981.

Lovejoy, Paul. *Transformations in Slavery: History of Slavery in Africa.* Cambridge, UK: Cambridge University Press, 1983.

——. "The African Diaspora: Revisionist Interpretations of Ethnicity, Culture and Religion under Slavery." *Studies in the World History of Slavery, Abolition and Emancipation* 2 (1997): 1–23.

——, ed. *Identity in the Shadow of Slavery.* 2nd ed. New York: Continuum Books, 2009.

Lovejoy, Paul, and David Richardson. "Pawnship in Western Africa, c. 1600–1810." *Journal of African History* 42 (2001): 67–89.

Lovejoy, Paul, and David Vincent Trotman, eds. *Trans-Atlantic Dimensions of Ethnicity in the African Diaspora.* London: Continuum, 2003.

Lydon, James. "New York and the Slave Trade, 1700–1774." *William and Mary Quarterly* 35 (1978): 375–394.

Mackie, Erin. "Welcome the Outlaw: Pirates, Maroons, and Caribbean Countercultures." *Cultural Critique* 59 (2005): 24–62.

Mann, Kristin. "Shifting Paradigms in the Study of the African Diaspora and of Atlantic History and Culture." *Slavery and Abolition* 22 (2001): 3–21.

Mann, Kristin, and Edna G. Bay, eds. *Rethinking the African Diaspora: The Making of a Black Atlantic World in the Bight of Benin and Brazil.* London: Frank Cass, 2001.

Manning, Patrick. *Slavery and African Life: Occidental, Oriental, and African Slave Trades.* Cambridge, UK: Cambridge University Press, 1990.

Manoukian, Madeline. *Akan and Ga-Adangme Peoples of the Gold Coast.* London: Oxford University Press, 1950.

——. *The Ewe-Speaking People of Togoland and the Gold Coast.* London: International African Institute, 1952.

Marcus, Jacob R., and Stanley F. Chyet, eds. *Historical Essay on the Colony of Surinam, 1788.* New York: KTAV Publishing House, 1974.

Marshall, Emily Zobel. "Anansi Tactics in Plantation Jamaica: Matthew Lewis's Record of Trickery." *Wadabagei* 12 (2009): 126–150.

——. *Anansi's Journey: A Story of Jamaican Cultural Resistance.* Kingston: University of the West Indies Press, 2011.

Mathurin, Lucille. *The Rebel Woman in the British West Indies during Slavery.* Kingston, Jamaica: Herald Limited, 1975.

Matthews, Gelien. *Caribbean Slave Revolts and the British Abolitionist Movement.* Baton Rouge: Louisiana State University Press, 2006.

M'Baye, Babacar. *The Trickster Comes West: Pan-African Influence in Early Black Diasporan Narratives.* Jackson: University Press of Mississippi, 2009.

McCaskie, T. C. "Anti-Witchcraft Cults in Asante: An Essay in the Social History of an African People." *History in Africa* 8 (1981): 125–154.

——. "Accumulation of Wealth and Belief in Asante History." *Africa: Journal of the International African Institute* 53 (1983): 23–43, 79.

——. "Komfo Anokye of Asante: Meaning, History and Philosophy in an African Society." *Journal of African History* 27 (1986): 315–339.

——. *State and Society in Pre-Colonial Asante.* Cambridge, UK: Cambridge University Press, 1995.

———. "Denkyira in the Making of Asante c. 1660–1720." *Journal of African History* 48 (2007): 1–25.

McFarlane, Milton. *Cudjoe the Maroon*. London: Allison and Busby, 1977.

Mehta, Varad. "Sparta in the Enlightenment." Ph.D. diss., George Washington University, 2009.

Meillassoux, Claude. *The Anthropology of Slavery: The Womb of Iron and Gold*. Chicago: University of Chicago Press, 1991.

Mencken, H. L. "Designations for Colored Folks." *American Speech* 19 (1944): 161–174.

Meredith, Henry. *An Account of the Gold Coast of Africa: With A Brief History of the African Company*. London: Hurst, Rees, Orme, and Brown, 1812.

Meyerowitz, Eva. *Akan Traditions of Origin*. London: Faber and Faber, 1952.

———. *The Early History of the Akan States of Ghana*. London: Red Candle Press, 1975.

Miller, Christopher L. *The French Atlantic Triangle: Literature and Culture of the Slave Trade*. Durham: Duke University Press Books, 2008.

Miller, Joseph C. "Nzinga of Matamba in a New Perspective." *Journal of African History* 16 (1975): 201–216.

———. *Way of Death: Merchant Capitalism and the Angolan Slave Trade, 1730–1830*. Madison: University of Wisconsin Press, 1988.

Mintz, Sidney, and Richard Price. *The Birth of African-American Culture: An Anthropological Perspective*. Boston: Beacon Press, 1992 [1976].

Moitt, Bernard. *Women and Slavery in the French Antilles, 1635–1848*. Bloomington: Indiana University Press, 2001.

Monroe, J. Cameron, and Akinwumi Ogundiran, eds. *Power and Landscape in Atlantic West Africa: Archaeological Perspectives*. Cambridge, UK: Cambridge University Press, 2012.

Monteith, Kathleen, and Glen Richards, eds. *Jamaica in Slavery and Freedom: History, Heritage and Culture*. Kingston, Jamaica: University of the West Indies Press, 2001.

Morgan, Jennifer L. *Laboring Women: Reproduction and Gender in New World Slavery*. Philadelphia: University of Pennsylvania Press, 2004.

Morgan, Philip D. "Slaves and Livestock in Eighteenth-Century Jamaica: Vineyard Pen, 1750–1751." *William and Mary Quarterly* 52 (1995): 47–76.

———. "The Cultural Implications of the Atlantic Slave Trade: African Regional Origins, American Destinations and New World Developments." *Slavery and Abolition* 18 (1997): 122–145.

———. *Slave Counterpoint: Black Culture in the Eighteenth-Century Chesapeake and Low Country*. Chapel Hill: University of North Carolina Press, 1998.

Morrish, Ivor. *Obeah, Christ and Rastaman*. Cambridge, UK: James Clarke, 1982.

Mullin, Michael. *Africa in America: Slave Acculturation and Resistance in the American South and the British Caribbean, 1736–1831*. Urbana: University of Illinois Press, 1992.

Murray, Deryck. "Three Worships, an Old Warlock and Many Lawless Forces: The Court Trial of an African Doctor Who Practised 'Obeah to Cure' in Early

Nineteenth Century Jamaica." *Journal of Southern African Studies* 33 (2007): 811–828.

Mustakeem, Sowande'. "'I Never Have Such a Sickly Ship Before': Diet, Disease, and Mortality in 18th-Century Atlantic Slaving Voyages." *Journal of African American History* 93 (2008): 474–496.

Northrup, David. "Igbo and Myth Igbo: Culture and Ethnicity in the Atlantic World, 1600–1850." *Slavery and Abolition* 21 (2000): 1–20.

Nwokeji, G. Ugo. *The Slave Trade and Culture in the Bight of Biafra: An African Society in the Atlantic World.* New York: Cambridge University Press, 2010.

Odotei, Irène. "The History of Ga during the Gold and Slave Trade Eras." Ph.D. diss., University of Ghana, 1972.

Olmos, Margarite Fernandez, Joseph M. Murphy, and Lizabeth Paravisini-Gebert, eds. *Creole Religions of the Caribbean: An Introduction from Vodou and Santeria to Obeah and Espiritismo.* New York: New York University Press, 2003.

Olmos, Margarite Fernandez, and Lizabeth Paravisini-Gebert, eds. *Sacred Possessions: Vodou, Santeria, Obeah, and the Caribbean.* New Brunswick: Rutgers University Press, 2000.

Opoku-Agyemang, Kwadwo. *Cape Coast Castle: A Collection of Poems.* Accra: Afram Publications, 1996.

Oppong, Christine, ed. *Female and Male in West Africa.* London: George Allen and Unwin, 1983.

Painter, Colin. "The Guang and West African Historical Reconstruction." *Ghana Notes and Queries* 9 (1966): 58–66.

Painter, Nell Irvin. *Soul Murder and Slavery.* Waco, TX: Baylor University Press, 1995.

Palmberg, Mai, ed. *Encounter Images in the Meetings between Africa and Europe.* Uppsala: Nordiska Afrikainstitutet, 2001.

Palmer, Colin. *Human Cargoes: The British Trade to Spanish America, 1700–1739.* Urbana: University of Illinois Press, 1981.

———. "Defining and Studying the Modern African Diaspora." *Journal of Negro History* 85 (2000): 27–32.

Palmié, Stephan, ed. *Slave Cultures and the Cultures of Slavery.* Knoxville: University of Tennessee Press, 1995.

Parés, Luis Nicolau. *The Formation of Candomblé: Vodun History and Ritual in Brazil.* Chapel Hill: University of North Carolina, 2013.

Parish, Jane. "From the Body to the Wallet: Conceptualizing Akan Witchcraft at Home and Abroad." *Journal of the Royal Anthropological Institute* 6 (2000): 487–500.

———. "Anti-witchcraft Shrines among the Akan: Possession and the Gathering of Knowledge." *African Studies Review* 46 (2003): 17–34.

Parker, John. *Making the Town: Ga State and Society in Early Colonial Accra.* Portsmouth, NH: Heinemann, 2000.

Paton, Diana. "Punishment, Crime, and the Bodies of Slaves in Eighteenth-Century Jamaica." *Journal of Social History* 34 (2001): 923–954.

———. "Witchcraft, Poison, Law, and Atlantic Slavery." *William and Mary Quarterly* 69 (2012): 235–264.

Patterson, Orlando. *The Sociology of Slavery: An Analysis of the Origins, Development and Structure of Negro Slave Society in Jamaica.* Madison: Fairleigh Dickinson University Press, 1967.

———. "Slavery and Slave Revolts: A Socio-historical Analysis of the First Maroon War, 1655–1740." *Social and Economic Studies* 19 (1970): 289–325.

———. "Rethinking Black History." *Harvard Educational Review* 41 (1971): 299–304.

———. *Slavery and Social Death: A Comparative Study.* Cambridge, MA: Harvard University Press, 1982.

———. *Rituals of Blood: The Consequences of Slavery in Two American Centuries.* New York: Basic Civitas Books, 1999.

Perbi, Akosua Adoma. *A History of Indigenous Slavery in Ghana from the 15th to the 19th Century.* Legon-Accra, Ghana: Sub-Saharan Publishers, 2004.

Pestana, Carla Gardina, and Sharon V. Salinger, eds. *Inequality in Early America.* Hanover, NH: University Press of New England, 1999.

Phillips, U. B. *American Negro Slavery: A Survey of the Supply, Employment and Control of Negro Labor As Determined by the Plantation Regime.* Baton Rouge: Louisiana State University Press, 1966.

Pitman, Frank Wesley. "Slavery on British West India Plantations in the Eighteenth Century." *Journal of Negro History* 11 (1926): 585–650.

Postma, Johannes Menne. *The Dutch in the Atlantic Slave Trade, 1600–1815.* Cambridge, UK: Cambridge University Press, 1990.

Price, Richard. *Saramaka Social Structure: An Analysis of a "Bush Negro" Society.* Rio Piedras: University of Puerto Rico, 1973.

———. *The Guiana Maroons: A Historical and Bibliographical Introduction.* Baltimore: Johns Hopkins University Press, 1976.

———. *Maroon Societies: Rebel Slave Communities in the Americas.* Baltimore: Johns Hopkins University Press, 1996.

Price, Sally, and Richard Price. "Saramaka Onomastics: An Afro-American Naming System." *Ethnology* 11 (1972): 341–367.

———. *Maroon Arts: Cultural Vitality in the African Diaspora.* Boston: Beacon Press, 1999.

Priestley, Margaret. "The Ashanti Question and the British: Eighteenth-Century Origins." *Journal of African History* 2 (1961): 35–59.

———. *West African Trade and Coast Society: A Family Study.* London: Oxford University Press, 1969.

Quartey-Papafio, A. B. "The Use of Names Among the Gãs or Accra People of the Gold Coast." *Journal of the Royal African Society* 13 (1914): 167–182.

Rath, Richard Cullen. "African Music in Seventeenth-Century Jamaica: Cultural Transit and Transition." *William and Mary Quarterly* 50 (1993): 700–726.

Rattray, R. S. *Ashanti.* Oxford: Clarendon Press, 1923.

———. *Religion and Art in Ashanti.* Oxford: Clarendon Press, 1927.

Rediker, Marcus. *The Slave Ship: A Human History.* New York: Penguin Books, 2007.

Reese, Ty M. "'Sheep in the Jaws of So Many Ravenous Wolves': The Slave Trade and Anglican Missionary Activity at Cape Coast Castle, 1752–1816." *Journal of Religion in Africa* 34 (2004): 348–372.

Richardson, David. "Shipboard Revolts, African Authority, and the Atlantic Slave Trade." *William and Mary Quarterly* 58 (2001): 69–92.

Riley, James C. *Poverty and Life Expectancy: The Jamaica Paradox.* Cambridge, UK: Cambridge University Press, 2005.

Roberts, John. *From Trickster to Badman: The Black Folk Hero in Slavery and Freedom.* Philadelphia: University of Pennsylvania Press, 1989.

Robinson, Carey. *The Fighting Maroons of Jamaica.* London: William Collins and Sangster, 1969.

———. *The Iron Thorn: The Defeat of the British by the Jamaican Maroons.* Kingston: Kingston Publishers, 1993.

Ross, Doran H. "The Iconography of Asante Sword Ornaments." *African Arts* 11 (1977): 16–25.

Rucker, Walter. "Conjure, Magic, and Power: The Influence of Afro-Atlantic Religious Practices on Slave Resistance and Rebellion." *Journal of Black Studies* 32 (2001): 84–103.

———. "African Americans and an Atlantic World Culture." In *The Blackwell Companion to African American History.* Edited by Alton Hornsby, Jr. 235–254. Malden, MA: Blackwell, 2005.

———. *The River Flows On: Black Resistance, Culture, and Identity Formation in Early America.* Baton Rouge: Louisiana State University Press, 2006.

———. "'Only Draw in Your Countrymen': Akan Culture and Community in Colonial New York City." *Afro-Americans in New York Life and History* 34 (2010): 76–118.

Sanders, James. "The Expansion of the Fante and the Emergence of Asante in the Eighteenth Century." *Journal of African History* 20 (1979): 349–364.

Sangree, Walter. "Secondary Marriage and Tribal Solidarity in Irigwe, Nigeria." *American Anthropologist* 34 (1972): 1234–1243.

Sarpong, Peter. *The Sacred Stools of the Akan.* Accra-Tema: Ghana Publishing, 1971.

Schaffer, William C., and E. Kofi Agorsah. "Bioarchaeological Analysis of Historic Kormantse, Ghana." *African Diaspora Archaeology Newsletter* (March 2010): 1–12.

Schildkrout, Enid, and Carol Gelber, eds. *The Golden Stool: Studies of the Asante Center and Periphery.* New York: American Museum of Natural History, 1987.

Schuler, Monica. "Akan Slave Rebellions in the British Caribbean." *Savacou* 1 (1970): 8–31.

———. "Ethnic Slave Rebellions in the Caribbean and the Guianas." *Journal of Social History* 3 (1970): 374–385.

———. "Afro-American Slave Culture." *Historical Reflections* 6 (1974): 121–137, 138–155.

Scott, James C. *Weapons of the Weak: Everyday Forms of Peasant Resistance.* New Haven: Yale University Press, 1985.

———. *Domination and the Arts of Resistance: Hidden Transcripts.* New Haven: Yale University Press, 1990.

Scott, Kenneth. "The Slave Insurrection in New York in 1712." *New York Historical Society Quarterly* 45 (1961): 43–74.

Seeman, Erik R. "Reassessing the 'Sankofa Symbol' in New York's African Burial Ground." *William and Mary Quarterly* 67 (2010): 101–122.

Sharples, Jason T. "The Flames of Insurrection: Fearing Slave Conspiracy in Early America 1670–1780." Ph.D. diss., Princeton University, 2010.

Shaw, Rosalind. *Memories of the Slave Trade: Ritual and the Historical Imagination in Sierra Leone.* Chicago: University of Chicago Press, 2002.

Shepherd, Verene, ed. *Working Slavery, Pricing Freedom: Perspectives from the Caribbean, Africa and the African Diaspora.* New York: Palgrave, 2002.

———. "From 'Numbered Notations' to Named Ancestors: Finding Contemporary Meaning in Vincent Brown's *The Reaper's Garden.*" *Small Axe* 31 (2010): 212–218.

Sheridan, Michael J., and Celia Nyamweru. *African Sacred Groves: Ecological Dynamics and Social Change.* Oxford, UK: James Currey, 2008.

Sheridan, Richard B. "Africa and the Caribbean in the Atlantic Slave Trade." *American Historical Review* 77 (1972): 15–35.

———. "The Jamaican Slave Insurrection Scare of 1776 and the American Revolution." *Journal of Negro History* 61 (1976): 290–308.

Shumway, Rebecca. *The Fante and the Transatlantic Slave Trade.* Rochester: University of Rochester Press, 2011.

Shyllon, Folarin. "Slave Advertisements in the British West Indies." *Caribbean Studies* 18 (1978): 175–199.

Sidbury, James, and Jorge Cañizares-Esguerra. "Mapping Ethnogenesis in the Early Modern Atlantic." *William and Mary Quarterly* 68 (2011): 181–208.

Siguret, Roseline. "Esclaves d'Indigoteries et de Cafeières au Quartier de Jacmel, 1757–1791." *Revue Française d'Histoire d'Outre Mer* 55 (1968): 190–225.

Simpson, George Eaton. *Black Religions in the New World.* New York: Columbia University Press, 1978.

Smallwood, Stephanie E. "African Guardians, European Slave Ships, and the Changing Dynamics of Power in the Early Modern Atlantic." *William and Mary Quarterly* 64 (2007): 679–716.

———. *Saltwater Slavery: A Middle Passage from Africa to American Diaspora.* Cambridge, MA: Harvard University Press, 2007.

Smith, Katherine A. "Forging an Identity: British Virgin Islands' Slave Society 1672–1838." Ph.D. diss., Howard University, 2009.

Smith, Michael G. "Secondary Marriage in Northern Nigeria." *Africa* 13 (1953): 298–323.

Smith, Theophus Harold. *Conjuring Culture: Biblical Formations in Black America.* New York: Oxford University Press, 1994.

St. Clair, William. *The Door of No Return: The History of Cape Coast Castle and the Atlantic Slave Trade.* New York: BlueBridge, 2007.

St. George, Robert Blair, ed. *Possible Pasts: Becoming Colonial in Early America.* Ithaca: Cornell University Press, 2000.

Steady, Filomina Chioma, ed. *The Black Woman Cross-Culturally.* Rochester, VT: Schenkman Books, 1985.

Stewart, J. M. "Akan History: Some Linguistic Evidence." *Ghana Notes and Queries* 9 (1966): 54–58.

Stuckey, Sterling. "Through the Prism of Folklore: The Black Ethos in Slavery."
    Massachusetts Review 9 (1968): 417–437.
——. *Slave Culture: Nationalist Theory and the Foundations of Black America.*
    New York: Oxford University Press, 1987.
——. *Going Through the Storm: The Influence of African American Art in History.*
    New York: Oxford University Press, 1994.
Sweet, James H., *Recreating Africa: Culture, Kinship, and Religion in the African-
    Portuguese World, 1441–1770.* Chapel Hill: University of North Carolina Press,
    2003.
——. *Domingos Álvares, African Healing, and the Intellectual History of the Atlan-
    tic World.* Chapel Hill: University of North Carolina Press, 2011.
——. "Defying Social Death: The Multiple Configurations of African Slave Family
    in the Atlantic World." *William and Mary Quarterly* 70 (2013): 251–272.
Taylor, Eric Robert. *If We Must Die: Shipboard Insurrections in the Era of the Atlan-
    tic Slave Trade.* Baton Rouge: Louisiana State University Press, 2006.
Thompson, Alvin O. *Flight to Freedom: African Runaways and Maroons in the
    Americas.* Kingston: University of the West Indies Press, 2006.
——. "Symbolic Legacies of Slavery in Guyana." *New West Indian Guide* 80
    (2006): 191–220.
Thornton, John K. "A Resurrection for the Jaga." *Cahiers d'études africaines* 18
    (1978): 223–227.
——. "On the Trail of Voodoo: African Christianity in Africa and the Americas."
    The Americas 44 (1988): 261–278.
——. "African Dimensions of the Stono Rebellion." *American Historical Review*
    96 (1991): 1101–1113.
——. "Legitimacy and Political Power: Queen Njinga, 1624–1663." *Journal of Afri-
    can History* 32 (1991): 25–40.
——. *Africa and Africans in the Making of the Atlantic World, 1400–1800.* 2nd ed.
    New York: Cambridge University Press, 1998.
——. "The Coromantees: An African Cultural Group in Colonial North America
    and the Caribbean." *Journal of Caribbean History* 32 (1998): 161–178.
——. "The African Experience of the '20. and Odd Negroes' Arriving in Virginia
    in 1619." *William and Mary Quarterly* 55 (1998): 421–434.
——. *Warfare in Atlantic Africa, 1500–1800.* London: University College London
    Press, 1999.
——. "Cannibals, Witches, and Slave Traders in the Atlantic World." *William and
    Mary Quarterly* 60 (2003): 273–294.
Thornton, S. Leslie. "'Obeah' in Jamaica." *Journal of the Society of Comparative Leg-
    islation* 5 (1904): 262–270.
Todd, Janet, ed. *Aphra Behn Studies.* Cambridge, UK: Cambridge University Press,
    1996.
Trouillot, Michel-Rolph. *Silencing the Past: Power and the Production of History.*
    Boston: Beacon Press, 1997.
Tyson, George. "The Contributions of Africans to the Establishment of Chris-
    tiansted, 1735–1755." *Crucian Trader: Celebrating St. Croix History, Culture and
    People.* (2010): 2–7.

van den Bersselaar, Dmitri. *The King of Drinks: Schnapps Gin from Modernity to Tradition*. Leiden: Brill, 2007.

van Kessel, Ineke, ed. *Merchants, Missionaries and Migrants: 300 years of Dutch-Ghanaian Relations in Ghanaian History*. Legon-Accra, Ghana: Sub-Saharan Publishers, 2002.

Vansina, Jan. *Paths in the Rainforests: Toward a History of Political Tradition in Equatorial Africa*. Madison: University of Wisconsin Press, 1990.

van Stipriaan, Alex. "Watramama/Mami Wata: Three Centuries of Creolization of a Water Spirit in West Africa, Suriname and Europe." *Matatu: Journal for African Culture and Society* 27 (2005): 323–337.

Velzing, Ineke. "The Berbice Slave Revolt of 27th February 1763." *History Gazette* 29 (1991): 2–13.

Venkatachalam, Meera. "Between the Devil and the Cross: Religion, Slavery, and the Making of the Anlo-ewe." *Journal of African History* 53 (2012): 45–64.

Vivian, Brian. "Recent Excavations of Adansemanso." *Nyame Akuma* 46 (1996): 37–41.

Vogt, John. *Portuguese Rule on the Gold Coast, 1469–1682*. Athens: University of Georgia Press, 1982.

Voyages: The Trans-Atlantic Slave Trade Database, http://www.slavevoyages.org/tast/database/search.faces (accessed July 3, 2012).

Walker, Sheila, ed. *African Roots/American Cultures: Africa in the Creation of the Americas*. New York: Rowman and Littlefield, 2001.

Warner, Jason. "Understanding Cyber-Crime in Ghana: A View from Below." *International Journal of Cyber Criminology* 5 (2011): 736–749.

Watson, Richard L. "American Scholars and the Continuity of African Culture in the United States." *Journal of Negro History* 63 (1978): 375–386.

Wax, Darold. "Preferences for Slaves in Colonial America." *Journal of Negro History* 58 (1973): 371–401.

Weik, Terry. "The Archaeology of Maroon Societies in the Americas: Resistance, Cultural Continuity, and Transformation in the African Diaspora." *Historical Archaeology* 31 (1997): 81–92.

Welch, Pedro. *Slave Society in the City: Bridgetown Barbados, 1680–1834*. Miami: Ian Randle, 2003.

Westergaard, Waldemar C. *The Danish West Indies under Company Rule (1671–1754)*. New York: Macmillan, 1917.

———. "Account of the Negro Rebellion on St. Croix, Danish West Indies, 1759." *Journal of Negro History* 11 (1926): 50–61.

White, Deborah Gray. *Ar'n't I a Woman?: Female Slaves in the Plantation South*. New York: Norton, 1985.

White, Shane. "Pinkster: Afro-Dutch Syncretization in New York City and the Hudson Valley." *Journal of American Folklore* 102 (1989): 23–75.

———. "'It Was a Proud Day': African Americans, Festivals, and Parades in the North, 1741–1834." *Journal of American History* 81 (1994): 13–50.

Whitten, Jr., Norman E. "Contemporary Patterns of Malign Occultism among Negroes in North Carolina." *Journal of American Folklore* 75 (1962): 311–325.

Wilks, Ivor. "The Rise of the Akwamu Empire, 1650–1710." *Transactions of the Historical Society of Ghana* 3 (1957): 99–136.

———. "A Note on Twifo and Akwamu." *Transactions of the Historical Society of Ghana* 3 (1958): 215–217.

———. *Asante in the Nineteenth Century: The Structure and Evolution of a Political Order.* Cambridge, UK: Cambridge University Press, 1975.

———. "Wangara, Akan and Portuguese in the Fifteenth and Sixteenth Centuries: The Struggle for Trade." *Journal of African History* 23 (1982): 463–472.

———. "Asante: Human Sacrifice or Capital Punishment? A Rejoinder." *International Journal of African Historical Studies* 21 (1988): 443–452.

———. *Forests of Gold: Essays on the Akan and the Kingdom of Asante.* Athens: Ohio University Press, 1993.

———. "Slavery and Akan Origins? A Reply." *Ethnohistory* 41(1994): 657–665.

———. *One Nation, Many Histories: Ghana Past and Present.* Accra: Ghana Universities Press, 1996.

Williams, Joseph J. *Voodoos and Obeahs: Phases of West India Witchcraft.* New York: Dial Press, 1932.

Wilson, Kathleen. "The Performance of Freedom: Maroons and the Colonial Order in Eighteenth-Century Jamaica and the Atlantic Sound." *William and Mary Quarterly* 66 (2009): 45–86.

Wiredu, Kwasi. *Cultural Universals and Particulars: An African Perspective.* Bloomington: Indiana University Press, 1996.

Wood, Peter. *Black Majority: Negroes in Colonial South Carolina from 1670 through the Stono Rebellion.* New York: W. W. Norton, 1974.

———. *Strange New Land: Africans in Colonial America.* New York: Oxford University Press, 2003.

Wright, Michelle M. *Becoming Black: Creating Identity in the African Diaspora.* Durham: Duke University Press, 2004.

Yarak, Larry W. "Elmina and Greater Asante in the Nineteenth Century." *Africa: Journal of the International African Institute* 56 (1986): 33–52.

———. "The 'Elmina Note:' Myth and Reality in Asante-Dutch Relations." *History in Africa* 13 (1986): 363–382.

———. *Asante and the Dutch, 1744–1873.* Oxford: Clarendon Press, 1990.

Young, Jason R. *Rituals of Resistance: African Atlantic Religion in Kongo and the Lowcountry South in the Era of Slavery.* Baton Rouge: Louisiana State University Press, 2007.

Zips, Werner. *Black Rebels: African Caribbean Freedom Fighters in Jamaica.* Princeton: Markus Wiener, 1999.

INDEX

BLACKS IN THE DIASPORA

EDITORS

Herman L. Bennett
Kim D. Butler
Judith A. Byfield
Tracy Sharpley-Whiting

FOUNDING EDITORS

Darlene Clark Hine
John McCluskey, Jr.
David Barry Gaspar

A Question of Manhood: A Reader in U.S. Black Men's History and Masculinity. Volume 1: "Manhood Rights": The Construction of Black Male History and Manhood, 1750–1870. Edited by Darlene Clark Hine and Earnestine L. Jenkins

A Question of Manhood: A Reader in U.S. Black Men's History and Masculinity. Volume 2. The 19th Century: From Emancipation to Jim Crow. Edited by Darlene Clark Hine and Earnestine L. Jenkins

A Refuge in Thunder: Candomblé and Alternative Spaces of Blackness. Rachel E. Harding

A Turbulent Time: The French Revolution and the Greater Caribbean. Edited by David Barry Gaspar and David Patrick Geggus

African American Women in the Struggle for the Vote, 1850–1920. Rosalyn Terborg-Penn

African Cinema: Politics and Culture. Manthia Diawara

Africanisms in American Culture. Edited by Joseph E. Holloway

Africanisms in American Culture, Second Edition. Edited by Joseph E. Holloway

Africans in Colonial Mexico: Absolutism, Christianity, and Afro-Creole Consciousness, 1570–1640. Herman L. Bennett

"All the World Is Here!" The Black Presence at White City. Christopher Robert Reed

Archaeology of Atlantic Africa and the African Diaspora. Edited by Akinwumi Ogundiran and Toyin Falola

Artists, Performers, and Black Masculinity in the Haitian Diaspora. Jana Evans Braziel

The Atlantic World: 1450–2000. Edited by Toyin Falola and Kevin D. Roberts

Barriers between Us: Interracial Sex in Nineteenth-Century American Literature. Cassandra Jackson

Between Slavery and Freedom: Philosophy and American Slavery. Howard McGary and Bill E. Lawson

Binding Cultures: Black Women Writers in Africa and the Diaspora. Gay Wilentz

Black Female Playwrights: An Anthology of Plays before 1950. Edited with an Introduction by Kathy A. Perkins

Black Police in America. W. Marvin Dulaney

Black Women in America: An Historical Encyclopedia. Edited by Darlene Clark Hine, Elsa Barkley Brown, and Rosalyn Terborg-Penn

Gendering the African Diaspora: Women, Culture, and Historical Change in the Caribbean and Nigerian Hinterland. Edited by Judith A. Byfield, LaRay Denzer, and Anthea Morrison

God Almighty Make Me Free: Christianity in Preemancipation Jamaica. Shirley C. Gordon

The Great Migration in Historical Perspective: New Dimensions of Race, Class, and Gender. Edited by Joe William Trotter, Jr.

Haitian Revolutionary Studies. David Patrick Geggus

Hine Sight: Black Women and the Re-Construction of American History. Darlene Clark Hine

Historians and Race: Autobiography and the Writing of History. Edited by Paul A. Cimbala

Legacy of the Lash: Race and Corporal Punishment in the Brazilian Navy and the Atlantic World. Zachary R. Morgan

Life for Us Is What We Make It: Building Black Community in Detroit, 1915–1945. Richard W. Thomas

Mammy and Uncle Mose: Black Collectibles and American Stereotyping. Kenneth W. Goings

Maria W. Stewart, America's First Black Woman Political Writer: Essays and Speeches. Edited by Marilyn Richardson

Materialities of Ritual in the Black Atlantic. Edited by Akinwumi Ogundiran and Paula Saunders

Mau Mau and Kenya: An Analysis of a Peasant Revolt. Wunyabari O. Maloba

Modernity, Freedom, and the African Diaspora: Dublin, New Orleans, Paris. Elisa Joy White

More than Chattel: Black Women and Slavery in the Americas. Edited by David Barry Gaspar and Darlene Clark Hine

"NAACP Comes of Age": The Defeat of Judge John J. Parker. Kenneth W. Goings

Nation of Cowards: Black Activism in Barack Obama's Post-Racial America. David H. Ikard and Martell Lee Teasley

"New Negroes from Africa": Slave Trade Abolition and Free African Settlement in the Nineteenth-Century Caribbean. Rosanne Marion Adderley

The Other Black Bostonians: West Indians in Boston, 1900–1950. Violet Showers Johnson

Our Mothers, Our Powers, Our Texts: Manifestations of Àjé in Africana Literature. Teresa N. Washington

Private Politics and Public Voices: Black Women's Activism from World War I to the New Deal. Nikki Brown

Race for Sanctions: African Americans against Apartheid, 1946–1994. Francis Njubi Nesbitt

Richard B. Moore, Caribbean Militant in Harlem: Collected Writings, 1920–1972. Edited by W. Burghardt Turner and Joyce Moore Turner

Rumba: Dance and Social Change in Contemporary Cuba. Yvonne Daniel

Santeria from Africa to the New World: The Dead Sell Memories. George Brandon

Screenplays of the African American Experience. Edited by Phyllis Rauch Klotman

WALTER C. RUCKER, Associate Professor of African diaspora and Atlantic history at Rutgers University, is the author of *The River Flows On: Black Resistance, Culture, and Identity Formation in Early America*. With Leslie Alexander, he is coeditor of *The Encyclopedia of African American History*. Before joining the History Department at Rutgers in 2014, he was an associate professor at the University of North Carolina at Chapel Hill, an assistant and an associate professor at the Ohio State University, and an assistant professor at the University of Nebraska–Lincoln.